How to Start and Build a Law Practice

Platinum Fifth Edition

Jay G Foonberg

ABA **LawPracticeManagementSection** | **American Bar Association**
MARKETING • MANAGEMENT • TECHNOLOGY • FINANCE | **Law Student Division**

Library of Congress Cataloging-in-Publication Data

Foonberg, Jay G., 1935–
   How to start and build a law practice / Jay G Foonberg. — Platinum
5th ed.
      p. cm.
   Includes index.
   ISBN 1-59031-247-3
   1. Practice of law—United States. 2. Law—Vocational guidance—
United States. 3. Law firms—United States. I. Title.

   KF300.F66 2004
   340′.068—dc22

                                                    2004008218

08 07   9

Discounts are available for books ordered in bulk. Special consideration is given to state bars, CLE programs, and other bar-related organizations. Inquire at Book Publishing, American Bar Association, 321 N. Clark Street, Chicago, Illinois 60610.

For information on audiotapes and videotapes or other works by Mr. Foonberg, contact the National Academy of Law Ethics and Management, 1-800-55-NALEM.

Horace
Quintas Horatius Flaccus, aka Horace, Roman poet
Epilogue from Horace's third book of Odes.
23 B.C.
I have erected a monument more lasting than bronze
And taller than the regal peak of the pyramids . . .
I shall never completely die.
Exegi monumentum aere perennius
Regalique situ pyramidum altius . . .
Non omnis moriar.

Contents

Part VIII: Resources and Advice

Part IX: Quality of Life

Preface to the First and Second Editions

This book, by its nature, is money-oriented. Its purpose is to assist the new lawyer in starting and building a law practice on a firm economic basis. Do not quote the book or sections out of context.

To succeed in the practice of law over a period of years requires a deep and sincere desire to help people. If you are looking upon your license to practice law simply as a ticket to making money, or as a one-way ticket out of the ghetto or barrio, then you are making a serious mistake. I would advise you not to proceed as a lawyer. You will do better as an insurance salesman or a teacher or an engineer. If you are entering the legal profession solely to make money, you are making a serious mistake. You might get lucky and make money in a given year, but over a period of years, you won't make it.

I repeat: to succeed in the long run, the practice of law requires a deep and sincere dedication to helping people. With proper management and proper client relations skills, the economic rewards will follow the rendering of high-quality legal services.

You are about to enter into a thirty- or forty-year career as a lawyer. Don't do it unless you really and sincerely want to help people.

Preface to the Third Edition

The sum of money required for technology and equipment can be substantial, so chapters have been added on doing a cash-flow budget, earning a living until you open your practice, financing your practice with bank credit cards, and practicing from your home.

Disciplinary efforts have increased against lawyers at every level. There is a 10 percent likelihood that someone will file a disciplinary complaint against you. The adoption by many states of the ABA's Model Rules of Professional Conduct has given disciplinary staffs specific guidelines for deciding when to investigate and prosecute a lawyer. The disciplinary staffs sometimes have a consumer-protection, anti-lawyer, prosecutorial mentality. They often are under pressure from their legislatures to investigate and discipline lawyers.

Four new chapters dealing with professional conduct and the Model Rules have been added. I hope these chapters, which include "Ten Rules for Avoiding Disciplinary Complaints" and "Fifty Ways to Win or Avoid the Ethics War," will cause you to examine your professional responsibility, both on a macro (profession-wide) and on a micro (personal) level. It was my intention to include the ABA Model Rules of Professional Conduct as an appendix to this book, but it proved impossible to do so. In fact, reliance on the ABA Model Rules can lead to problems for you, as many jurisdictions have rejected or modified sections of the Model Rules. I recommend that you contact your local licensing jurisdiction for a copy of the rules that will apply where you practice. The expansion of the section dealing with professional responsibility recognizes that an increasing number of law schools use this book as a supplementary source in the course on professional responsibility.

Lastly, the explosion in the number of lawyers has greatly affected how a practice is started and built. Lawyers and law firms aggressively market to get and keep clients. Many firms now hire in-house marketing people to try to take clients from other firms. Large sums of money are spent on public relations firms and media advertising in marketing efforts. I personally have helped firms by teaching their lawyers and even their nonlawyers the fundamentals of marketing. The lawyer who wants to start a law practice in today's competitive market must know marketing, a subject never taught in law school. I have included more tips for a new lawyer in this third edition.

In summary, this third edition includes the most current information you need to start and build a law practice.

Jay G Foonberg
Beverly Hills, California
April 1991

Preface to the
Millennium Fourth Edition

This one book will help you succeed in starting a law practice, alone or with others.

In this single millennium fourth edition, you will find the basic tools necessary to succeed as a lawyer.

The current ABA list of ABA Publications recommended for solo and small firm lawyers recommends as many as 246 books. I have written this one book to identify what the new lawyer needs to know to succeed.

Since the last edition was published in 1991, there have been five major changes affecting starting your law practice. These are

1. The increased demands of clients and potential clients for excellent client relations when choosing or recommending a lawyer.

2. Technology is reducing the need for lawyers.

3. The lack of training opportunity for new lawyers before opening their practice.

4. "Involuntary solos" who have been forced out of their law firms or corporate employment due to merges, downsizing, outsourcing, etc. Many lawyers now starting a practice are really starting a second career.

5. Quality-of-life issues.

Technology

Foonberg's rule "If it works, it's obsolete" exemplifies the impossibility of highlighting anything other than basic technology in any book.

1. *The new lawyer fresh out of law school probably has better equipment and electronic skills than most existing law firms.* The Internet, voice recognition, OCR, and other forms of information transfer and retrieval are radically changing and will continue to radically change law practice. The library and research sections in this book have been updated to give greater effect to the Internet and electronic research methods.

On the other hand, I have tried to ease the burden of shifting from a paper library and office, and from a paper file system to an electronic system keeping in mind that many lawyers coming from a large firm or corporate atmosphere will have to learn new ways to be cost effective with reasonable fees.

2. *Increasingly, lawyers starting a practice have no practical or clinical training in how to practice law beyond recognizing legal issues.* Law school courses in practice management, although beginning, are still rare. Law school courses in how to create and maintain good client relations (what physicians would call "bedside manner") are virtually nonexistent. This book is used successfully by many law schools to provide management and client relations skills.

The ABA MacCrate Report issued in 1992 identifies specific skills and values considered necessary to practice law. This book has recognized those needs since it was first published in 1976. This fourth edition provides materials needed by new lawyers and law schools to meet the issues addressed by the MacCrate Report.

I have added new chapters on how to meet client expectations and have added many interview forms, practice forms, form letters, and checklists to help the new lawyer recognize and systemize essential issues.

3. I have added a chapter on how to create a business plan and another chapter on how to handle student loans. Thousands of lawyers have told me they never throw this book away, but continually refer to it for guidance and as a refresher course. Accordingly, I have added a chapter with over 500 tips, which you will find useful to review from time to time to improve your practice after it is going well.

4. *As with prior editions, forms, checklists, and other tools to maintain excellent client relations are found throughout the book.*

5. *Lastly, quality of life is increasingly an issue for lawyers who have delayed having families or who are not willing to trade a quality of life and family for money or position.* I have added a section,

including practicing out of the home, to help the new lawyer or senior lawyer who seeks more out of life than working sixteen hours per day, six days per week. Also included are tips for dealing with difficult clients, difficult lawyers, and difficult judges.

In this millennium edition, I have worked hard to continue to provide in a single book the basics of what a new lawyer in practice needs to succeed.

There are hundreds of books, articles, videos, etc., that cost thousands and thousands of dollars that could augment or supplement parts of this book. This book continues to provide the best help available regardless of price.

Over the years, more than 100,000 lawyers have used this book. Hundreds of lawyers and their spouses have written or called me to tell me how this book made possible their successes and to suggest improvements and changes. I welcome these comments.

Jay G Foonberg
Beverly Hills, California
January 1999

Preface to the Platinum Fifth Edition

This book is intended to help you succeed by giving you, in a single book, what you need to start your legal career or to start a law practice. It is designed to save the time and the cash of the new lawyer. Even if you elect to become employed in a firm, this book will often help you understand how a law firm functions.

Several major changes have occurred since the fourth edition, which was written five years ago. Many of the changes affect the new lawyer—or any lawyer starting a firm alone or with others.

Most of what is in this book will never change. What lawyers do for clients and what clients need and expect from their lawyers is basic. The mechanics of how lawyers do things for their clients may change from time to time. Lawyers continually tell me that they keep prior editions of the book in their upper right-hand desk drawer to read and re-read and to refer to when they have a problem. About 10 percent of the book may someday become dated because of new methods of doing things and because of new areas of law replacing other areas. There will also be some changes both in the way lawyers help clients and the economic environment in which law is practiced.

There are several "new" topics that this fifth edition addresses, including:

1. E-mail and the Internet
2. Law firms merging to become mega-firms
3. Law firms of all sizes breaking up
4. The globalization of legal practice
5. The increasing size of student loans
6. Increasing attempts to convert the profession of law into a law business

7. Aggressive marketing being done by firms of all sizes, including cold calling by larger firms and the hiring of nonlawyer salespeople to seek clients for the firm

8. An aging population creating greater opportunities for serving senior clients and prompting the growth of elder law as a practice area of law

9. The huge increase in the number of nonlawyer consultants

10. The decreasing ability of courts to process the increased litigation needs of a growing population, causing an increasing use of alternate dispute resolution, which is often mandatory

11. When and how to safely and ethically close or destroy files

12. A brief history of some of the changes in our profession and the changes in law practice management

13. How to overcome the fears caused by lack of experience

The five major issues addressed in the fourth edition of this book are still with us and are addressed in this fifth edition. They are

1. Increased expectations of the lawyer by clients

2. Client technology changing the clients' needs for lawyers

3. Lack of training of new lawyers by firms that are expecting billable hours from the untrained new lawyers

4. Lawyers finding themselves unemployed through no fault of their own

5. Quality-of-life expectations

Yesterday my first grandchild was born. My son and daughter-in-law elected to have a "natural" delivery with no anesthetics or surgery. The baby was born at a hospital with millions of dollars of equipment and thousands of employees. In the delivery room were an obstetrician, a pediatrician, a doula, a midwife, and several nurses. In the final analysis, notwithstanding all the people and equipment, the delivery was a matter between the obstetrician and the mother. Similarly, in the final analysis, the rendering of legal services is a matter between the lawyer and the client, notwithstanding all the nonlawyer staff available and all the new technology in the office.

Tomorrow, I shall be teaching several hundred new admittees (baby lawyers, if you will), as part of a Bridging the Gap program. I will collect several hundred audience questionnaires from these new lawyers. The hundreds of questions from the thousands of new lawyers whom I have taught for more than thirty years become, over the years, the questions that are answered in this book.

As in prior editions, I have followed Foonberg's Rule of Technology, which is "If it works, it's obsolete." It is almost impossible to name any new equipment or software that will still be the latest available by the time the book is transformed from manuscript to print. The highway of law practice management is littered with the wrecks and corpses of "the latest technology." Consultants and companies have simply gone out of business, leaving the lawyer with equipment that is little more than scrap metal and applications and systems that are worthless. Accordingly, there are very few references in the book to hardware or software unless I believe it is worth the new lawyer's time and money to look at it. There are also very few references to other publications for the same reasons. The American Bar Association Law Practice Management Section has dozens of excellent books that are well written by knowledgeable authors and that could help a lawyer or a staff person do their job, but I have not recommended them unless I believe they would meet the needs of new lawyers who must learn basics and conserve cash.

As in the past, many hundreds of lawyers and their spouses have told me how this book was the key to their success when they began their careers.

This book has worked for them. It can work for you.

Jay G Foonberg
Beverly Hills, California
March 2004

A Short History of
Law Practice Management

This piece has been added to give you a sense of perspective. It is often easier to understand where you are and where you are going if you understand where you have been.

The goals of management of a law practice have not changed much in a thousand years. It is only the means of accomplishing the goals that have changed. It would be fair to say that there have been more changes in the twentieth century than in the previous thousand years. Accordingly, many of the changes may be within your memory.

In general, lawyers and their predecessors have always concerned themselves with the following:

1. Obtaining facts.

2. Classifying the facts to be within specific areas of law.

3. Obtaining or creating forms or oral or written presentations appropriate to combine the facts and the law to produce new information in a document or position of advocacy.

4. Printing or producing the information in a readable format, with copies as required.

5. Storing the new finished product in a manner allowing recovery of the product to be used again for similar fact situations.

6. Communicating the information and products produced by the lawyer to clients and third parties as required.

While there are some variations on the theme, almost all of the advancements in law practice management deal with how the above steps are accomplished. The following dates indicate when some of the major changes occurred. All dates are approximate.

Equipment

4,000 B.C.—Clay tablets were the medium of the information and bronze tools were used to carve the information on to the tablets. The Romans used sheets of wax which could be permanently inscribed or which could be melted and reused.

2,000 B.C.—Romans made reusable sheets of wax for tablets and melted the tablets and reused them when creating new information.

1,000 B.C.—The Chinese used brushes made of hair to record information.

"Documents" were often written on parchment, which is the skin of an animal.

500 B.C.—The Egyptians used "pens" made of reeds with frayed ends which were dipped into ink and written onto papyrus reeds, which had been made into sheets.

600 A.D. to 1850 A.D.—The quill pen was used. It was dipped into ink and information was written onto a variety of media, parchment and paper being the principal media used. A goose feather could be shaped into a nib (what we would call a pen point) and the hollow shaft of the feather could hold a supply of ink that was adequate to write out a few words at a time before more ink was needed.

One goose could supply about ten good quills. Thomas Jefferson, for example, raised a huge flock of geese to provide a supply of quills. The nibs (points) of the quills needed continual recutting and shaping as they wore out.

Lawyers (and others) had to use a small cutting knife to continually reshape the nib. The knife came to be called the pen knife.

1850—The steel pen began to be used. The points could be cheaply produced by stamping tempered steel sheets to produce the basic shape, slit (to hold the ink), and the tip.

The steel-tip pen was the single most significant development in law offices, allowing rapid production of documents with uniform width of ink stroke and no spattering or blobs. The steel-tip pens were cheaply produced and children in school began learning penmanship.

Law offices could now produce documents cheaply using semi-skilled workers who did not have to understand what they were writing. The workers were called clerks or draftsmen and were the forerunners of word processors. Copies would be made using a process called tracing, whereby thin tissue sheets were dampened to absorb ink from the original document and then pressed onto a blank sheet of paper.

The invention of the steel-tip pen was the most significant event in the history of law office management.

1808—Carbon paper was invented, but was not often used because if enough pressure were applied in making the original, the ink would blot on the original.

1868—The typewriter was patented by Christopher Sholes, an employee of Remington Arms.

1873—The Remington 1 typewriter was patented, but did not have a "shift key" to produce both upper-case and lower-case letters.

1840—The English postal system using postage stamps allowed easy sending of information back and forth. Adopted in America in 1847.

1850—The fax machine was invented but was not heavily used because equipment had to be identical at both ends of the message.

1878—The Remington 2 was patented with the shift key and the ability to produce both upper-case and lower-case letters. Printing was now possible in an office setting using multiple carbon copies.

1902—Transmission of photos and images over telephone wires became popular.

1937—What we now call Xerography (Greek for "dry writing") was invented by an American law student who became a patent lawyer. IBM was not interested in the process and Chester Carlson started a company known as the Xerox Corporation. Information, both typed and handwritten could now be easily and cheaply made into multiple copies. Changes and corrections only had to be made on the original, not onto carbon copies.

1940—The ballpoint pen was patented by Laszlo Biro, a Hungarian who had fled the Nazis and was living in Argentina. The British Air Force needed the pens because fountain pens leaked at high altitudes.

Law offices could now produce written documents in great quantity with uniform shapes and sizes (fonts) and carbon paper to produce multiple copies simultaneously with the production of the original.

1950—The Xerox machine and process became available to lawyers, and law offices became "paper mills," turning out multiple copies of everything using the Xerox machine.

1960s—Telex and limited dedicated modem to modem fax transmission allowed communication over telephone wires.

1969—The ARPA was invented at UCLA and became the Internet.

1970s—Computers called main frames were being used in law offices. They were sold without programs, which the law firm paid for separately and which often cost more than the computer.

1981—IBM personal computer (PC) came on to the market.

1984—Apple MacIntosh computers came on to the market.

1990s—Computer prices fell and Internet and e-mail was being used.

Digitalization allowed electronic messages to be sent to and from modems and other devices made by different manufacturers to a single standard.

As an example of the rapid changes in communication technology, one need only consider that in the late 1990s, more than two-thirds of all lawyer to lawyer and lawyer to client communication was done by fax. Within five years, more than 90 percent of these communications were changed to e-mail. From the 1840s, when the postage stamp and postal systems came into being, until the 1990s, almost all communication was done by mail.

1990s. Computer prices began collapsing. As an example of the increase in available technology, one need only consider that for less than $1,000 retail, one can walk into any computer store and buy more computer power than the entire United States had when we sent a man to the moon and brought him back. Computer prices continue to fall.

Digitalization allows communication by fax and modem to modem information transmission.

Late 1990s—the Internet and e-mail changes the availability and transmission of information.

Staffing

1776 to 1870s—Lawyers sometimes used a male clerk or a scrivener and a law student who was "reading the law." (Abraham Lincoln never finished any school, nor went to high school nor college nor law school. He "read the law" under the supervision of a lawyer.)

Staff historically was made up of male lawyers, scriveners, and clerks, often law students.

1870s to 1900s—Advent of female secretaries and typists.

1970s—Increasing numbers of female lawyers.

1970s—Introduction of paralegals, legal assistants, and first paralegal school in Philadelphia.

1990s—More female law students than male law students.

21st Century—Law firms heavily staffed by nonlawyers doing administrative work, including Information Technology, Sales and Marketing, Personnel, Accounting etc. Lawyers doing their own typing.

Marketing

Historically not possible. The word "advocate" means (the one who is called), stemming from the Latin advocare (to call). The client had to call for the lawyer.

1970s—Bates and Osteen adv. Arizona approved attorney marketing.

1976—Shapero vs. Kentucky allowed direct mail advertising.

Currently almost all forms of advertising are permissible including solicitation. Large firms have "sales" departments that cold call for clients.

With the aggressive marketing now used by firms of all sizes, almost anything is permissible provided it is truthful.

Billing and Pricing

Prior to 1964, billing done annually or quarterly. Bar associations published fee schedules. Lawyers could be disciplined for charging less or more than the bar association fees.

1964—Goldfarb v. Virginia led to abolition of fee schedule.

1969—Missouri Bar survey proved time-keeping essential to determine a "fair fee."

1970s—Lawyers began billing monthly and quarterly instead of annually or completion of matter using handwritten time records.

Firm Size

Prior to 1900—Most law firms were one to five lawyers, often all partners.

1920—Firms especially on Wall Street began enlarging—ten to fifteen lawyers still considered "huge."

1973—American Bar Association forms Law Practice Management Section (then called Economics of Law Practice Section) classifying lawyers by firm size: solo practitioners; small firms, two to five lawyers; medium firms, six to ten lawyers; large firms, more than ten lawyers.

2004—85 percent of American lawyers practice in firms of five lawyers or less, 15 percent of American lawyers in firms of more than 5 lawyers, some firms having more than 1,000 lawyers.

2000s—Law firms of 1,000 or more lawyers becoming common. Firms forming national and international affiliations common.

Hopefully, this historical review of law practice management will demonstrate that what lawyers do hasn't changed much. How lawyers do it has changed and will continue to change.

A Very Short History of
Our Legal Profession

I am personally mystified why law schools don't devote fifteen to thirty minutes in a three-year curriculum to teach students the history of our profession.

Knowing a little about our profession can be helpful when dealing with clients and potential clients who from time to time ask a few questions of you.

There is a play titled "The History of the World in One Hour" in which a very abbreviated review is made of world history.

You may wish to call this piece "The History of American Law in a Little More Than One Page."

The Roman Empire ruled over most of Western Europe, including England, imposing Roman Law. Under Roman Law, citizens could take their disputes to courts or forums run by nonlawyers. If they felt they needed help they could get help from a person known as an *advocatis* (friend). The Latin verb *advocare* means to call out for help. The person who helped them was an advocatis (friend), and the position of this advocatis when he was in court was *advocatis*. This is the origin of the word *advocate*.

In 349 A.D., the Emperor Constantine declared Christianity to be the official religion of the former Empire, thus bringing Judeo-Christian concepts into the law. In 535 A.D., the Emperor Justinian codified the Roman Law. One of the results was the Civil Code, which created the position of the Notary. Lawyers went to court or a forum. That's all lawyers did. Today we would say they were trial lawyers. What we would call transactional work (deeds, loans, mortgages, corporation, immigration, contracts, partnership, etc.) were done by Notaries. Even in the twenty-first century, in most civil law countries advocates (abogados, etc.) only go to court for litigation and Notaries who may or may not also have a legal education do transactional work. A person in a civil law country normally can only be one or the other, an advocate or a notary.

England was part of the Roman Empire. The common law governed after the Battle of Hastings in 1066, however legal practice was still divided between advocates who went to court (called Barristers) and notaries (called Solicitors) who did transactional work.

Henry the Eighth broke away from the Catholic Church in 1535, declaring the Anglican Church to be the official church and reducing the power of the notary to just witnessing signatures and protesting bills of exchange. His reason for transferring transactional work from the notary to the solicitor was that all notaries were appointed by the Vatican. Solicitors normally could not go to court. (They did not have the right of audience.)

The American Colonies being part of England were part of the English legal system of Solicitors and Barristers until the American Revolution, when most of the Barristers and Solicitors fled to Canada or the Caribbean or England.

The new United States needed an entire legal system, and new states needed constitutions and laws and courts. The shortage of lawyers allowed a person without any law school education to become a lawyer (Abraham Lincoln never attended high school, college, or law school). Faced with a shortage of lawyers, there never was a division between court and transactional work in the United States.

Lawyers have been critical to the establishment and continuance of the American system. Our 1789 Constitution was created by a committee of fifty-five people, twenty-nine of whom were lawyers. Two-thirds of the Presidents of the United States have been lawyers. More than 60 percent of legislators have been lawyers.

Our legal system goes back at least as far as the Roman Law, and we are reminded of it when in some states, lawyers still refer to themselves as "Attorney & Counselor at Law," a reminder of the Advocate and the Notary or the Barrister and the Solicitor. In most states we call ourselves "Attorney" or "Lawyer."

Acknowledgments

My first acknowledgment is to Lois, my wife and partner for more than 45 years. So often she saw only the back of my head while I was writing this edition and the four prior editions of *How to Start & Build A Law Practice* over a period of more than 30 years. She was always available to give me an opinion on the best way to express a thought. (The reader may not appreciate that at times I spend hours to seek the best way to express a single thought in a way that will be helpful to the reader.) Lois also had to sit through innumerable bar association lunches and dinners and meetings throughout the world that often went along with the programs I was doing.

Many other people have helped me with the writing of this Fifth Edition.

Chair Greg Siskind and my fellow members of the Publishing Board of the ABA Law Practice Management Section offered many useful suggestions reflecting their areas of expertise. Gary Munneke, in addition to being a writer of many books for lawyers, is also a Professor at Pace University School of Law in White Plains, New York. On many occasions he and I worked together when matters of legal ethics and legal history were being reviewed. In addition, several of his students, along with a young associate of Rick Feferman of Albuquerque, reviewed the previous edition of this book to identify any dated phrases or terminology that might detract from the timelessness of the book's lessons.

Many LPM Practice Management Advisors, especially Reid F. Trautz, Gisela Bradley, Laura A. Calloway, Dee Crocker, Ellen Freedman, Steve Gallagher, Janean Johnston, Courtney Kennaday,

Linda Oligschlaeger, JR Phelps, Pete Roberts, Jill Rothstein, Carol Seelig, and Pat Yevics offered helpful suggestions based on the problems they observed in their states. Their suggestions would require another book in and of itself, and prove just how knowledgeable they are and how important they can be in helping lawyers. In addition, Dan Coolidge of New Hampshire gave input on the use of current technology in the practice of law. I have tried to use his suggestions where they are applicable to new lawyers starting a practice.

I am grateful to the members of the ABA General Practice, Solo, and Small Firm Section for their continued support of this book and other books I have written over many years.

I am grateful to the lawyers—and especially the new lawyers—who each year ask me the thousands of questions that make this book responsive to current needs.

I am grateful to the more than 100,000 lawyers who have bought this book, and the hundreds of lawyers who each year tell me how this book helped them with their legal careers when they most needed help.

My law firm of Bailey & Partners in Santa Monica, California, to which I have been Of Counsel for more than eight years, has made many contributions deserving of acknowledgment. Patrick Bailey has always supported my efforts in attending bar association meetings and new admittee programs, where I obtain many of the current questions of new lawyers that are answered in this book. Stephen Hofer has always been available to me when I would seek the correct word or phrase to describe a concept. My assistant-secretary (and marathon-running partner), Yolanda Ornelas, was of great help in preparing the original manuscript and multiple drafts and revisions of the new materials and changes from previous editions.

Saving the best for last, I wish to acknowledge the ABA LPM Book Publishing staff of Beverly Loder, Neal Cox, and Tim Johnson. We haven't always agreed on everything, but have somehow managed to work together to produce the best, most useful book possible. Special kudos are due to Beverly Loder, one of the hardest-working staff members at the ABA, who somehow always found time to put me and my ABA books first.

Beverly and I have had many heated discussions over what I want to communicate and the best way to communicate it. There is an ongoing problem in that I write like I speak and I speak like I write. I don't care what the style manuals say is correct. At times I prefer to use digital numbers rather than words. Don't blame Beverly when you see the number "1/3" or "3" instead of the words "one-third" or "three" (or vice versa). Beverly did her best, but I can be stubborn. Give her credit when the various style manuals and ABA policies are complied with and blame me when they have been ignored or disregarded.

I love Beverly dearly for her hard work, even if she had to compete with the needs of my paying (and sometimes nonpaying) clients who took priority over the ABA publishing dates and goals. Without her prodding, it probably would have taken another year to complete this edition, and *How to Draft Bills Clients Rush to Pay* might never have gotten finished. The ink is not quite dry on this Platinum Fifth Edition and Beverly is already prodding me for the workbook on closing a law practice. When the ABA book of heroes is published, Beverly Loder's name belongs at the top of the list.

Part I
Getting Started

Why Has This Book Been Written?

Why has this book been written? It has been written because there is a need for it. I have spoken to and worked with tens of thousands of new admittees throughout the United States over the last four decades. I know that the new lawyer needs and wants this information, and the information in this book cannot be found in any other single book. To get the information in this book, one would have to comb hundreds of periodicals and publications to get the raw information that would then have to be distilled; and unfortunately, the new lawyer doesn't know which raw information is needed, nor how to distill it.

Law schools are turning out about twice as many lawyers as the nation needs. Simultaneously, nonlawyers working under the general supervision of lawyers are doing work formerly done by lawyers. "Do-it-yourself" divorce, bankruptcy, and immigration enterprises are flourishing. The Internet and bookstores make free and low-cost legal service available of varying quality. No-fault liability insurance will have a significant effect on law practices. One-third of all small businesses fail within one year. Law firms of all sizes from two-lawyer partnerships to megafirms merge, break up, and go out of business.

The lawyer who enters the economic arena of private practice in an entrepreneurial capacity must know and master the principles of this book or else be independently wealthy to survive initially, and to flourish ultimately. The lawyer who heeds the lessons of the book will probably succeed. The lawyer who ignores them will float along from year to year, rolling up and down from an occasional "good year" to the more common struggling years, until he or she learns the lessons of this book or fails completely.

A successful law practice is similar to a three-legged stool. The three legs are legal skills, practice management skills—including technology—and client relations (marketing) skills. Unless all three legs are present, the stool will topple.

With due apologies to the world of academics, I have used a "nuts-and-bolts" approach in this book. Until recently, the law schools have not taught the materials in this book. Whether the reason is lack of qualified instructors or some other reason is immaterial. The end result is that at the present time, most law schools don't teach these materials, and this book is necessary.

For example, I have entitled one part of the book "Setting Fees" and have drawn upon empiric observations of my practice. In an academic setting, I might have done two or three years of research with surveys and two or three grants to end up with a chapter entitled "Socio-Economic Factors Considered by Providers of Professional Legal Services in Relation to the Socio-Economic Resources of Recipients of Professional Legal Services as Correlated to the Intricacies and Time Demand Factors Inherent in the Services Provided." I trust that the reader will appreciate this alternative "nuts-and-bolts" approach.

One of the beneficial offshoots of public criticism of the legal profession was the response of the law schools with respect to legal ethics and professionalism as well as some exposure to management. In the 1960s, when I first started participating in teaching new admittees *How to Start and Build a Law Practice,* about 10 percent of the new admittees knew what a trust account was. In January of 1975, at the height of the Watergate disciplinary publicity, almost one-half of the new admittees knew what a trust account was. In 1983, when the State Bar of California implemented mandatory trust account procedures, less than one-third of the lawyers had complied. By 1991, many states required courses in ethics or professional responsibility as a prior condition to admission. Among new admittees, however, about 80 percent know what a trust account is. I personally would expect 100 percent of new admittees to know and understand trust accounts, but accept that 80 percent is better than 10 percent. I believe the 1976 disclosure of these statistics has prompted law schools to spend forty minutes out of a three-year curriculum on this important subject, and to include trust accounts in the bar exams. In 1996 I wrote *The ABA Guide to Lawyer Trust Accounts* to provide instructions on how to maintain trust accounts. It is sad that so many lawyers are expected to manage huge amounts of client money, yet receive no law-school training in trust account management.

The individual chapters of this book appear to be unconnected or not in sequence. This is intentional. In most cases, each chapter is intended to stand on its own without reference to other chapters. I have done this so that the new admittee can most easily find the general information needed. This results in some blank spaces and some repetition, which may be aesthetically unsettling but that simplify use of the book.

A number of times in this book I refer to the ABA Model Code of Professional Responsibility and its successor, the ABA Model Rules of Professional Conduct. Every law student and lawyer should have copies of these important documents, as well as applicable state and local rules.

In 2002 I sent a free one-hour videotape on trust accounts management to every teacher of law school ethics and professional responsibility in an effort to allow every law student to painlessly learn trust accounts management. I also sent a complimentary copy to every law school library. If your law school does not have a copy, notify me and I will send them another copy. I am hopeful that one day every law school graduate will have received at least one hour of training in trust accounts management to avoid disbarment.

The History of This Book

This book was the first book published by the Law Practice Management Section of the American Bar Association.

I first began teaching new lawyers "How to Start and Build a Law Practice" in the 1960s, along with three other lawyers who like myself were also CPAs. I taught the course in California four times a year in Northern California at Berkeley and in Southern California in Los Angeles, timing the course to coincide with the results of the bar examination. About 15 percent of new admittees attended the programs. I still teach that course twice a year in Los Angeles as part of the "Bridge the Gap" program.

In 1973 in San Francisco, we voted to transform the Economics of Law Practice Committee into the Economics of Law Practice Section of the American Bar Association.

At that meeting where the structure of the section was being constructed, I asked to be appointed Chair of the New Lawyers In Practice Committee. On creation of the section, I received that appointment and chaired the New Lawyers In Practice Committee for fifteen years.

In 1974 and 1975 I was asked to do the program outside of California and did so, eventually teaching in every one of the fifty states and every one of the ten Canadian provinces.

In 1973 I began writing this book to provide guidance to new lawyers who were considering starting a practice.

In 1976 I published the book using a client to print it. The book was enormously successful. I tried to give the book to the ABA Economics of Law Practice Section, but I was told they wouldn't accept it because I advocated written fee agreements, which I had learned about from my accounting experience. I refused to delete the chapter.

Lynne Gold (now Lynne Gold-Biken), Chair of the Law Student Division, wanted to publish the book as a Law Student Division book with the client fee agreement chapter in the book. I then returned to the Economics of Law Practice Section and offered them half or zero at their option, with the fee agreement chapter intact. They accepted one-half, and the book was published in 1976 by the two entities.

You may note that I own the copyright on the book. This is to prevent any tampering with the contents should they not be in accord with ABA or other policies. I have written this book and updated it in 1984, 1991, 1999, and 2004 to be able to provide beneficial, unbiased help to new lawyers, answering their questions.

I practice law in Santa Monica, California, and speak ten to fifteen times per year, which is where I get the information to keep the book current.

About 90 percent of this book is basic. It will never change. The means of delivering legal services will change as technology advances and the needs of American public changes. 10 percent will probably be obsolete within five years, but the remaining 90 percent will always help you, no matter how many years you practice law.

To answer a frequently asked question, "No, I do not make any money from this book. I give half of the sales revenues to the Law Practice Management Section and half to the Law Student Division, where I am told it helps to fund their Minority Scholarship Program. I don't keep one cent." The book has made in excess of $1 million for the ABA and is approaching the $2 million figure. There are no records for the earlier years, but our best estimate is that about 150,000 to 200,000 copies of the book have been sold. It is easily the all-time bestseller of the American Bar Association Law Practice Management Section.

This book is one of my ways of "Giving Back" to the profession that I love so dearly and that has been so good to me. Where else but in America could the son of a bankrupt immigrant butcher be invited to the White House to meet with the President, to the Vatican for an audience with the Pope, and to the Queen's Garden Party at Buckingham Palace?

I would remind the reader of this book that we only have a life estate in the profession. We are obligated to improve the remainder for those who follow us.

Have Confidence—You Can Do It
An Historical Perspective

This book will help you overcome any fears you may have. It answers your questions and tells you what you need to know to start a practice. You need not be afraid to start your practice, alone or with others.

You are competent. You became competent when you were sworn in and admitted after passing the bar exam. You simply are not yet as experienced as you might wish to be. Don't worry. No lawyer ever feels that he or she has all the experience a lawyer could have. Law is a profession. You apply the problems you learned about in law school to the real live factual problems of your clients. People will always have more questions than you have answers. Don't be nervous. Don't worry that you can't always advise a client about what to do until you look up the latest law on the subject. You can always ask other lawyers for help if you are unsure. No lawyer would ever turn down the request of a new lawyer for help.

As an inexperienced new lawyer, it took me 15 hours to draft my first motion for summary judgment. My second took 6 hours, my third 2 hours and eventually I could prepare the motion in 30 minutes. I was competent when I drafted my first motion, I simply was not experienced.

I have an extensive collection of books on law office management going back to 1610, the year the English legal profession began writing books in English rather than Latin or Norman French.

The oldest book I own on how to start and build a law practice was published in 1654 and was titled *A Perfect Guide for a Studious Young Lawyer: Both Delightful and Profitable for Any Gentleman* (there were no female lawyers at that time). The book is based on the teachings of Coke, Bacon, Denny, and other giants of the English legal profession. It was authored by Thomas Fidell of Furnivalls Inne and it took him thirty years to write the book, indicating that he first felt a need for the book in 1624.

My collection also includes a book written in 1919 by Frederick J. Allen of Harvard, *The Law as a Vocation*, with an introduction by William Howard Taft and acknowledgments to Dean Wigmore, among others. That book quotes advice given to a young man by Abraham Lincoln in 1855:

> If you are absolutely determined to make a lawyer of yourself the thing is more than half done already. It is a small matter whether you read *with* anyone or not. I did not read with anyone. Get the books and read and study them in their every feature, and that is the main thing. It is no consequence to be in a large town while you are reading. I read at New Salem, which never had three hundred people in it. The *books* and your *capacity* for understanding them are just the same in all places. . . . Always bear in mind that your own resolution to succeed is more important than any one thing.

The challenges inherent in *How to Start and Build a Law Practice* have been with new lawyers for hundreds of years and will continue to be with the legal profession. Problems of lawyer overpopulation, unequal allocation of legal incomes, some failures and some successes are not new problems. These problems have previously been faced and conquered and you also can conquer them.

It took Fidell thirty years to write his book in 1654. It has taken me more than thirty-five years to write this fifth edition and the four predecessor editions of the book. This book answers the same questions that were asked 350 years ago. The questions are the same. The answers are different. This book represents the hopes and fears and questions and solutions of the almost two hundred thousand lawyers who have previously bought it or read it and the more than one hundred thousand lawyers whom I have taught face-to-face. These new lawyers have gone before you.

As Abraham Lincoln advised, your desire to succeed is one-half of the battle. This book will help you with the other half.

Go for it—you can do it!

Should You Start
Your Own Practice?
(You Can Do It)

Lawyers who start their own law practices usually fall into one or both of two categories:

A. They have to.

B. They want to.

Lawyers Who Have to Start Their Own Practices

Frankly, I expect that many, if not most, of the new and experienced lawyers who start their own practices today have no choice. They would prefer to get jobs, but can't for various reasons, including:

1. They are in the 95 percent of a law school class who are not in the top 5 percent of the class.

2. They were forced out of a job or partnership in a law firm or a job in a corporation due to factors beyond their control.

3. They are disgusted with the life they are leading and want a career that includes a quality of life and time to enjoy life and family.

4. They need a flexible professional setting to accommodate a child care or parental care problem.

5. They don't have a rich relative who can pressure a law firm to put a son or daughter on the payroll or risk losing the family's company as a client to the law firm that hires the son or daughter.

6. Neither they nor their parents belong to the "right" clubs or churches.

7. They didn't attend the "right" colleges or law schools.

8. They buy their clothes "off the rack" rather than having them custom tailor-made and therefore wouldn't have the proper appearance with clients.

9. They lead a lifestyle that doesn't fit in with firm images.

10. Their wives or husbands just aren't the "type" to be social with partners' spouses.

11. They are the "wrong" (or right) color or were born to the "wrong" (or right) parents.

12. They are considered "too old." There often is a fear that the older experienced lawyer will want to do things "their way" instead of the firm's way.

All of the above may or may not be valid reasons for being denied appropriate employment. I submit that *none* of the above reasons has the slightest correlation to success or failure as a practicing lawyer. (I expect those persons who satisfy all or part of the above list of requirements to disagree.)

Many of the people reading this book simply can't get the jobs they need or want as lawyers to use their legal training so they must either start their own practice or leave the field of law. *This is a perfectly valid reason to start your own law practice.*

Lawyers Who Want to Start Their Own Practices

I opened my own doors right out of law school. To satisfy your curiosity I will tell you that I turned down several unsolicited job offers and walked away from my successful practice as a CPA to open my doors.

A classmate of mine went to work for a firm. My classmate told me, "Jay, you're crazy. You'll be worrying about getting clients and overhead and collecting fees, while I'm getting my paycheck. It will take you years to make up the difference between your earnings and my paycheck. At the end of five to seven years, with luck, you'll be a partner in a good firm and so will I. You're doing it the hard way."

To some extent he was right and to a great extent he was wrong. Let me list some of the factors with pros and cons:

1. *Personality.* I could take three months to two years in law libraries doing the scutwork of other lawyers, while I was being looked at with a magnifying glass for fear I might say or do something to embarrass the firm. When I believe another lawyer is wrong on the law I tell that person so (*after* documenting my position). I didn't want candid criticism of a legal position to cost me my job.

2. *Client Contact.* Three years of law school was enough. I wanted contact with clients and the responsibility of making deci-

sions immediately. Another year of apprenticeship held no appeal for me. I had been an "apprentice" in two different unions and an "apprentice" with a CPA firm. To me an apprenticeship seemed more a matter of getting cheap profitable labor than of improving the quality of the work done by the apprentice.

3. *Practical Training*. Law firms hire associates because there is work to be done, not because the firm is interested in teaching new lawyers. In many firms there is no formal training program and in many others the training program is not functioning because the partners have little or no time to teach you anything. If they had that time they wouldn't need the associates. Increasingly, clients refuse to pay for "second lawyers" in trials, depositions, etc. A partner who takes time to teach an associate will be penalized with lower income. Many young lawyers tell me they are forced to work unsupervised in areas where they don't know what they are doing in order to create billable hours. Therefore, in many, if not most, instances you'll get just as much training in the law on your own as with a firm.

4. *Money*. My friend was simultaneously right and wrong. It took me five years until my cumulative earnings as a self-employed lawyer equaled what my cumulative earnings as an employee would have been. In my fourth year of private practice I was earning more than my classmates, but I had yet to make up for the difference of the first three years.

After the fifth year I was ahead of my friends, my employed classmates, etc. I've never fallen behind either on a year-by-year basis or on a cumulative basis.

After ten years some of my classmates had weathered the selection process and became junior partners in the large prestige law firms. They still earned less than I did.

I suppose that at some point I may or may not have fallen behind some of my classmates with the large firms when they attained senior partnership or were relegated to nonequity partnerships. On the other hand, I believe that those of my classmates who initially or ultimately started their own practices are earning about as much as I am.

5. *Type of Legal Work*. As a CPA I had to work on matters where I frankly didn't care for the client or type of work or what the firm was doing for the client. I didn't want the problem as a lawyer of doing work on matters or for clients for whom I had no respect simply because they had money to hire lawyers and I was a lawyer.

As my own boss I have greater freedom (not absolute freedom) to turn down cases and clients when I disagree morally with the legal principle espoused by the client.

6. *Security.* Except for some civil service situations, there is no such thing as job security in legal practice. If anything, I feel more secure standing on my own two feet than being dependent on the success or failure of an organization that I cannot control.

I've seen banks fire their entire legal division to "experiment on cost savings using outside counsel." If the experiment is a failure, some vice-president will shrug it off and the careers of some good lawyers who thought they had security will have been destroyed.

I've seen private law firms fire associates on a mass basis when a large client leaves.

Some of the largest law firms in the United States have gone under or merged, leaving lawyers unemployed who gave their lives to the firm, often at the cost of delaying children and forsaking spouses, children, and parents as well.

I've seen law firms and corporations where there are two lawyers in line for every promotion. The better lawyer (better-liked lawyer may be more accurate) gets promoted and the other gets fired, and the competition starts again.

In the 1990s, law firms split up and merged and split up again like amoebae. Whole departments and individual lawyers suddenly found themselves unemployed and forced to start a law practice.

The economic downturn of the early 2000s put many lawyers in the street trying to get a job or start a practice after a lifetime of loyalty to a firm.

Except for some civil service positions, there is no security as a lawyer, other than what you carry under your hat. Security is both relative and illusory. Your best helping hand is the one at the end of your arm.

7. *Fringe Benefits.* Obviously there are many other fringe benefits to being your own boss:

    a. *Vacations.* Go when *you* want to go.

    b. *Tax Benefits.* There are huge tax benefits in being self-employed, compared with being on a job (including loss carry-forwards). These benefits, however, in the main are more significant to you after a few years in practice. At the beginning you need more income, not deductions.

c. *Prestige.* A firm name with your name carries more prestige than working for another name firm. Being "self-employed" sounds better than being "unemployed."

d. *Freedom.* You'll have the freedom to turn down or refuse to represent a client or case you truly despise (with some limitations).

8. *Avoiding Burnout and Career Dissatisfaction.* Many young lawyers accept high-paying jobs with megafirms and then are forced to work long hours to justify the high salaries. After two or three years, the lawyer is burned out or feels "used up" and quits the practice of law.

You'll have to work long hours in your own firm, but you'll feel good about it because you're doing it for yourself and your family. You'll grow to love, not hate, the practice of law.

Risks of Failure

Nothing in life is guaranteed except death, and some religions claim they can guarantee against even death. There is a substantial risk of failure in opening up your own law practice. There is also risk if you accept a job with a law firm. Law firms "downsize," merge, are absorbed, and go out of business. Megafirms open and close branches or dissolve, leaving lawyers unemployed. There is also an element of luck involved. This is no more or less true with a law practice than with any other activity. Marriages fail, children and parents divide, even some of the largest corporations in the world have gone bankrupt. I would not be candid if I didn't make clear the possibility of failure.

Should You Start Your Own Practice?

Are the risks justified by the rewards? In my opinion, YES. If you will follow the lessons of this book, you'll increase the rewards and decrease the risks. Go ahead. Whether you make it or not, you'll never regret having tried. The lessons of failure are more bitter than the lessons of victory, but they are valuable lessons, nonetheless. There truly are no failures, only learning experiences. Even if you don't make it, you'll be a better lawyer and a better person for having tried. You may even find yourself able to get a job with a law firm since some law firms now look for lateral hires of experienced lawyers. Considering all the pros and cons, if you care enough about opening your own practice to be reading this book, you probably have what it takes to make it and successfully "start and build your own law practice."

How Soon Should You "Open Your Doors"?

As soon as possible. Student loans need to be repaid. You will quickly develop a liking for the "finer things in life," such as fine cars, skiing, recreational travel, clothing, nice restaurants, spectator events such as theatre, football, basketball, etc., not to mention a good apartment or home in addition to your student loan payments. These fine things slowly but surely creep into your standard of living, imperceptibly raising your cost of living. It is easier to "bite the bullet" *before* developing a taste for these things than *after* you have all these personal expenses.

Am I Competent to Give Legal Advice?

I am asked this question at almost every law school class I teach and at almost every new admittee Bridge the Gap course I teach.

The answer is YES! Upon passing the bar and being sworn in, you were declared competent to practice law in your state. You are competent, but you may not yet be experienced in the particular problem your client may have. This will happen to you many times as a lawyer, no matter how many years you may practice. Law is a profession. You never stop learning. Don't worry about it.

Try to get the facts from the client before the client comes in and do a little homework on the issues before the client arrives. If you are stuck, ask another more-experienced lawyer for help. (This is one of the advantages of practicing in a location with other lawyers.)

If you don't have time to check out the law or discuss the matter with another lawyer before meeting with the client, be truthful. Tell the client something like, "No one has ever asked me this question before. I need some time to think about it before I can recommend a plan of action." You might also say, "I'm pretty sure I know the answer" (if you do), "but I want to double-check to be sure the answer hasn't changed since the last time I dealt with this issue."

Don't panic just because you haven't previously handled a matter in an area of law. It frequently happens to all lawyers and it will happen to you many times in your career. Remember: You are competent. You just are not yet experienced.

Lastly, do not under any circumstances quote a fee or give advice until you feel you have either learned or looked up the law involved and applied it to the facts to come to an answer.

Should You Work on a Job "for Experience" Before Starting Your Practice?

Notwithstanding that you have a license to practice law and have been declared competent to practice law by your Supreme Court, you probably have some doubts about your ability to competently represent clients in court and give advice.

Working in Private Practice

I don't think that the "crutch" of six months' or a year's experience will assist you that much. Your "experience" may consist of doing research or making minor court appearances or preparing lesser documents. You will have relatively little client contact in most firms. The associates or partners to whom you are assigned will have relatively little time to spend with you discussing the case or "grading" what you turn in. Lack of supervision and review is a common complaint of new associates. Increasingly, first- and second-year associates tell me they are worried about their malpractice and ethics exposure because their firms are forcing them to do unsupervised work where they have no experience in order to build up chargeable hours to a file. Partners don't get compensated for mentoring and clients won't pay for two lawyers on a case. The associates would rather go into their own practice than continue working under those pressures. If the firm had a lot of free time available to supervise and teach, it wouldn't need associates.

Except in very few firms, there is relatively little formal training.

The "experience" you are seeking usually consists of access to the firm's form files, a few minutes of advice now and then from a slightly senior associate, and even less advice from a partner.

It is my opinion that there is no great detriment in developing your own forms using form books available from the law library and government forms available from the Internet, and scanning the incoming forms developed by others (see chapter on "How to Build a Good Form File"). In litigation matters, the clerks of court and other attorneys from whom you get work give you at least as much counseling as you would have gotten in a firm. Many of the court forms and instructions are available on the Internet.

The limited amount of supervision you would receive in six months to a year on a job does not, in most cases, justify delaying starting your practice.

Obviously the attorney who makes a commitment of one to five years in accepting a first job is taking a great risk and should be sure such a step will really be beneficial.

Working in Civil Service

At the time of the writing of this book, most, but not all, lawyers in civil service were receiving pay and fringe benefits equal to or in excess of those lawyers in private practice in medium-sized firms for the first few years.

My objections to civil service as a career are threefold:

1. *Limited Range of Professional Challenge.* In some jobs one can get five years of experience in five years. In other jobs one gets the same six months' experience ten times over. Some, if not many, civil service positions fall into this second category.

2. *The Pay Trap.* At the end of one, two, or five years, a lawyer in civil service has earned and is usually earning more than a counterpart in private practice. One often is limited in subsequent pay increases (but not limited in title promotion) because of rules not to earn more than a supervisor, etc. This results in a triangle with a small apex and a broad base. There is nowhere to go. The lawyer in private practice, however, can increase earnings without limitation.

3. *Limited Maximum Salary.* Even though a civil service lawyer can't go much farther in compensation, there are substantial pay and fringe benefits that would be reduced in private practice. Also, having proved ability in civil service, the lawyer must now prove ability in private practice.

There are some people who definitely are well suited for some civil service careers, but I doubt that many of them would be reading this book. The job security of civil service, lack of client pressures, little or no night or weekend work, generous retirement and medical plans, all combine to make it appealing to some lawyers.

Being a Contract Lawyer to Get Experience and Money While Building Your Practice

Drastic changes in the legal marketplace and in the structure of law firms have created new opportunities for contract lawyers to earn money while getting some experience and some training or mentoring. As firms downsize and outsource, contract lawyering is becoming a major factor in the dynamics of getting experience by new lawyers.

Because contract lawyers are typically paid by the hour, they often receive much more targeted direction, training, and mentoring than associates who are paid by the month.

I am frequently consulted by young lawyers who are concerned over their ethical and financial responsibility for trying to do work they can't do without guidance. They are often instructed to run up hours on a file, doing work they feel they are not competent to handle, with the partners and other associates refusing to train or supervise for fear they will lose chargeable hours by teaching. It is an ironic twist that outsiders will often receive better training and direction than the associates in the firm.

Definition of a Contract Lawyer

For purposes of this chapter, a contract lawyer is a lawyer who does work as an independent contractor for other lawyers, which can be either independent law firms or corporate counsel (sometimes called house counsel). The contract lawyer is typically hired by a lawyer or firm to work on a client matter often without the input or even the knowledge of the client.

19

The concept of the contract lawyer has been with us for more than fifty years, but only recently has become an important form of practicing law. In the 1930s, 1940s, and 1950s, women lawyers were only hired by Wall Street firms to work on large nonrecurring matters such as antitrust. During the case they were not considered as being part of the firm and at the conclusion of the case they were unemployed. Women lawyers were also hired to do estate or trust work where the executrix or trustee was a female. If the trustee were to be replaced by a male or institution, the lawyer became unemployed. In the 1960s and 1970s, firms began using contract lawyers to exclude them from the coverage of the pension and profit-sharing plans, which were then in vogue due to high income tax rates. In the 1980s and 1990s, firms began using contract lawyers to exclude nonrainmakers and to reduce training and health care coverage costs, among other reasons.

The large number of firms and corporate general counsel who now use contract lawyers has spawned a new type of employment agency or divisions in existing agencies specializing in placing or finding contract lawyers.

I have always recommended that young lawyers solicit business from older lawyers and overworked lawyers. Typically the work solicited and received is of the garbage type. Common examples would be taking or defending depositions in remote or distant places or making a court appearance to save the lawyer a trip to a distant or local courthouse on a minor or nonproductive case. In some cases the older lawyer will want to get rid of problem cases or garbage cases or problem clients or low-profit matters, all of which can become money, experience, and clients to the new lawyer. I strongly advocate that the young lawyer take great care not to steal clients from the referring lawyer and not to accept repeat work from the referred client without the permission of the referring lawyer, which typically might involve some form of a referral fee.

The classic centuries-old method of older lawyers helping younger lawyers with this arrangement has drastically changed due to two reasons:

1. The older lawyer may need the business and have little or no overflow to refer.

2. Many large firms and some bar associations have adopted the position that there is nothing wrong in stealing clients if the

client wants to make the change, and further, that agreements not to steal clients are unethical restraints on the clients' rights to choose counsel.

When lawyers are associates in firms, they are normally allowed some contact with clients. The amount of contact and the level of contact with the client may depend on the firm and its fear of a client liking the associate better than the partner in charge of the matter, resulting in the client following the associate when the associate leaves the firm. The contract lawyer often may be allowed absolutely no direct contact with the client, with all client contact coming through the firm.

Of Counsel

In many respects, a lawyer who is designated Of Counsel can be considered a contract lawyer. However, a lawyer who is Of Counsel usually has a long-standing relationship to one or more of the lawyers in the firm. Other aspects of the Of Counsel relationship will be treated separately.

Getting Work

Getting contract work is typically a lawyer-to-lawyer thing. You have to network with other lawyers through bar association activities. You have to meet them face-to-face and you have to communicate with them by mail and by periodic telephone calls reminding them you are available. Do not be upset by rejection. You have to keep trying. There is a large element of luck involved. You have to reach them when they happen to need you. Just because they don't need you in October doesn't mean they won't need you in January when someone in the office collided with a tree while skiing and will be out for a month, or in June when someone had to take a one-month emergency leave to take care of a sick or dying relative, or in April when the firm got substituted into a major litigation matter and is shorthanded, or in November when one of their existing clients needs help in an area of law in which you happen to have expertise the firm doesn't have. Develop an e-mail or fax-blast list of lawyers you have met. If you are going to use "snail mail," be sure to use high-quality engraved stationery.

Getting Paid

In some jurisdictions, a contract lawyer being neither a partner nor associate cannot receive any part of a fee paid by the client unless the rules on division of fees are followed. This may require the client's consent to a division and may require your being identified to the client. This is a newly developing area of law on division of fees. Check your local rules.

Your Contract Lawyer Agreement: Twenty-One Questions to Be Answered

You may increase your chances of getting the work if you have already prepared an agreement to be used in the hiring process. The agreement ought to address the following questions.

1. *Who is hiring you?* The law firm? The individual lawyer? The corporate counsel? The corporation? The employment agency? The client?

2. *For what task are you being hired?* If you fail to get new agreements for other work you may do, will this agreement serve to cover the new or additional work as well?

3. *What are your time periods and deadlines for doing the work or reporting?*

4. *Where you may do your work?* Anywhere you choose? Anywhere they choose? Their offices? Your home or office?

5. *Facilities and personnel: What law firm personnel or facilities (if any) will be available to you?* May you use an online or paper library, photocopy equipment, computers, the office, a conference room, and/or parking facilities?

6. *Who provides malpractice insurance?* Ask for a letter from them or their insurance agent confirming you are covered for the matters for which you are hired. Get a letter from your own agent confirming that this type of work is covered. You may wish to put a clause in your independent contractor agreement providing that for purposes of malpractice insurance only, you have agreed that you will be considered an employee of the hiring firm for malpractice insurance purposes only. Some insurance companies will sell malpractice insurance by the hour.

7. *Have you addressed your independent contractor status?* The hiring firm will want lots of independent contractor language to exclude you from any employee benefits, burdens, or taxes. This is

the firm's problem more than yours, but you may wish to cover it. Check out the latest rulings under state and federal laws concerning independent contractor status.

8. *How is your work to be delivered?* Via paper? On disk? Via modem? Via e-mail? Via fax? Via telephone? Some combination of media? What word processing programs are acceptable to them? Be sure to keep copies for your personal files for malpractice reasons and to be able to apply for specialty certifications.

9. *How frequently must you report?*

10. *To whom must you report?*

11. *Who will be available to answer your questions?* When will they be available? What is their turnaround time? (This is important if they have given you time deadlines.)

12. *When is the work due?* Will it be reviewed in stages to be sure they will not later complain you have missed the boat?

13. *How frequently will you be paid?* What billing documents or other documentation will you need to get paid?

14. *Are oral reports or questions and answers permissible or can you depend on instructions and help in writing?* (Remember, you may have almost no contact with the lawyer or client while you are doing the work.)

15. *Who provides or pays for various out-of-pocket costs?* Common sources of disagreement to be anticipated include secretarial or word processing services, messengers and delivery services, online research, parking, long-distance phone charges, and faxes.

16. *What type of time records or billing records must be maintained?* Must you conform to the firm's or its client's systems? Who must pay for inputting these records? Must you provide a disk for their systems?

17. *Have you and the firm checked for any conflicts of interests?* Check with your local ethics hotline to determine whether you have to be concerned that the work you do for the other firm will cause the other firm's client to become either your client while you are doing work for the firm or your former client at the conclusion of the matter. If there is a concern, you may wish to receive your assignment without names of clients or parties or without any more information than you absolutely need. This is a new area of concern and the dust hasn't settled. I personally would opt for anonymity if there is a concern.

18. *Should you identify the client?* Although you may wish for anonymity because of conflicts, in some states, a lawyer is deemed to be the agent of the client in hiring assistants and you may be able to sue the client directly if the lawyer or firm doesn't pay you as agreed. This is a very effective collection technique when a lawyer doesn't pay.

19. *Subcontracting: Do you have the right to choose assistants at your own expense?* Can you use paralegals or hire other lawyers or must you personally do the work?

20. *Have you considered a minimum fee or termination penalty?* If the amount of work anticipated is significant—more than 100 hours for example—you may have to give up other work or refuse other work to take this one matter on. In such a case, there's no harm in asking for a minimum fee or a termination penalty if the work dries up. To occupy and plan your time most effectively, you should ask for a minimum fee.

21. *Is payment of your fee contingent on payment by the client?* If so, you may have a "Division of Fees" problem, which must be addressed. It may be necessary to get client consent in writing.

In summary, contract lawyering is becoming a significant part of the legal profession. It is replacing and supplementing associate hiring and should be considered by new lawyers seeking fees and experience.

Earning a Living
Between Graduation
and Opening Your Practice

Some lawyers have no choice but to start a law practice on a part-time basis while working at a full- or part-time job. This is totally contrary to my best advice, yet I recognize the facts of life are that some lawyers have no choice due to financial obligations or personal obligations—they will, in fact, start a law practice while working at another job.

Some of the more common reasons expressed to me for deferring the opening of a law practice include:

1. They want to wait for a spouse to finish school, job training, or military training to then be assigned to a city. Only then will the lawyer know where he or she will be opening a practice.

2. They know where they want to practice, but for some reason have to wait a year or two before they can get there to open a practice.

3. They graduated law school heavily in debt and need money to repay student loans. (See chapter entitled "Managing Your Student Loan.")

4. They want to accumulate as much cash as possible before starting a practice in order to have a year's living expenses on hand.

5. They want to earn money to enable them to purchase high-tech computers, printers, fax machines, software packages, etc.

6. They have personal problems or commitments due to timing in taking the bar exam, getting the results, or getting sworn in, any of which will necessarily delay the start of a law practice.

Lawyers often ask me for information on the kinds of work they can get with a law degree, other than traditional clerking jobs. This is not a book on how to get a job. Many such books written by job experts are available; and there are many consultants who will tell you everything you have to do to get a job, from what color paper to use for a résumé, to how to sprinkle the salt and pepper on your entrée. This also is not a book on what kind of law you should seek a career in. There are a myriad of articles and books on that subject.

My purpose in adding this chapter is to give you some additional ideas on how to earn a living between law school and opening a practice. I've tried to point out whether or not the experience you would get in a particular nontraditional job will be of value to you when you open your own practice.

This chapter is based in part on an article I wrote for the *National Law Journal* and has been reprinted many times by state and local bar journals. It is not intended to include every job possibility; it is intended to get you thinking about ways to earn a living with your law degree until you can open your own practice. If you want to refer to the original article, it is titled "Nontraditional Jobs Where You Can Use a Law Degree."

1. *Corporate Counsel (formerly called House Counsel)*. This area of law is frequently referred to as corporate counsel, law division, or a similar title. Traditional law firms often price themselves out of the corporate legal market through overpricing of services. A law division or corporate counsel generally can provide many, if not all, of the same services as the traditional law firm at much less cost. The higher cost of traditional law firms is due to many factors, including the refusal or inability of the traditional firm to adopt modern techniques and personnel management. Mismanagement of resources, which I feel is prevalent in traditional law firms, would not be tolerated in a corporate environment. Business consumers of legal services are now forming and enlarging their in-house legal staff. It has been said that a traditional law firm has a variety of clients with a variety of problems. Corporate counsel has a single client with a variety of problems. This is definitely a growth area. Depending upon the particular job you secure, the experience may or may not be of value when you open your own firm.

2. *Legal Assistants and Paralegals*. (I have lumped these two together because I am tired of arguing about the differences, if any, between the two.) If you can get a job as a legal assistant, the experience will be of great help to you in understanding the proper (and improper) utilization of legal assistants in a law firm. In law school you learned *why* law is practiced. As a legal assistant you can learn

how law is practiced. A legal assistant can and should do anything a lawyer does except make court appearances and make decisions concerning legal rights and responsibilities. Accordingly, as a legal assistant you may get training and supervision that new associates in a firm do not get.

For various reasons, many law firms absolutely refuse to hire lawyers as legal assistants. One of the reasons for their refusal is that the firm feels the lawyer is not looking for serious permanent employment as a legal assistant. When you meet this resistance you can honestly reply that you intend to work as a legal assistant for only six months, one year, or for whatever your schedule is. You should ask if they have any substantial client matter in the office or coming up that would make it in the firm's best interests to hire you for the duration of that matter. The firm then could consider you for temporary employment, or for employment for only that one case.

3. *"Rent-A-Lawyer" Temporary Agencies.* There are agencies that serve as a clearinghouse between lawyers seeking part-time or additional work and firms that need a lawyer for a particular case or for a limited period of time. Often a firm wants to take on a case for a particular client rather than refer it to another law firm, even though it cannot handle it without increasing its permanent staffing. These firms (and lawyers seeking work) go to an agency to match needs and availability. Some bar associations run these agencies. Typically, the lawyer is paid between forty and seventy-five dollars per hour and the agency gets an additional 10 percent as its fee. It may be worthwhile to familiarize yourself with as many of these agencies as you can. Be sure there is a written definition of responsibility for malpractice coverage. There is a sort of "grab bag" element of luck in terms of the work being of value to you in opening your own practice.

4. *Government.* Government, both state and local, has been in the past and will be in the future a major consumer of legal talent. It has been estimated that government at levels from local to federal employs between 10 and 15 percent of all lawyers. There are as many different jobs as there are government agencies. Some of these agencies hire lawyers in governmental areas where one might not ordinarily consider a lawyer for the job.

With government jobs generally, as with house counsel, whether or not the experience can be of value to you when you open your own practice will depend on the job you get and the practice you start.

a. *Law Enforcement.* FBI and Treasury Agents and IRS Criminal Investigators are examples.

b. *Military.* The military services hire civilian lawyers to do work similar to the work done by career military officer lawyers. Contracts and litigation are common areas where military and civilian lawyers work side by side.

c. *Other.* Get a Washington, D.C., telephone directory, a telephone directory from your state capital, and a local telephone directory, and simply send a form letter to the personnel section of each agency or department listing, asking if it hires lawyers. It may take some time to coordinate timing of applications, interviews, and the ultimate hiring. Many jobs that require lawyers are not civil service and, accordingly, may not be subject to the usual procedures. This is why it is necessary to write to each agency and department separately.

Government is definitely a growth area for lawyers. People want increased regulation and layers of new laws on top of old laws, which require an increased number of lawyers to draft and administer these laws.

Notwithstanding a Proposition 13, anti-growth sentiment on the part of the public, government will find a way to grow, making government law definitely a growth area.

5. *CPA Firms.* The practice of accounting is very similar to the practice of law in many aspects. After traditional law firms and house counsel, CPA firms may be one of the largest employers of lawyers. Some CPA firms actually own law firms as profit centers. The international CPA firms tend to be the main employers, although local CPA firms also hire lawyers. Some of the uses of lawyers in CPA firms are:

a. *Tax Departments.* Even small local CPA firms often hire lawyers to work in their tax departments. Typical work would include research and tax opinions given to a client or given internally to a department, such as the audit department. The extent of active use of lawyers in a CPA firm varies from firm to firm. In some firms the lawyer may go to Tax Court or to an administrative or local tax hearing, but not to a U.S. District Court. In some firms the lawyer may review documents prepared by the client's counsel for tax effects. In some firms the lawyer may draft legal documents.

b. *Litigation Support or Litigation Services.* Many CPA firms work closely with and compete with law firms to lend support in such areas as document analysis, or to assist a law firm in handling major litigation.

    c. *International.* International CPA firms often use lawyers in the international department's offices to assist in a variety of ways.

    d. *Management Services.* CPA firms offer management advice to law firm clients, such as assistance in data processing and information technology.

    6. *Law Firm Management.* Many law firms have specialized administrative staffs. This is a phenomenon that began in the 1980s and 1990s. Law firms need management personnel to the same extent that any going business needs management. If you have had courses or experience in areas such as sales, marketing, advertising, public relations, printing, finance, personnel administration, training, accounting, budgeting, etc., you may be able to get a position in a law firm where, although you won't be practicing law, *per se*, your experience will stand you in good stead when you open your own practice. Many law firms prefer to hire a person who has a law school education to work better with lawyers and lend credibility. In some cases, however, law firms deliberately avoid using someone with a law degree.

    7. *Computer and Hi-Tech Experience.* If you can spell PC, as in personal computer, there is a job in a law firm for you, either as an employee or as a consultant. Many law firms now know *what* they can do with a computer, but don't know *how* to do it. Frankly, it doesn't require much technical ability to put computer applications into law firms. Unfortunately (possibly fortunately for you), many lawyers over fifty can't figure out how to turn off a PC, much less program simple applications. Having a law degree will be helpful in understanding what the lawyers and support staff are doing. The experience also will help you when you open your own practice.

    8. *Law Firm Consulting.* This is similar to law firm management except that it is done by outside consultants. This again is a new area that began opening up widely in the 1990s. I believe that the large international CPA firms may share, if not take, the lead in this area.

    9. *Law Firm Marketing Administration and Consulting.* Specialized and full-time law firm marketing has been given candid recognition by the profession only recently. The National Association of Law Firm Marketing Administrators (NALFMA) came into

being about 1985 and has grown to more than one thousand members. The criteria or qualifications for becoming a law firm marketing administrator are varied and in a state of flux. As a lawyer, if you are admitted to practice, you legally and ethically can share fees with the firm you work for. You may be able to convince a law firm that it needs a marketing administrator. If you are the firm's first marketing administrator and do not understand the function of a marketing administrator, buy a copy of my book *How to Get and Keep Good Clients*, Second Edition. Read the book. It'll probably take you about a year to install in the firm the various techniques described in the book. The experience will stand you in good stead when you open your own practice.

10. *Newsletter Writing and Publishing.* Writing and selling newsletters for lawyers and for their clients seems to be an exploding industry. I frequently get invited to be on the editorial board or to write for some new newsletter. Many law firms write their own newsletters, which they use as a form of advertising to get new clients and/or to communicate with existing clients. Some law firms buy "canned" or pre-written newsletters and send them to clients, passing them off as material developed by the firm. If you have any ability or interest in writing newsletter-style publications, you may be able to earn income writing or ghostwriting for these publications. The experience may not do much for you in terms of your own practice, unless you intend to put out your own newsletter when you begin a practice. These newsletters typically are devoted to "recent developments in the law" or "how our law firm can help you," and require a hard-hitting writing style that is not consistent with the way most lawyers write.

11. *Government Regulation.* I am describing a career that does not yet exist in the United States. In Brazil, there is a profession known as *economista*. The profession is not equivalent to the American profession of economist. The *economista* has the responsibility of determining all government laws, regulations, etc., of the various administrative agencies that apply to the business. The *economista* also is responsible for advising the company on how to comply with these regulations. Normally, the *economista* is responsible directly to the president and occupies an important position within the enterprise. In some companies, the *economista* takes the place of house counsel, while in others, the *economista* assists the regular house counsel staff. Since this profession does not yet exist in the United

States, it is difficult to create a name for the position. Perhaps the title should be "Corporate Vice-President, Governmental Regulations" or "Governmental Affairs," "Regulation Compliance," or some similar title.

12. *Banks and Insurance Companies.* Banks and insurance companies require large numbers of house counsel due to the scope and size of operations, and as government regulation of their activities increases. Many of the observations applicable to banks and insurance companies also will apply to house counsel in other industries.

  a. *Litigation.* Many banks and insurance companies maintain a litigation firm that ostensibly is outside counsel. These firms typically defend cases where the institution feels the exposure is low compared with the costs of a defense, which could be high (relative to the exposure) if outside counsel were used. Often the lawyers employed in these firms are allowed to work on their own cases as long as it does not interfere with their regular workload. Insurance companies also use this type of firm for subrogation, and banks often use the firms for routine collection-type work.

  b. *Forms.* Banks and insurance companies must generate a myriad of forms that have to comply with a myriad of regulatory rules and laws. These forms are more cheaply produced by house counsel than by outside counsel for a variety of reasons.

  c. *Corporate.* Banks and insurance companies frequently have multiple corporate subsidiaries or affiliates, all of which require the typical corporate minutes, resolutions, etc.

  d. *Administrative Regulation Compliance.* See "Government Regulation," above.

  e. *Securities Law, Bankruptcy.* Secured creditor work, or "workouts" (agreements between a debtor and a creditor when the debtor is in default), are common for banks and insurance companies because of the large number of investments they make. The complexity of creditor rights laws often requires a lawyer to do the workout.

The experience gained as house counsel generally is helpful to a point for a lawyer starting a practice. Often a house counsel position becomes repetitive and boring after six months to a year. Since you will be staying only long enough to open your own practice, the experience probably will be of value. If you are fortunate, you may be able to make some good contacts and get some office procedure experience that could be of help to you.

13. *Investment Banking.* For reasons that I truly do not understand, a large number of lawyers are being hired to do nonlegal work in investment banking (possibly in a capacity similar to a retail stockbroker). I do not see any relationship between working for a brokerage firm and opening your own law office, but I pass on to you that this may be a way of earning a living until you are ready to open your own firm.

14. *Labor Law (sometimes called Human Resources Law).*

a. *Classic Labor Law.* Both unions and management hire large numbers of lawyers to advise the union or the employer of the limits of permissible conduct. Union lawyers also may provide various forms of workers' compensation law or FELA law for their members when they claim work-related injuries. Often the union lawyer represents both the union and the worker.

b. *Age, Gender, and Other Forms of Prohibited Discrimination.* Many special-interest groups hire lawyers to litigate or otherwise protect their members or constituencies from prohibited discrimination or harassment. Employment lawyers are always in great demand, especially during recessions.

c. *Employer-Group Prepaid Insurance Plans.* I include this category because this area of law often is controlled or sponsored by unions, although certainly many nonunion groups also have these plans. This is an area of law where a group member pays, or has the employer pay, a certain amount of money per year or month or hour. The "legal group" of lawyers agrees to provide a certain quantity of legal services in specified areas for some part of the prepaid fee. The theory is that the legal group will lose money on many prepaid members but make up the losses on volume or on the occasional contingency fee. I seriously question the long-term economic viability of these plans as presently constituted. Certainly this may represent an area where a lawyer can get experience in "preventative law." In any event, you can gain experience in a rather limited area while waiting to open your own practice.

15. *Legal Aid, Poverty Lawyers, Legal Defense Clinics, Store-Front Lawyers, and Other Pro Bono Publico Work.* It takes a special kind of person to do this kind of work. One must be highly motivated to provide legal services to people who otherwise might not be able to afford them. I've heard lawyers who work for these organizations compare the experience to that of being an intern in the emergency room of a county hospital: grueling hours of under-com-

pensated work, but a wealth of hands-on experience. These law firms sometimes take on a caseload far beyond their financial ability. The results can be a legal job of questionable quality for a client with little or no ability to pay for the amount of work and resources required. Many of my books, forms, articles, etc., are used by these groups, and I willingly help them.

Although *pro bono* cases offer you exposure to a wide variety of work, you may not be able to give any one client or case the highest level of professional quality of law required. Your compensation probably will be more psychological than financial. In most cases, you must have passed the bar to secure this type of employment, but in some situations a law degree without a license is sufficient. It may be difficult or impossible to repay student loans out of what you can earn doing this work. It is my hope that someday lawyers who do this type of work will have their student loans forgiven or deferred while working for legal services that do pro bono work.

16. *Mediators, Arbitrators, Conciliation Counselors, etc.* Alternative dispute resolution (ADR) is a rapidly growing area. Many people and companies are now turning to mediation, arbitration, or conciliation as an alternative to litigation. Many large corporations submit to arbitration and mediation of consumer and employee complaints. Many lawyers are becoming mediators.

If you have some special skill outside of legal training, you may be able to serve as a well-compensated arbitrator or mediator. A telephone call to your local American Arbitration Association office or American Association of Mediators is a good starting place. It will be worth your while to spend the money to get the required number of hours (typically forty) of training to be a certified or approved mediator or arbitrator. The money will be well spent if you have it.

17. *Employment Agencies.*

a. *Using an Employment Agency.* Often a company with no hiring experience will employ an employment agency to locate a lawyer it needs. Such an agency may be called an executive search firm, headhunter, or a variety of other names. You should consider using an agency to get a job only if no fee is to be paid by you. (The company should pay all fees.)

b. *Working for an Employment Agency.* You may wish to work for an employment agency on a commission basis. Working for an agency is not likely to give you experience you can use in your practice, but it can give you insight into the "hot" areas of law in your region, based on what kinds of lawyers law firms need most.

18. *Consider Moving.* On behalf of the State Bar of California, I did an informal survey of state bar groups to find out who was "importing" lawyers. In the survey, I discovered that some states don't have enough local law school graduates to meet their needs and must bring in lawyers from other states. Although the survey is a bit dated, the results remain the same. States importing lawyers include Delaware, Hawaii, North Dakota, Arizona, Nevada, Colorado, North Carolina, Rhode Island, Idaho, Nebraska, Mississippi, Oregon, New Hampshire, New Jersey, Wisconsin, Alaska, Indiana, Louisiana, and Maine.

19. *Continuing Legal Education.* CLE is a growing area of law and should be considered as a possible employment area. The Association of Continuing Legal Administration (ACLEA) is a good contact organization.

20. *Bar Association Administrator.* Bar associations typically get bigger rather than smaller and often hire lawyers for various jobs. The National Association of Bar Executives (NABE) is a good contact organization.

21. *Law Firm Consultant.* Many lawyers who have experience or skills in allied fields become "consultants" to lawyers in various areas, including technology.

Conclusion

The number of jobs available for lawyers in nontraditional areas is extensive. You will have to use imagination and ingenuity. In this chapter, I've tried to give you some ideas to stimulate you to do your own thinking.

As my dear friend J. Harris Morgan of Dallas suggests (and I consider him the greatest mind on the delivery of legal services):

"Begin! The rest is easy."

Should You Start with Another New Lawyer?

Two new, inexperienced lawyers without an established clientele starting out together are similar to the blind man carrying a legless man on his back with the latter doing the navigating for both. In theory, the combination should work. In practice, it only works on a temporary basis. Therefore, as a general rule, two new lawyers getting together will accomplish very little except to prove that two can starve to death at least twice as fast as one. I recommend against it.

On the other hand, I know from experience that many teams of inexperienced lawyers have set up practice together for noneconomic reasons such as long-term friendships. A few teams will make it. Therefore, although I generally recommend against two brand-new lawyers getting together, I'll give you some suggestions that may increase your chances of success.

1. Don't form a partnership for at least one year. A bad partnership can be financially worse than a bad marriage. Your spouse can only cost you everything you have. Your partner can cost you your future. Get together on an expense-sharing basis. Each of you can be "of counsel" to the other. For example, there could be two sets of stationery as follows:

BRAND NEW LAWYER JONES 123 Main St., Anytown	INEXPERIENCED LAWYER SMITH
INEXPERIENCED LAWYER SMITH Of Counsel	123 Main St., Anytown BRAND NEW LAWYER JONES Of Counsel

Check local rules for this situation.

2. Put your expense-sharing "of counsel" agreement in writing.

3. Be sure clients are informed in their written fee agreements that the other lawyer and you are not in the same firm. Require the other lawyer to do the same. This may be necessary in order to divide fees. Be sure the client consents in writing.

4. Verify in writing your malpractice insurances coverage.

5. Work together to formulate your business plan. (A sample business plan is included in this book.)

6. Pick someone who complements you rather than who merely duplicates you. Remember, you need as much exposure as possible.

a. If you have the same friends, belong to the same church and clubs, have the same interests and hobbies, then you'll make great friends but will lose one of the chief benefits of association, which is multiple exposure to clients and potential clients.

b. Unless you have some reason for trying to start a specialty practice your first day, you should associate with someone who has different legal interests. The most common example I have seen is that one is interested in "Trial Law" areas such as criminal and divorce and the other is interested in "Business Law" areas. Usually, the practice ultimately tends toward the activity of the better business-getter.

c. Be flexible and ready to change your plans. Since the practice will gravitate toward the activity of the better business-getter, the other lawyer may have to readjust career plans. The "Trial Lawyer" will have to start doing corporation formation and leases, or the "Business Lawyer" will have to start getting clients bailed out of jail. If this adjustment doesn't occur, there will be a falling out when the better business-getter realizes that he or she is doing all the work and needs an associate rather than a partner.

7. Be sure your "partner" is adequately financed. You don't want to come into the office one morning and find that you are the "stuckee" on the rent, library equipment payment, payroll taxes, etc., because your good friend couldn't bear half of the burden.

8. Cover in advance the problems of split-up.

a. Telephone number. A telephone number, and a fax number, and an e-mail address or a Web site are exceedingly important assets to a lawyer. Whoever gets the phone and fax number, e-mail address and Web site may get cases originally intended for the other.

b. Unpaid payments. Who is going to pay for what?

c. Who moves? Who stays? The office location has a small value. Clients get nervous about lawyers who keep changing address.

d. Who gets the forms file?

e. Who will be responsible for which files (storage and distribution)?

f. Who will get ownership of the Web site?

g. Provide for arbitration of differences. Individual litigation can be expensive and bitter. In short, if you're smart, you'll have a written agreement.

9. How about a new lawyer getting together with a lawyer with two to three years' experience? In my opinion, this makes much more sense than two new lawyers getting together. The best way to improve your bridge, your tennis, or your chess is to play against someone slightly better than you. The same is true in law. A new lawyer can learn a lot from a lawyer with experience, and the experienced lawyer can take advantage of the willingness of the new lawyer to follow instructions and do the work outlined. I recommend this arrangement as opposed to the two-new-lawyers arrangement.

10. How about buying a practice? This is a newly developing area and will be treated in another chapter. See also **www.Senior Lawyers.org**.

Practicing with Your Spouse

I have been married more than forty years (to the same spouse) and it is beyond my comprehension how two people can be together almost twenty-four hours a day experiencing the same experiences, not getting "space" or enough privacy when privacy is needed.

On the other hand it appears I am wrong. Many lawyers have written to me and told me that they practice law with their spouse and find the experience very rewarding. They often tell me that this book was their "bible" in getting started and they constantly refer to it to settle law practice disputes.

These couples relate to me that they feel they have a higher quality of life. They share child rearing, often bringing the children into the office, and they share errands and tasks. Working together gives both of them the flexibility to take care of children and parents and themselves and their home without loss of income.

I am certain that there must be couples who found working together to be a disaster, but I have never met them or heard from them while, as indicated, I've heard from many who have found great happiness and satisfaction working together. I don't understand how they do it, but it seems to work, so I must advise you to at least think about practicing with your spouse (after formulating your business plan).

I am frequently corrected by those who want to include "partner, cohabitee, or other person" with whom one may have a significant relationship within the scope of the word "spouse." I do not mean to exclude them. I use the word "spouse" to include these various relationships to avoid lengthy repetition.

Should You Practice Another Business or Profession While Starting Your Law Practice?

If you can do so, it will probably be in your best interests financially to limit your activities to law until you are fairly well established as a lawyer. In my opinion, your second business or profession is more likely to be a brake than a booster on the development of your law practice. A few people can successfully maintain two businesses or professions with both growing profitably, but they are the exception, not the rule.

If you have another business or profession, I advise you to sell it or become as inactive as possible and devote your full time to the development of your law practice. I know from past experience that my advice will probably be ignored because you'll be afraid to give up your known income for unknown income in a new profession. Three or four years from now you'll say that I was right and you should have taken my advice earlier, but until then you'll hang on to your other practice or business out of fear.

If, on the other hand, you are earning enough from your second business or profession so that you have no immediate interest in creating a full-time law practice, then you can practice another business or profession, subject to certain restrictions:

1. *Attorney-Client Privilege Problems.* You must segregate activities as a lawyer from your other activities. When a client seeks legal advice from a lawyer, there is an attorney-client privilege. When the same person seeks nonlegal assistance from the "lawyer" acting in the other, nonlegal capacity, then the attorney-client privilege does not apply. You must take care to protect the client's privilege.

2. *Malpractice Insurance Problems.* Here again you must be careful. For example, if you are both a lawyer and a CPA and you sign a gift tax return as a CPA, your accounting professional insurance should protect you. If you sign as a lawyer, your legal professional insurance should protect you. If you don't identify your capacity, you may find that your accounting carrier will claim you're not insured because you were practicing law, and your legal carrier may claim you are not insured because you were practicing accounting. You can conjure up similar hypothetical problems for the lawyer who is also an insurance agent and gives estate-planning advice, or the lawyer who is also a bank or insurance company director and advises the bank or insurance company.

3. *Advertising and Solicitation Problems.* Disciplinary Rule 2-102(E) of the Code of Professional Responsibility as adopted by some bar associations states: "A lawyer who is engaged both in the practice of law and another profession or business shall not so indicate on his letterhead, office sign, or professional card, nor shall he identify himself as a lawyer in any publication in connection with his other profession or business."

Disciplinary Rule 2-103(A) states: "A lawyer shall not recommend employment, as a private practitioner, of himself, his partner, or associate to a nonlawyer who has not sought his advice regarding employment of a lawyer."

These rules are possibly not constitutional, but where they are still in effect, require you to, in effect, hide your second business or profession from your legal clients, and not to recommend yourself as a lawyer when you discover legal problems.

While acting in your nonlawyer capacity, there is significant debate among reasonable people as to whether the prohibitions and restrictions on advertising and solicitation were or are for the benefit of the public or for the benefit of the established law firms who wish to eliminate open competition for clients. There is also an ongoing question as to whether the prohibitions and restrictions are themselves illegal under First Amendment or antitrust laws or as deprivations of the public's "right to know."

The winds of change are blowing strongly in the fields of advertising and solicitation. My personal belief has always tended toward informing the public of the qualifications and fees of a lawyer so that the public can make informed choices when selecting a lawyer. This, however, may not be the state of the law, and the new lawyer would be well advised to follow the dictates of DR 2-102(E) and 2-103(A) or the applicable local rules unless he or she is interested in a three-to-five-year battle with the organized bar and is willing to bear the expense and stigma attached to such a fight. Each of these rules, in my opinion, represents a compromise between conflicting theories and, for that reason, is worthy of respect.

4. *How to Handle Dual Businesses or Professions.*

a. Maintain two filing systems. Don't mix the legal files with the nonlegal files.

b. Maintain separate bank account systems including separate trust accounts. Don't mix legal fees with nonlegal fees.

c. Maintain separate stationery and calling cards.

d. Maintain separate billings to the client.

e. Maintain separate phone and fax and e-mail numbers.

f. If, in the course of your nonlegal representation, you discover a legal problem, bring it to the attention of the client and offer to assist the client's lawyer. Don't offer to handle the legal problem. Explain to the client that you may not have any attorney-client privilege due to having discovered the problem in your nonlegal capacity. If the client insists on your handling the problem as a lawyer, protect both yourself and the client by sending the client a letter indicating:

(1) That the client is not obligated to use you due to your discovery of the problem and your willingness to cooperate with any other lawyer the client might wish to use;

(2) That you will be functioning as a lawyer from that point on at your standard rate for legal fees and that from that point on there will be an attorney-client privilege.

5. *Starting Your Own Practice While Working as a Full-Time or Part-Time "Flex" Lawyer.* "Flex" lawyers often work full-time as lawyers for state and federal governments and commercial companies where they can have "flex-time" schedules. They try to build a practice by servicing client needs while adjusting their employment hours and days to accommodate their new practice (and vice versa). They sometimes end up practicing their personal practice from their employer's facilities. There can be serious problems as to improper or unauthorized use of the flex employer's facilities.

In my opinion, the flex lawyer approach is not a good way to try to start a law practice. I don't recommend starting a practice while you have another full-time job, if you have a choice.

6. *Multidisciplinary Disciplinary Practice (MDP)*. MDP is fundamentally contrary to the American legal system. It is a plan for nonlawyers to practice law and lawyers to be in various businesses and for the lawyer and the nonlawyer to share money gotten from a common client. It has been soundly defeated by the ABA House of Delegates, but may become part of permissible fee-sharing in one or more states.

Should You "Specialize"?

I, personally, do not recommend you consider "specialization" until you have been in practice for six months to one year. I believe you need this time for two reasons:

1. To find out the areas of law for which there is a need for lawyers in your area.

2. To get a feel for different areas of law to determine the area or areas you enjoy practicing.

On the other hand, successful new lawyers starting a practice tell me they get a faster start in their practice by partially limiting their area of practice from the very beginning. They report they get more immediated referrals from older lawyers and from other professionals by stating they "specialize" or "concentrate" or "limit their practice to" or "emphasize" a specific area of law. (The exact wording you can use will depend on the rules in your state.)

The new lawyers tell me they ask other lawyers in the community where there is a need for lawyers in terms of the area(s) of law involved. The new lawyers then tell the practicing lawyers they are willing to do those areas. The new lawyers then begin getting referrals immediately in the chosen areas of law. As time goes on the new lawyers also get cases and clients in other areas of law in order to broaden their experience.

A possible solution would be to announce to professionals that you have a "specialty" (again, your state rules will dicate what you can say), but to accept work in as many areas as possible to get a taste of other areas of law.

After your practice gets going, I suggest you have two specialty areas plus general practice, or two specialty areas. Clients will feel more comfortable feeling that you "specialize" in their problem area. On the other hand, it is dangerous to put all your eggs in one basket. Areas of law practice could get eradicated by a single court decision or legislative act. You don't want to find yourself a "specialist" in a nonexistent area of law practice without a fall-back area of law practice. You also wish to be in a good position whether the economy is up or down.

Naming Your Law Firm

Major law firms have long recognized the value that can attach to a firm name. Major firms have long used names of people who were dead before some of the lawyers in the firm were even born. The rules are changing in many jurisdictions, allowing lawyers to use fictitious names.

In my opinion, you should name your law firm with your own name. As a new lawyer, you want to get your name out to as many potential clients and referrers of clients as possible. Having your name as the firm name gives you status. Accordingly, I would go with "Law Office of Mary Smith" or "John Smith, Attorney-at-Law," or whatever similar naming is appropriate in your community and permissible under your rules. I believe that the words "Law Office" on the card and letterhead of a new lawyer creates a sense of permanence and responsibility. Clients and potential clients know they are dealing with the decision maker, the most important person in the firm. Simply saying "Attorney-at-Law" doesn't connote your stature. One could be an employee of another firm with the words "Attorney-at-Law." In some jurisdictions, you must, in fact, have an office if you use the words "Law Office." One lawyer related to me that he had earned a huge fee as a new lawyer because he used the words "Attorney & Counsellor at Law" on his card. A client chose him from among many lawyers she interviewed because she thought that he had more training or experience than an attorney who was not also a counsellor.

On the other hand, the rules are changing rapidly and you may wish to choose a fictitious name for your practice, especially if you are starting a specialty or niche practice or a practice with one or more other lawyers. Law firms could call themselves "The Litigation Group," "The High Technology Group," "The Real Property Firm," or other names designed to convey to clients and potential clients one or more areas of competence. Some lawyers choose a fictitious names for purposes of listing placement in telephone or other directories.

I highly recommend that you reserve your Internet name immediately before someone else "cybersquats" it. At the very least, reserve your own name. **Johnsmith.com** or **Johnsmithlaw.com** are good examples. My Internet site is **http://www.Foonberglaw.com**. (Check it out.) I also use **www.estatecontests.com**, **www.trustcontests.com**, **www.willcontests.com**, as well as **www.FractionalJetOwenership.com** for my practice. You can reserve your Internet name(s) without actually having a Web site or using the reserved name. You might even consider trademarking the name(s) you reserve.

Be sure you check local rules before you do anything out of the ordinary. Where the rules permit you may wish to practice under two different names, one being your own name (Mary Jones) and the other indicating your area of law (The California Divorce Lawyer). [I made up this name as an example.]

You may also have to register your name as a fictitious name with the Bar and to comply with local laws.

Sole Practice v. Partnership v. Shared Office

1. A partnership can have some economic and psychological advantages over sole practice, especially for a new lawyer. The principal advantages of partnerships are

a. Each partner can develop an expertise or specialty in specific areas of practice, relying on the other partner(s) to cover the other areas of practice.

b. Someone is earning money for you when you are sick or on a vacation (or vice versa).

c. There is someone to "watch the store" while you are out of the office for short or long periods of time. Your client emergencies can be temporarily handled in your absence.

d. The overhead per lawyer may be slightly less for a two- or three-lawyer partnership than for two or three lawyers practicing solely. (In my opinion this factor is greatly overrated and in itself does not justify forming a partnership.)

e. You have a "sounding board" in the office to discuss your theories or issues. You can easily get a second opinion on a case.

f. A bank loan is easier to get with two signatures.

g. A simple Partnership Agreement Form is easy to write. See the earlier chapter "Should You Start with Another Lawyer?" for some points to cover.

2. Sole practice (also referred to as solo practice) has the following advantages and disadvantages:

a. You don't have to feel guilty about spending large amounts of time on cases that really interest you.

b. You come and go as you wish.

c. You can turn down cases and clients you hate.

    d. When you do earn "the big fee," it's all yours.

    e. You're stuck with all the administrative tasks of running a law firm.

    f. You lose the larger or complex cases you have to refer out when you don't have the expertise or personnel to handle the case.

    g. Many clients equate small law practices with ability to handle only small legal matters.

    3. In a shared-office arrangement, sometimes called an incubator suite, you can remain a sole practitioner and still have many of the advantages of partnership in group practice. Normally you are a tenant in the suite along with the others in the suite, or possibly you will simply be sharing expenses. The proximity of the other lawyers will give you the second opinion and the coverage you need, plus some possible additional referral work.

    In the past I was somewhat hesitant about space sharing, but with ever-escalating costs due to inflation, I now recommend it to the lawyer who wants to be in sole practice but still have the advantages of a partnership without actually having a partnership. I specifically recommend the concept of the "Fegen Suite" (see p. 78). You should include a sentence in your standard fee agreement that the client understands that the other lawyers in the suite and you are not in the same firm. You should require all lawyers in the suite to include similar language in their agreements to reduce the likelihood of your being sued by a client of another lawyer who reasonably thought you and the other lawyer were in the same law firm.

    4. Choosing your form of entity is important. In general, a new lawyer in practice for himself or herself would be wise to stick with the sole proprietorship form of practice unless there was some overriding reason not to do so. On the other hand, if the lawyer is going into practice from a firm taking a major client or case along, then there may be tax or other advantages in considering practicing as a professional corporation or a limited liability company (where permitted).

    If the new lawyer is starting with other lawyers in what would ordinarily be a partnership, then the lawyers should consider a professional corporation or limited liability company or limited liability partnership. Tax considerations may dictate whether a C or an S corporation would be preferable. Creditor liability may be a factor in opting for a limited liability company or S corporation. There are sometimes financial risks in going into business with another person who can make financial commitments that can bind you.

The Written "Business Plan"

Having a business plan does not mean that the profession of law is a business, concerned only with making money and ignoring professional responsibility. The practice of law is an economic activity that requires efficient utilization of resources, but it is not a business. A business plan is a commonly accepted term to refer to a concept of planning efficient utilization of resources. A written business plan is of great help in successfully starting a law practice.

Creating a written business plan forces you to consider and evaluate your strengths and your weaknesses, your resources, and where you need to obtain additional resources. The plan gives you both a road map and a timetable for where you want to go and when you hope to get there. The plan, after creation, gives you a tool to measure your progress and to spot small problems before they become big problems.

If you intend to go into practice with others, the creation of the plan will create a common goal so that you and the others will have a team effort and be pulling in the same direction with the same short-, medium-, and long-term objectives. If you and the others with whom you are starting a practice cannot agree on the business plan, you might have to reconsider either where you are going or with whom you are going to practice, or both. Be sure all of you sign the plan to ensure you are on the same track.

A written business plan can also be a valuable marketing tool. Having a written business plan will impress bankers and other people you may be looking to for financial resources or for client referrals or for legal work. You can ask these people to review your business plan for their comments and input. They will be impressed that you think enough of them to ask them for business and career advice and they will psychologically become part of your team, wanting you to make it and trying to help all they can.

The process of creating the plan forces you to seriously consider factors you might not otherwise even think of. A written plan is critical to be sure you have covered all bases and to have a document to refer to when there is a problem concerning a decision reached or to be reached.

The creation of the plan with other people can be divisive in that problems will arise that point out differences of goals or methods. It is better to face and resolve these differences before committing your time and your money and possibly your career than to ignore the differences and hope they will somehow resolve themselves when the problems arise.

Whole books have been written on how to put together a business plan. Graduate business schools teach courses and entire curricula on creating and implementing business plans. In this chapter, I will list most of the factors for you to consider in starting and building a law practice. Most of the listed factors are treated at length elsewhere in this book and you'll have to pull information from those other chapters, or simply start from scratch to put together your own business plan. Simply copying someone else's business plan won't help. You have to create your own. It is not necessary to pay large amounts of money to write a business plan. There are many free business plans available on the Internet.

1. *Time periods.* I recommend you try to focus your time periods as follows:

1.1 Before opening the office (The cash really flows out.)

1.2 The first month of being open (Cash continues to flow out.)

1.3 The first three months after the office is opened

1.4 The second three months after the office is opened

1.5 The second six months after the office is opened (By now you should have a small positive cash flow.)

1.6 The second year of practice (You hopefully are drawing a little out of the practice.)

1.7 The third year of practice (By now you should have a good feeling as to whether you are in the right place at the right time with the right people.)

1.8 The fourth year of practice (By now you should be considering whether to add people and resources or narrow your practice focus.)

1.9 The fifth year of practice (You should be rolling along, making a living with a good feeling about your long-term prospects.)

1.10 The sixth year of practice (You should have a new five-year plan.)

2. *Reviews.* You must review your business plan and your progress at least quarterly to determine if you should change the plan and to look for serious problems developing.

3. *Flexibility.* A business plan is not carved in stone. It can be amended and changed as appropriate. Time and financial and size goals can be accelerated or extended, provided you understand why you are changing the plan.

4. *Face problems immediately.* If it is cold outside and you close the windows, it will still be cold outside. Don't avoid problems by pretending they aren't there.

5. *Be willing to admit errors and mistakes.* If something isn't working after three or four months, be willing to abandon it or change it. As a lawyer in Newfoundland, Labrador, once told me, "If you have to eat crow, eat it while it is young and tender. Don't wait until it is old and tough."

6. *Clients.* Where will clients come from?

7. *Family relationships.* Are your family and spouse or significant others with you and supporting you and willing to sacrifice in the short run to help you, or do you have problems at home that may affect success?

8. *Where to locate the office.* City or state or street?

9. *Where to locate the office.* Law suite, incubator, home, alone?

10. *Go it alone or with others?* Partners, associates, space sharers, of counsel?

11. *Form of practice.* Sole proprietorship? Professional corporation? Partnership?

12. *Strategic alliances with potential client references.* Banking relationships, accountant relationships, insurance agent relationships, other law firms and lawyers, etc.

13. *Fictitious name.*

14. *Web site design and responsibility for maintaining.*

15. *Mentors.* Have you identified mentors who can help you with your problems, or do you know where to look for them? (See **www.SeniorLawyers.org.**)

16. *Computer, hardware, and software needs.*

17. *Communication needs.* Telephones, fax lines, computer lines, e-mail, answering machines, phone company voice mail, own voice-mail systems.

18. *Other equipment needs.* Desks, chairs, reception or conference furniture, etc.

19. *Office layout.*

20. *Office supply needs.*

21. *Library needs.* Electronic and paper.

22. *Marketing.* What proactive marketing do you intend to do?

23. *Type of practice you hope to develop in the first year and thereafter.*

24. *Personnel needs.* Secretary, reception, word processor, do-it-yourself, part-timers, alternatives, etc.

25. *Cash flow budget.*

26. *Profit and loss budget.* (Not the same as cash flow budget.)

27. *Cash flow resources.* Savings, family, spouse, other income, credit cards, other loan sources.

28. *Timekeeping and billing systems.*

29. *Trust account and bookkeeping systems and maintenance.*

30. *Insurance needs.* Malpractice, general liability, life, disability, medical.

31. *Licenses, permits, tax registrations needed.*

32. *Exit plan.* If it doesn't work, how do you exit so you can correct the problems or do it over differently?

33. *Where to get help.*

34. *There are many other factors that can be added to the plan,* depending on your own situation and desire for detail. Some examples include:

    34.1 Child care or elder care considerations

    34.2 Spouse's occupation and possibility of transfer

    34.3 Health problems

    34.4 Media advertising

    34.5 Mission statement

    34.6 Defining the business you want to be in

    34.7 Practice area goals or limitations

34.8 Gender and diversity considerations

34.9 Responsibility for management

34.10 Time and money budgets for bar activities, community activities, marketing, continuing education, improving the administration of the office.

34.11 Responsibility for personnel hiring, training, and firing

34.12 Responsibility for technology advances

34.13 Quality of life (overtime, nights, weekends, vacations, family time)

34.14 Resolution of intra-firm conflicts

34.15 Preparation of written agreements for all persons in the new firm

Your own business plan can be developed by using this format, customizing to your personal goals and needs.

Managing Your Student Loan

The law and economics of managing student loans changes rapidly. The information in this chapter rapidly changes. This chapter hopefully will help you to determine the major issues and possible solutions.

It is no longer uncommon for a law student to graduate from law school with $75,000 to $100,000 or more in student loan debt. Married couples are often well over $100,000 in debt. However, student loan debt need not prevent you from starting your practice. With some advance planning you can still start a law practice even though you owe money on your student loan(s).

The laws and procedures related to student loans are continuously in a state of flux. Two rules will always apply:

1. Never ignore or lose communication with your lender.

2. Make a record of all your attempts to communicate. As of the writing of this chapter, there are at least two major agencies that can help you plan for dealing with your student debt when you start your practice. There is also at least one agency that helps consolidate student loans, including your spouse's loan(s).

One agency is called The Access Group, which is a nonprofit organization. The membership consists of all or almost all ABA-approved law schools. The agency may be able to help with a consolidation loan or refer you back to the appropriate lender for help in rescheduling your student loan(s). It is located in Wilmington, Delaware, with a toll-free number of 1-800-282-1550. It maintains that its members account for most of the law school debt.

The second major agency is Sallie Mae, which is discussed in greater detail later in this chapter.

Based on reports I have received, I strongly recommend that you keep a complete file of every conversation you ever have with anyone concerning your student loans. Make a record of the time, date, and with whom you speak, as well as what was said. In some cases, you may find yourself dealing with telephone operators who are trained to answer only the most routine of repetitive questions and who may tell you something can't be done when your situation strays the slightest bit from what they do. Insist on talking to supervisors or managers when you get either a "no" answer or someone who is obviously confused. Many of the telephone operators may refuse to give you their names or a code to get back to them or to quote. If people refuse to identify themselves, consider tape-recording your conversations (if permitted by law). You may never deal with the same person twice and you'll need to document what was said.

Before going into the mechanics of arranging your student loan, let me point out that the law and the regulations change frequently and not all lenders will necessarily do the same thing.

About 40 percent of all student loans are carried by Sallie Mae. The people at Sallie Mae are friendly and helpful, and their current toll-free number is 1-888-2-SALLIE. Their offices are in Lawrence, Kansas, but they are most helpful by telephone. You can also access their Web site at **http://www.salliemae.com/**. I personally prefer using the telephone over using the Internet when I have a question. Internet responses by e-mail are often anonymous, and you may have difficulty making printed copies of your inquiry or the response. Telephone contact gives you the ability to indicate time, date, and with whom you spoke, getting a person's name or position.

About 60 percent of student loans are carried by a variety of lenders. These lenders are governed by "Servicing Guidelines," which are promulgated by some federal government agency that is remarkably unapproachable. They are serviced by some private company that appears to be remarkably dense. This servicing company either doesn't know who hires them or refuses to disclose the information, encouraging you to call some 800 number and leave a message although you won't know for whom you are leaving the message. For purposes of this chapter, I am assuming that these private lenders are similar to Sallie Mae in their structure, rules, procedures, and final decisions.

As you begin to navigate through the waters of student loan servicing, it is imperative that you distinguish between deferments and forbearance.

Anyone who makes normal progress toward obtaining a law degree will get an automatic six-month deferral beginning with the day he or she gets a law degree. This will normally cover the period between law school and the bar results.

After the six-month period, anyone who is unemployed and seeking employment will get from twenty-four months to thirty-six months of unemployment deferment, depending on whether the debt is pre- or post-1993 debt. During this twenty-four to thirty-six month period, no payments are due and if the loan is a subsidized loan, the federal government will make the interest payments.

You can be both self-employed and unemployed at the same time!

According to the current definition of being unemployed you can be self-employed until you get a job, as long as you are listed with a bona fide agency seeking employment. You may not limit your job availability to being a lawyer. You must be available for any type of job in any field that you would be willing to accept. You are not required to take any particular job unless you really want it, but you must be available for and consider all jobs, including nonlegal jobs. Accordingly, you can simultaneously start and build your law practice while being unemployed and can get from twenty-four to thirty-six months of deferment on your loan.

In addition to deferrals for schooling and unemployment, you can obtain up to twenty-four months of forbearance during the life of the loan. These forbearances are usually considered and granted one six-month period at a time. You can request a twelve-month forbearance and it will be given serious consideration, but the length of the forbearance period is normally six months at a time.

To recap, you can get one six-month deferral after finishing law school if you made normal progress toward your law degree. You can get from twenty-four months to thirty-six months of unemployment deferral provided you remain listed with a bona fide agency and will give consideration to nonlegal jobs. (You don't have to accept them; you only have to consider them.)

After all the above, you can get also get twenty-four months of forbearance. You should try to use up your deferrals before you use your forbearance, which you may need at a later time.

As a minor inconvenience, the periods of deferral and/or forbearance might extend the seven years during which you can't go bankrupt on the student loan. There is some case law that appears to say that while a student loan may not be dischargeable in bankruptcy, a loan that is used to pay off a student loan may be dischargeable in bankruptcy.

Another possibility that may be worth considering is the consolidation of student loans. As of the writing of this chapter, one can consolidate existing student loan(s) including the student loan(s) of your spouse. There are a variety of repayment programs including plans in which the amount of monthly payment is contingent on the amount of your annual income. The period of repayment can be for as long as thirty years. The plan can be changed from year to year. The loans are called Direct Consolidation Loans and the program is administered by the Direct Loan Servicing Center in Utica, New York. (The telephone number is 1-888-868-1391, and the current fax number is 1-800-848-0984.) As with all government programs, annual budgeting may cause elimination or expansion of the program.

In summary, you'll have to get updated by whomever is servicing your loan(s), but with some careful planning your student loan debt need not prevent you from starting your law practice.

Check into refinancing your student loan from time to time; interest rates go up or down. You might benefit by refinancing your loan with the same or a different financial institution. It doesn't hurt to ask about reducing your payments.

The ability to go bankrupt on a student loan or into a chapter proceeding changes from time to time. The answer to your questions may depend on whether you are dealing with the original loan or a refinanced loan. Get the answer from a bankruptcy lawyer.

Get more information. The best source of information I have found concerning student loans is found in *Student Lawyer,* the magazine published by the Law Student Division of the American Bar Association. It is worth subscribing to that publication just for these articles if you are concerned about your loan(s). (See **http://www.abanet.org/lsd** for more information.)

Again, the rules and economics are in an ever-changing state of flux and must be brought current when you want more accurate information.

Part II
Getting Located

Where Is the Best Place to Open Your Office?
(From a Client-Getting Point of View)

If you have a choice, don't practice out of your home. Clients will not appreciate your low overhead. They may think that you're a lawyer who can't make it. Additionally, clients don't want to be seen by your family or hear a television set or garbage disposal.

If you really can't get an office, use the attorney conference room of the local law library or the attorney conference room of the local courthouse, or meet the client at his or her place of business. But don't use your home. (However, if you must practice out of your home, see my chapter on "Practicing from Your Home.")

Generally, I recommend starting in a suite or area where you can get overflow work from other lawyers.

I know one lawyer who opened his office in a store on a corner by a bus stop that was a major bus transfer point and was across the street from a large phone company office. In a few months he had a very successful practice of telephone company operators and administrative people who had the usual amount of divorces and accident cases. By opening his office at 7 A.M., he also was able to accommodate other people on their way to work between bus transfers.

The lawyer told me that this was all planned and that he bought out the lease of a dry cleaners after he had concluded that the location was right. Several lawyers have told me they outfitted minivans with computers, word processors, faxes, cell phones, and the like. They drive from client to client, making house calls for the elderly, accident victims, and others who are not mobile.

The moral of the above stories should be obvious: "Go Where the Clients Are." If you are from a community where you have a lot of friends and family, then this is where you should locate.

If you've gone away from home for college and away from home for law school and you haven't much family, then you should consider moving into an area where there will be a need for you.

As that eminent speaker on law practice management J. Harris Morgan teaches, you should look for a community where there is only one lawyer. As the second lawyer in town you'll get the cases where there is a conflict. Obviously the same lawyer can't represent both the creditor and the debtor or the claimant and the insurance company.

When I first wrote this book I didn't know much about rural or small-town practice. I went to Los Angeles High School, UCLA as an undergrad, and UCLA Law School. We lived in Los Angeles because that's where the family was.

After presenting more than one thousand programs in every state of the Union, every Canadian province, and every continent, I have learned vicariously about rural, small-town, and suburban law practices. The problems are very different, but the rewards are often greater in terms of lifestyle and community life and professional growth.

A practice starts with friends, relatives, and professional acquaintances. Therefore, the best place to start your career is where they are.

If no one knows you, it's going to be difficult to start your practice. In a small community you become known more quickly. If you cannot start your practice where people know you, then find a place and make yourself known there.

Being unknown can lengthen the time you need to become established.

Geographic Location Checklist

1. Where are your friends and relatives (the best place)?

2. Pick a growing rather than a decaying section of the country. Watch out for blight and decay.

3. Choose urban, rural, or suburban practice. Consider possible changes in economic patterns due to escalating energy costs.

4. Analyze whether you can really be happy in a rural or small-town atmosphere or in an urban atmosphere. This is a matter of your personality and background.

5. Use demographics and economic data to locate. If all other criteria fail, you can locate in a geographic area where there is the best ratio of lawyers to population or lawyers to economic activity.

You may have to get some help from a local realtor or the census bureau or a state office that solicits industries to locate in the state.

The national ratio of general population to lawyers in 1995 was about 290 to 1. By 2010 the official estimate is that the ratio will be about 235 to 1. Compare that to when law firms were all doing great in the 1980s with a ratio of 403 to1.

If you might end up with some litigation, access to a courthouse is important. (About 40 percent of all legal fees are in litigation, so there's a strong possibility that you will have some litigation in your early practice).

Draw a circle with the courthouse in the center and a radius of about a twenty–to–twenty-five-minute drive from the courthouse. Look for points on the circle where a twenty-minute circle would give you the best lawyer/population ratio. Decide if the people in that area are likely to need legal services they can afford in the areas of law you think you are interested in.

You can also buy demographics by zip code. Simply designate the income levels and the ratios of lawyer/population you think you will want and there are professional market research companies that can give you that data using information from the Census Bureau.

See the chapter entitled "Epilogue" to read about more than one hundred lawyers who successfully started solo practices.

Quality of Life Checklist

(Also see the chapters on "Quality of Life.")

1. *Quality of Professional Life.* What kinds of cases and clients can be gotten where you will practice?

2. *Quality of Social Life.* Do you want or need proximity to museums, symphonies, dance clubs, or other young intellectual people?

3. *Quality of Atmosphere.* Smog and pollution or clean air and water?

4. *Quality of Recreational Life.* Do you want proximity to swimming, skiing, boating, hiking, hunting, etc.?

5. *Quality of Home Life.* Is the area safe for your spouse and children? Will you have to be afraid to go out at night or afraid to sleep with the windows open? (See the chapter on "Quality of Life.")

6. *Quality of Economic Life.* What kind of money can you earn? You probably have to compromise some items to obtain others.

There is no right or wrong. Think about where and how you wish to spend the next thirty or forty years of your life.

7. *Juggling the Three Balls.* It seems as though we all have to juggle three balls: the first is how much money we earn, the second is the quality of our professional time and life, and the third is the quality of our personal, family, and social life. It seems that every time one ball goes up, two come down. With some planning two will go up and only one down. If you are truly fortunate and plan well, all three might go up simultaneously.

Where Should You Locate Your Office for Your First Year or Two?
(From a Cost Point of View)

I strongly recommend that for the first year or two you try to locate your office in a suite where there are as many lawyers as possible and in a building that has as many lawyers, law firms, and similar suites as possible.

The other lawyers in the suite and in the building can be a source of legal fees and practical advice to you.

For purposes of this book, a suite is defined to be a place where more than one lawyer practices, with the lawyers having no economic relationship with each other beyond the sharing of certain common expenses, such as reception space, library, etc.

These suites are more and more available on a commercial basis; there are now companies that set up these suites for lawyers. Even if there is not such a company, you may find in your community one or more suites where there is an association of lawyers, or a law firm that has excess space and wishes to rent it out.

It should be self-evident that the cost per lawyer of a law library is less when there are anywhere from four to twenty lawyers sharing the costs than if only one lawyer is paying for it. Additionally, such features as photocopying, receptionist, conference rooms, etc., are much less expensive when several lawyers are sharing the costs than if only one lawyer is covering them. With a nice conference room, you may wish to meet all clients in the conference room and go for cheap in your personal working office. Ask lawyers already in the suite how long they have been in the suite and what they like or dislike about the arrangement. Be careful to control your own phone number.

Be sure that all the lawyers in the suite have a clause in their fee agreements explaining that the other lawyers are not in the same firm (to avoid erroneous malpractice suit exposure when another lawyer faces a claim).

After you have been in practice a year or two and have gotten over the initial hump of economic survival, you can select an office that you feel fits the needs of your practice.

Additionally, you normally can rent space in suites on a month-to-month basis or with a one-year maximum lease liability. If you find that you've chosen the wrong location or you don't like the other lawyers in the suite, or they don't send you the business you expect or don't mentor you, you can cut your losses short and change locations without worrying about a long lease liability.

Neighborhood/Building Checklist

1. Proximity of office to public transportation for staff and clients.

2. Proximity to eating places for client entertainment and meetings.

3. Proximity to law library.

4. Proximity to major anticipated clients.

5. Type of practice hoped for. For personal injury, workers' compensation, and criminal law, proximity to courts and administrative hearing locations or jails may be important.

6. Proximity to other lawyers for advice and possible overflow work and library is important.

7. Will the office and building be accessible for people on crutches or in wheelchairs or for elderly people (that is, have ramps, wide doorways, elevators, nearby parking)?

Low-Rent High-Quality Building

Many cities, states, and counties will grant tax incentives to locate in a specific neighborhood. These neighborhoods are sometimes called "Economic Redevelopment Districts or Zones" or "Special Incentive Zones." There are often property tax, sales tax, income tax, business tax, or other incentives and benefits available. While these benefits may not be of much value to you in your first years of practice, they may be of great value to a landlord who can offer you a cheaper rent in a new building. These buildings are commonly located in former slums or poor neighborhoods. There may be income tax credits or deductions available.

If a client or potential client asks you why you located in that area, you can answer, "The city made me such a good deal I couldn't say no."

Budget Office in Luxury Suite

I know of one lawyer in a suite who had one chair and an orange crate for a desk with a telephone on the floor and a notebook computer on the crate. He met with all clients in the suite's luxurious conference rooms. Meeting them in the luxurious reception area, he led them to the conference rooms through hallways covered with expensive art. He used the suite's common facilities and an outside secretarial service, keeping his costs low.

Should You Trade "Space for Services"?

The basic concept of "space for services" seems to be a good idea. A lawyer with extra space provides that space to a new lawyer in exchange for a certain number of hours per month. There are various additional services that might be involved, such as office furnishings, telephone answering, client reception, reproduction services, library use, etc. Although secretarial services could be included, they rarely are.

The lawyer with space usually guarantees specified hours of work to the new lawyer and the new lawyer promises to be available for that number of hours.

This system is very appealing to the new lawyer who is afraid to lay out cash for overhead. It is also very appealing for the established lawyer who is trading excess capacity for a part-time associate without cash outlay.

Sometimes this space-for-service arrangement is intended as a "trial marriage" before any job commitment or before any merger.

In theory, this system has mutual advantages and should be a big success. Unfortunately, space for services rarely works for reasons that I will set forth. It usually ends rather quickly with a lot of bad feelings on both sides.

Because this system rarely works, I recommend against it. On the other hand, if both the new lawyer and the experienced lawyer face the problems that I've set forth (and others), then perhaps you can make it work.

Typical Problems in Space for Services

1. *Are Hours Cumulative or Noncumulative?* If twenty hours per month is the agreed number, what happens when only eighteen are used? Is there a "debt" of two hours to carry over to the next month? Is reduction in services justified?

2. *Suppose New Lawyer Doesn't Want to Handle the Matter Because of Conflict in Schedules.* Typically, New Lawyer owes five hours and the last day of the month comes and New Lawyer wants to interview a prospective client and Experienced Lawyer wants New Lawyer to handle a matter seventy miles out of town.
Who wins this conflict?

3. *Suppose New Lawyer Doesn't Want to Handle the Matter Because of Personal Dislike of the Case or Client.* There may be good or no reason for New Lawyer not to want to handle a matter or client. Does New Lawyer have the right to say "No"?

4. *Are Hours During the Working Day?* Does New Lawyer have to go down to the jail at 3:00 A.M. on Sunday morning or meet with a client when he or she has tickets to take a new client to a Sunday football game? Is there time and a half or double time for nights and weekends?

5. *Who Is to Arbitrate Claims of Excess Time Spent?* When Experienced Lawyer says that fifteen hours research was insane, unwarranted, and wasted, who is to arbitrate?

6. *Is New Lawyer Obligated to Do Only Legal Work?* If there is time to burn on the last day of the month, can Experienced Lawyer use New Lawyer for tasks such as picking up personal laundry and cleaning? Experienced Lawyer will claim the right to use New Lawyer in any capacity.

Recommended Alternatives

Frankly, I feel that unless the two lawyers can work out the above problems in advance, they should avoid time-for-space arrangements. I recommend, instead, exchanging checks with no promises. New Lawyer pays a fair rental and may accept or reject work assignments as desired. Experienced Lawyer pays an agreed hourly rate (about six or seven times the federal minimum wage) for work performed. If Experienced Lawyer doesn't like New Lawyer's work, the work stops. A ninety-day termination period should be provided so New Lawyer can find another situation.

Consider Trading Technology Services for Space

If you recently graduated from law school you are more technologically advanced than 80 to 90 percent of practicing lawyers, especially older lawyers. E-mail, the Internet, electronic research, OCR, voice recognition technology, and a long list of required legal skills are needed by practicing lawyers.

Reverse Mentoring—Many senior lawyers and many nonsenior lawyers are "technologically deficient!" They cannot effectively use e-mail, the Internet, or electronic research. They panic when a computer jams.

Senior lawyers often require special training methods. You can find help on teaching seniors at **www.SeniorLawyers.org**.

Offer to trade computer and technology work and training for space. You can then, little by little, work your way into rendering legal services. (See **www.SeniorLawyers.org/ProjectReverseMentoring**).

How Do You Get
the Best Space Arrangement?

Make Contacts to Find Space

Sources of information such as your local legal newspaper are very good; nonlegal local papers are all right; local bar association journals are often helpful. A commercial broker may be a good source, if the space you require is not too small. Other lawyers can be of assistance. If there is a particular building in which you want space, try a form letter sent or delivered to every existing tenant and building manager. This is a good source of leads on sublet space when offices move or firms break up, often creating an opportunity for reduced rent.

Determine True Rental Cost
in Order to Comparison-Shop Prices

Always ask for the net square footage figure from the broker or landlord, and put it into the lease. Divide monthly or annual rent by net total square footage to get cost per net square foot, which is the only true way to measure rent cost. There can be a 20 percent difference between net square footage and gross square footage, due to poles, beams, corridors, windowsills, ducts, stairwells, irregularly shaped premises, etc.

Consider Cheap Space in an Expensive Building

Inside, non-window space is very cheap. No one wants it. With imaginative drapes, lighting, and decorating, the client won't realize that the offices are inside offices. Cost savings in rent can be very significant. Indicate that you are willing to accept inside space for price or other considerations. If you are willing to meet all clients in the conference room you can avoid expensive personal office decoration.

Be sure there are adequate telephone lines and electrical outlets for computers and e-mail.

What Size Office Will You Need?

How many square feet do you need for an office? Generally speaking, you'll need about 400 to 600 square feet per lawyer, as follows: Personal office 150 to 200 square feet (smaller is OK if you have access to a conference room for client meetings). Secretarial area 150 to 200 square feet (try to defer this for a few months, if possible). Reception area, storage, copy machine, etc. 100 to 200 square feet.

What to Negotiate and Include in Your Lease or Office Rental Agreement

1. Parking for yourself, staff, and clients at fixed prices. Don't automatically accept the story that parking is a concession. Buildings often make parking a part of the lease if pushed.

2. Access to office at night or on weekends. Will air conditioning, heating, and lights be available at no extra cost? Is there any form of building security after hours?

3. Is there any furniture from the outgoing tenant you might have?

4. Right of first refusal on additional space in building if you expand.

5. Air conditioning and heating thermostat controls for your part of the suite.

6. Be sure telephone, computer, fax, and electrical outlets are where you will need them or get the landlord to move them.

7. Carpet cleaning or replacement.

8. Painting or other wall treatment replacement or cleaning.

9. Drapes often can't be cleaned; insist on new ones.

10. A one-year term, with two one-year renewal options, is best for a starting lawyer. You can stay or move after one or two years' experience.

11. Minimum maintenance such as trash removal, carpet maintenance, etc., and frequency of maintenance (daily, weekly, etc.).

12. Try to delay the effective date of start of rent for as long as possible in order to gain time for delivery of furniture, announcement printing and addressing, etc.

Practicing in a Law Suite

The law suite may be the best way for the sole practitioner or small firm (up to five or six lawyers) to reduce occupancy, personnel, and technology costs.

By definition, a law suite is a large office where many different lawyers practice. These lawyers may be sole practitioners or they may be small firms, but they are not the tenants of the owner of the building. They are subtenants or licensees of the tenant and they share the cost of reception, conference rooms, library, and common areas through their rent charges.

I must confess that for many years I was opposed to the concept of a law suite. I valued total privacy and possession of my own library, my own receptionist who knew all my clients by name, my own reception room, my own photocopy machine, etc. Times have changed and I have changed with them. Those luxuries were worthwhile when office rents were low and could be planned without cost-of-living increases. Today they are unwarranted luxuries. Inflation in the costs of operating law offices—especially rent, salaries, library costs, and the costs of communications and copy equipment—have caused me to change my opinion. I now strongly support the concept of the law suite as a vital tool in reducing costs. I especially recommend the law suite for the lawyer starting a practice alone or with a partnership. Be careful to include a sentence in your fee agreement where the client acknowledges that you and the other lawyers in the suite are independent and not in the same firm. Insist the other lawyers do the same in their fee agreements. You don't want to be sued by other lawyers' clients (and vice versa). Ask the master tenant or operator if there is a section of the lease or rules requiring disclosure.

It is only common sense that if twenty-five lawyers share the cost of a receptionist or photocopy machine or library, the cost would be less than twenty-five lawyers each paying for a receptionist and photocopy machine or library. If the cost of a receptionist increases by $100 due to inflation, it could cost a sole practitioner $100 more to have his or her own receptionist, but only $4 more if there were twenty-five lawyers sharing the burden of the increase.

In accounting terms, a law suite allows individual lawyers or groups of lawyers to amortize fixed costs over a greater amount of production.

A lawyer who occupies a 225-square-foot office in a traditional law office arrangement will need an additional 225 to 425 square feet for secretarial area, library area, reception area, photocopy area, hallways, employees' lounge, conference room, and other common areas. The law suite reduces the "common area" by spreading the costs over a large number of lawyers. The additional space drops down in amount to 125 square feet per lawyer.

A law suite gives the lawyer a flexibility unattainable in the traditional landlord/tenant relationship because the lawyer can take additional offices or space in the suite (as available) for associates, partners, paralegals, etc. The lawyer can also leave or reduce the amount of space occupied by simply giving a thirty-day notice, without having to find a subtenant or worry about a lease liability or liability on library contents, etc.

In addition to expanding or contracting the space within the suite, you may also be able to expand or contract the facilities or services you wish to pay for and use.

As an additional benefit, you may get some overflow work or other referral work from other lawyers in the suite. Alternatively, you can refer work to the other lawyers and maintain continuing contact with both the client and the lawyer in order to receive forwarding fees (as allowed by the rules of your jurisdiction).

For the new lawyer it is important to be near other lawyers who can help with advice on how to handle new cases or clients that the new lawyer is encountering for the first time. The more experienced lawyers will also be a good source of current information on fee charging and other information. This is always helpful for all lawyers but especially helpful for new lawyers.

Services and Facilities to Expect from a Law Suite

A law suite can provide a large variety of facilities and services, depending on what the suite has to offer and how much you are willing and able to spend. Try to find a flexible law suite that allows you to add space and services and facilities as you need them. When you first start out, you will have the time and temperament to do a lot of things yourself. As your practice expands you will want others to do what you used to do and you will have additional technology and equipment needs.

1. Employees are not your employees. Unless you have your own employees, you will save the costs of payroll accounting and payroll tax accounting, employment and workers' compensation, and other tax reports and returns.

2. Library use according to your need and what the suite has. Expect to use electronic research from your desk at your cost unless the suite has a special deal. (See the chapter on "Library Needs and Costs.")

3. Use of the suite's mailing address.

4. Receptionist during specific hours on specified days.

5. Live telephone answering during specified hours on specified days. (Cost may be based on a flat rate or specified number of calls per day or per month.)

6. Use of the suite's automated voice mail system and equipment.

7. Specified number of "special call handling" calls. (Emergency calls, giving or receiving information other than name, hours, mailing address, fax number, e-mail address, etc.)

8. Specified number and location of phone lines, and data lines for faxes, modems, etc.

9. Specified number of hours per week or month for use of large, medium, and small conference rooms.

10. Availability of coffee service to your office or conference room.

11. Availability of mail handling for sending or receiving, regular or special U.S. mail handling, messenger services, package services (Federal Express, DHL, UPS, etc.).

12. Rental of office furnishings (desk, chairs, computer work station, art work, etc.) for your personal office.

13. Use of high-speed Internet and fax and copy equipment with or without a key operator.

14. Use and cleanup of kitchen and refrigerator, freezer, chairs, tables, and microwave ovens.

15. Possible availability of word-processing equipment and full-time or temporary word-processing personnel. Be sure to cover client confidentiality if others do work on your clients' matters.

16. Possible availability of nonlawyer personnel to assist with practice administrative filing, special projects, etc.

Advantages

To recap, the principal advantages of a law suite are:

1. A greatly reduced monthly occupancy expense due to sharing of common expenses.

2. Flexibility to move out (on thirty days' notice in most cases) if you find a "better deal" or want to move into another law office.

3. Flexibility to expand or contract space, facilities, and services within the suite as your needs change.

4. A known, fixed, monthly occupancy expense subject to your contract.

5. Relief from the administrative problems of maintaining a library, hiring a receptionist, negotiating lease clauses, etc.

6. Close-by temporary secretaries and in-house word processors available on an "as needed" basis.

7. Access to other lawyers for their help in case handling or fee setting in new matters.

8. The possibility of some overflow work and fee sharing.

Disadvantages

There are some disadvantages to law suite practices, but they are relatively minor. They should, however, be noted:

1. Inconsistency of practice mix. Another lawyer in the suite may have a personal injury or workers' compensation, mill-type of practice. There may consistently be mobs of people in the reception room in factory clothes with their kids because they can't afford a baby-sitter. Your tax and corporate clients may wonder what kind of practice you really have and they may feel uncomfortable in the reception room. Your clients won't be able to distinguish that these people are not clients of your firm or of you. (The reverse may also be true; i.e., your personal injury and workers' compensation clients may feel uncomfortable with the tax and corporate clients.)

2. Receptionist indifference. The receptionist probably won't be able to offer your clients any special welcome or treatment to make them feel comfortable. The receptionist won't bring coffee, soft drinks, etc., out to your client. If your clients or any lawyers waiting to see you want to call their office, count on the receptionist coldly informing them that there are no phones available to them.

3. Access to offices at night and on weekends and holidays may be a problem due to lack of air conditioning or security procedures. This is a problem with all law offices, not just suites.

4. Books missing from the library when you need them will, from time to time, be a problem, but no more or less than the same problem in a large law firm.

5. The interior walls and hallways are bare of decoration, creating a hotel hallway feeling when going from the reception room to the individual lawyer's office.

Paul Fegen (pronounced FEE-jin) is the pioneer in the concept of the law suite. It is to his credit that the law suite is also known as the "Fegen Suite." Paul and I are contemporaries. I have known him since he first began his concept in Beverly Hills, California, where his headquarters are now located. His company, Attorneys Office Management, Inc., now rents to thousands of lawyers throughout the United States. I would recommend that any lawyer considering the opening or the relocation of offices contact Paul before making a move. By visiting a Fegen Suite and getting prices you'll have a rough idea of how low your cost per lawyer for occupancy can be.

6. Limited or no storage facilities for your current or closed files.

7. Omission of name from building directory or suite entrance. This is a negotiable point.

Practicing from Your Home

I wish to distinguish between working at home one or two days a week instead of at your regular office (a practice I recommend) from working only out of your home.

Additionally, there is a difference between (1) a new lawyer starting a practice with little or no client base where the new lawyer has to establish herself with a potential client, and (2) an older experienced lawyer with an existing client base. Loyal clients often don't care from where you practice. They would follow you if you practiced out of your garage or basement. New clients may be wary of lawyers who practice out of their home.

Until recently, I have always been opposed to practicing law from your home as your principal office. I have always advised new lawyers and older lawyers starting a new practice to defer starting their practice until they can get into an office somewhere. Notwithstanding my opposition to practicing from the home, more and more lawyers are, in fact, practicing from their homes. Typically, they practice from their homes for a variety of reasons including child-care or elder-care responsibility. Sometimes they just cannot get the money together to get a minimum amount for furniture, first and last month's rent, and telephone costs. Some lawyers simply want to practice out of their homes because of the lifestyle they have chosen, such as practicing in remote mountain or rural areas where there really is no meaningful "downtown." Some lawyers want to be home with their children to share the "growing-up years." There are many reasons why lawyers want to practice out of their homes.

Because of the advent of cheap, reliable technology, I have softened and indeed almost dropped my opposition to practicing from the home based on competency and ability to deliver quality legal services. The PC, the Internet, and other office technology gives "David" a bigger and better "slingshot" in the fight against "Goliath." Some have called the PC and Internet access "The Great Equalizer." With a PC and the technology of the Internet, online services, e-mail, good software packages, printers, scanners, fax, and telephone systems, a lawyer practicing from the home can have the same research and library and communication resources as the largest firm in the state. Good telephones and e-mail and chat groups make it easy for a new lawyer to get help from other lawyers all over the world on the best way to handle a client's problems or a firm problem. (The listserv "**solosez@abanet.org**" has thousands of lawyers giving and getting help from all over the United States and many foreign countries.) **Www.SeniorLawyers.org** is great for senior lawyers, who can learn e-mail and the Internet and share problems and solutions.

The facsimile and e-mail render it much less important to be near multiple mail pick-up and deliveries. Optical character reader (OCR) scanners reduce the amount of skilled word processing labor necessary to input data into form files. Automatic-dialing telephones make it easier to get hold of another lawyer to exchange ideas on the best way to handle a case or problem. Conference telephone calls reduce the number of face-to-face meetings required to properly represent a client.

In other words, by making full use of computers and modern technology and communications equipment, one can now practice from the home and deliver a competent, quality legal product almost equivalent to the product delivered by the largest firms. Accordingly, I am more satisfied that clients can now receive competent legal care from lawyers who practice out of their homes.

My principal remaining objections relate to the circumstances of the attorney-client relationships, especially getting new clients. How does a client or potential client react to the following:

1. A child answers the telephone;
2. A client hears toilets flushing;
3. A client hears radios, televisions, family arguments, or children fighting;
4. A client smells cooking;
5. A client uses a washroom and sees the lawyer's personal toiletries;
6. Children, parents, spouse, or a pet walk into a conference;

7. You get up and leave a conference to answer a door for mail or a delivery service or a neighborhood child who wants to play with your child. Many lawyers who do practice out of their homes tell me that some clients think that the lawyer is practicing law as a hobby and they do not take the lawyer or the lawyer's invoices seriously. Sometimes clients think the lawyers do not "need" the fee income because the client does not see the trappings of overhead.

The lawyer who practices out of the home has to be imaginative. Some suggestions are:

1. Meet clients out of the office whenever possible. Be creative. Breakfast meetings at fashionable restaurants are good. Use the lawyer conference rooms at the courthouse or bar association offices or your local law school, or at the law library or the city hall or other government buildings. Meet at the client's place of business, or a restaurant. Court reporters may give you a conference room for free or at a low hourly rate to get your deposition business. Check out hourly-rate business centers. I've used airline clubs and conference rooms at airports. Because of post-9/11 security controls, it may be necessary to register nonpassengers in advance. Ask another lawyer if you can use his or her conference room or library.

2. Do not volunteer that you practice from your home, but do not lie about it either.

3. Tell people that you have your office in your home for several reasons, including your being more available to your clients in the evening or on weekends or holidays when office buildings have no air conditioning, and being more available to share your child's development (if applicable).

4. Tell people you have "an office" in your home rather than saying you have "your office" in your home.

5. Tell people you want to access the clients' files and information and your computers when office buildings are closed.

6. Do not try to justify your home location based on money or cheapness.

7. Have a separate businesslike office in which to meet your clients; have lots of law books and law journals in evidence to keep reminding the client they are in a law office.

8. Be sure your office in the home is soundproofed from other house or neighborhood sounds.

9. Do not let children use or answer business telephones or come into the office area or answer the office door.

10. When you are with a client or out of the office, be sure your telephones are covered by an answering machine or voice-mail system or your secretary, or an adult trained in telephone reception.

11. Have someone available to answer the door when you are with a client.

12. Have separate dedicated fax, modem, computer, and telephone numbers and systems for your practice and your home.

13. If you are practicing from an apartment use "Suite 306" instead of "Apt. 306" to give the appearance of being in an office building.

14. Use a P.O. box or mail-drop address on your business card rather than your home address if your home address is readily identifiable as being a home. If asked why you use a P.O. box instead of a street address, you may reply (if true) that you find greater access at nights and weekends to the mail or that you sometimes save a day on receipt of mail, especially on weekends.

15. Investigate the cost and use of a "shared services suite" that typically will list you on the building directory, but not on the door. They will receive mail and phone calls for you as well as provide conference rooms by the hour. They can forward or hold the mail.

16. Encourage clients to use e-mail or fax instead of snail mail to deemphasize your street address.

17. Have a backup system to send and receive mail, messengers, express services, deliveries, etc., when you are not in the office.

18. Do not meet clients in the home unless you really have no options. If you are going to meet clients in your home, remember that you may be subject to multiple governmental requirements, including ADA requirements for ramps, toilets, faucets, wide doorways, fire exits, zoning, business permits, etc. Be sure you have appropriate insurance because your typical homeowner's policy may exclude all commercial coverage.

19. Use a headset when on the phone to eliminate household noises such as children playing or crying, toilets flushing, sirens and cars passing by, doorbells, street and airplane noises, etc.

20. If you have child-care responsibility you must have a fail-safe backup child-care system in case you have to suddenly leave the house for a court appearance or for any unexpected reason, including meeting a new client. (Typically, good results are obtained with a nearby retired grandmother with free time who loves kids and who

is willing to accept $10 or $20 per week just to be on call plus being paid hourly when needed.)

21. If you are going to see clients in your home office, either on a regular or occasional basis:

21.1 Be sure your office is soundproofed to keep out the household and neighborhood noises and smells.

21.2 Do not allow family members into the office or use of the client restroom.

21.3 Keep lots of law books and legal journals in the office to reinforce that you are a lawyer rendering professional services.

21.4 Try to use a separate entrance for clients to protect their identity from family members.

22. Be active in bar associations and local business groups and go to meetings. Practicing outside the presence of other lawyers can be lonely and create a sense of isolation from the professional and business world.

23. Try to avoid hiring employees to work in the house unless you can comply with OSHA and state and federal laws covering employee workplaces. Use temporary agencies and independent contractors where possible.

24. Your equipment and communication needs in a home office are not much different than in a "regular" office. I recommend against "multi-function" machines and recommend stand-alone dedicated equipment. Buy refurbished if cash is a problem. (See Part III on "Getting Equipped.")

25. Try to dress and have hair styled and makeup as though you were going to an office outside the home. You'll feel more professional and businesslike than if you were to try to work in your bed clothing or yard clothes.

26. Lastly, have a life. Leave the office behind you when you leave the work area to go into your living area. Turn it off. Your children are entitled to a parent and your spouse is entitled to a spouse. If you are going to take or make business calls at night, go into the office to do it. Don't inadvertently create the impression that your practice and clients and their needs are more important than your family.

No matter what you say or do, many potential clients will have little or no confidence in a lawyer practicing out of the home. The client will not believe you are a "real" lawyer with a "real" office.

They may expect cheap prices for small matters and then go to a "real" lawyer with a "real" office when they have a significant problem.

In most cases, practicing from the home still seems to be a temporary or transition phase in starting a practice. Most of the lawyers I have met who practice from their homes would rather practice from an outside office and most intend to do so when they can. Often, lawyers who practice from their homes just feel isolated from the mainstream of the professional community and business life and for that reason move their office from their home to an outside office as soon as they can. Many lawyers who practice out of their homes miss the nearby physical presence of another lawyer to discuss cases and problems for a "backup" or second opinion.

In summary, I have somewhat lessened my opposition to practicing from the home, when there are compelling reasons to do so. I now believe that a lawyer practicing from the home using modern technology can deliver a competent product. I am still greatly concerned by the attitude or reaction or expectations of clients who use lawyers practicing from the home, and I am concerned as to whether lawyers who practice from their homes are truly finding professional satisfaction from their work. Perhaps we will have some accurate data in the not-too-distant future.

Virtual Law Offices

Increasingly, the Internet makes your office location less and less important. I have received clients and referrals from all over the world from people I have never met. They find me on the Internet, contact me on the Internet, and all communication is by e-mail and telephone, without the client ever coming to my office or seeing my office or me.

The nature of parts of my practice (will contests and trust contests) requires people from all over the world to find a California lawyer, which they do on the Internet. We then communicate without a face-to-face meeting until there is a deposition or mediation. Another part of my practice (fractional jet ownership) requires expertise that only a handful of lawyers in the world possess. Again, all contact is via e-mail and telephone without face-to-face meetings.

Even though the Internet may someday replace the physical law office, that day is not yet here and you will be well-advised to follow the advice in this book concerning your office location and furnishings.

As the balance shifts from physical law offices to virtual law offices you may wish to start early in your practice to emphasize the virtual aspects. For a new practice, money invested in a Web site is better invested than spent on a couch.

Part III
Getting Equipped

How Much Cash Do You Need to Start Your Practice?

Regardless of inflation, recession, boom, or depression, the answer to this question remains the same: You need enough cash (or guaranteed income) to support yourself and your family for one year. In other words, assume that even though your practice grows, you will not be able to take any cash out for one year.

You should plan to have some combination of the following:

1. One year's living expenses in a savings account.

2. A working spouse or other income-earning person with enough income to support the family for a year.

3. A bank loan of the funds to live on for a year. (This will be almost impossible to get from a bank unless you have the right co-signer or guarantor.)

4. A wealthy parent, in-law, or other relative to:
   a. lend you the money or
   b. give you the money or
   c. guarantee your bank loan.

In addition to the funds for living expenses, you will need money to buy and pay for the following:

1. Announcements, stationery, calling cards, postage, etc.

2. First and last month's rent (possibly, you will need first and last two months' rent).

3. Down payment on modest desk, chair, two or three client chairs, and some modest decorating of your office.

4. Initial payment to telephone company for equipment, line charges, directory listings, optional services and features, etc.

5. Malpractice insurance.

6. PC with word processing package and good printer.

I cannot emphasize strongly enough the necessity of starting with adequate capitalization for your living expenses. It is theoretically possible that you will be able to take cash out from your practice in six to nine months, but an error in calculation here can be fatal. Do not plan for only six or nine months in living expenses. It won't be enough. You'll be forced to leave your practice and get some kind of job to help support your family and this will be the death knell of your practice.

If you can keep your doors open for a year, you'll probably make it, as you'll have a backlog of receivables and work-in-progress that will start producing a steady cash flow. On the other hand, if you go under after six months, you'll take clients with you, and these are the clients who would otherwise have been the foundation of your practice's growth, if you had been adequately financed.

If you open your doors, then close your doors, then open your doors again, you won't get the same clients the second time around. They will remember that you didn't make it the first time and will be afraid to trust you the second time. You will have doomed yourself to perpetual failure with your first failure.

Lawyers have gone under the first time and somehow made it the second time, but this is a rarity. The lawyer who couldn't successfully start a practice the first time probably won't be successful the second time.

Do not neglect your student loan obligations. Try to extend or defer your repayment schedule if you can. In at least one state, being in default on your student loan(s) is considered grounds to prevent you from being admitted to practice.

If I had to choose between opening my doors immediately with only six months' living expenses, or working as a laborer for two years to have enough living expenses for a year, I would choose the latter course of conduct. As a matter of fact, I worked for accountants and as a cab driver to accumulate funds. I also had a working wife, which made it possible to save cash to start the practice.

Even though you are able to make money in your practice right away, this doesn't mean you can withdraw it. You will need cash for many purposes, including:

1. Investigators' fees for personal injury cases.

2. Court filing fees to commence litigation. Even though you may earn a large fee ultimately from a probate or divorce or personal injury matter, the fee will be received one or two years from

the time you get the case started, and you need the filing fees immediately.

3. Electronic research and law books are exceedingly expensive, as you will soon find out. (See the chapter on "How to Buy Law Books.") There is no end to how much money you can spend on the bottomless pit called a law library. It is difficult enough to succeed when you are adequately financed. It is almost impossible when you are inadequately financed.

If you happen to own your home, you should consider refinancing your home to use the cash to maintain you for the year. If a relative owns a home, you might be able to convince them to refinance their home to get the cash you need.

How to Get a Rich Relative or Friend to Finance Your Start-up Costs by Offering Tax Advantages

It's hard to swallow your pride to ask a relative to lend you money for your furniture and equipment. It's no pleasure to ask a relative to guarantee a bank loan for you.

Frankly, the relative may wish to follow Polonius' well-known advice, "Neither a borrower nor a lender be." Additionally, the relative may have serious doubts about your ability to repay the loan or the bank. (You also may have these doubts.)

One way to entice your rich relative or friend to help you is to offer tax advantages as follows:

1. You select the furniture and equipment you want. List the price and where the equipment can be obtained. (You are doing the legwork.)

2. Give your list to your friend or relative.

3. Have your friend or relative buy the equipment in *his or her* name and deliver it to you.

4. Have your friend or relative lease the equipment to you. (You draft the lease.)

5. Your relative or friend gets the following tax advantages:

   a. Investment credit tax benefits.

   b. Depreciation expense benefits (technically, cost recovery).

   c. The interest deduction if he or she borrows the money from a bank.

   d. The ability to claim that he or she is in the equipment leasing business in order to deduct appropriate expenses for use of home as office, telephone expenses, auto expenses, other appropriate expenses. (The amount of these expenses to the extent they are appropriate may or may not be worth the bookkeeping and calculation time.)

e. Assuming both you and the relatives are cash-basis tax-payers (you probably are), the equipment should be acquired and put into use as close as possible to December 31, and the first payment of rent by you should be some time in the following year. Under current tax law your relative gets 100 percent of the investment credit and also gets depreciation (cost recovery) in the first year, with the rental income starting the following tax year. You will get the appropriate experience in drafting an equipment lease and become an instant expert on the subject. Be sure to get updated on the current tax law on such areas as:

(1) Length of lease relative to equipment life (for investment credit and depreciation purposes).

(2) Payment of 15 percent or whatever the then-current tax law is for operating expenses.

(3) Complying with UCC filing requirements as appropriate in your jurisdiction to protect the relative if things go downhill.

(4) Getting a "dba" or fictitious name for the leasing company.

(5) Deciding whether to expand the indicia of an active business for the leasing company with city license, sales tax number, personal property tax registration, separate employee identification number, etc.

(6) Whatever you as a lawyer would do in advising a third-party client on such a transaction.

As a new lawyer you do not need deductions. They would be wasted. On the other hand, your friend or relative will get immediate tax benefits for helping you.

Checklists of Needs for New Law Office

Get Telephones, Computer Lines, Fax Lines, and Internet Lines Ready

1. Estimate number and kind of instruments needed, as well as number of lines needed by meeting and locations with a phone company marketing representative. Keep in mind that until you are busy, you may not need a lot of extra equipment that will quickly become obsolete before you need it. Consider using services that the phone company can provide. Call forwarding, call waiting, delay call forwarding, speaker phones, remote access to call forwarding, three-way calling, caller ID, high-speed Internet access and other features can be added or dropped on a monthly basis as needed.

2. Order equipment (may be delay of two to six weeks).

3. Order installation date (may require two or three days of work to complete installation).

4. Get telephone and fax numbers and e-mail address reserved in advance of opening office, so you can give them to your printer for announcements, cards, and stationery before opening the office.

5. Consider microwave transmission subscription service if you will have a lot of long-distance calls.

6. Get directory publication dates for telephone or other directory listings.

7. Consider Yellow Pages advertising.

8. Try to get low cash deposit on telephone equipment.

9. Get an answering service used by other lawyers or by doctors.

10. Don't forget eventual secretary, receptionist, and client usage of your telephone.

11. Get an e-mail address or domain name and a Web site if you want to attract international clients.

12. Get separate dedicated lines for your fax machine, computer, and/or modem, or get switching devices.

13. Cell phones. The world of cell phones and their usage is rapidly expanding. Check out the costs and advantages and disadvantages of using cell phones instead of land lines. Keep in mind the transportation of a cell phone number if you change offices or think you might change office location.

14. High-speed Internet. Most major cities and most communities have some form of high-speed Internet capacity available via telephone or cable TV, as an alternative to dial-up service. Get the highest speed service you can afford.

Order Furnishings

1. Determine if major items can be rented instead of being purchased.

2. Determine if used (sometimes called refurbished or remanufactured) furnishings are available (should be about 60 percent of new furnishing price).

3. Read ads in local legal newspapers for used furnishings.

4. Minimum furniture for office:

    a. Framed photo of spouse and children for desk;

    b. Lawyer's desk at least six feet wide with overhang in front and treated to protect against scratches and spills;

    c. A table, desk, or desk return for your computer equipment;

    d. One "judge's" chair for you. Try it out next to the desk you have selected. Be sure the chair has wheels or roller balls to roll over to your computer if not on your desk;

    e. Two to four straight-back chairs for clients;

    f. Wastebasket to match desk;

    g. Clear floor pad for chair if office is carpeted. (Don't skimp on pad size, or chair will roll off edges.)

    h. Floor lamp, if office is not light enough;

    i. Potted plant.

5. Problem: Remember that new furniture may take from two to six months to deliver. Consider furniture rental.

6. Keep in mind that subletting an office from a law firm or other lessor may provide a completely furnished office.

7. Second telephone extension for client's usage in office.

8. Bookshelf for those books you need or want in your office.

9. Minimum furnishing for reception room:

   a. Four straight-back chairs;

   b. Magazine rack or table;

   c. Reading light for magazines;

   d. Client telephone;

   e. Bookshelf for books;

   f. Coat rack and umbrella stand.

Order Equipment

1. Determine if secretarial service can provide you with dictating equipment as part of its service.

2. Determine if equipment can be rented rather than purchased.

3. Determine if used (sometimes called refurbished or remanufactured) equipment is available (should be about 60 percent of new equipment price).

4. Read ads in legal and local papers for used equipment and for equipment specials.

5. Minimum equipment:

   a. Secretarial desk (with return for typewriter);

   b. Secretarial chair (if possible, let secretary choose own chair);

   c. Small copy machine or scanner, unless one is available nearby;

   d. Dictating equipment lawyer unit, transcription unit, and two portable tape recorders, one for briefcase and one for car;

   e. Word processing. Use your law school computer until you have a good understanding of what you need in the way of programs and equipment. Get a laser-quality or ink-jet printer if you don't already have one. Go for laser if you can. Color is nice, but not necessary, and color inks can be expensive. Get the fastest (highest number of pages per minute) black and white laser printer you can afford for printing information and lengthy documents and downloading. Time spent watching a slow printer, waiting for the printed copy, is not time well spent. Use a software program that is most commonly used by lawyers. WordPerfect (Corel) and Word

(Microsoft) are the most common. Keep an old electric typewriter on the premises as a backup to your system and for odd forms, etc.

f. Word-processing equipment and programs. This requires a whole treatise. Get advice from secretaries, administrators, and other lawyers. Read ABA publications. Don't depend on vendors alone. WordPerfect (Corel) and Word (Microsoft) are the most common.

g. Accurate postage scale and postage meter. This will save you a considerable amount of money over the year. Investigate using online Internet postage.

h. Read the chapter on personal computers and other office technology later in this book.

Arrange for Supplies

Get some office-supply catalogs from two or three nearby office-supply stores. Open charge accounts with the stores. Ask for a discount from the list prices in the catalogs. Ask your secretary or another lawyer's secretary to make up an initial "order list" for you. In addition to stationery, equipment, and furnishings, consider supplies such as staplers, paper clips, scissors, two-hole punch, three-hole punch, telephone message pads, rubber stamps and inking pads, scratch pads, legal pads, paper cutter, felt-tip markers, staple removers, Scotch® tape, desk calendars, pens and pencils (use blue ink), manila envelopes, Rolodex® files, coffee cups and equipment, check protector, fireproof safe for wills, documents, receivable records, etc.

Don't Overlook Office Supply Centers and Copy Service Centers

The traditional separations between office furniture companies, office supply stores, office supply catalog suppliers, and copy centers have disappeared.

Office supply centers now sell everything from computers and paper by the case and desks and chairs to tea bags and candy along with computer rentals and high-speed copy services. Similarly, copy services now manufacture and sell stationery, office supplies, and computer rentals. Many offer twenty-four-hour service.

Before actually spending money on buying your initial setup of supplies, it will be worth your while to go to a few of these stores and get an idea of prices and availability. What you see and learn in these stores may affect some of the services you do or don't buy from a landlord or law suite.

I am hesitant to name specific examples like Kinko's or Home Depot because many of the chains, although gigantic, are regional and they constantly merge with other chains, changing their names and consolidating stores. Almost all major suppliers also sell on the Internet, where the price including taxes and shipping and handling may be cheaper.

Buying Supplies on the Internet

Consider Internet purchasing. I have made Internet purchases of supplies and equipment. I have never had a problem. I keep expecting to have a problem but it hasn't happened yet. I suppose it might happen in the future. I make no recommendation as to buying or not buying equipment or supplies via the Internet with big savings.

Office Supplies and Procedures

Having good office supplies and procedures makes the practice of law more enjoyable and more profitable. It's frustrating when you are out of supplies or have the wrong supplies. At such times, your attention gets diverted from the client's legal problems to your own administrative problems, and you waste otherwise profitable time on minor administrative matters. Having good supplies and procedures is like having good health. When you have it, you don't think about it; when you don't have it, it's continually on your mind.

Jimmy Brill of Houston, Texas, one of the finest lawyers you will ever meet, has written a copyrighted article entitled "The Thrifty Fifty," which he also uses as the basis of a delightfully entertaining and informative speech by the same name. "The Thrifty Fifty" is a list of "Fifty time- and money-saving ideas that you can begin to implement on Monday morning," to quote Jimmy.

I have heard Jimmy's seminar presentation many times and, like wine, it gets better with the aging. Jimmy's seminar inspired me to add this chapter for lawyers starting a law practice.

Parts of this chapter are based on Jimmy's seminar, modified by me to meet the special needs of a lawyer opening a practice for the first time. You should read this chapter in conjunction with the chapter that includes the checklist for opening your first law office.

Vendor Identification

In some cases you may not know of a source to get the supplies described in this chapter. I've identified some vendors for you with their principal city or phone number. I do not intend to recommend, and cannot vouch for, any of the vendors as being right for your practice and personality, or having better or worse products or services or prices than their competitors. This is a book on how to start a law practice and I'm simply trying to give you a starting point from which you eventually can develop your own sources. I encourage you or your secretary to shop around to find the supplies and procedures best for you. Additionally, vendors merge, change names and go out of business. If you can't get the product or service from the listed vendor, look for other vendors selling what you want.

1. You can buy a "canned" or prepackaged personnel testing kit that includes a dictation test cassette, interview forms, and evaluation forms for screening and testing secretaries, word processing operators, or people who need secretarial or word processing skills. For about $75, you will get enough materials to do about 25 applicant tests (Law Publications, Inc., Los Angeles).

2. You can buy inexpensive prepackaged tests for clerical skills (The Psychological Corporation, New York) and general intelligence (Wonderlic & Associates, Northfield, Illinois) to use as hiring aids.

3. If you share a photocopier with other lawyers, there are devices and systems to control who uses the machine and to record usage by user, and in some cases by client. Ask the photocopy machine vendor for recommendations for your particular equipment.

4. Even if you do much or most of your own typing (keyboarding), you'll still need dictation equipment or digital recorders. Using dictation equipment properly greatly increases the efficiency and cost effectiveness of your office. Dictation equipment allows you to give oral instructions and can go with you anywhere without a special carrying case. The batteries are small, last a long time, and are easily replaced. You can use your equipment in your car and other places you can't use a word processor. Most of the equipment manufacturers (Sony, Lanier, Dictaphone, IBM, etc.) offer free-of-charge short guides on dictation procedure, or you can buy a book on effective dictation from the Association of Information Systems Professionals in Willow Park, Pennsylvania. If you want a free fifteen-minute circus act, ask the vendor to demonstrate all the things you can do with its equipment. You'll feel like you're watching the man demonstrating the vegetable slicer at the county fair and you'll learn a few things as well.

Portable machines cost from one-half to one-fourth the price of a desktop model. I recommend using a lot of portables instead of buying desk models. You get much more for your dollar using a lot of machines even though the quality of a desktop model is slightly higher.

Don't be cheap by buying and using only a few dictating tapes or digital recorders. You should use a lot of tapes and dictate only one or two items on each one. By using multiple tapes, you can prioritize the transcription of the tapes rather than limit their transcription to the sequence dictated. You also can divide the work among more than one word processor or secretary, and can use outside dictation services for tapes when you have insufficient in-house capacity. Long tapes can be debilitating psychologically to the transcriber in that they make the job to be done seem more burdensome than does a series of short tapes. Most inexpensive tapes are adequate for word processing dictation even if they are not of concert quality. Be sure to give complete instructions with the tape when you send it to be transcribed.

5. Digital recorders are replacing tape recorders. They are cheaper and smaller. Unfortunately it is difficult to divide a recording into short segments for transcription by multiple transcribers. Multiple digital recorders are a substitution.

6. Consider using only blue ink for signing documents and letters. Fax machines and photocopy machines generally copy only in black. Copies are often so good you need a different color ink to distinguish the original.

7. If you are thinking of changing your word processing equipment, you should consider how you are going to get your existing forms and information from one system into the other. When the time comes, you may be able to use electronic disk converters or OCR scanners. The cost of outside disk conversion can be expensive.

8. Choosing the right software is covered extensively in the chapter on computers, but it is worth repeating that the ABA maintains a Legal Technology Resource Center (LTRC) that can provide general legal technology assistance to firms and corporate law departments of all sizes. Additionally, I highly recommend many of the publications produced by the Law Practice Management Section, including their books, *Law Practice* magazine, and their online and e-mail resources, which provide detailed and current information on software vendors and products for law office use. Your local or state bar practice management advisor may also be of help.

9. I advocate using colored file folders and using them in numerical sequence (see my chapter on "Simple Hard-Copy Filing Systems for the New Lawyer"). Some lawyers use colored file folders

based on the substantive area of law; others use them based on the client.

10. Consider using different colors of paper stock for your printer or photocopy machine (yellow copy to file, green copy to lawyer file, blue copy for follow-up, canary for interoffice memos, pink for memos of phone conversations, etc.).

11. For opening a new file, you can design your own new file information form or contact Safeguard (Fort Washington, Pennsylvania), Lawdex (Minneapolis, Minnesota), Law Publications, Inc. (Los Angeles), or All-State Legal Supply (Mountainside, New Jersey) for their printed forms.

12. I do not care to use three-ring notebooks, but some lawyers use them for office files and in some cases for client files. Some trial lawyers prefer these notebooks for case management. You may want to consider them, too.

13. Ask your stationery supplier to punch holes in your yellow legal pads and in the stationery or paper you use for file copies. Have the supplier punch two holes across the top for standard Acco fasteners for legal files and three holes along the side for three-ring notebooks. You can purchase your stationery from dealers who sell prepunched stationery as a standard catalog item, but any supplier should be able to punch your stationery supplies holes for you at little or no cost. Alternatively, you can buy a two-hole or three-hole punch and waste your time or a secretary's time needlessly punching holes in paper.

14. You can buy recycled inkjet and laser cartridges for about half the cost of new. You can get recharged and rebuilt cartridges for printers, photocopiers, and fax machines at a much lower price than new ones. I personally have never used recycled or recharged supplies for fear of a malfunction damaging a machine or voiding a warranty or service policy. But if you are interested, look for ads in your legal paper or journals and scan the Internet ads you receive via e-mail.

15. You can save stationery when replying to letters received by writing your response in the margin of the original, putting a sticker on it and returning or faxing it after making a photocopy for your files. You can get the stickers from Law Publications, Inc., Los Angeles, or other supply houses. I personally would restrict those stickers to situations where I felt the recipient would approve of this procedure. The stickers refer to the speed or convenience of returning the original document with a handwritten response. Sometimes

when I receive these stickered responses, I am impressed that the other person is efficient and saves the client or customer money by reducing unnecessary expenses. At other times, I think the respondent can't afford good stationery or a secretary. It depends on how I feel that day.

16. Proper postage procedures and supplies can save you a lot of money over a period of years. Develop your own office postal manual and place it near the mailing area so temporaries and new hires will be able to get the mail out properly.

17. Remember that the second ounce and subsequent ounces cost less than the first ounce for first-class postage. For example, a first-class letter (in 2004) costs 37 cents for the first ounce but only 23 cents for the second ounce, which means that two ounces costs 60 cents, not 74 cents. You can't use the transitional stamps A, B, C, D, E, F, G, etc., for international postage.

18. By putting the magic words "Address Correction and Forwarding Requested" on your outgoing mail, the post office will deliver your letter to the addressee and notify you if there is a new address. If you ask only for address correction, you get the new address when they return your letter to you undelivered. It costs only about 30 cents for each such change to keep your mailing lists updated. Put those words on your invoice envelopes and on your "Season's Greetings" mailings.

19. When you send mail, be sure to give the complete address, including the suite number. When mail was addressed to me at my office address without a suite number, the postal service often returned it to the sender for incomplete address, even though I had been in this ten-story building for eight years. I encountered a similar problem with my returned outgoing mail. When I moved from the tenth floor to the ninth floor of the same building, the post office returned all mail to senders that was addressed to me at my former location on the tenth floor, even though I had filed a change of address and the same mail carrier delivered to both floors.

The problem of letter carriers refusing to deliver your mail without a current suite number can prejudice your clients' substantive legal rights seriously if notices are effective when sent.

It seems to me that the U.S. Postal Service has seriously deteriorated at a time when the service and reliability of competitors such as private couriers and fax and the Internet has greatly improved.

Mail sent without a zip code frequently takes a day longer to get to you; mail sent with your nine-digit zip code (coded zip plus four) frequently gets to you a day sooner. Mail sent to you with the wrong zip code can take weeks to get to you. Be sure your zip code is clearly legible on stationery and faxes.

Using a post office box can reduce problems with incoming and returned mail if a post office is convenient to you. You also can get your mail on weekends and evenings with a post office box. Be aware that if you send a letter with both a post office box and street address, the post office will deliver it to the first one you list as the address.

20. Use airmail stickers, stamps, and envelopes. All first-class mail in the United States goes by airmail, whether or not you print "airmail" on it. International mail goes by boat unless you mark it "airmail." You can put on all the postage in the world and the letter will go by boat, and train, and mule unless you specify "airmail" on the letter.

21. Express Mail is an overnight service provided by the U.S. Postal Service and is cheaper than couriers (DHL, Federal Express, Purolater, UPS, etc.). It costs about one-half the others' prices. I personally have had very bad results with Postal Service Express Mail. (They once lost all of the printed briefs marked for filing with the U.S. Supreme Court. This cost me the time of making a motion and getting new printing done, etc. To add insult to injury, it had no record of what happened to the originals because it didn't make or keep any records of mail going to agencies of the U.S. government.) I've had fantastically good results domestically with Federal Express and internationally with DHL. Their tracking systems are excellent.

22. Buy preprinted, postage-paid envelopes. If you do not mind waiting a long time (six weeks to two or three months) for delivery, the U.S. Postal Service sells envelopes with both your return address and postage printed on the envelopes. These preprinted envelopes cost you 33 to 40 percent of the cost of getting the same printing done by a print shop. They are great for paying bills and sending invoices. Do not forget to add "Address Correction and Forwarding Requested" on the printing order.

23. Be sure your oversized envelopes have green diamond borders and the words "First Class" printed on the front and back or the post office may treat the letter as a "flat" and deliver the mail with the same priority as bulk-rate advertising.

24. Next to the paper clip, "Post-it^{TM}" note pads are the office supply product I most wish I had invented. You can get them printed if you wish with messages, designs, logos, forms, etc.

25. There are at least twenty newsletters and magazines relevant to office management. If you want to start with one magazine, I'd suggest *Law Practice*, the ABA Law Practice Management (LPM) Section magazine, followed by your state bar practice management publications. The others are good, but there is a limit to how much a new lawyer has time to read. If you have delegated office management to a nonlawyer, this individual can join the ABA LPM Section as an associate member and receive *Law Practice* magazine. The nonlawyer also should consider joining the Association of Legal Administrators in order to receive its publications. (If you can afford it, you should pay for the nonlawyer's dues.)

26. As noted earlier, Jimmy Brill's seminar inspired me to write this chapter. Jimmy has a printed speech outline of "The Thrifty Fifty" that covers many items not covered in this chapter. You can get Jimmy's entire outline for $8 to cover copy and postage costs by writing to him at P.O. Box 22870, Houston, Texas 77227.

27. Almost all office-supply stores have a catalog with list prices in it. There also are several companies that publish catalogs and sell by mail through toll-free numbers. You should get on the mailing list of five or six of these companies and spend a few minutes to flip through the catalogs to look for new products that can help you. You'll be able to keep up on what's new with a minimum investment of time and no money. If you routinely trash catalogs without skimming through them, you deprive yourself of good information on what's new.

When you are ready to order, compare prices among the catalogs and then ask for your discount. Local catalog list prices are just that, list prices. Discounts run from 10 to 40 percent off that price, depending upon how badly the store wants or needs your business. If you can pay by credit card and also get a cash discount, you may find it both profitable and convenient to do so.

Some catalog companies (with current telephone numbers) are:

Stuart F. Cooper Co., Los Angeles
(800) 421-8703

The Drawing Board, Dallas
(800) 527-9530

Law Publications, Inc., Los Angeles
(800) 421-3173

The Reliable Corporation, Chicago
(800) 621-4344

New England Business Service
(800) 225-6380

28. You'll soon learn that time devoted to increasing revenues usually is better spent than time devoted to reducing expenses. On the other hand, that's no reason to ignore expenses or to needlessly waste money. Don't forget that running out of supplies interrupts your ability to generate revenue when you "stop everything" because you've run out of stationery, envelopes, or photocopying machine toner. To avoid this, you, your secretary, or office manager should keep an updated file card for each item of office supplies, indicating cheapest source, fastest source, minimum order vendor will handle, prices (including quantity discounts), and time necessary to fill the order. You should predetermine reorder levels for supplies and inventory your supplies at least monthly. In time, you'll develop your own sources and your own procedures.

Your Equipment Purchases

1. It is false economy not to have adequate equipment.

2. The right equipment makes you and your staff more productive and more profitable. The dollars you spend on equipment, if wisely spent, earn hundreds of dollars.

3. How much equipment you buy is usually a function of how much time you have available to do the work manually that equipment could be doing for you. If you don't have cases and clients, then you can rationalize not buying equipment because you have nothing better to do with your time and you have a higher need for the cash. As you start getting busy, you are foolish to waste time that could be earning money, doing work that equipment could be doing for you.

4. It has been said that you can create and store just about anything except time. This is not totally true. Having the right equipment creates more time for you by doing the job faster so you spend less of your time doing the mechanical things. Your time has a great value, and equipment that is efficient, in effect, creates more time for you.

5. Having the right equipment and technology allows the smallest of firms to appear to be big firms, when the equipment turns out

a product of the same or higher quality. The equipment, especially the computer, becomes "the great equalizer" of firms.

6. Don't underestimate the equipment you need and can use to be more profitable. Be alert to possibilities for equipment making your job easier. It shouldn't take many trips to the copy store to convince you that you should have your own in-house copy equipment, if for no other reason than you save the time spent going back and forth to drop off and pick up copying.

7. Technology and prices change so rapidly that any article or book becomes obsolete between the time it is written and the time it is printed. Accordingly, be prepared to use this book only as a starting point. Read the ads in bar journals and computer magazines to learn what vendors claim can be done.

a. Fax machines are an essential. Plain paper faxes are more expensive and slower. Dedicated paper fax machines are extremely inexpensive. If you know what you are doing, consider adding a fax card to your computer for data you generate. You'll need either a scanner or another fax machine to send out information created by someone else. I personally think your money is better spent on a fax machine than on computer software and hardware, although PDFs and attachments will reduce the need for fax.

b. Cheap copiers and minicopiers are adequate until you have huge volume or complex needs, like magnifying, reducing, collating, etc. Go for cheap and don't be afraid to upgrade. When you upgrade, take the slower, obsolete equipment home to create office facilities in your home.

c. Printers. Start with an inkjet printer. Be sure you get professional print quality. A good inkjet printer does 80 to 90 percent of what a laser printer does, at less than 50 percent of the cost.

d. Computers. Computer prices, technology, equipment, etc., change almost daily. In general, go for computers that allow you to upgrade speed and memory and then add the speed and memory as you need them. Newer and better software programs require more and more memory and speed. Additional memory and speed are cheap. No matter where you start, you'll find your equipment and programs too slow in a short period of time. People tend to underestimate what they need in order to conserve cash. This is understandable when starting a practice.

Personal Computers, Word Processing, and Office Technology

Rule 1. If it works, it's obsolete. Anything you buy will be obsolete in thirty months due to improvements and lack of vendor support for what you are using.

Rule 2. If it ain't broke, don't fix it, but if your clients or practice truly need something, don't hesitate to get it. You must be current to provide legal services competently and cost efficiently.

Rule 3. If your clients require it, don't wait.

A few words to younger lawyers:

From time to time you may find some part of this book to be so simple or elementary as to be almost demeaning or insulting to you.

Please be patient or forgiving. Many older lawyers have become involuntarily self-employed due to mandatory retirement, law firm mergers, or breakups, or expulsion. Often these lawyers simply don't have the technical skills you attained in your education. You can use the Internet, but they can't even arrange a three-way telephone conversation. You've been doing word processing on your notebook computer in college and law school and printed out your assignments. Many of the older lawyers have never touched a keyboard.

You can use your technical skills to tutor one of these older lawyers in technology in exchange for their tutoring you in the law or client relations or getting a job (see **www.SeniorLawyers.org**).

This book is used as a text in many foreign countries where available technology is limited and some of the information that is old and simple to you is new to them.

A few words to senior lawyers:

From time to time you may find parts of this book overwhelming. It may seem like you just can't keep up with the technology you need to effectively practice law. You may try to practice the way you used to practice, but eventually you'll find that you're so far behind that it all will seem completely foreign to you. The books you used to use no longer exist and the clients insist on modern communications. E-mail and Internet access are essential to being able to practice law (or be employed at nearly any job) and to maintain personal independence.

I personally have found the best way to learn or to catch up is to get a private tutor or trainer. You may be able to find a young lawyer or law student who is willing to teach you or you can hire the same trainers used by larger firms. You may be able to find a tutor for free at **www.SeniorLawyers.org/ProjectReverseMentoring**. You had what it took to go through law school and to pass the bar exam, and you have what it takes to learn the technology you need. As my dear friend and mentor J. Harris Morgan would say, "Begin! The rest is easy." (See **www.SeniorLawyers.org**.) It has been estimated that 60 percent of the energy required to start and complete a project is used in starting the project. Once you start, the rest is easy.

The typewriter, telephone, dictating machine, photocopier, and facsimile (fax) equipment have each, in their own time and place, radically affected the way lawyers practice law. Now, the personal computer (PC), with a modem and software for document production, information storage and retrieval, and electronic communication has created momentous changes in the way information can be transmitted, stored, and used. The PC, the Internet, e-mail and other new technology have caused a renaissance in the methodology of delivery of legal services. We lawyers are using the computer for communication and computation in ways that were considered science fiction only a few years ago. A computer and a modem enable us to obtain, send, store, and utilize almost unlimited amounts of information. We are just beginning to understand and use the potential facilities of the Internet for the marketing and delivery of legal services. The utilization of advanced technology has enabled us to create a new "golden age" in the delivery of legal services.

In this chapter, I've deviated from my normal writing style of delivering information in "bite-size" quantities. This chapter combines information on computers, word processing, and office technology in general. In addition to describing what is used in a law office, I'm also describing how it is used, what it costs, and how to buy it.

Different readers will have varying levels of expertise in each of these areas. Some will be technology experts or "techies"; others will be computer-phobic or have no idea of what a law office really needs in the way of office technology.

Rather than breaking this chapter into many smaller chapters based on levels of sophistication in each area, as I've tended to do with other subjects in this book, I've put all this information into one larger chapter. I leave it to you, based on your personal level of expertise and experience, to skim or skip a section or to study it slowly.

I'm not a computer or technology expert. I can help you by explaining what you can do with a PC or other equipment and can give you some assistance on how to go about it. I'm the first to admit, however, that I haven't the foggiest idea about the engineering of how or why computers or other equipment do what they do. I can set my wristwatch alarm, but I can't repair a watch.

You must have one or more PCs as the central point in your law office. Just about anything you do with a computer can be done without a computer, but with a computer you get the job done faster, cheaper, and more accurately. You can cross the continent by flying in an airplane or by driving a wagon and team of oxen. You'll probably get there either way. It's just a question of the time, money, and effort needed to accomplish the feat.

Basic Rules for Acquiring Computer Equipment and Office Technology

Before launching into specific uses, I'd like to pass on some general advice on acquiring office equipment, based upon managing my own practice. These basic rules will assist you not only in opening your first office, but also in managing your practice your entire professional life.

Ask Around

Try to avoid reinventing the wheel. As with other areas of law office management, some other lawyer somewhere has already faced and solved the problems you now are facing. Ask around and locate that lawyer.

Before you spend a huge amount of time talking to vendors and waste a lot of money buying things that won't work for you, see if you can find someone else's solution to copy and use for yourself. Use the Internet to find information available for free. Get about two years' back issues of *Law Practice Management*, the periodical of the ABA Law Practice Management Section. Also, get about two years' back issues of the *Lawyer's PC*, and *ABA Journal*. Get the current issue of the ABA LPM Section's publications catalog. Other publications, such as the *National Law Journal* and state and local bar journals, also can be helpful. There is a plethora of new publications covering law office technology. There is no limit to how much time you can spend reading these publications for isolated articles of help. Read the articles written by lawyers on computer applications in which you're interested. Scan the ads to see what vendors claim can be done. The few hours invested in reading these materials will save you many hours in wasted time meeting with vendors. I would estimate that you'll need ten to twenty hours to do the above research, which could save you thousands of dollars avoiding mistakes. In addition, by using office technology, you will earn tens or hundreds of thousands of dollars over the years through increased productivity. By reading the articles and the ads, you may find exactly what you're looking for, and you'll get some new ideas, as well. You will have a rough idea of what is currently "state of the art" and what are current prices. If you're really ambitious, you can go to the Internet or to the quarterly Law Office Information Service (LOIS) indexes and find every article ever published on the subject you're interested in. You will then have a better understanding of prices and value for equipment.

In general, when you start doing your research, give more weight to articles written by practicing lawyers, law firm administrators, or others who themselves have recently practiced law than to consultants, who often may not understand the dynamics of attorney-client relationships or attorney-staff relationships. Some consultants want you to modify the way you practice law to conform to their engineering and accounting precepts. A great deal of what consultants and vendors do is geared to the big firm, big consulting fee situation rather than toward the solo practitioner, small firm, or young lawyer starting a firm. This, of course, is a generalization, but in my opinion practicing lawyers best understand the problems of practicing lawyers and can better advise other lawyers on how to solve a problem after having successfully solved similar problems themselves. A lawyer writing an article is usually motivated to help other lawyers by sharing information on what he or she did to solve a problem. A nonlawyer on the other hand, may write an article as part of a public relations campaign to get business, and may make promises that are neither realistic nor cost effective for you as a new lawyer.

I do not wish to imply that one should never use outside consultants who have not practiced law, but I do feel that the best starting point for a new lawyer is information produced by lawyers who have had to live with their successes and failures.

Form a Group

Form your own mini office management group. Have a monthly two-hour breakfast meeting with about eight other lawyers at your stage of practice and share problems and solutions and opinions.

Practice Management Advisor

After you think you have a rough idea of what you might need, call your state bar practice management advisor if your state has one.

Don't Wait—Begin

Foonberg's rule is: "If it works, it's obsolete." At one time lawyers measured the "useful life" of their equipment at ten to fifteen years for desks, typewriters, etc. (Oversimplified, "useful life" refers to how long you'll be able to use something before it becomes physically worn out or so technologically obsolete as to require replacement.) With the advent of accelerated depreciation for tax purposes, useful life was cut back to five to ten years and in some cases written off in the year of obtaining the equipment. Today's high-technology equipment such as computers and software are estimated to have a thirty- to thirty-six-month life. Accordingly, when a piece of equipment has been on the market a year or so and has gotten a reputation for being useful, there'll be something newer and better along in about one year.

No matter what you buy, someone will come along and say that some other company has a newer, faster, or cheaper item than the one you just bought. Don't be upset or overly concerned. No matter where or when you acquire your equipment or software, there will soon be something better, faster, or cheaper. No matter when you buy, you'll soon have obsolete equipment. Don't wait forever to take the plunge. If you pick good equipment and a good system, the vendor will update it for many years. Vendors want to sell you something new, so eventually they do stop updating and supporting older equipment and software. Make your decisions on today's prices and availability rather than waiting for the next generation of technology or lower prices.

Follow Up on References, Support, and Warranties

Ask vendors and your practice management advisor for the names of lawyers in your community who have bought their products. Ask those lawyers if they're happy with the purchase and whether they'd recommend it to you. Lawyers generally will be helpful to, and honest with, other lawyers.

Find out what kind of vendor support you can expect after you buy the product or service. Do they have a toll-free telephone number with someone online to help you after a reasonable time on hold, or will you have to wait hours or days or until after the weekend for a service person to call you to set up an appointment? Is their support facility available during your time-zone requirement? Is there loaner equipment available for you while yours is being serviced?

Don't take or accept delivery until you're ready to use the equipment. Most equipment has a ninety-day parts and labor warranty. Some retailers have only a ten- or fifteen-day return or exchange period. There's no point in letting equipment sit in a box unused while the warranty is expiring.

Find out what choices you have concerning service or maintenance contracts. Does the company do its own servicing or does it farm it out to some company that will service your high-tech equipment along with washing machines, water heaters, carburetors, and cheese cutters?

A choice of post-warranty policies may be available to you. Often, there is a reduced-price service contract if you bring the equipment to the dealer or company for repair rather than require the service person to come to your office. Is that service facility nearby?

Ask if you can get a guarantee of trade-in value if the equipment is no longer sold or supported by the vendor.

Stick with brand-name merchandise unless you really know what you are doing. You can waste a lot of time and money trying to correct mistakes and make minor adjustments to get your equipment working. You may have to call in outside people or services to start up the equipment. It can cost you more to get the equipment going than you saved on the price of it. Sometimes clones of brand-name equipment do not accept all the programs or instructions that the original would accept. Buying by mail order can be a big mistake if you buy something you're not familiar with. If the equipment doesn't work properly, you won't know if it is defective or if you just haven't learned how to use it correctly.

Don't Forget to Charge Your Clients for Your Equipment and Technology

If a piece of equipment costs $10,000, has a maintenance cost of $2,000 per year, lasts 2.5 years, and will be used 4 hours per day, be sure to add $6 per hour to the operator's time when you bill your client. ($10,000 + $5,000 = $15,000 cost. 2.5 years = 125 weeks × 5 days × 4 hours = 2,500 hours usage. $15,000 + 2,500 hours = $6 per hour.) You should add at least this $6 cost figure to the hourly rate charged for the operator.

Use existing equipment and technology as long as it gets the job done for you in an acceptable manner. Don't abandon what you have for something new unless you really need the new product to serve your client.

Buying Used, Refurbished, or Obsolete Equipment

You can save a lot of hard-to-come-by cash by buying used (often called refurbished or remanufactured) equipment, if you are careful and know what you are doing. You also can make some disastrous mistakes. These suggestions will help you.

1. Try to buy equipment that has been, and still is or will be, under service contract. Equipment that has been under service contract or has been remanufactured is normally in pretty good condition.

2. Be sure you still can get a service contract for the equipment after you buy it. I've heard of vendors or maintenance companies that service equipment only as long as it's owned by the original buyer.

3. Be sure you can get all of the manuals and or instructions (including tutorials) from the seller or from the company. Without

the manuals, you'll waste a lot of time trying to figure out how to make the equipment do a particular task. These manuals are sometimes provided in print and sometimes on diskette.

4. Find what it will cost to protect your investment in used equipment when you want to upgrade. For example, you may get a fantastic buy on obsolete word processing equipment that works perfectly. You will be proud of the money you've saved until you learn it will cost a fortune to get all of your forms and product and records into the format required for the next-generation equipment. Worse yet, you may find out there is no way to convert or upgrade your system, and you'll have to start all over again or pay a fortune for someone to transfer disks from one format to another.

I was shocked to find that my IBM Display Writer disks were useless in terms of using them for an IBM PC with a printer and software package. (One solution to this problem is to print the documents you want to keep onto hard copy and then to feed the hard copy into an optical character reader (OCR) to get the document into the new system. Another solution could be to e-mail the information from your old computer to your new computer.) Accordingly, if I were to sell my old Display Writer system to you, you would buy the equipment at a fraction of the price of new equipment. The equipment would continue to work perfectly for you (under contract), but you would incur a lot of expense getting off Display Writer and onto a different system when you want to upgrade.

5. Do not buy a "boat anchor." Much of available used equipment is bulky, heavy, slow, and unmaintainable under service contract. Its highest and best use would be as an anchor for a rowboat.

6. Ignore the original cost of used equipment when deciding what price to pay for it. Because of the rapid advance in technology and equally rapid price reductions, it is totally immaterial what someone originally paid for new equipment. What is material is what new, more modern equipment would cost in today's market.

7. Used and refurbished equipment is great for backup and for expansion. If you have an equipment system that's old but still does the job, you should buy similar or identical used equipment as it becomes available. Since you already have that type of equipment, you can use the spare for backup when your regular equipment is down, for part-time people during busy periods, or for expansion when you add people. The price of used backup equipment is usually

cheap and will more than pay for itself in keeping your production up when your regular equipment is down.

8. You should understand that much used equipment cannot be upgraded to current levels of performance or technology. This is deliberate because the manufacturers want to sell you the new models rather than peripherals or conversions to upgrade old equipment. Although you won't be the first owner of the used equipment, you may be the last owner. Often, you can find a company other than the vendor or original manufacturer that sells the peripheral (or add-on equipment) or programs that the manufacturers won't sell to upgrade your equipment.

9. Factory sales. Manufacturers often sell discontinued, used, refurbished, and cosmetically blemished equipment directly. IBM, Compaq, Hewlett Packard, and many others publish daily lists of what's available via fax on demand and lists on the Internet. There are terrific bargains available, but you have to know what you want and need before you buy.

10. "Refurbished" equipment. The concept of refurbished equipment is relatively new in the marketplace, but is well accepted. Manufacturers accept returns of equipment for various reasons (scratched, floor model, had to be fixed, etc.). They then sell the refurbished equipment with new equipment guarantees for very low prices, but you are limited to what they happen to have available on a given day. Major retailers sell refurbished equipment with new equipment warranties.

Miscellaneous Equipment

Fax Equipment

In the US and most modern cities, the Internet has essentially replaced fax machines, but the use of fax is very much alive and frequently used where Internet availability is limited or not available.

Fax use is cheap and it is still essential to practicing law although it has been replaced by e-mail in most parts. Until recently more than two-thirds of all lawyer-to-lawyer mail was by fax. Many law firms no longer even bother to send follow-up confirming hard copies of the fax by U.S. mail (often called "snail mail"). Fax letter transmission saves time, is cheaper than snail mail, and eliminates arguments over whether mail was sent or received. Fax is also an excellent way of communicating important information to clients at any hour of day or night, whether or not the client is there to receive the fax. (You should clear fax communication with a client before sending faxes due to problems of the fax being read by third parties, employees, etc.) Fax is more private and secure than e-mail. A computer hacker can get to your e-mail but not to your stand-alone fax equipment.

Fax is sometimes called facsimile, telefacsimile, or telecopier. It is not e-mail, although sometimes e-mail systems are utilized as part of the system of sending and receiving the fax.

This equipment allows you to transmit or receive documents through online hard-wire telephone or cellular telephone lines from any place in the world to any place in the world. You can transmit a letter, diagram, or photo and receive a copy at the receiving end. You don't have to rely on mail or messengers. You can get messages to or from your firm or client or other lawyers instantly. Notebook computers and other small, single-purpose machines are available that you can take with you when you travel. Your office and clients can transmit your correspondence or documents from a file to an electronic mailbox for you to retrieve while you're on the road overnight or at home on a weekend or on a long trip. Some courts and governmental agencies allow service of process and filing by fax. I send all mail of up to ten pages first by fax or e-mail, then by regular mail for confirming backup.

Although you can probably buy a used (sometimes called refurbished or remanufactured) fax machine cheaply, they are so cheap new (as low as $100 or less for a stand-alone machine), I wouldn't fool around with buying a used one. On the other hand, if you can get one for free or next to free, they seem to last forever and there's no reason not to use existing old equipment when starting a practice. If you use old equipment, be sure it is automatic (can send or receive twenty-four hours a day even though unattended) and that it has an automatic page cutter if it is an old-fashioned not plain-paper copier. You need a memory of at least twenty pages for out-of-paper reception (about 256 KB).

If you do get a plain-paper fax machine, be sure that documents longer than letter size are printed on multiple pages, actual size, rather than being "scrunched up" to fit on a single letter-sized sheet of paper. Many legal documents created before the 1980s in the U.S. are "legal length," and most legal documents currently being produced outside the U.S. are longer than the standard American letter size of $8^1/_2 \times 11$. Many plain-paper copiers make these documents illegible by "scrunching" them to fit on a single letter-sized sheet of paper.

Dedicated fax telephone lines. A dedicated phone line for your fax machine and dial-up email is cheap and recommended, but is not absolutely necessary. For about $35, you can buy a device that can tell if your phone line is being called from another telephone or from a fax machine and go to the fax if it is a fax calling or e-mail. I use the dial-up as a back up to my DSL Internet. I personally use a single dedicated telephone line for my PC, for my e-mail, my online services, Internet, and my fax, leaving my other phone lines free for telephones.

Sending and receiving faxes via computer. Many word processing and communications software packages allow you to send and receive faxes directly to and from a PC without a stand-alone fax machine, using the PC's printer to print out incoming faxes. If you are competent with computers, this may work for you. Otherwise I recommend against using your computer for incoming faxes. There seem to be too many problems with receiving faxes, and almost everyone I have questioned recommends against using the computer for incoming faxes, especially when stand-alone fax machines are so cheap and the $35 device will divert faxes to the fax machine.

On the other hand, sending faxes to an electronic mailbox to be retrieved by a computer seems to work fairly well, if you are disciplined to regularly check your electronic mailbox(es).

If you will have more than one lawyer in your office, consider a private fax machine for each lawyer near that lawyer's desk.

I have predicted and continue to predict that fax and e-mail will have a greater impact than the photocopy machine on the way law is practiced in America.

Modems
If you know about modems, skip this section.

All sorts of new and developing technology may affect modem choices. ISDN, DSL, Cable, T1, T3, Wi-Fi and other technology, direct broadcast satellite broadcasting systems, modem cable systems, and digital satellite systems are in various stages of development, but for most lawyers 56 kbps is going to be adequate and affordable. If you know what you are doing, you can use an external modem and use the same modem for different computers. I believe that external modems are a false economy because of all the tweaking problems from computer to computer. Use an internal modem set for the host computer unless you enjoy wasting time tweaking computers when you could be using your time more profitably practicing law or getting clients.

The modem is the device that sends and receives information from one computer to another over telephone lines. It doesn't create the information, it converts the information into and out of a digital format so the information can go over telephone lines.

You need a modem (and software) to receive or send e-mail and to access the Internet, among other uses.

Some modems are faster than others. The faster the modem, the faster the information flows over the phone lines. Speed is important when you pay by the minute for telephone lines or when you are sending or receiving a huge amount of information and have better things to do than watch the grass grow while waiting for all the information to be sent or received. This is especially important when sending huge amounts of information via e-mail or downloading huge quantities of information from the Internet.

Modems also are part of the system in sending and receiving faxes. Modems, if they are accompanied by the appropriate software, can also be part of an overall communications system including voice mail, data conferencing, etc. Modem speeds are measured in bits per second (BPS) or thousands of bits per second (KBPS). Most fax machines send/receive through a 78 KBPS modem and most Internet dial-up is at 56 KBPS. High speed is about 10 times faster than dial-up.

Remember my "Foonbergism," "If it works, it's obsolete."

Scanners

If you know about scanners, skip this section.

Scanners are also called optical character readers (OCRs) or optical scanners. A scanner is sort of a reverse photocopy machine. You put a sheet of paper into or under a scanner and the scanner "reads" what is typed or printed on the paper. It transfers that information into your computer. (Technically, it transfers the characters onto the medium.)

An inexpensive scanner can cost less than a hundred dollars and can slowly read most typewriter printing, allowing you to copy almost any legal document produced by another lawyer. Scanners costing a lot more can read just about any print, including almost any form found in a form book.

In addition to the scanner, you must buy some peripheral equipment to integrate into your word processing system.

With a scanner, you can copy other lawyers' products into your system and then print it out on your own printer. This enables you, without keyboarding, to use other lawyers' forms or the parts of them you like better than your own, or to use their forms in addition to yours. Scanners also are useful for copying the other lawyers' documents into your system so that you can print the final version of a document for your client to sign. This gives you control over the possibility of the other lawyers "accidentally" omitting a word or phrase in a long document. (Incidentally, there are word processing packages such as CompareRite that will permit you to compare your copy of the document with that of the other lawyer, and then will highlight discrepancies between the two documents.)

I once drafted four seventy-five-page settlement agreements for four consolidated cases. The cases were similar yet differing from case to case, as were the settlement agreements. I took the documents to the other lawyer's office to negotiate various aspects of the agreements. While we were discussing the first agreement, his staff was feeding the other three agreements to the scanner(s), and then later they input the first agreement into his word processing system. We made the agreed-upon changes and I left his office with finalized documents produced by his word processors, having used my documents as the starting point. You could accomplish the same results by bringing your word processing disk with you or asking the other lawyer for his or her document on disk. By using PDF and other formats documents can easily be sent via Internet.

Research articles from periodicals applicable to a case or portions of a case from a book can be scanned into the computer, into the client file, or into your general research files.

Tax and court administrative forms also can be read into your word processing system without inputting by keyboard. The forms then can be filled in and printed out on your system.

Paper Shredders

I was shocked to learn that police agencies and private investigators routinely go through the garbage produced by lawyers to look for evidence or information that can be used against the lawyers' clients. It is my understanding that in most states no warrant is necessary to search a lawyer's trashed documents once they leave the lawyer's office. If the possibility of police agencies or your client's competitors or adversaries having access to your trashed documents concerns you, you should consider a paper shredder for use when appropriate. Proper document and file disposal procedures are part of a lawyer's ongoing obligation to maintain client confidences, even after the case is closed or the client no longer is a client. You should know that even shredded files can be reconstructed back to the original and the only way to be sure paper has been destroyed is to burn it or turn it into pulp.

Telephones

There is no limit to the number of features you can add onto a telephone system by either purchasing your own equipment or by obtaining services from the telephone company for a monthly fee. Voice mail, call forwarding, paging, caller ID, and many other features can be purchased. I recommend using monthly service from the telephone company rather than buying equipment or software you may never need. You can have features such as redialing and music for callers on "hold" built into the instrument, and you can get features such as conference call capability from the phone company. The important features to you are the number of instruments and lines the system can handle. Leave room for future stations and lines. You cannot depend on being able to get additional equipment later on because companies quickly discontinue one line to start a newer line with more sophisticated technology and features.

A cellular phone allows you to return client calls and be in touch with your office while commuting or going to and from court. I recommend them. Try to get a car speakerphone or earphone and microphone so you can keep your hands on the wheel while driving and talking. You can also access the Internet for e-mail, etc.

Telephone Answering Machines and Systems (Sometimes Called Voice Mail)

I am generally opposed to answering machines for after-office hours and prefer answering services with live operators who are trained to handle hysterical callers or forward voice mail to reach the lawyer. If you are going to use an answering machine, there is a feature available that I like. The new feature is called remote call transferring. When a caller leaves a message and hangs up, your answering machine dials your remote pager, your remote home telephone, or any other number. You then call your own number to get the message that was left on the machine. This system can give you twenty-four hour availability and coverage using a machine. Many telephone communications features are available for monthly charges from your telephone company with no "up front" cash needed.

Voice mail is also used for screening calls and is frequently used to avoid unwanted calls from telephone solicitors, unhappy creditors, nuisance clients, etc.

Overcoming Technology Phobia

If you already are a "techie," skip this part and go on to the next one. If you are not a techie (or don't even know what a techie is), then continue reading.

If you have the ability to operate a car, you have the ability to operate a computer, but you first have to learn how. Just as you aren't born knowing how to drive a car, no one is born with computer skills. It takes a certain amount of time and practice to learn and to keep current.

If you take lessons, it's important that you take your lessons with students of equal or lesser ability. If you progress at the same rate or faster than the others, you'll feel good. If you are significantly slower than the others, you'll feel foolish and give up. No one wants to appear slow or dense, and if you feel "out of it," you'll probably quit the class.

After all, you went through high school, college, and law school with good grades because you were a fast learner. To appear to be a slow learner is a big blow to your ego. It's because of this fear of appearing slow that many lawyers prefer to learn in private using tutorials. These are software programs that interact with the students so that they advance at their own pace without others knowing how slow or fast they learn.

Some experts feel the best way to learn is for two people of approximately equal age and position to sit side-by-side and share a computer. The two students encourage and help each other and are more apt to advance at the same speed. If you can afford it, get a private tutor to teach you what you have to know. If you are a senior lawyer, check out **www.SeniorLawyers.org/ProjectReverseMentoring** for a system of matching tutors with seniors.

PC Software for the Sole Practitioner or Small Law Firm

If it works, it's obsolete. Publishers of software want their software to become obsolete in order to sell you upgrades and new applications. Competition readily makes software obsolete. Throughout this section I'll cover the applications most important to a new practice or a newly started office. I will mention several different packages. It is not my intention to recommend any of them or to downgrade their competitors. I feel that by giving you the name of a system already used by lawyers, or which vendors claim will work for lawyers, I'll be helping you in two ways:

1. You'll have an idea of what can be done with a PC;

2. You'll have a starting point of at least one specific package that you can look at and with which you can compare others.

Some software is free or low cost and can be obtained by downloading it from the Internet. Other software packages can cost between $70 and $3,000. Most software that a new lawyer would want or need is in the $100 to $350 range.

Some lawyers have their own favorite software or hardware and will be concerned that I did not mention something important. If you feel I've neglected some system that's three times as good, four times faster, and one-tenth the cost of those I mention, you're right and I apologize in advance.

Word Processing

Choosing a word-processing software package is very important because lawyers tend to stay with the first system they learn. The lawyer (or secretary) who becomes used to a system does not want to change, and compares all other packages to that one.

If a lawyer achieves success and comfort with a word-processing system, the lawyer is more likely to go on to other PC software packages and systems. A bad result with word processing tends to make the lawyer hesitant to use a PC for new applications or to maximum advantage.

WordPerfect historically has been and still is one of the more popular software packages used by lawyers, especially for lawyer to lawyer communication of legal documents. It is reported by the experts to be easy to learn and use. It has good support and does most of the things lawyers need from a word-processing package, including (according to many lawyers) good document appearance, page and paragraph numbering and renumbering, underlining, title centering, spell checking, and automatic creation of tables of contents and/or index of words used. Most importantly it has a "reveal codes" feature. Microsoft Word also is a very popular software system used by lawyers, according to those who review software packages. You should have the capability to use both WordPerfect and Word.

Microsoft Word is commonly used by nonlawyers because it often comes included with the computer without extra cost.

The ABA's Legal Technology Resource Center (LTRC) does not specifically recommend or evaluate law office software, but it can provide general legal technology assistance to firms and corporate law departments of all sizes. For more information, call the LTRC at 312-988-5465, e-mail **ltrc@abanet.org**, or visit **http://www.aba net.org/tech/ltrc/**. Your bar-sponsored law practice management advisor may also have recommendations.

CompareRite is a system that is supposed to eliminate or reduce the need for two people proofreading to compare documents. You can input by scanner or by keyboarding (the fancy word for typing on a computer) your original document via an OCR scanner into your PC. CompareRite will highlight the differences between the two documents, giving you the equivalent of a blue-line or red-line version of the document and covering the possibility of the other lawyer's "inadvertently" forgetting to tell you about changes made in your document. This matching process is sometimes called "redlining." Although this program may be expensive, it will help prevent malpractice in document negotiation and presentation.

Spell Checking and Thesaurus

If you don't get a software package that contains spell checking, you can buy a spelling package very cheaply. Typically, the dictionary contains about 75,000 words. If a word in your document doesn't match up to a word in the list, the package highlights the differing word and gives you a choice of possible correct words. I strongly recommend this feature. It is especially important if you are going to rely on a high-school graduate secretary or word processor to do your post-graduate spelling. Having a spell checker does not relieve you of the responsibility of reading everything you sign before you sign it. A spell checking error can make you look incompetent as a lawyer and can even result in a malpractice suit. Add your clients' names to the spell-checker dictionary. A spell checker is just a mechanical device. It cannot select the right word. The term "spell checker" isn't even in most spell-checker dictionaries. Some software packages have a thesaurus. This package brings up synonyms to the screen to help you compose a letter or document when you can't find just the word you need.

Cite Checking

If your legal work includes a lot of law and motion or appellate work where you'll be citing a lot of cases, there are software packages that check cites against the *Harvard Blue Book*. CiteRite is a relatively well-known product.

Form Creation and Retrieval

When you input a form, you can retrieve it to use again when you need it. You can input your forms much the way you would on a typewriter, or you can input other lawyers' forms using a scanner. Wills, trusts, pleadings, discovery, and myriad commonly used forms can be created and stored in your PC on a disk unit ready to use.

For example, many ABA Law Practice Management Section books come with a disk featuring forms, checklists, and other information that can be tailored to your law practice. Many forms can be downloaded for free from government agencies on the Internet Government and other organizations make forms available on the Internet to avoid the labor and postage expense of sending forms to people requesting them.

Most books that feature forms also have a disk containing the forms.

Clients, Contacts, and Conflicts

It is extremely important for a new lawyer to start and maintain a list or database of just about everybody the lawyer meets in the course of being a lawyer. Everyone you know should be on this list. Everyone you meet should be added to this list.

You will be able to use the list for practice development purposes including the sending of announcements, newsletters, Christmas cards, birthday cards, etc. The list can also serve as a resource for checking conflicts of interest. The list will be useful in locating a person in a given geographic area or with a special attribute you need. It will be of great value in getting help from others and in establishing and reestablishing relationships and contacts years after you meet people and have long forgotten their names or what they did or why you knew them. Be sure to include lawyers representing all adverse clients.

You can create your own database or look to a commercially available program such as ACT or Goldmine. Be sure to list fax numbers and e-mail addresses.

Litigation Support

If you are fortunate enough as a new lawyer to get a big case, then litigation support systems using a PC, scanners, etc., may enable you to handle a case competently that you otherwise would have to refer to a larger firm. You can keep track of thousands of documents and be able to find what you need when you need it. You can project and calculate damages using a spreadsheet. You can analyze and organize a deposition with a PC by using key words and phrases. There are several programs available for deposition analysis. Ask your friendly deposition reporter for recommendations as to what is currently available. In some large cases you may wish to use an intranet.

Office Management

Your PC should be used to run your office. Some examples of what the PC can do for your office include:

1. *Calendar and Docket Control.* Your PC can be used to maintain a calendar to manage your office and docket controls. You can schedule appointments, court dates, conferences, depositions, etc., with reminders before the events take place and follow-up dates after they pass. You also can schedule birthday cards, anniversary cards, will revisions, reminders of lease renewals, reminders of directors' and shareholders' meetings, probate and trust accountings, tax returns, etc.

2. *Accounting and Billing Systems.* Many different accounting and billing systems are available. The ABA's Legal Technology Resource Center (LTRC) can provide suggestions. For more information call 312/988-5465. Ask your CPA to suggest reports you need from the system.

3. *Time Recording.* Some lawyers recommend the most recent version of Timeslips or Time Matters as an easy-to-learn way of keeping good time records for the purpose of preparing a bill to the client and reviewing the status of work in progress.

4. *Check Writing and General Ledger Accounting.* Some systems (Quick Books is an example) allow you to write checks and distribute the checks through the accounting system all the way to the general ledger and income tax return.

5. *Electronic Mail (e-mail).* This is an electronic mailbox system. E-mail ability is a necessity. Many clients will insist on document transmission via modem rather than fax. Using your computer and modem, you can send a letter over a telephone line and the Internet to another electronic mailbox. The letter is received at the mailbox the instant it's sent. You can check your mailbox for mail at any hour of the day or night from your computer or wireless device. E-mail is a fraction of the cost of "snail mail." There are a great many e-mail programs available. Your Internet service provider will automatically include e-mail capacity.

6. *Fax.* Faxes can be sent and received via your computer, but I recommend a stand-alone fax machine. They are cheap and you don't have to be concerned about your computer being on or off.

7. *Conflicts.* As indicated, you can use your contacts program to check every potential new client against every current and former client to find potential conflicts of interest.

8. *Telephone Directory and Dialing.* You can program a computer to look for a client's telephone number (after you've input it). You punch a key and the computer will dial the client's number through the modem. Some programs will also record or meter the time spent on the phone for billing purposes.

Research and Databases

Your PC at your desk is where you should do most of your legal research. Online services such as Lexis and Westlaw are less than half the cost of CD-ROM. CD-ROMs can be less than half the cost of books. A new lawyer should try to use fixed-price online research and CD-ROMs. A lot of research material is available for free through the Internet. Many governmental bodies and law schools and law firms make their libraries available via the World Wide Web. With your modem and a CD-ROM you can do legal research from anywhere, including the courtroom during a trial.

Most local bar associations have negotiated flat monthly rates for online services.

In addition to purely legal research, there are millions of pages of information available for free from the Internet as well as thousands of databases available for a cost through Lexis, Westlaw, and other online research providers.

Your law school librarian or local law librarian can make recommendations based on your needs.

If you are an older lawyer who just can't properly handle electronic research you can get very low-priced research help from the Wisconsin Law Library at 1-800-322-9755. It will charge very little and is available to all lawyers, not just Wisconsin lawyers. The staff can research anything anywhere ranging from parking tickets to Security Exchange Commission litigation. If you are a senior lawyer or know one who needs email and Internet help, check out **www.SeniorLawyers.org/ProjectReverseMentoring/**.

Desktop Organizers

Lawyers often scribble time records and notes on random pieces of paper. A desktop organizer does all that through a keyboard without paper all over the desk. You simply input (type) the data you used to scribble, and it's in proper form for filing and bill preparation.

Spreadsheets

Among many things you can do with a spreadsheet is to set up your computer to accumulate data, organize it, and list it in any sequence you wish. You then can ask the computer "what-if" situations and the computer will give you the answer based on the way you set up the spreadsheet.

Substantive Law Systems

Starting with admiralty and administrative law and going alphabetically down to veterans' benefits, wills, and workers' compensation, there are software packages designed for almost every area of law. Many continuing legal education suppliers sell software for substantive systems. Wills, corporations, bankruptcy, taxation, and litigation management commonly are available. There is more commercial software for federal practice areas than state practice areas because of the larger market. On the other hand, much of the information for state practice areas can be obtained for free or at low cost through BBSs. Additionally many governmental agencies publish forms and instructions for use of the forms on the Internet for you to download and use. They use the Internet to save postage and printing expense.

Miscellaneous Computer Equipment

Computer Tables and Cabinets

Specialized furniture to accommodate a PC, manuals, and peripherals is available. Wrist guards to reduce carpal tunnel syndrome and ergonomic chairs to prevent back strain are also available. Some desks accommodate computers under the desk with the monitor at tabletop level.

Flat Wiring

If your landlord or contractor wants a lot of money to bring electrical or telephone wires in conduit through the roof, ask about flat wires for electricity and telephones that go under pressure-sensitive, easy-release carpet tiles.

Modem

The modem is the device that connects your PC and your fax to the telephone for both incoming and outgoing information. As of this writing, a 56,000 baud modem was pretty much the capacity of most telephone lines unless you have DSL, ISDN, cable, or other newer technology telephone lines.

Since you might pay by the minute for telephone time and access time on databases, you want to be able to send or receive quickly. What you spend on a modem you'll usually save on time access charges. (Some databases charge by the line instead of by time when you unload with a faster modem.)

Printers

There are various types of personal computer printers available at prices ranging from less than a hundred dollars to several thousand dollars. Laser printers are small desktop machines, and produce letter-quality documents that you can send to your clients and opposing counsel without embarrassment. I recommend using laser printers for letters rather than inkjet printers. Inkjet printers are satisfactory for making internal memos or as a backup but really should not be used for client correspondence. You should use different stationery for laser printers. This type of stationery is called "low impact." In large-volume reproduction, it is often cheaper but slower to use laser printers than to use photocopying machines. (Stuart F. Cooper Stationery Company in Los Angeles will be happy to assist you in selecting paper and stationery.)

Color printers are cheap. A word of caution, the biggest cost of printers over a period of time is the cost of inks or toner. Try to estimate usage for a year or two and then look at the total cost of the printer and the supplies.

PDAs

There is a huge variety of PDAs on the market as of the writing of this chapter. It would be almost impossible to list everything that can be done with a PDA.

Should You Do Your Own Word Processing?

In general, I recommend that you not do your own word processing (typing). Many new lawyers and some law firms think they are saving money by not hiring a secretary or a word processor. It is a false and foolish economy to try to be your own secretary. You can handwrite at about 15 words per minute. You can type at about 50 or 65 words per minute, and you can speak at about 160 to 175 words per minute. Obviously, speech is the most efficient way to transfer information from your brain to paper.

Some lawyers believe that being a fast typist justifies doing their own typing. They are generally wrong. You can dictate twenty-five or more letters in an hour and charge a standard time of fifteen minutes or thirty minutes per letter. There is no way you can type that many letters. In a matter of seconds you can dictate instructions into a digital recorder or tape recorder that would take five to ten minutes for you to compose at a word processor.

For example, you could dictate into a tape recorder "Ms. Jones. Send a letter to Mr. Petersen on the Main Street property matter. Tell him that we received a set of interrogatories and that he should read the questions and call me within ten days for an appointment to discuss the answers, which will be due on March 10th. Enclose a copy of the interrogatories. Send a copy of the letter and the interrogatory to Ms. Thomas the CPA with a note to please review the questions. Calendar to February 20th to call Mr. Petersen if he hasn't called me."

It might take Ms. Jones a half hour or more to pull up all the appropriate addresses and file numbers and salutations, spell check the letters, make the necessary copies and enclosures, calculate and affix postage, and calendar on the manual and computer tickler system. In the meantime you have dictated ten more letters with instructions, charging for your time.

Your secretary or word processing person can be producing documents and letters for you and minding your telephone while you are earning fees in court or in deposition or with a client. If you don't have legal work to do you should be out of the office developing clients while your word processing person or secretary is doing the letters or document revision or input.

With a digital recorder and dictating equipment, you have a portability you won't have if you do your own typing. Keep a small portable dictating unit or digital recorder in your desk, in your briefcase, in your car, and by your bedside. Give the tape or recorder to your secretary or word processor and go out and practice law or market or go to a CLE program.

If you haven't got much cash or working capital, get an intern (sometimes called extern) from a junior college, high school, or business college to do your word processing.

Some lawyers can compose long original documents on a computer better than they can dictate or write on a yellow pad. If you are one of these lawyers, then by all means do your own inputting of these long documents. Inputting large amounts of mechanical data (batch processing) should be done by a secretary or word processor.

One of the advantages of working with a secretary as part of your team is that you will be reviewing his or her work and vice versa. When you do it yourself, no one is reviewing what you do and you are not likely to catch your own mistakes.

If you communicate with your clients by e-mail, you still should have a word processing person and then send your e-mail when you are confident it is error-free. You wouldn't send out unreviewed and uncorrected first drafts of documents and correspondence by "snail mail" (U.S. mail), and you shouldn't send out first drafts by e-mail.

Voice-recognition word processing, if you can master it, further frees you up to do legal work by dictating drafts to be cleaned up by someone else while you do marketing of the practice. Many lawyers are employed by firms that want to keep overhead low by not providing word processing support.

Notwithstanding, my recommendation is that you not do your own word processing. You may disagree.

Voice recognition systems may or may not work for you. They require a significant investment in software that requires powerful hardware and sound cards which must be matched to each other. Expect to devote huge amounts of time practicing to effectively use the equipment. It's my best estimate (based on the seminars I do) that about 75 percent of all lawyers have tried voice recognition systems and that less than 5 percent continued using voice recognition. I tried it and gave up. Too much time learning and practice time was required. You may be able to use it.

Should Your Office Furnishings Be Lavish?

Any ten lawyers are likely to have at least thirty opinions on this subject. Perhaps there is no answer. My advice is for you to do whatever makes you feel comfortable, and whatever you personally think your clients will like. I have been in offices of lawyers who make well into six or seven figures a year. Some offices appear to be "Early Salvation Army," and others are garish with rare and expensive furniture and works of art. I have also seen the offices of lawyers who went under and found the same discrepancies. I therefore have come to the conclusion that your office furnishings will not determine your success or failure.

I will repeat here some "maxims" that I have heard over the years and leave it to you to make your own decision.

1. In a "neighborhood practice," heavy with divorce, criminal, and accident work, the prospective clients want a "successful" lawyer, and will be impressed by your success if you have garish, obviously expensive furnishings.

2. In a "neighborhood practice," heavy with divorce, criminal, and accident work, the prospective clients will be frightened away if they see expensive furnishings. They will be afraid of being charged high fees, knowing that in the final analysis, their fees pay for the furnishings.

3. Business executives don't want to pay for your unnecessary overhead. They know that the quality of the furnishings is unrelated to the quality of the legal services.

4. Business executives want a successful lawyer, and they will expect high fees when they see expensive offices.

There are many, many more "maxims." Frankly, I don't believe any of them. Do whatever makes you feel comfortable.

I do recommend, however, that during your early practice you avoid buying expensive furniture for a year or two. You can anticipate several office changes during your first few years, and a piece of furniture that fits perfectly in one office may not fit at all in your next office. As a new lawyer, put your money into having a good conference room for meeting clients. Your personal work area can be outfitted with cheap, mismatched, functional furniture if you confine client meetings to the conference room.

Also, give serious consideration to buying or renting used furniture. Your local legal newspaper will have ads from lawyers who learned the hard way that they no longer need the furniture they bought. When big firms go broke, their fancy furniture can often be purchased cheaply.

I recommend the following furniture for your office:

1. Formica-top lawyer's desk, at least six feet. Be sure the desk has an overhang in front, so that your client can come up close to the desk without banging knees. (Don't waste your money on fancy natural woods.)

2. One judge's chair for you.

3. Two to four straight-back clients' chairs. Remember that clients who are old or who have injured bodies have difficulty getting out of soft chairs.

4. Wastebasket to match your desk.

5. Potted plant. Don't buy items for your desk such as memo pads, ash trays, paper clip holders, pen sets, desk TVs and radios, etc. You will be deluged with gifts of these items from well-meaning friends and relatives.

6. If having lavish furnishings and surroundings is important to you, consider subletting an office in a law firm that has the kind of surroundings you want.

7. Computer cabinet or table configured with the equipment you need placed where you need it.

Diplomas, Degrees, Admissions to Practice, Etc.

Your parents were very impressed with all of your certificates. Your clients won't be. They will assume that you have graduated from law school and are admitted to practice. It's not necessary to prove it to them or to reassure them. It may, however, be reassuring to you to put these on a wall in your office. If so, do the following:

1. Put them on a wall behind your desk. This will be close enough for the clients to see you have them, but far enough away that they can't see the dates.

2. Get them framed in glass, rather than sealed in plastic. I learned, to my dismay, that the fancy gold seals of the court and university were permanently squeezed flat beyond recognition by the heat-pressure combination. If you want to preserve the lettering on the seals, get the certificates framed or at least investigate what you are doing when a relative, such as your mother, offers to pay the cost of the plaques.

Announcements, Stationery and Professional Cards, Christmas Cards, and "Mailing Lists"

Stationery in General

Your stationery is a legitimate form of advertising and you should use only the very highest quality of engraved stationery. Clients, prospective clients, adverse parties, adverse attorneys, judges, etc., may never see you face-to-face, but they will see your stationery.

I shudder when I see the cheap heat-process stationery or photocopier-produced stationery where the ink chips off or causes the paper to stick together. I mentally downgrade the lawyer, and I suppose I also downgrade somewhat that person's client and that client's case. Whether this reaction is or is not a proper reaction is immaterial. The important thing is that you, your clients, and your clients' cases may be judged in part by your stationery. So use only the highest quality. Saving money on stationery is a false economy.

Follow up e-mail messages and faxes with a letter whenever possible. The letter is a tangible reminder to the client of what they are paying for.

It has been estimated that it costs about $6 in secretarial time and overhead to type a letter, fold it, put it in the envelope, and carry it to the mailbox for mailing, as well as getting the copy into the file, etc. The postage stamp will cost 37 cents or more, and the letter may be the only tangible manifestation of your legal work (besides your bill) that your client will ever get.

Your client will probably never throw your letters away. Your client (mentally) may be paying from a few dollars to hundreds or even thousands of dollars for the one letter from you, or for a few letters from you, embodying your sage advice.

I personally believe that a judge or client or opposing counsel or third party will have a higher opinion of your legal skills, your client, and the merits of your client's position when they receive high-quality paper and engraved stationery from you. Cheap do-it-yourself stationery in my opinion conveys a negative or lesser status than engraved high-quality paper.

For a lawyer to use cheap stationery, to me, is comparable to a jeweler's wrapping a fine diamond ring or watch in an old newspaper.

Legal services, like jewelry, are a relatively expensive commodity to the consumer, and, in my opinion, should be well packaged when sent out. Please keep in mind that I am referring in this section to your letterhead, letterhead envelopes, billing stationery, and professional cards. I am not advocating this high-cost stationery for scratch pads, forms, or other similar materials.

You will need engraved letterhead paper, "copy" paper (stationery identical to the letterhead with the word "copy" on it), envelopes, professional cards, and statement paper. In order to save the cost of die cutting, the printer may try to sell you an introductory "package" of some of each of the above, using the identical die, which looks like this:

BRAND NEW LAWYER
ATTORNEY AT LAW
123 Main Street, Suite A
Anytown, USA 00000-1234

Telephone: 312/123/4567
Fax: 312/765/4321
e-mail: **BNLaw@law.com**

The die or computer design is used on all your cards and stationery except that the contact numbers are left off the return address. It is very tempting to order this package due to what appears to be a special price. The printer may tell you that if you order the package you can get delivery in ten days, but it will take four or five weeks to get a special die or computer design. Often there is nothing "special" about the special price. It only appears special because you are ordering everything at one time instead of ordering piecemeal at intervals. The major cost of printing is the labor cost of setup. Once the presses or printers are set up, the cost of feeding additional stock is negligible. You should keep this in mind and try to order several stationery needs at the same time wherever possible. In other words, if you are about to order letterhead stationery, check all your printing needs.

My objection to the package is that it is obvious to other lawyers that it is a package. I recommend not using the package and instead having something prepared that makes it obvious that you are not using the package.

Be prepared to use your computer to produce stationery on an emergency basis only. Self-designed stationery using your fonts and copy paper, in my opinion, degrades the quality of your communications.

Die Costs

Depending on local custom and law, the die the printer makes for you may legally be your property. If so, don't be embarrassed to ask for the die if you change printers.

Fax and Photocopy Quality

The fax machine and the photocopier have greatly revolutionized the way law is practiced and the way legal printed information is transmitted and received.

In the real world of practicing law, your documents and letters will be faxed and scanned and photocopied.

Stationery designers and printers and commercial artists are often totally ignorant of the need for legal written letters and documents to be capable of being faxed and scanned and photocopied. They sometimes produce stationery that is great when you hold it in your hands, but is almost totally worthless in the real world of fax and photocopy and email.

Faxability

Test your stationery by sending yourself a fax typed on your stationery. You may be amazed to learn that the printing that is perfectly clear and legible in the original form is not legible on a fax transmission or when scanned. The problem is compounded when a receiving fax is a low-quality machine or uses low-quality paper or low-quality printing. Some plain-paper fax machines only print out on $8^1/_2 \times 11$ paper, and compress larger documents down to that size, thus further worsening the problem of illegible stationery. You should assume the worst possible receiving equipment and design your stationery (or ask your printer to design it) to take into account the possibility of low-quality fax reception where you send your faxes.

If you find that your printed stationery is not clear and legible when faxed, consider larger type (fonts), and consider a more generous use of bold type and fonts. There is no substitute for trial and error to determine what works best for you.

When in doubt go for large, bold type, especially if you want seniors as clients.

Photocopyability

As previously indicated, almost every letter and document you produce will be photocopied at some point in time. It is extremely important that your stationery be capable of photocopying. You will send copies to clients and third parties. Clients will photocopy the letters and documents for others in the organization. What you produced may be copied for extensive distribution.

Every time someone reproduces one of your letters and distributes it, they are in effect advertising and marketing for you. Be sure your stationery is legible when photocopied. I have seen a lot of white on white embossing which looks nice when you hold the letter in your hand, but is worthless when you try to photocopy it.

Creating Your Own Stationery

Most word processing packages include a large variety of fonts, which allow you to create your own stationery.

Unfortunately, the flat letter ink jet or laser printing on inexpensive copy paper does not begin to carry the same authority as engraved high-quality paper stationery.

Legal services are expensive and you should not deliver a high-priced product on cheap paper.

Time Lag in Printing

When considering opening or changing your office, remember that printers are worse than lawyers when it comes to delivering their work product. Time delays of two weeks to two months are not unusual. Asking your printer for your die to give to another printer can sometimes decrease the waiting time for an order.

Announcements

To whom you may send announcements is largely a matter of local custom. See DR 2-102(A)(2) or whatever is your local equivalent. As a general rule, you can, and should, send your announcements to anyone with whom you have any preexisting relationship. Again, the acceptable practice varies greatly from jurisdiction to jurisdiction. For a new lawyer, announcements accomplish the dual purpose of telling people that you passed the bar and where your office is. You may find a substantial delay due to printers and getting your phone numbers confirmed. Don't be concerned if the announcements don't arrive until after you've moved in. Order some extra announcements to send to people you overlooked on your first list. For a decent interval of time, you can send these overlooked people your announcement.

When people receive your announcement, they will read it and say, "That's nice." They may then put your phone number and address in a book and throw your expensive announcement immediately into the wastebasket. (Except for your parents, who may frame it or put it in a scrapbook.)

I personally think you will be doing more for your friends and relatives if you include a professional card with your announcement. The small card can be easily placed in a wallet to be available when your client needs you right away.

Announcement Mailing List

Your announcement mailing list is a valuable asset. Keep it updated with new addresses and clients. Eliminate people with whom you have no contact. Announcements to people you have not had prior contact with may be a form of improper solicitation. (See section on clients, contracts, and conflicts.)

Christmas Cards

Every year I send personal "Season's Greetings" cards to my clients. Invariably, the cards serve as a reminder to some of them to take care of some legal matter such as updating a will. A divorce lawyer told me that couples stay together through Christmas and New Year's Day and start divorce proceedings in January and February. If this is so, then I suppose "Season's Greetings" cards are a very good investment, as you may be reaching two potential clients.

Senior lawyers tend to decrease the number of Christmas and Holiday cards they send. This is a serious mistake unless they are intentionally reducing their practice. Clients need to be reminded that the senior lawyer is neither dead nor retired.

I try to be clever and distinguishable from others on my holiday cards. Holiday cards are a good investment. Ordinarily you get more than enough response to pay the cost of the printing and mailing. Many of my overseas clients send me fax greetings, which are often quite clever.

Here again, local practice varies from jurisdiction to jurisdiction, and you should ask other lawyers what is permissible. In some areas, you cannot use a firm name on the card and in some you can.

I also receive e-mail greetings, especially from overseas clients and lawyers. When considering the cost of postage and the time and uncertainty of delivery, e-mail greetings may be a better way to go.

After forty years of practice, I can unequivocally state that sending Christmas cards (or the equivalent Holiday Greetings) is the most important marketing you can do. At my peak, I sent more than 6,000 cards/year. As I cut back my practice, heading toward retirement, I kept reducing the number of cards each year and the practice decreased in direct proportion to the number of cards sent.

Use Yellow Legal Pads

Carry a yellow legal pad with you whenever you go to a public place. When you have a yellow pad with you, you are loudly, but nonintrusively, proclaiming to everyone who can see the pad that you are a lawyer. Everyone knows that lawyers use yellow pads and that very few people who are not lawyers use yellow pads.

People cannot use you for legal services if they don't know you are a lawyer.

Many lawyers have related to me how they first met good clients and received good fees and cases because a total stranger who saw them with a legal pad approached them with the opening question "Are you a lawyer?" This was followed by a recitation of their problem and a statement that they wanted to talk with a lawyer, but didn't know how to find the right one.

I personally have been approached many times by total strangers who came over to talk to me because they saw my yellow pad and assumed I was a lawyer. I've picked up some good clients because I had a yellow pad with me where total strangers could see me and my yellow pad.

Some law firms have their name and phone number imprinted on the pad itself across the top on the front. Everyone in the firm is encouraged to take the pads home and to use them in public. Many firms go out of their way to give the pads to clients and others who use them at meetings. These personalized pads should be placed at every spot at the conference table, and in every lawyer's individual office where the pad can be given to the client for the purposes of note taking with the client taking the pad with him or her at the end of the meeting.

There is a rumor, which is not true, that yellow paper cannot be recycled. You may wish to use recycled pads that have imprinted on the bottom of each sheet the message, "Made from recycled paper." Although this does not say the yellow pad itself will be recycled, it carries the message that the firm is environmentally conscious and aware and probably would not be using paper that cannot be recycled.

Do not cover the yellow pad with a fancy leather folio. This would hide the fact that you are a lawyer. If you are concerned over client confidentiality (and you should be), begin your notes on the second page of the pad, using the first page as a cover sheet. Use the standard $8^1/_2 \times 11$-inch size, not the old-fashioned legal length. Most legal and nonlegal file systems and notebooks today are set up for the standard size and potential clients will not use the pad or take it with them if the paper won't fit in their file system.

Carry the yellow pad in your hand where it can be seen, even though you have a briefcase with you where you could put it (and hide it).

Remember, the potential client solicited you, you didn't solicit the potential client.

Part IV
Getting Clients

How to Handle Friends and Relatives

It is a fact of life that many, if not most, of the new lawyer's clients and sources of clients will be friends and relatives. If the new lawyer can't be trusted by friends and relatives to handle a legal matter, then who will trust him or her?

Most lawyers have unhappy experiences representing their friends and relatives, and it is usually the fault of the lawyer. No matter how hard the new lawyer works on the case, no matter how fantastic a job the new lawyer does, no matter how successful the result, friends or relatives honestly believe that they are the recipients of third-rate legal services. They honestly believe they did the new lawyer a favor by giving him or her the case "for experience." Regardless of the fee, friends or relatives think they are being overcharged.

Face reality. You had better satisfy your friends and relatives and their referrals if you expect to make it as a new lawyer. They will be the source of much, if not most, of your practice your first few years.

There are several things you can do to improve your image with them:

1. *Be friendly* when they seek free legal advice at social events and on the telephone at night.

2. *Get them into the office.* Don't conduct your law practice in an atmosphere of blaring television, screaming children, or orchestras at weddings. Tell them the case sounds very interesting, and if they can please come to your office, you'll be able to concentrate on their problem and get the facts down correctly. Tell them you don't like to interview clients outside the office because you can't make the notes essential for the proper handling of their case.

3. *Don't reveal confidences.* Go out of your way to tell the client that you can't or won't discuss the case with your mutual friends or relatives. Tell your cousin Mary that you can't and won't discuss her case with her mother, Aunt Jane, or your mother who is Mary's aunt. Tell cousin Mary that if she wants Aunt Jane to know about the case, that she'll have to tell her because you won't. This touch of professionalism goes a long way toward solidifying the attorney-client relationship.

Early in my career, I represented some very close friends in the early stages of an adoption just before and just after the baby was born. I never told my wife. A few weeks later we went to the friends' house for a long-planned social gathering. At the party my wife found out for the first time about the new baby, and promptly let out a stream of not-too-kind comments for my not having said anything about the baby. (All the other couples had brought baby gifts and we hadn't.) The adopting parents tried to alleviate my wife's embarrassment by saying that they assumed I would tell my wife about the adoption and hadn't called her with the good news. I stated that I couldn't say anything about the new baby because I couldn't disclose a client's confidence. Over the years, I've gotten a lot of business and a lot of referrals from the people at that party and that couple. If my friends had doubts about my professionalism before this episode, the doubts were over afterward.

4. *Billing friends and relatives.* It is very important that you bill friends and relatives properly. Suppose $750 is a reasonable fee for your services, but your friend or relative only has $250 to pay you, and you are willing to take this case for $250 because:

    a. You want the experience;

    b. You are tired of playing solitaire in the office;

    c. The phone company is threatening you about your unpaid bill.

The proper way to bill someone like a cousin is as follows:

Flaky Cousin
123 Main Street
Anytown, USA
RE: Professional Services Rendered
Cousin adv. People
Case C123456

One-half day trial in traffic court to defend charges of speeding violation of Vehicle Code Section 5976. Preparation of trial brief to exclude improperly obtained confession and attempting to exclude eye witnesses. Obtaining letter from employer asking court not to suspend driver's license.

Services rendered January 3, 7, 11, and 14, 20xx.
Total fee	$750.00
Less family discount	$500.00
Balance now due and payable	$250.00

Thank you.

The reason for showing the $750 price and $500 discount is to let the cousin know the value of what was received. He or she has no way of knowing your services were worth $750 unless you say so. A relative will think he or she was only worth $150 and you were overcharging. (Remember, relatives think they do you a favor by letting you get experience.)

Additionally, you want relatives and friends to refer you $750 cases, not $250 cases. If they don't know the value of the services, they'll recommend people to you telling them you only charge $250. Your cousin will be grateful to you for the $500 "discount."

In summary, friends and relatives will be the beginning of your legal practice. Treat them professionally, and they will recommend clients to you. Treat them with scorn and disdain, and your practice may never get a good start.

5. *Always send a bill even if nothing is due.* A friend or relative might think you forgot to send a bill and might be afraid that if they return for future work, that you will discover the unbilled matter and charge them for the earlier matter. By not sending a bill you may lose further referrals.

How to Market Your Services

Start on Announcements

1. Prepare e-mail and postal mailing lists:
   a. Law school class (get addresses from alumni association);
   b. Undergraduate classmates (get addresses from alumni association);
   c. High school classmates, if appropriate (get addresses from alumni association);
   d. Church members, if appropriate;
   e. Family (your mother will be glad to help you);
   f. Organizations you belong(ed) to/sports clubs, social clubs, philanthropic clubs (get addresses from club secretary);
   g. Professional associations you belong to.
2. Get sample announcements from printer.
3. Get time and cost estimates from printer.
4. Decide on style of announcements (listing or not listing areas of practice).
5. Remember to order professional cards and enclose one with announcements.
6. Don't use cheap announcements or cards (be sure you get them engraved, on good stock).
7. Get cost and time estimate from professional addressing service for addressing, stuffing, and mailing announcements.
8. Start addressing envelopes while announcements are being printed.
9. Consider buying old postage stamps from stamp dealer for postage to attract attention to the announcement when it is received.
10. Consider sending "cutesy" items. Depending on your budget, you should consider sending enclosures with your announcements.

Refrigerator calendar magnets, wallet calendars, letter openers, pens, and Rolodex cards are commonly sent and appreciated items that the recipient will probably keep as a constant reminder of you.

Order Stationery

Allow up to two months' delivery time for high-quality stationery. Get a catalog with samples from a national supplier such as Stuart Cooper, or a local company. Order letter-size bond letterhead, and second sheets. Also order blank letter-size bond, letter-size envelopes, professional cards, announcements, Will paper, and Will covers. Get some engraved rag content. Don't use self-printed copy paper for client communication.

If your state allows or requires letter-size pleadings, don't use "contract" or "pleading size" stationery. Some courts may require "recycled" paper for pleadings.

Also get "cheap" envelopes for bill-paying from the post office. Order billing stationery and window envelopes.

Get Started Now

If you are reading this book as a textbook in law school or while waiting for bar results, get started immediately. Don't wait. It takes a lot of time to obtain, assemble, update, and input names and addresses.

Start a good client contact database that you can update and use your entire career. Goldmine and ACT are among the many available. Put just about every name you can think of on the list. It will be invaluable over the years for marketing purposes and for conflict search purposes. Be sure you can combine your contact database with a mailing list software package for addressing and salutations. If possible, anticipate needing fax numbers and e-mail addresses for marketing purposes.

How to Get & Keep Good Clients

How to Get & Keep Good Clients is another book I have written. As the title indicates it is primarily a practice-building book. I recommend it for lawyers who have been lawyers for more than two or three years. It has been revised and updated several times. More information about the book can be found at my Web site **www.Foon berglaw.com/products**.

Cost-Effective Media Advertising

In this chapter, I wish to touch upon lawyer advertising as it affects the lawyer just beginning a practice.

What is in this chapter is my experience in discussing advertising with tens of thousands of lawyers all over the United States. A particular lawyer in a particular community may have contrary experiences but I believe that on balance these observations are correct.

1. *Yellow Pages Advertising.* Increasingly, the American public is using the Yellow Pages to find a lawyer. It's estimated that 22 percent of blue-collar America uses the Yellow Pages to find a lawyer for accident, criminal, divorce, workers' compensation, bankruptcy, and other noncorporate legal problems. About 15 percent of middle-class America uses the Yellow Pages for legal needs including small businesses and probate along with a Web site. Yellow Pages telephone directory advertising is probably the most cost-effective advertising there is for the new lawyer, if done correctly, because the persons looking believe they need a lawyer. If done improperly, however, the cost-effectiveness is questionable. Unfortunately there may be a significant time lag between arranging for the ad and the date of publication of the directory.

a. *Space Ads.* Improper (least cost-effective or noncost-effective) advertising is too general and tells the potential client too much. A poor advertisement might read like this:

JOHN DOE

123 Main Street	(123) 555-1212
Business Law	Probate
Family Law	Workers' Compensation
Criminal Law	Civil Trials

FREE INITIAL CONSULTATION

The proper (cost-effective) advertising lists the principal types of case(s) you hope to get from the advertising in simple individual ads:

JOHN DOE	JOHN DOE	JOHN DOE
Drunk Driving	Divorce and Family Law	Auto Accidents
(123) 555-1212	(123) 555-1212	(123) 555-1212

JOHN DOE	JOHN DOE	JOHN DOE
Will and Estates	House Purchases	Purchases and Sales of Business
(123) 555-1212	(123) 555-1212	(123) 555-1212

The multiple "one-inchers" are extremely cost-effective, according to the people who use them. I haven't done any formal marketing research into specialization, but I believe that the American public wants lawyers who specialize in the kind of problem that they have. Thus the "one-incher" is cost-effective.

    b. *Full-Page Ads.* As of the printing of this edition, the currently available information is that full-page Yellow Page ads are the most effective and produce $10 in fees for every dollar spent. These ads, however, often take a lot of cash outlay and accordingly are too expensive for the new lawyer. If the new lawyer can afford the cash outlay, I recommend full-page ads in the Yellow Pages.

    2. *Newspaper Advertising.* Here again there is cost-effective and noncost-effective advertising.

    Metropolitan newspapers, generally speaking, are not cost-effective. I believe that when people read the metropolitan newspaper they skim it and have no time to study or remember lawyer advertising. I have heard that the average person spends eleven minutes skimming the local metropolitan newspaper and remembers very little of what he or she saw.

    Smaller newspapers, such as neighborhood papers, military base papers, shopping news, and local throwaways, are extremely cost-effective, according to the reports I get. For some reason, college newspapers and newspapers in college areas are very effective. It is my personal opinion that the people who have the inclination to read this type of publication apparently have the time to read the paper or study it carefully.

    It appears that in newspapers the display ad is not any more effective than the classified ad. (Again, those people who have the time to read these papers have the time to read them carefully.) It would appear that it is sufficient simply to state:

JOHN DOE
ATTORNEY AT LAW
(123) 555-1212

a. *Frequency of Ad*. Very few ads are worthwhile, however, on a one-shot basis. To be successful, almost all ads must run over a period of time. People will look for a lawyer when they need one. Therefore your ad must run continuously until there is a matching of your availability and the client's need for a lawyer.

3. *Radio Advertising*. Lawyers in small towns and rural areas tell me that radio advertising is cost-effective. Lawyers in big cities tell me it is a waste of time and money other than for general name recognition by the largest law firms. I personally worked long and hard to experiment with radio advertising of Lawyer Referral Services and the ads were an economic disaster.

Radio advertising can be inexpensive and may be worth experimenting with if you are in a rural area.

4. *Television Advertising*. For reasons that I don't understand, people just don't want to believe the truth about TV advertising for lawyers. I continually tell groups of lawyers my observations in the area and then immediately encounter reservations or disbelief from the lawyers in the group. When I ask if anybody can report contrary evidence no one raises a hand. When I ask who in the audience has tried TV advertising a few hands go up and then they tell me their experiences. Their experiences match the experiences of other lawyers throughout America, yet the rest of the audience still seems hostile and disbelieving.

With a few possible exceptions, TV advertising is generally not cost-effective and should be avoided by new lawyers. Many lawyers have related to me that the TV advertising money they spent was totally wasted. The two exceptions are as follows:

First, there is cable TV. Lawyers have reported limited success on cable TV advertising in reaching very targeted interest and geographically located groups.

Second, there is one law firm I know of that claims that TV advertising is cost-effective for developing new business. They sell what, for all intents and purposes, amounts to a franchise for a neighborhood law office and then promise to spend the investor's money on TV ads (at least they did so in the past). I am not aware of any independent verification of their claims, and I don't doubt that the investor's money was spent on TV ads, but I don't know if there is any benefit to the investing firm from a cost-effective point of view. I have my doubts about the cost-effectiveness, but I repeat the claim that at least one firm has found television advertising worthwhile.

In summary, in my opinion, I wouldn't spend my precious dollars on TV ads when I could spend the money on Yellow Pages, Internet, and neighborhood newspaper classifieds.

Advertising and Marketing on the Internet and via E-mail

I personally am a firm believer that the Internet will completely redefine how people decide where and how they will buy goods and services, including legal services. I predict that the Internet and e-mail will have a greater impact on law practices than did the word processor and the fax machine.

The Internet is increasingly replacing the printed directories used by clients to "check out" a lawyer before hiring the lawyer or firm. Almost every law firm gets some new clients via the Internet.

People can find you on the Internet search engines and can then e-mail you via your Web page e-mail link. Just having a Web page will attract people looking for a lawyer in your community or a lawyer in your area of law. People in 105 countries from all over North America, Europe, Asia, South America, and Africa have found me on the Internet.

How and what to advertise on the Internet is still in the early stages. Senior citizens and students spend a lot of time on the Internet. Legal services for these groups are effectively sold via the Internet. I highly recommend as an introduction to this subject the ABA book *The Lawyer's Guide to Marketing on the Internet*, Second Edition, by Gregory H. Siskind, Deborah McMurray, and Richard Klau. I personally do not seek new business via my Web page (**http://www.Foonberglaw.com**), but rather people who know me can find me and then send e-mail to me.

E-mail will be a way to reach unlimited numbers of people at almost no cost.

Both Web pages and e-mail are strongly recommended by me for new lawyers. Be sure you have an appropriate disclaimer on your Web site and e-mail disclaiming any attorney-client relationship unless there is a signed retainer agreement. You should also disclaim compliance with Lawyer Advertising Regulation except in your home state.

Letter for Prospective Clients and Turn Downs

Ms. Telephone Caller
123 Main Street
Anytown, USA 12345
Re: Appointment for Interview

Dear Ms. Caller:

Thank you for your call of January 2nd, concerning your case. I am looking forward to meeting you in person at our office meeting of January 10th. Please bring with you all documents you might have concerning the matter.

I am sure you understand that at this point we have not agreed to represent you or to undertake any professional responsibility. We could only agree to representing you after we have met and gotten all the facts, made a written fee arrangement, etc. We could only do this after an interview and review of documents to get all the facts.

Additionally, we ethically could not agree to represent you until we have checked our system to be sure there are no conflicts of interest. In our brief telephone interview you gave us the names of the principal parties known to you. We are in the process of checking our files and personnel to be sure there are no ethical conflicts.

(Optional) The first part of the initial interview will be to investigate possible conflicts. We will not investigate the facts beyond determining whether a conflict exists. If a conflict exists, we will conclude the interview at that point. If a conflict does not exist, we will investigate the facts.

(Optional) There will be no fee for the initial consultation. There will be no fee until you have engaged us and we have agreed in writing to represent you.

(Optional) There will be no fee for the first thirty minutes of the interview. Time beyond thirty minutes will be billed if we accept the matter.

(Optional) There will be an initial consultation fee of $250. Further fees will depend on whether you wish to engage us and whether we wish to represent you in the matter. The initial consultation fee will apply even though you do not wish to engage us to do further legal work or we do not accept representation because of conflicts or because of any other reason.

I am enclosing some information about the firm, which you may find of interest.

Looking forward to meeting you on the 10th.

Very truly yours,

Ketchem, Holdem & Skinnem
By:

Letter Turning Down Representation but Keeping the Door Open

Mr. Telephone Caller
123 Main Street
Anytown, USA 12345
Re: Your Telephone Call of January 2nd

Dear Mr. Caller:

Thank you for your telephone call of January 2nd. As I indicated to you by telephone, we unfortunately cannot assist you with this matter at this time.

Please do not accept our inability to represent you at this time as any indication of the merits of your matter.

I have suggested that you call the County Bar Association Lawyer Referral Service at (123)123-4567 for a referral.

[Alt]. I have recommended the following three law firms to you:

1. John Smith, Jones, Jones and Smith (123) 234-5678

2. Mary Petersen, Norge, Svenska and Dansk (123) 345-6789

3. Arthur Bagle, Beagle, Bagle and Bugle (123) 456-7890

Each of these three lawyers has been alerted by my secretary to expect your call.

Although we are unable to accept your case or to accept any professional responsibility for you at this time, it is possible that we may be able to assist you in the future. We have enclosed some information about our firm and have added your name to our friends and associates mailing list. You will receive more information about us in the future.

We wish you luck in finding the right lawyer for your case.

Very truly yours,

bcc: Prospective Client File

Letter Turning Down Representation

Dear Mr. Nudge:

Thank you for your telephone call of January 2nd. We regret that we cannot be of assistance to you at this time.

We have not accepted any professional responsibility nor rendered any advice to you.

Very truly yours,

bcc: Prospective Client File

The Internet and
Your E-mail Addresses

The Internet is not only the future, it is both the future and the present.

The Internet is radically changing the way clients find lawyers and lawyers give advice.

You will have clients from all over the world whom you have never met, who found you on the Internet and with whom you communicate only by e mail and who will pay your legal fees.

Learn all you can about the world of Internet communication and be willing to try trial and error until you can find an Internet system that works well for you.

The learning curve is not so steep that you shouldn't learn.

Your e-mail addresses are important. If possible, use your full name in at least one address, for example, **JayFoonberg@aol.com** in addition to **Jay@Foonberglaw.com**. A client or potential client should not have to try to remember or look up whether it is **Jfoon berg@aol.com** or **FoonbergJay@aol.com**. I believe Internet addresses are not case-sensitive. You can also get Internet addresses for areas of practice or geographical area in which you practice. You might wish to use **NewYorkFamilyLawyer@xxx.com** and also be **NewYork AccidentLawyer@xxx.com** and also **NewYorkDivorceLawyer@xxx .com**. The list of possibilities is endless.

All of your e-mail messages can be forwarded to a single address.

With some imagination, you could construct more than one worthwhile and helpful e-mail address.

Your Web Site(s)

It is critical that you have one or more Web sites for the following reasons:

1. Many clients will check you out on the Internet before hiring you. If you're not there, they simply go on to another lawyer.

2. Your Web site(s) can attract clients from all over the world.

3. I get an average of one or two low five-figure cases a month through two different Web sites.

1.) **Fractionaljetownership.com** deals with buying fractional interests in business jets with the money average transactions being more than $3 million.

2.) **EstateContests.com**, **Willcontests.com**, and **Trustcontests.com** are all the same Web site found by people using different search words. The fees are good and we are building both a reputation and a following using the Web as almost our only major marketing activity.

Have a Web site for each area of law in which you practice. Different clients and search engines use differing methods for searching.

You can have the "contact" e-mail from every Web site go directly to you.

There are hundreds of "experts" in setting up and managing Web sites. Be sure you get one who has successfully worked with lawyers. If you can't afford an expert, learn to do it yourself. One good resource is the ABA book *The Lawyer's Guide to Marketing on the Internet*, Second Edition, by Gregory H. Siskind, Deborah McMurray, and Richard P. Klau. Web site design and maintenance will be critical to your entire career.

The Importance of Accepting and Promptly Returning Telephone Calls

Don't let the sun set on an unreturned call. If you can't return the call let someone else in your office return the call. Try to return calls within two hours or have someone return the call for you within two hours. Tell your clients of the time slots in which you try to return calls or will be available to receive calls.

I needed a lawyer.
I couldn't reach you.
I reached another lawyer.
I don't need you anymore.

In terms of good public relations, this may be the most important chapter of this book. Unless God made you clairvoyant, you won't know in advance why people call. When Ms. Jones calls, you don't know if she's pestering you about her complaint about the apartment owner turning off the hot water, or if she is trying to reach you because her husband fell down the unlit stairwell and has two broken legs and a broken back. Some studies indicate clients expect a return call within two hours.

Most clients feel that lawyers' telephone calls are excessively screened and not returned promptly enough. Failure to maintain communications with clients is the single most common complaint to bar associations. Increasingly, lawyers are being disciplined for ignoring clients' calls and letters. (Do not discard old telephone bills. They may be your only proof of having returned a call.)

Unless you have a storefront office, most if not all of your new clients will call you before coming in. Your telephone is your lifeline to new clients and new matters. Receptionists spend 95 percent of their time dealing with incoming telephone calls and less than 5 percent dealing with waiting people. If you can't return a call, have your secretary or another lawyer return the call for you so you won't lose that new client who is trying to reach you. Try to block 11:00 A.M. to 11:30 A.M. and 3:30 P.M. to 4:00 P.M. for returning telephone calls. Your secretary or receptionist can then return the ones you didn't return. Be sure your receptionist knows how to pronounce clients' names and be sure the receptionist can recognize and immediately route new business inquiries from prospective clients.

I think it's good public relations for you to return calls at night and on Saturdays and Sundays. Tell the client you are concerned about his or her call and didn't want to wait until the next morning or until after the weekend to return it. The client will really appreciate your concern.

Be sure you use a duplicate phone message system for all telephone messages to protect yourself from the client who claims to have called you ten times and you didn't return any of the calls. When you try to return the call without success, note on the message itself your efforts.

Sample notations would be:

3/1/04	10:04 a.m.	BY/Busy
3/1/04	10:30 a.m.	BY/Busy
3/1/04	1:00 p.m.	N/A, No Answer
3/1/04	5:00 p.m.	N/A, No Answer
3/2/04	9:00 a.m.	WCB, Not in, left message, will call back

You might even send the client a speed letter or form letter by fax and e-mail as follows:

Dear Client:
  I tried five times to return your call of March 1. Please call me or drop me a note so that we can help you if necessary.

  Very truly yours,

  John Novice

Logging Incoming Telephone Calls. I don't. Some lawyers do. If the client connects on the call, I have notes in the file and my time records to verify the call. If the client doesn't connect, I have my return message copy. I've never needed a log of incoming calls. In some situations they might be worthwhile, but I doubt it. Be sure to make notes of incoming voice mail messages, and to write a written record of your hearing the message and of your return call. Senior and super busy lawyers should log all incoming calls to prevent forgetting to return a call and as a reminder of follow-up tasks promised.

Telephone. Telephones are your lifeline to new clients. Use a speakerphone or telephone headset so you can take notes during conversations and can go through files for information while talking on the phone. Get an extension phone in your office so your client can listen in. Get multiple lines to prevent busy signals. Three to four lines should be adequate during your first year. A client who gets a busy signal may call the next lawyer on the list. List yourself in as many phone books as your local ethical rules permit. Never use another lawyer's phone number. Get your own number. Clients often will take the first lawyer they can get hold of. Don't use mechanical answering devices. Use an exchange instead. If you use voice mail on nights and weekends use a system that allows the caller to enter a number that goes to your pager.

Clearing voice mails. Be sure that you or another person clear your voice mails at least once a day, preferably twice a day at 11:30 a.m and 4:00 p.m. to allow time to return the call before the client goes to another lawyer with their problem.

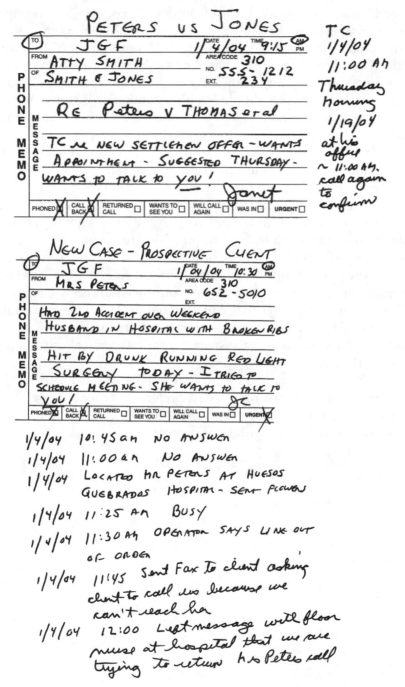

PETERS vs JONES

TC
1/4/04
11:00 AM
Thursday
morning
1/19/04
at his
office
~ 11:00 AM.
call again
to
confirm

PHONE MEMO

TO: JGF   DATE 1/4/04   TIME 9:15 AM
FROM: ATTY SMITH
OF: SMITH & JONES   AREA CODE 310   NO. 555-1212   EXT. 234

MESSAGE

RE Peters v THOMAS et al

TC re NEW SETTLEMENT OFFER - WANTS
APPOINTMENT - SUGGESTED THURSDAY -
WANTS TO TALK TO you!

Janet

PHONED ☒ CALL BACK ☒ RETURNED CALL ☐ WANTS TO SEE YOU ☐ WILL CALL AGAIN ☐ WAS IN ☐ URGENT ☐

NEW CASE - PROSPECTIVE CLIENT

PHONE MEMO

TO: JGF   DATE 1/04/04   TIME 10:30 AM
FROM: MRS PETERS
OF: AREA CODE 310   NO. 652-5010   EXT.

MESSAGE

HAD 2ND ACCIDENT OVER WEEKEND
HUSBAND IN HOSPITAL WITH BROKEN RIBS

HIT BY DRUNK RUNNING RED LIGHT
SURGERY TODAY - I TRIED TO
SCHEDULE MEETING. SHE WANTS TO TALK TO
you!

JC

PHONED ☒ CALL BACK ☒ RETURNED CALL ☐ WANTS TO SEE YOU ☐ WILL CALL AGAIN ☐ WAS IN ☐ URGENT ☒

1/4/04   10:45 am   NO ANSWER
1/4/04   11:00 am   NO ANSWER
1/4/04   LOCATED MR PETERS AT HUESOS
         QUEBRADOS HOSPITAL - SENT FLOWERS
1/4/04   11:25 AM   BUSY
1/4/04   11:30 AM   OPERATOR SAYS LINE OUT
         OF ORDER
1/4/04   11:45 Sent Fax to client asking
         client to call us because we
         can't reach her
1/4/04   12:00 Left message with floor
         nurse at hospital that we are
         trying to return Mrs Peters call

PUT MESSAGE FORM IN CLIENT FILE WHEN CALL IS RETURNED.

Managing Written Communication

Bombard your clients with paper and e-mail. Good written communication with clients is critical to having happy clients who pay their bills and who recommend more clients to you.

There is also a very high correlation between failure to communicate and nonmeritorious malpractice claims and disciplinary complaints. It is tragic that most of these claims and complaints are totally unnecessary and easily avoidable.

Managing written communication is relatively easy for the lawyer to do as most of the work is done by others on an automatic, systematic basis.

Good written communication is an extremely effective practice builder in addition to being a problem avoider. Good written communication creates happy clients who come back for more legal work and who refer you more clients. Good written communication is good lawyering since it keeps the client involved and informed in their legal matters. Good written communication projects effort to the client, and while the clients may not be ecstatic about paying for legal fees, they will pay their bills more readily and quickly when they have been kept up to date on the progress of their legal matters.

For most law practices, good written communication simply involves a few automatic procedures and a lot of form letters. Whether the form letters are computer-generated or photocopy-generated or handwritten is much less important to the client than the fact that the client has received something in writing from the lawyer.

The legal profession generates enormous amounts of paperwork. The paperwork is created because lawyers must create, communicate, and preserve their legal product. Paperwork is so significant that many nonlawyers refer to the "law industry producing product" rather than the legal profession producing legal services. Paperwork is the tangible representation and evidence of the law firm's intangible services.

Electronic mail (e-mail) is used for lawyer-client communication by counsel and clients. Since e-mail is frequently printed out as hard copy by the recipient, it is included within the scope of client written communications. E-mail has a unique marketing advantage. When a client receives an e-mail that the client wishes to share with others, it is easy to simply forward copies to those people who might become clients when they realize you know the subject matter.

This chapter will include principles, procedures, and product. The product section will contain a series of form letters that any firm can modify to become part of its system of communication. The lawyer or firm is encouraged to modify them and to add more form letters to fit individual practices. Some written communication forms have been added that are more related to the firm's overall program of good client relations than to the specific legal services being rendered.

Principles

1. The client gets a copy of every piece of paper that goes into the file including both incoming and outgoing letters, pleadings, correspondence, e-mail, memos to the file, documents, etc.

2. The client gets the copy of the paper in all cases unless the lawyer gives instructions NOT to send the information.

3. The lawyer has the control and power to hold back copies from the client, but unless the lawyer gives specific instructions not to send information, the information is to be sent automatically without waiting for the lawyer to give instructions or approval.

4. Information should be sent to the client AFTER the lawyer has seen it and BEFORE it gets filed in the file, but should not be unduly delayed if the lawyer is not available.

5. Memos and information that the lawyer does not want sent to the client should be coded in the word processing system or printed out on specially colored paper. A suppressible code can be built into the word processing system coding those documents.

6. It is the responsibility of the lawyer to prevent information from going to the client, if the withholding of the information is deemed to be in the client's best interests.

7. All information going to the client must be checked by a responsible person in the mail department to be sure that the client's name is spelled correctly and that indicated enclosures either are enclosed or the notation "without enclosures" appears.

8. List all enclosures or attachments at the end of the letter or e-mail message even though the enclosures are referred to in the body of the letter. This procedure creates a written checklist to ensure everything is in fact enclosed or attached.

9. Adopt the mental attitude that "cc" means "client copy" rather than "courtesy copy." The client is paying for the work and the client is entitled to be kept informed as to what he or she is paying for and what is happening on the case.

10. If you insist on authorizing communications with clients on an ad hoc rather than systematic basis, develop a sticker or code such as "ccy" or "ccn" to mean "client copy yes" or "client copy no." Instruct personnel responsible for filing that nothing is to be filed into the client file until the document is coded ccy or ccn. (Or whatever code or sticker system you wish to use.)

11. Send clients copies of pleadings, depositions, discovery, research, intraoffice memos, and other items that you think clients wouldn't want or wouldn't understand. Leave it to the client to trash unwanted items AFTER they have seen them rather than deciding the client should be denied access to the information.

12. ANYTHING YOU SEND TO CLIENTS WILL REMIND THEM THAT THEIR LEGAL MATTERS ARE NOT BEING NEGLECTED.

13. Code your word processing program to flash "Is enclosure or copy attached?" whenever the words "enclosed" or "copy" appear in the body of the letter.

14. Add clients' names to the spell check program to try to catch obvious misspellings.

15. Develop a form letter or a form cover sheet for transmission of information when you don't need or want a response. If necessary, get a big red rubber stamp that reads "For your information only. No reply necessary."

16. Review the communication status of every file in the office at least every sixty days. If the client has not been communicated with (preferably by written communication) during the previous sixty days, send a form letter to the client indicating this lack of information is normal and their matter has not been overlooked or ignored.

17. Develop a calendar system to program future needs of the client that you know of now, even though the service won't be needed until some future time. Prepare form letters for this purpose. (See the sample time-triggered letters below.)

18. If there is a secretarial or word-processing bottleneck or delay in your office, consider handwritten faxes on preprinted message forms.

19. Do not send e-mail until after you have printed a file copy and read it to be sure it makes sense and that the proper wording or phraseology is used.

Product

The following represent sample form letters for keeping clients informed. An asterisk (*) following the description indicates that a sample form letter follows.

20. Fee and engagement letter. This is treated in the materials on fee disputes.

21. Expectations letter. This is treated in the materials on unrealistic client expectations.

22. "For Your Information" form word-processed letter.

23. "For Your Information" form cover sheet.

24. "No activity" letter.

25. Recent legal development that may apply to client's legal matter.

26. Disengagement letter.

27. Sample time-triggered letters.*

    27.1 Lease renewals.*

    27.2 Child attaining majority.*

    27.3 Union contract renewals.*

    27.4 Judgment abstract renewals.*

    27.5 Annual information filings.

    27.6 Corporate annual meetings of directors and shareholders.*

    27.7 Periodic tax returns.

    27.8 Expungement of criminal convictions.*

Time-Triggered Letters

These "time-triggered letters" are adopted from my book *How to Get and Keep Good Clients*. In that book they are described as part of a calendaring system to get ongoing future business from recently completed work done for an existing client.

To the new lawyer starting a practice, these letters can provide an opportunity to get immediate work from a new or potential client. Their applicability and the opportunity to use them will depend on your listening carefully when the new client or potential client makes casual mention of other matters handled without a lawyer or with a lawyer who has not previously advised the client of the work remaining to be done.

By listening carefully to people in social or professional situations, you may find a need for legal services that the client was unaware you could provide. You may get a new client.

In each case, the need for legal work is triggered by the passage of time after some other prior event.

These are "follow up" letters to set the stage for a telephone call or meeting.

Sample time-triggered letters:

Lease Renewals

Dear Mary Newclient,

At the Jones' cocktail party, you mentioned to me that the lease on your store (your home, your cabin, etc.) would run out this year (next year) unless you renewed it.

As I related, I don't like to discuss legal matters in a public place, so I am sending this follow-up letter [as I said I would].

I would suggest you read the lease carefully to determine if it is necessary for you to give some sort of formal notice within a certain number of days or months of the scheduled expiration date. Many leases require as much as six months or one year's advance notice of intention to renew to allow the owner time to find a new tenant or make other plans.

If you need help in understanding your lease renewal provisions or in properly giving the required notice, please let me know.

Sincerely,

Jay

Child Attaining Majority

Dear John,

I enjoyed meeting you at the Rotary Club Meeting. Your description of what you have to do to pay for your son Joe's college tuition was fresh in my mind, having recently had to work with my parents to raise the tuition for my law school.

I didn't feel it was appropriate to discuss your legal matters in a public place so I am writing you as I promised.

Since your son Joe has just entered college, he has become 18. In our state a child legally becomes an adult for many purposes on reaching age 18. If your children are mentioned in your will or trust, or if you have no will, it may be necessary for you and your wife to make some changes in your wills and/or living trusts to take into account that Joe is no longer legally a minor.

Additionally, if there is any chance that Joe might receive a significant inheritance from his grandparents or from you, it would be a wise measure for Joe to make his own will over vacation before going back to college.

Please let me know if I can be of any help. (Optional: I will call you later this week after you have had a chance to think about Joe's situation.)

Sincerely,

Jay

Union Contract Renewals

Dear Mary,

Last week at the Red Cross fund-raising committee meeting, you mentioned your concern over what would happen next year when the Union Contract is up for renewal. I said I would drop you a note or call you in the coming week.

I would suggest that you not wait until the last minute, but rather start making your plans and contingency plans as soon as possible rather than waiting until there is an emergency situation.

Please let me know if you want help. If necessary, I will help you find an employment lawyer who specializes in representing employers in union matters.

Sincerely,

Jay

Judgment Abstract Renewals

Dear Larry,

Your comments about the preacher's sermon, "Have You Paid Your Bill?" were very appropriate. You mentioned the man who owes you money on an old judgment, but who now takes expensive cruises, never having paid the judgment.

I said I would drop you a note, as I don't like to discuss people's legal matters in public.

In our state, a judgment is good for ten years. It then expires unless you take legal steps to renew it. You can renew it by a motion in court. Additionally, you can examine a judgment debtor to determine whether he or she has assets which you can reach to satisfy (pay) the judgment. Often people cannot pay a judgment when it is obtained against them, but can pay it several years later when the situation has changed. In the interim the judgment debt accrues interest at 10 percent per year.

These are very broad general statements based on general principals and you should not rely on them as legal advice at this point.

Please let me know if you want or need help in renewing the judgment or examining the debtor. You should not let your legal rights expire due to neglect.

Optional: I will call you in a few days to set up a meeting if you wish.

Sincerely,

Jay

Annual Meetings of Shareholders and Directors

Dear John,

At the PTA meeting you commented on the huge amount of paperwork required to do business. You said your late wife Mary used to take care of all corporate legal matters, but you had no idea of what you should have been doing in the three years since she passed away.

I said I would drop you a note as I don't like to violate client privacies by discussing legal matters in public.

It is very important that your corporate records reflect annual meetings of shareholders and directors. The proper documentation may be what saves the officers and directors from liability to creditors for bills or to the government for taxes. Certain transactions should be reflected in the minutes, including but not limited to transactions with shareholders, officers or directors; salaries; leases; changes in the Board of Directors or shareholders of record, etc. For example, is Mary still listed as a director?

Let's get together to be sure your corporate records are up to date.

Optional: I'll have my secretary call you to set up a meeting. It would be a good idea to bring copies of your corporate and personal income tax returns for the last three years.

Sincerely,

Jay

Expungements

Dear Mary,

Last week at the Jones wedding, you mentioned that many people can succeed if given a second chance, but felt that society wouldn't forget or forgive past problems.

You indicated that you (your son) had a problem with the law several years ago and the conviction prevented getting a second chance.

I told you I would send you a follow-up letter as I didn't want to discuss private legal matters in public.

In some situations, an individual can go to court and request that original records be expunged. Often if a person has "paid the bill" jail time or probation and subsequently kept out of trouble, the criminal records can be sealed forever.

I do not know if expungement is possible or not in your case (your son's case), but it certainly would be worthwhile to check out the facts to seek expungement or to set the stage to later seek expungement.

Let me know if I can help you or your son get a clean fresh start in life.

Sincerely,

Jay

Note: I am not creating letters for Annual Information returns or annual tax returns because on reflection, I don't think they will be of help to a new lawyer starting a practice.

Can You Get Clients from Organizations?

Can you get clients from social, civic, or charitable organizations? The answer to the question is simultaneously "Yes" and "No." If you join an organization solely to get clients, you will be wasting your time and money. The other members will see through you, and you won't get anything from them. On the other hand, if you belong to an organization because you sincerely believe in its purposes and you work hard for the organization, the other members will be impressed by your efforts and how sincere and dedicated you are, and they will come to you with their legal work.

If you are going to pick an organization to work for with the hope of getting legal work, stay away from organizations that are heavily constituted of lawyers. It should be obvious that if 65 percent of the members of an organization are lawyers, there won't be as much legal work as there would be if you were the only lawyer. Some charities are so heavy with lawyers that they have a "Lawyers Division."

Some lawyers claim that you can get business simply by belonging to clubs and occasionally attending a meeting and making some noise so people know who you are. I think this was true years ago when very few people knew even one lawyer and would go to the lawyer they knew. The number of lawyers has more than doubled in the last twenty years and most people now can choose from many lawyers. Perhaps in some lower socioeconomic organizations you can get business from the members simply by being the only lawyer and making some occasional noise, but it will be difficult.

The advice, "Above all, to thine own self be true" applies in this area.

Cold Calling to Get Clients

The very words "cold calling" conjure up the very worst in marketing and client reactions. We think of stockbrokers lying to our receptionists and secretaries to get through to us to sell us stocks and bonds. We conjure up images of telemarketers calling lists of unknown people or prison inmates calling us at home at night to sell us warranties for recently purchased appliances.

Yet, the truth is that cold calling works and the largest law firms in the world hire sales people with no legal background and use cold calling regularly to get a foot in the door and an opportunity to take clients away from other law firms. I personally don't like cold calling and refuse to do it, but my personal likes and dislikes should not dissuade you from doing permissible cold calling if you can handle the rejection that goes with cold calling.

In my book *How to Get and Keep Good Clients*, I explain many different types of cold calling that work.

One form of cold calling that is very effective for new lawyers is religious and charitable membership solicitation. Volunteer to serve on the membership or fundraising committee of a charity. Most people do not want to do membership solicitation and it should be easy to get on that committee. Cold call the potential members with an appeal for their membership along the following lines: "Hello, Mr. Jones. My name is Mary Smith. I'm a new lawyer here in Smith County calling to solicit your membership in the Smith County Cancer Society (or support of our charitable event or to join our church or charity)." Offer to take a membership prospect to lunch or meet you at your office.

Stating you are a new lawyer will immediately explain why the person has not heard of you before.

If you haven't got the courage to call yourself, hire a high school student to call for you saying, "I'm calling from the law offices of Mary Smith."

If the person being called does not seem interested, offer to send information about the charity or event. Send the information in one of your envelopes with a cover letter on your stationery and possibly a business card with your handwritten notation, "Call me if you have any questions about the XYZ charity."

Cold calling for a charity is a good way to call the people you want to reach. You can use the charity's mailing list or make up your own list to call.

Try to choose a charity or a calling list where you will reach the people you want to reach.

Getting Clients by Using Charities

As previously indicated, in my book *How to Get and Keep Good Clients* I cover this area in great detail, including publicity, cold calling, seminars, fund raising, etc.

As the bans on lawyers advertising have been lifted, the marketing of legal services has become extremely aggressive. Firms spend huge amounts of money and time to do marketing often hiring staff for just this purpose.

Cause-Related Marketing is a simple-enough concept. By joining forces in fact or in appearances with a reputable charity, clients can be gotten using very aggressive marketing techniques that might be considered in poor taste if no charity were involved. As one of many possibilities you could join a charity and volunteer to serve on the membership committee (a job no one wants).

You can then cold call targeted potential clients using a pitch along the following lines, "Ms. Jones. My name is Mary Smith. I'm a new lawyer here in town over on Main Street. I'm calling to solicit you to become active in our local chapter of the American Red Cross. I would like to send you some information and drop by your office to discuss how you can help the people in our community. May I do so?" Send the information with your personal cover letter and a card. Tell the prospect that you will from time to time follow up and that you will place their name on your firm mailing list. Offer to meet the prospect at his or her office or your office or for lunch or breakfast.

You have just opened the door by using the name of the charity. This is simply one example of Cause-Related Marketing.

You can also "sponsor" athletic events, community events, tribute dinners and seminars, charitable giving seminars, "charity nights" at theatre or other events, or marathon running (which I do), or creating a local chapter of a national charitable organization.

Insurance Claims Adjusters: A Source of Clients

Insurance claims adjusters can be a very profitable source of clients in the personal injury and casualty fields. Insurance adjusters frequently are asked by their insured to recommend a lawyer to represent them against the other parties. Sometimes the adjuster will recommend a lawyer, and sometimes not.

You must be very careful in your dealings with, and relations with, insurance adjusters. You can call for the claims manager and speak to the claims manager even though you suspect the claims manager will forward your call to the treasurer.

Honest insurance adjusters will recommend an accident case to you if they think you are sincere, hard-working and competent, and if they like you. Adjusters will not ask for, or expect, any remuneration for recommending a client. Stay away from dishonest adjusters. Remember, all the dishonest adjuster has to lose is a job. You have a license to practice law to lose.

The best way to meet insurance adjusters is in connection with the cases you already have. When an adjuster makes first contact with you on a case, ask him or her to join you for lunch. You owe it to your client to meet the adjuster. Impress upon the adjuster that you are ready, willing, and able to fight for your client to get your client what can reasonably be expected. Remember that impressions of you and your office may end up in the case file and may affect the amount of the settlement you can obtain for your client.

If the adjuster is impressed by you, you will obtain a better settlement for your client, and new cases may be referred to you.

Remember that the recommendations of an insurance adjuster carry a lot of weight with accident victims. Work as hard and rapidly as you can on the referred matter. Remember that the first matter the adjuster refers to you may be a "real dog," as he or she may be testing you.

A lawyer can build a very profitable law practice on the referrals and recommendations of a single insurance adjuster.

Just be very careful not to trespass the ethical prohibitions against soliciting and fee splitting.

Shmooze Your Vendors

As a new lawyer in practice you should make the time to shmooze with the vendors who call on you.

My very first client was the telephone man who installed my first phone.

I have received hundreds of thousands of dollars of fees and dozens of business clients from a CPA who was referred to me in my third month in practice by the book salesman who sold me my first set of tax books. The CPA referred by the book salesman still refers me clients many years later, and one of the clients referred to me produced thousands of dollars in legal fees in my first six months of practice.

I have received many good litigation referrals from the court reporting firm I used in my first deposition in my first year of practice.

I have received a lot of good estate planning referrals from an insurance agent from whom I bought life insurance in my first year of practice.

I have received referrals from my landlords and my auto mechanic.

We tend to forget that our vendors are also vendors to other professionals and businesses and are often in a position to recommend us. As a new lawyer in practice, you can make the time to shmooze for a few minutes with the salespeople who come to your offices. Later, as your practice grows, you won't want to take the time to talk to your vendors. You may even treat them as enemies because they detract from your billable time when you talk to them.

Your vendors can refer you a lot of business if you will just take some time to get to know them and let them know you would be happy to receive some referrals. Even if you don't buy something from a salesperson, he or she often will refer you a client, hoping you will eventually buy something or because the salesperson knows you are a new lawyer who wants and needs clients and has the time to do the work.

You want to work on those who have enough interest in you to come to your offices. A good comment would be something along the line of "Look, Ms. Jones, I truly don't know if we can help each other, but I certainly am willing to spend a few minutes with you learning about what you can do for me and what I might be able to do for you."

You will waste a certain amount of time, especially with the hard sellers, but you will also establish some good relationships with people who can and will send you business.

How to Accept Personal Injury Cases

I have written a special chapter on accepting personal injury cases because all lawyers, and especially new lawyers, run the risk of being called "Ambulance Chasers" if they act too quickly and "Negligent" if they act too slowly.

To begin with, the lawyer, when talking to the prospective client or family of the prospective client, should give the following advice (an exception to my warning about giving advice to people who are not yet your clients):

1. Engage a lawyer (whether it be you or somebody else) as rapidly as possible.

2. Do not discuss fault or facts with anybody except police officers until after they've consulted with a lawyer. (Usually there is a police report long before any lawyer is contacted.) If there is any possibility of criminal liability, then tell them not to talk to police officers either. The client or potential client must be made to understand that it is essential for your investigator to photograph vehicle damage before the damage gets repaired. The adverse parties' statement must be gotten before they are instructed not to give statements. Third-party witnesses must be interviewed while their memory is fresh and before they move away. The scene of the accident must be examined and photographed before it is altered. Torn and blood-stained garments must not be thrown away at the hospital. Bruised and broken bodies should be photographed before healing.

The client or potential client must be made to understand that insurance companies have millions of dollars available for investigators and it is reasonable to assume that the insurance company will be into the case as soon as the other party reports the case to his or her insurance agent.

Criminal suspects get a Miranda warning advising them of availability of counsel. Personal injury victims don't get any such advice. If anything, overzealous insurance adjustors sometimes tell the injured party not to get a lawyer, misrepresenting that the insured party will get a good recovery without the lawyer and that the lawyer is taking money that would otherwise go to the injured party. The injured person must be made to understand that the insurance company's primary concern is to defend a claim for damages rather than getting any funds for the insured for personal injury. The injured party must also be made to understand that a personal injury claim must be valued and that the injured party doesn't have enough experience or knowledge to value it properly. An insurance adjuster or company may have handled thousands of cases. The injured party only has his or her one case and doesn't know what to do or how to value the claim.

How to Protect Yourself

1. *Don't quote numbers or promise recoveries.* Tell the client orally and again in writing, "Based on the facts as they appear at the present time, it appears that you have a meritorious case. It is impossible to value the case until the full extent of injury, treatment, damages, and losses are known." Tell the client orally that anybody who promises or guarantees any specific recovery without knowing the extent of injury, etc., is either foolish or stupid or fraudulent.

2. *Get the client to sign more than one document.* We ask the client to sign and date the fee agreement and also to sign and date four "Authorities to Release Information." A client might say he didn't know what he was doing if he signed only one document, but he is hard-pressed to make this claim when he has signed five times in five different places and dates his signatures five times in five different places. (See sample forms on pages 186–187.)

3. *Try not to be present when the client actually signs and dates the fee agreement and authorities.* Have the client sign them out of your presence and either mail them back to you or have a friend or relative bring them back to you. If possible, have a friend or relative be with the injured party when the documents are signed. That friend or relative can later testify to your absence during the signing.

If necessary, leave the room yourself. Tell the injured party that you're going down the hall to the bathroom so that he or she can think about which lawyer to use without your presence. Knock on the door when you come back even if it's your own office you've left and come back to. Give the prospective client every reasonable opportunity not to use you.

4. *Begin work on the case immediately.* This is necessary not only to protect the client's own best interests, but also to substantiate the need for immediate legal help. If you told a client he or she needed a lawyer immediately and then did nothing for two weeks, you were either unethical for pressuring the client to sign or you were negligent in the conduct of the case, or both.

5. *Know your local rules.* In some states there are ethical or legal prohibitions against plaintiff's lawyers or their investigators to contacting an injurred person or relative of a deceased person for a certain number of days or in specific places such as hospitals. These restrictions often apply only principally to lawyers who would be helping a plaintiff. The rules change and should be learned immediately if there is any question over the propriety or legality of a contact. You don't want to do a lot of work and then find out you will not receive a fee for a violation of a rule.

6. *Communicate with the client.* If you decide not to take the case, send a nonengagement letter so the client knows you are not accepting professional responsibility. (See pages 188–189. See also the sample short-form nonengagement letter that follows the chapter "How to Say 'No' to a Client or Case.")

Re: Accident of _____ (date) _____

Dear Mr. (or Ms. Client):

This letter will confirm the details of our telephone discussion (our discussion in my office) on ____.(date)____.

Our firm will represent you in your claim for damages as a result of the above accident. Our fee will be one-third (1/3) of any amounts obtained by settlement if a lawsuit is not necessary or forty percent (40%) of all amounts received by settlement or judgment if filing of a lawsuit is necessary. If there is no recovery for you, there will be no fee.

We are enclosing herewith several authorities to obtain information. Please sign each where indicated by the red "X" as we need the authorities to obtain police reports, medical reports, etc. We also enclose a copy of our current fee policy, which contains further information. Additionally, please sign the enclosed copy of this letter and return the copy along with the authorities in the enclosed envelope. We cannot begin work until we have received back the copy of this letter and the authorities.

Very truly yours,

Arwee Honest & Howe

by Howard Howe

HH:ak

(On Copies Only)
THE ABOVE IS UNDERSTOOD AND AGREED TO.

_____   _____
Signature   Date

SHORT FORM LETTER TO ACCEPT A PI CASE
(PUT INCOMING OR TELEPHONE MESSAGE FORM
IN CLIENT FILE WHEN CALL IS RETURNED)

AUTHORITY TO RELEASE RECORDS

TO WHOM IT MAY CONCERN:

This is the authority for you to furnish to my lawyers, Arwee Honest & Howe or their representatives, all medical, police, and financial reports pertaining to my accident that occurred on or about _____, 20_____, at or about _____ , _____ , California.
         Street   City

_____   _____
            Dated   Signed

(Signed by _____ because victim is
                            (relationship)
minor/physically unable.)

_____
        D.R. No.

FOUR COPIES OF "AUTHORITY" FORM SHOULD BE SENT WITH
FEE LETTER

Re: Jones vs. Smith
Date of accident: x/x/z
Dear Mr. Jones:

It was nice meeting you at my office on Thursday. I wish to set forth in this letter what I related to you personally.

We are not accepting professional responsibility with respect to your auto accident of [date].

In our opinion the case is not economically sufficient to warrant proceeding. We have returned all of your papers to you and are doing nothing further in this matter. [Return originals—keep copy if you can. Enter name(s) or conflicts into marketing database.]

It is possible that another lawyer or firm might feel differently after examining the law and the facts. We encourage you to seek other lawyers' opinions, given they might disagree with us and be willing to accept your case.

You may wish to contact the County Bar Association Lawyer Referral Service at 123-123-4567 for assistance in finding a lawyer who may be willing to accept your case.

Although we are unable to assist you in this matter, we are happy that we had the opportunity to meet and we welcome your returning on another matter or referring other clients if you wish.

We are placing your name on our VIP mailing list and from time to time we will send you announcements and newsletters about what is happening.

We feel badly that we cannot help you at this time, but we hope you appreciate that we try to be upfront and truthful with our clients and potential clients, even when the news is not what they want to hear.

Again, you are welcome to contact us on another matter should you wish.

Very truly yours,

I.M. Attorney

SAMPLE SHORT FORM NONENGAGEMENT LETTER

RE: AUTO ACCIDENT OF X/X/20XX

Dear Mr. Jones:

We regret that we cannot undertake to represent you in connection with (1) your accident of [DATE] (2) your legal needs.

Please do not accept our inability to represent you as an opinion of the merits of your matter.

We have returned all documents or other items that you provided us.

You may wish to contact the County Bar Association Lawyer Referral Sevice at 555-123-4567 for assistance in finding a lawyer who may be willing to accept your case.

We have given you no legal advice and have not accepted any professional responsibility for your matter.

Very truly yours,

I. M. Attorney

How to Communicate Settlement Offers to Clients

Be sure that the client understands the difference between the *gross settlement* and the *net settlement* after costs, unpaid medical bills, and your fees. Send the client a letter explaining the breakdown and the *net* settlement. Clients are concerned about what *they* get, not about the gross settlement. When the insurance company sends a draft, get the client into the office to sign it. If you have to mail it to the client for signature, be sure to tell the client that it's a draft, not a check, and cannot be honored until *after* the insurance company compares your signature on the draft with your signature in its files. If you're stupid enough to endorse the draft before the client does, then you deserve to be deprived of your fee. Be careful about unpaid medical bills that have to be paid.

In some jurisdictions, you are required to communicate all settlement offers to the client even though you want the client to reject the offer. You can recommend against accepting the offer, but you still must communicate the offer. In some jurisdictions you must disclose referral fees paid and to whom (check your "division of fees" rules).

Some lawyers add a provision in their engagement letter getting a power of attorney, allowing the lawyer to endorse settlement checks in the client's name. Some lawyers use the power of attorney given to execute settlement agreements on behalf of the client. I recommend against both practices as being dangerous to your license. Get the clients' signatures even if you have to send messengers, although it is better practice to ask the client to come into the office. A client who is desperate for money might forge your name on a check or draft and negotiate it if you mail it to them. Failure to observe these rules is a very good way to get a complaint filed against you with the bar association. A sample letter follows.

Ms. (or Mr.) Client
Re:

Dear Ms. Client:

This letter will confirm our previous telephone conversation of __[date]__. We have an offer from __[insurance carrier]__ in the gross amount of _____.

The gross settlement would be disbursed as follows:

Gross Amount:		$
Less: Property Damage	$	
Out-of-Pocket Costs		
Police Report		
Medical Reports		
Filing Fee		
Service		
Total:	$_____	
	Balance:	$_____
Our Fee (as agreed):	$_____	$_____
	Balance:	$_____
Liens:		$_____
Dr.:	$	$_____
Net to You:		$_____

(Opt.) Please understand that the doctor bills are your responsibility and must be paid by you. If you have given the doctor a lien on your recovery we may be required to pay that lien directly from your share of the proceeds.

(Opt.) As we related to you by telephone, it is our opinion that your case has substantially more value. However, you would not realize this value for a significant length of time and we shall comply with your wishes to settle the case now. The case is your case and we undertook to prosecute it fully and had you wished, we would have rejected the offer and tried the case to judgment although this would have caused a substantial delay in your obtaining funds.

(Opt.) If the above is acceptable and agreeable to you, please sign and date the enclosed copy of this letter and return to me in the envelope provided.

(Opt.) Please understand we accept no responsibility for tax consequences. We suggest you contact your tax counsel.

(On Copies Only)—THE ABOVE IS UNDERSTOOD AND AGREEABLE TO ME.

Date:_____ Signed: _____

Representing Seniors

This is one of the longest chapters in the book. It should be re read at least once a year. When you represent seniors, especially when you get your first senior client, you can do well by doing good. Many seniors need special attention and many seniors are relatively wealthy. They understand what lawyers do and they are willing to pay for legal help.

Sooner or later you are going to have some senior clients. America is graying and elder law is possibly the fastest growing area of law practice and likely to continue as such for decades to come.

By the year 2010, 65 percent of the U.S. workforce will be aged 55 to 64 and 30 percent will be over 65. Similar trends exist in Europe where 35 percent will be over 65, up from 20 percent in 2004.

One of the warmest and best feelings you will have as a new lawyer is to help a senior. Helping people old enough to be your grandparents will make you feel good about having chosen law as a profession.

In your early years, you may occasionally do a simple will or health-care directive or draft a trust document. As time passes and your practice grows, you may get involved with conservatorships, probate, taxes, and the myriad areas involved in elder law.

If you can prepare for some of the concerns listed in this chapter, it will be easier for you and easier for the client.

Although we have added thirty years to our life span over the last century, longevity does have a price.

Our vision, our hearing, our memory and our ability to react quickly generally diminish with increased longevity.

As we slow down and as we get older, it takes us longer to run a mile or climb a flight of stairs or remember a face or a name.

Some seniors require just a bit more time to walk to your office. Some speak more slowly. Some require more time to fully understand a question and fully give an answer.

I am not an audiologist, a gerontologist, a kinesiologist, or any other "-ologist." These are my suggestions based on my years of practice and suggestions from seniors themselves and senior organizations. As always, health-care professionals have the best advice and should be consulted.

Representing senior citizens does not have to be difficult. Just remember the 3 Ps of working with seniors: Patience, Patience, Patience.

1. *Age*

There is no magic number for defining when someone is a senior. Historically, 65 was a magic number, but with increased longevity many people are physically and mentally fit well into their 90s. Don't be obsessed with numerical age as standing for anything.

2. *Your Office—Help the Client.*

Meet your client in the reception room and introduce yourself. If the client is carrying documents or a package, offer to carry it for him or her. If he or she is wearing an overcoat, offer to help remove it.

3. *Don't Rush.*

Ask the client to please follow you to your office. Be prepared to walk slowly, especially if the client is using a cane or a walker. The client may become confused if you suddenly disappear from sight and the client is in new surroundings.

4. *Borrow a Wheelchair.*

Practice going from the entrance to your building to the lobby or elevator to the suite door to your office pushing an empty wheelchair. If you followed the advice in this book, you made sure the doorways in your office would accommodate a wheelchair.

Although your building may comply with access building codes, your interior office doors may not need to be in compliance, and the building might be exempted from compliance for various reasons.

If your client cannot get to your office from the street in a wheelchair, have a plan "B" to meet the client elsewhere.

5. *Do You Have Thick Carpets?*

If the client is in a wheelchair, ask the client if he or she would want you to push the chair, especially if there are carpets to be navigated. Some clients will appreciate the help; some may appreciate the offer and decline help; some few clients may even resent your offer. Nonetheless, it is still best to offer to push the wheelchair.

6. *Chairs*

You should have at least one straight-back wooden or hard cushioned chair with arms for the client to use if necessary. You really should have two in the event you will be interviewing a couple. Keep the chairs someplace other than your office until you need them.

7. *Getting Home.*

Ask the senior how they plan to get home. You need to be aware of pick-up time if the client is being picked up or time deadlines if public transportation is used.

8. *Communicating with Hearing-Impaired Clients*

It is estimated that more than one-fourth of all adult Americans have some hearing loss. Hearing impairment is no longer the exclusive domain of seniors. Earphones and high-volume music have taken their toll on young people. Many people with hearing impairment will turn their heads slightly when talking to you. They are favoring their "better ear." The person may even cup his or her hand behind their ear to better hear.

9. *Hearing Aids*

Do not assume that hearing aids make everything normal. They often are almost useless. Anticipate that the presence of hearing aids indicates there will be a need for communication assistance.

10. *Get the Client's Attention.*

Get the client's attention by stating their name or touching them, if appropriate. When you want the client to listen to what you are asking or explaining, get their attention first. Instead of saying, "What happened?" say "John," and pause. Be sure John's looking at you and then say, "What happened?" If appropriate, touch the person's hand or arm to get their attention or make a hand gesture or raise a finger to get the listener's attention.

11. *Remain Calm.*

Don't get frustrated or upset. You will simply make the situation worse.

12. *Remember the 3 Ps.*

Remember the 3 Ps of working with seniors: Patience, Patience, Patience.

13. *Keep Your Mouth Empty.*

Don't smoke, chew gum, or eat anything while talking. The listener may partially read lips or depend on facial gestures.

14. *Get Close.*

Face the listener as close as is reasonable. Look up and speak up. Keep eye contact.

15. *Speak to the Client.*

Talk to the client, not about the client or around the client. If there is a child, spouse, or third party present, don't make the mistake of directing questions or comments to the third party if the proper person to be asked is the client.

16. *Remember Not to Say "Forget It."*

Do not say "Forget it." A frustrated lawyer may at some point want to give up and say "Forget it," and move on to another question or area if not understood by the hearing-impaired person. This may anger the hearing-impaired person. If you want to move on with the questioning to a different topic, do so without saying "Forget it." Saying "Forget it" communicates both frustration and anger on your part.

17. *Don't Get Frustrated.*

Inability to communicate can frustrate both you and the client. When you are frustrated, you may become even more impatient or even angry and do less than your best work.

18. *Quiet the Office.*

Get rid of background noises if you can. If your office has a control to eliminate the office music system (it should), then be sure the background music is off.

19. *Use Graphics.*

Use charts, diagrams, and visual aids. I find that seniors love it when I go to a white board and use colored marking pens to illustrate the flow of money or numbers or the steps in the case. Write key words, phrases, or questions on the white board or on your note pad. Use erasable slates, used by children and scuba divers. Many a senior has said to me, "You are the first person to explain things to me," when, in fact, other lawyers had explained things to the senior who could not hear or understand what the lawyer was saying. The graphs made things understandable.

20. *Write It Down.*

Have lots of paper, pens, and pencils. Either of you may want to write out questions or answers. Inability to communicate orally can stress both the lawyer and the client, causing lack of confidence on the part of both. Having alternative communication methods to help can calm the situation.

21. *Provide an Amplification Device.*

Consider purchasing a mechanical device for the client to use. A simple voice amplifier in a giant room may be adequate and not cost much.

22. *Slow Down the Questions.*

Do not ask rapid-fire questions unless you are getting rapid-fire answers. The hearing-impaired person may need time to organize thoughts or to remember something before answering.

23. *Repeat Questions.*

If you are going to repeat a question or comment, just repeat it as though you had not previously asked the question or made the comment. Repetition may make what you said to be understandable the second time you say it.

It is not necessary to say, "I'm going to repeat the question." The listener will know you are repeating the question. Your announcing the repetition of the question will simply highlight your possible frustration.

24. *Use Your Computer Monitor.*

Use a flat-screen monitor if feasible. You may be able to type out your question onto a computer monitor for the impaired person. Standalone flat screens can be turned around so the impaired person can see your typed question or comment. You can also print out your questions as a record of your interview. If you don't have a monitor that can be turned around, give the client a chair where you can both see the monitor, but remember not to face the monitor when speaking.

25. *Speak Slowly.*

Speak slowly, with exaggerated lip movements. Ask the other person in a slow voice with exaggerated lip movements, "Is it easier for you if I speak slowly?" If the person responds "yes," then do so. Some seniors want more time to be sure they fully understand what you are saying.

26. *Ask the Senior What You Can Do.*

Ask the client what, if anything, you can do to make it easier to communicate. The client may have a specific suggestion such as, "Try to speak to my left ear" or "Please don't cover your mouth, or touch my hand to get my attention."

27. *Look Up, Look At, and Maintain Eye Contact.*

If you believe the client may have a hearing impairment, look directly at the client when talking. Never cover your mouth with your hands or turn your head down or away or speak from behind the client. The client may be reading your lips and looking for facial gestures to help understand what you are saying.

28. *Sign Language*

The use of sign language or sign language interpreters is beyond the scope of this chapter.

29. *Don't Scream.*

Do not yell, shout, or talk more loudly than you usually speak unless the client asks you to do so. The hearing-impaired person may be able to hear you but not understand you. Yelling will not change that and can even make the situation worse because of the distortion of speech caused by the shouting. Hearing loss is often a matter of loss in specific ranges. A client may be able to understand the lower-range voices of men but not the midrange or upper ranges of women's voices. Shouting may have the unintended effect of decreasing understandability.

30. *Accents*

If English is not your first language or the first language of the client, understand that accents or lack of English vocabulary can worsen the communication problem. Use simple words if possible and use gestures.

31. *Don't Assume.*

Do not assume senility or mental deficiency when a senior has a hearing problem. Lack of hearing is not lack of intelligence.

One British patient in a hospital put a sign over his bed: "I'm Deaf, Not Daft."

32. *Some Seniors Need More Time.*

As we get older, we need more time to run a mile, more time to focus our eyes, more time to remember a fact, more time to absorb and understand a question, and more time to give an answer. Understand that a hearing-impaired person may need more time to answer a question or add to the conversation. The person may have heard bits of your communication with only some words or sounds being familiar. They have to match what they have heard with what they have seen in your facial expressions and put your question or comment in the context of the subject matter being discussed. All this must be done before the person can respond to you.

33. *Watch for Concealment.*

Be aware of hearing impairment concealment. Unfortunately, there are many reasons why people conceal hearing loss. It has been said that they are victims of their vanity. The underlying causes are complex and an appropriate discussion is beyond the scope of this book. A few reasons include:

The wearing of a hearing aid is considered by some to be an admission of aging and mortality.

Some people fear they will be treated poorly by those who discriminate against the elderly if a hearing aid is worn.

Hearing aids often require adjustment and the person is embarrassed to remove the hearing aid, adjust it, and return it to the ear.

Some women are concerned that their hearing aid will interfere with their hairdo and vice versa.

There may be a sense of frustration at comparing hearing aids to eyeglasses. Eyeglasses immediately convert poor vision to excellent vision. Hearing aids rarely restore hearing to its original ability, but more often simply make only a slight difference in a person's hearing ability.

If you suspect concealment, simply ask the senior again if you can do anything to be sure the client understands your question. Turning his or her head to have the better ear closer to you or answers that are not responsive to the question asked are signs of a hearing problem. Cupping a hand behind the ear to direct the shell of the ear toward you is another sign.

34. *It's Worth the Effort.*

Communicating with a hearing-impaired person requires work on the part of the lawyer and assistance on the part of the client. It is a rewarding feeling when you know you have successfully communicated with a hearing-impaired person and are helping him or her.

Remember the keys to good communication: Look Up! Speak Up! Look to! Speak to!

35. *Avoid Back Lighting.*

Be sure your face is well lit so the hearing-impaired person can see your lip movement and facial gestures. Do not stand or sit with your head in front of a light or sunlight or a window because the senior needs to see your lips and face.

36. *Offer to Repeat the Question.*

Ask if they want you to repeat or rephrase what you just asked. Hearing the same question a second time gives the hearing-impaired the opportunity to recognize a word that was not recognizable the first time.

From time to time, rephrase what you have just covered to be sure you and the senior are understanding each other. Cover three, four, or five points each time you rephrase and review. Remember that the process of rephrasing may in and of itself aid additional communication problems.

37. *Schedule Seniors for Morning Appointments.*

They often are more alert in the morning and you also may be more alert. When you are tired, you do a poor job of being patient and you may violate many of the rules of communication.

38. *Loneliness*

It is a sad fact that some seniors are lonely and eager to talk to anyone who will listen to them. They may over-answer questions because they are happy to have someone listening to them.

You may find it helpful to say something like, "That is really interesting. I hope that someday we will have the time for you to tell me more. You should consider writing it down for others to read. Right now we have to finish our work together, or we may run out of time." Or you may wish to say, "Ms. Jones, your stories are fascinating and I could listen all day, but I have to base my fees on the amount of time required. If you are willing and able to pay me to listen, I'll be glad to charge you, but I'm sure you have better uses for your money." Believe it or not, some seniors are so lonely they will pay you your hourly rate just to listen to them. I leave it to your conscience what you should do if you have a large number of senior clients who simply want someone to talk to. You should consider hiring a "listener."

39. *Repeat the Question.*

Ask if the person understands the question as often as necessary, especially for key matters. Remember that not understanding a question is a sign of hearing deficiency, not mental deficiency or incompetence.

40. *Mental Impairment and Lack of Competence*

Neither law school nor practice qualifies you to distinguish between simple forgetfulness, slight dementia, advanced dementia, early Alzheimer's or advanced Alzheimer's or any classification of mental impairment.

41. *Sample Interview Questions*

I have personally devised a series of questions that I have used over the years to rule out competence problems. When I do find what appears to me to be a possible competence problem, I suggest to the client that I would like a letter from his or her doctor stating that in the doctor's opinion, the person is competent to make a will or make a gift or execute a health-care directive, or whatever the proposed work involves. I explain to the senior that this is in the senior's best interest to prevent a fight where someone is claiming the senior might not be competent. Without that letter, I simply refuse to do the work. I would rather lose a client and a fee than find myself as a defendant or witness in litigation where I will not be paid for my time.

When asking these questions, it is preferable that the client be alone with you. If there is going to be a third person present, spouse, child, care giver, etc., explain that the presence of the third party might impair attorney-client privilege and the third party really should leave the room. If it is not possible to exclude the third party, be careful to note whether the client was able to answer the questions or whether the third party was providing the answers. If the third person gave the answer, try to note whether the client did or did not repeat the information as being accurate or in some manner independently state the information as covered.

A sample line of questions (which I use in will interviews and other situations) includes the following questions. You may wish to change them to fit the needs of the legal matter involved.

1. What is your full name?
2. What is the name on your birth certificate?
3. When and where were you born?
4. What is your telephone number?
5. What is your social security number?
6. Did you serve in the armed forces? If so,
   a. What was your serial number?
   b. In what branch did you serve?
   c. When and where were you discharged?
7. Are your parents living or dead?
   a. What is (was) your mother's name including her maiden name?
   b. What is (was) your father's name?
   c. When and where did they die?
8. Do you have any living brothers and/or sisters? If so, what are their names, their approximate ages, and where do they live?
9. Do you have any deceased brothers or sisters? If so, when and where did they die?
10. Do you have any living children?
11. Do you have any deceased children, and if so, when and where did they die?
12. Do you have any grandchildren, and if so, when and where do they live?

The preceding questions are designed to put the client at ease. The following questions are the more serious ones.

13. Do you know who I am?
14. Do you know what I do?
15. Do you know where you are?
16. Do you know why you are here?

17. Tell me what you hope to accomplish today.

18. What are your principal assets? (If the person is there for a will)

19. Tell me what the assets of the trust are? (If the person is there for an amendment of a trust or to create a trust)

Indicate in your notes whether the senior answered from memory, looked at a document, depended on a third person to get an answer, or didn't have an answer.

42. *The Folstein Mini-Mental Status Test (MMSE)*

You probably are not competent to administer a Folstein Mini-Mental Test, but you should be aware of what it is. The Folstein Mini-Mental Status Examination (often called the MMSE) is used by health-care professionals and others concerned with determining various aspects of competency to screen for possible cognitive dysfunction. It is commonly used with hospitalized or medically ill patients. You should not try to administer it or to interpret the results, but you should know what it is as you may see references to it.

> The tested person may be asked to answer some or all of the following:
> Orientation—Year, Season, Date, Day, Month, State, County, Town, Hospital, Floor, Address
> Registration—Recite three consecutive objects (ball, flag, tee).
> Calculation—Count and subtract backwards by multiples of 7: 93-86-79-72-65
> Attention—Spell the word "world" backward.
> Recall—After a five-minute delay, name the three objects in the registration above.
> Language—Name two objects (book and pencil). Pick up this book with your right hand and put it on the floor. Close your eyes. Write a sentence. Copy a simple design (circle, triangle, square, etc.).
> Level of Consciousness—Alert, Drowsy, Stuporous, Comatose.
> Points are assigned to each part of the test and then added up and interpreted by the test giver.

43. *Videotaping or Audiotaping the Interview*

Videotaping and/or audiotaping can be a two-edged sword. The decision by you to tape can be interpreted as an acknowledgment by you that taping was necessary. Some lawyers routinely videotape interviews of all clients over the age of 70 or 75, which can then lead to accusations of age discrimination and the incurring of unnecessary expenses.

I suggest the best solution might be to simply discuss the subject of taping with the client and asking the client if he or she wants to be taped to lessen the possibility of a will contest.

44. *Vision*

As we pass age 30, our vision ability decreases. We may need glasses to read at a relatively early age. Several things are simultaneously happening to our eyes that can affect our ability to read. We may need more light, more contrast, and/or larger type letters to read a document even while wearing glasses.

Consider doing the following:

1. Type your letters and documents in larger type (size 16 font) and/or in bold letters. (Highlight the document or letter and click "Bold.")

2. Have available a large rectangular magnifying glass for the client to read documents while in your office.

3. Be sure your professional cards and stationery contain your telephone number in larger bolder-type numbers.

4. Avoid darkened rooms.

5. If a projection will be required, try to avoid darkening the room.

45. *Ethics*

Representing seniors sometimes presents ethical problems.

You have to be most careful to determine that you are doing what the senior wants rather than what a third party says the senior wants.

In general, you must be especially careful when there is more than one person in the room with you. You must ask "Who is the client?" and "Why is the other person present?" The presence of third parties may put you in the middle of a malpractice suit. This is especially true if the third party will benefit from what you are being asked to do. In some cases, you will simply have to decline representing the senior. You are better off losing a fee than being in the middle of a civil law suit and a bar complaint.

Regardless of how many years you have practiced law, you will feel good about helping seniors.

Can You Get Clients by Running for Political Office?

I once had the good fortune of spending a day with and interviewing former President Gerald Ford. The purpose of the interview was to learn how he had started his law practice and to get information for this book. President Ford related in the interview that he would advise new lawyers to get involved in politics. He felt that in politics you learn to listen to people, determine their needs, and try to provide practical solutions to their problems, which is exactly what you do as a lawyer. President Ford felt that politics is good training for law and vice versa.

However, as to getting clients, I really can't answer this question for you. The answer will depend on your area. I've listed this question solely to call the possibility to your attention.

Running for office will give you exposure. You will address many groups and may get radio, television, or newspaper coverage. You will get good insights into what people feel are the significant issues in your community. People who see and hear you or read about you will learn your views. Some of these people may identify with you and wish to use you as a lawyer.

On the other hand, if you run and lose, people may avoid you and want to go to the winner. The time, energy, and money you invest in an unsuccessful political campaign may have been much better spent in your practice.

If you are thinking of running for political office with the plan or hope of increasing your practice through publicity whether you win or lose, I would suggest some homework on your part before you start. If you plan carefully you might be able to meet and work with the lawyers or others who give out government legal work.

These people will be around even if you lose and often can be of great value in the future after the campaign.

President Ford impressed me with his charisma and honesty. He is one of the finest people I have ever had the privilege of knowing. I would trust him to handle any legal matter I might have. I have met many political figures in my career. Whether they learned to be good lawyers through politics or to be good politicians through law, I don't know. I do believe that the ability to listen to people and to demonstrate concern for them is critical to success both in law and in politics.

Contact some of the lawyers in your community who ran for office and lost during the last few years. Ask them if, on balance, the campaign exposure enhanced or damaged the development of their law practice. Ask them if they would do it again.

Based on my very limited questioning, I believe that running for political office and losing might help you in rural areas but might be disastrous in an urban area.

Getting Paid Work from Lawyer Referral Services

List yourself with every lawyer referral service that will accept your listing. The listing fees are relatively nominal, in addition to the cost of the bar association dues, and the lawyer referral service will refer you many matters over the years.

Lawyer referral services are allowed to advertise to the general public in phone books and in other places. People new to a community often turn to such lawyer referral services for help in selecting a lawyer.

Not too many years ago, people went to a bar association for referral because they simply didn't know any lawyers. Today, I suspect people go to bar associations for referrals because they know too many lawyers and don't know how to select one. They believe that the lawyers who list themselves as being available through the bar association are likely to be the better lawyers, or they believe (sometimes erroneously, sometimes correctly) that the bar association lawyer referral service will refer them to a lawyer most likely to be able to help them. The public is aware of the fact that all lawyers specialize to some degree and that not all lawyers are willing or competent to handle all cases.

Many lawyer referral services call themselves Lawyer Referral and Information Services, since on a national basis 60 percent of the callers need something other than a fee-earning lawyer. Accordingly, the people referred to you by the service will have been screened for you.

There is no way of knowing or guessing whether you'll get your first significant matter in weeks, months, or years. However, sooner or later you will get a significant matter, and the investment will be repaid handsomely. Additionally, you are helping the public by making lawyers (including yourself) available.

In recent years, some bar association referral services have switched from being a public service to benefit both the public and the lawyer to being simply a source of non-dues revenue for the bar association. If you are not getting referrals or only getting the worst of the contingency dog cases, it is possible the bar association is sending the better contingency and hourly cases and clients to a favored few lawyers and firms where the association feels the most revenue can be obtained for the bar association. These firms may "pay back" in subtle ways such as buying ads in the journal, or whole tables at meetings, or "donations" to some fund.

I recommend that you make the financial investment in joining the lawyer referral services. The ABA maintains a list of local associations, most of which are affiliated with lawyer referral services.

Getting Legal Fees and Work
from the Government

With the recent huge increase in the number of new lawyers, this kind of work is becoming increasingly difficult to obtain. How much of this work is available and how well or poorly it is compensated depends upon your local situation.

All I can do is to give you some typical examples and typical sources and you'll have to get the information yourself.

Types of Work

1. *Conflict of Interests.* It is common where there are multiple defendants that a single lawyer or department cannot represent some of them, and either the court or the government agency appoints and pays for the representation of the others.

2. *Juveniles.* It is common for a probate or juvenile court to appoint a lawyer to represent the interests of a child or unborn child.

3. *Appeals.* Commonly, because of indigency or conflict of interests, a lawyer can be appointed for the appeal even though another lawyer or government agency represented the appellant or respondent at trial.

4. *Indigents.* Indigents generally are entitled to free representation (meaning someone else is paying), both in civil and criminal matters. There are various agencies that pay for private lawyers for indigents.

Sources of Work

Getting this type of work may be very easy or very difficult, depending on how profitable (or unprofitable) it is and depending upon the method of lawyer selection.

1. Judges (federal, state, and local) are the most common sources of appointments. Sometimes each judge has his or her own list or own system of choosing lawyers and sometimes judges are obligated to use a master "approved" list. Ask the judge's clerk how the judge picks or selects a lawyer when a court-appointed lawyer is necessary. If the judge makes the selection, make an appointment to see the judge to tell him or her you are available. If there are too many judges, ask around to see which judges or departments make the largest number of appointments. See those judges and mail a resume to the other judges. Tell the other judges that you are a new lawyer available for appointments. Ask them to keep the letter for several months even if there is no immediate need for you.

2. Public defender and legal aid (federal, state, and local) attorneys. Contact responsible people in the offices to find out how outside lawyers are selected in conflict cases and how you can get on the list.

3. Contact appeals court clerks (state and federal) to find out about getting appointed for indigent appeals.

4. Contact various state, federal, and local administrative agencies that seek private-practice lawyers. Naturally, you won't know which ones do until you ask. In some jurisdictions, this conduct may not be permissible. Therefore, you will have to ask how to ask the agencies ethically.

5. Identify decision makers. It's important to identify the decision makers—the persons who decide you are eligible to receive work. The decision may be made by an elected official to reward a campaign worker (possibly you) or a campaign contributor (someone you know who has given money to a campaign). The decision maker may be a clerk at a lower level. Sometimes elected officials make the decision; sometimes the elected or appointed legal officers make the decision. It will not always be easy to determine who the decision maker is.

6. Females and minorities. If you are female and/or a minority be sure to communicate this information. Some governmental agencies give a fixed percentage of their work or priority to females or minorities.

Be Persistent

Getting some of this work may be difficult. Sometimes clerks will tell you that the judges have no time to see you. This may be true, but possibly the clerk has some favorites and wants to keep you off the list. These government appointments might be someone's private political slush fund. You may step on a few toes, but you may also end up with some cash fees and experience right away.

Getting Legal Work and Fees from Other Lawyers

Can you get legal work from other lawyers? You not only can get legal work from other lawyers, I recommend that you should actually seek work from them. Referrals from other lawyers can provide 25 percent or more of a new lawyer's fee income.

Solicitation of work from another lawyer is perfectly proper. Solicitation from the laity is improper. Ethical Consideration EC 2-22 and Model Rule 1.5(e) allow a lawyer to associate with a lawyer outside of his or her firm with the consent of the client.

DR 2-103's only prohibition is recommending yourself for employment to nonlawyers. There is no prohibition against recommending yourself to lawyers.

Many lawyers, especially sole practitioners, have low-fee legal work that they don't want to handle, or can't economically devote the time to. Additionally, overburdened and underpaid lawyers, particularly sole practitioners, are an excellent source of immediate legal fees and immediate work for the new lawyer. The problem is one of making your availability known to sole practitioners. They frequently are so busy that they have no time to see you even though they need your help as badly as you need income.

Most sole practitioners dislike leaving their office for minor matters. Most have a backlog and an ongoing flow of relatively low-pay, low-profit matters that they are only too happy to refer out to you if they know you exist.

The following kinds of cases can be obtained from overburdened lawyers:

1. *Low-pay domestic relations matters*. There are many people who just don't qualify for legal aid or other public lawyers but who

need legal services and can pay a little. Five hundred dollars may be a reasonable fee for default divorce, but the client may only be able to pay $175 or $200. The established practitioner with established overhead can't economically handle this case. You can, because you don't have the overhead yet. It's a quick fee and some legal experience for you.

2. *Landlord-tenant disputes*. No lawyer or client enjoys this kind of work, representing either the landlords or the tenants. Here again you can handle an eviction proceeding for a relatively low fee due to your lack of overhead and need for experience, and at the same time relieve another lawyer of an unwanted matter.

3. *Out-of-office minor court appearances and minor proceedings*. Lawyers don't like leaving their office for a whole morning for some simple matter that will take a short time. Typical examples include perfunctory court appearances for such matters as continuances or minor judgment/debtor examinations. Attendance at depositions (where the deposition is a great distance from the office), perfunctory court appearances, debtor examinations, and attendance at medical examinations are other examples.

In short, you do both yourself and the sole practitioner a favor when you handle a relatively minor matter at $50 to $75 an hour plus 35 cents a mile. The $150 or $300 you are paid for the morning will enable a solo to earn $500 or more staying in the office.

There are several organizations that hire lawyers to make "one shot" minor court appearances, which can provide the new lawyer with some modest income and some court experience. Be aware of malpractice insurance issues.

4. *Research, pleadings, investigations*. These areas are covered by professional organizations and, unless you are in a geographic area where they don't yet exist, you shouldn't try to sell yourself to other lawyers on this basis. Once you "get your foot in the door" with the sole practitioner, you will get work of this nature, but you are competing with nonlawyers such as law students, etc., who actively solicit this business.

5. *Minor low-pay criminal and traffic court matters*. Here again there are people who want to contest a speeding ticket, but who can't pay more than $300 to $500. The established practitioner can't handle the matter at this price, but you can and should, both to fulfill the client's need for legal services and to earn some money as well as get experience. To obtain this work, you have to make the

other lawyer aware of your existence and availability to do this kind of work. The easiest way is to locate yourself as close to as many sole practitioners as possible. Locate yourself in a suite of sole practitioner lawyers or in a building with sole practitioners or in a block or in a neighborhood or town with as many sole practitioners as possible, as close as possible. Introduce yourself to each of them. Sit next to them at the bar association meetings. Tell them plainly and simply of your availability to do the kind of legal work described above.

Go to bar association luncheons as often as you can and network, network, network. Don't be embarrassed or ashamed to sit down at a table of eight or ten lawyers and introduce yourself, exchanging cards. Immediately upon your return to the office send each of the lawyers a letter relating how you enjoyed meeting them at this bar association meeting and are available to handle their overflow. Tell them you will call on them to ask in person, and then follow up with the lawyers whom you called. Don't steal clients. Remember, you are being selected by the lawyer, not by the client. You want more work from the lawyer who is paying you. Therefore, when the "client" asks you to handle another matter, you are obligated to refer the client back to the referring lawyer.

Remember, the overburdened sole practitioner wants to give you the work to get it off his or her desk. You must be aggressive and make yourself known to these lawyers as being available. Get close to them physically by being in the same suite, block, or area. Take them to lunch. Walk in on them during the working day and announce yourself. You have nothing to lose.

At least one state bar is attempting to match the new lawyer's need for fees with the overburdened sole practitioner's need for help in a statewide service with a view toward giving the low-fee private-practice client good service. In my opinion, this "matching" process may be the greatest impetus to private-practice growth since casualty insurance.

6. *Remote or distant courts.* If you live near a distant court house, you can let lawyers know you are available for minor court appearances, saving them the travel time to get there and back. An ad in a bar journal or an e-mail blast is a relatively cheap way to announce your availability.

Prepaid Legal Plans

Prepaid legal plans can bring new clients to a lawyer. The work is often only marginal in terms of profit or quality, but it does provide some experience and some cash. Prepaid plans seem to be most successful in rural or small-town, nonmetropolitan areas.

Minority and Affirmative Action
Work and Money

Minority Work

In this section I only wish to suggest a concept. The particular fact situation is so complex that all I can do is make some general suggestions and give you a few examples, and then it's up to you to start making telephone calls and writing letters. The availability or nonavailability of what I call "minority work" changes according to your particular locality and the politics of your particular minority or location.

What I call "minority money" is also called "set-aside" money or "affirmative-action" money or other names. Many agencies' rules require private companies and semi-public entities such as public utilities and investment firms to set aside funds to use minority firms.

Many federal and state appropriation bills contain requirements and corporate policies that a certain percentage of the legal work must be awarded to minority-owned or -operated businesses depending on the particular person administering the particular program at the particular time. This may or may not vary to include awarding contracts to minority law firms to do some of the legal work. Sometimes this minority legal work is awarded as a matter of policy rather than a matter of law, so you'll have to dig around until you find the person in the government agency or the company who is responsible for "affirmative action" programs. You may find that the company or agency has a well-defined policy or program that includes lawyers or you may have to convince them that you should be the first lawyer firm hired under a new program that you will help design.

Minority Money

Again depending upon the time, the place, and the facts, there may be minority money available to you if you can qualify.

Often banks as a matter of company policy or the Small Business Administration or other agencies may loan or guarantee loans to minority businesses. I have heard of white lawyers going into partnerships with black lawyers or lawyers with a Spanish surname to get access to the money for starting a law practice.

If you are a minority lawyer, or know a minority lawyer, you should consider this avenue of financing. Unfortunately, you'll have to do the legwork to get more information.

American Bar Association Commission on Racial and Ethnic Diversity in the Profession (formerly the Commission on Opportunities for Minorities in the Profession)

The Minority Counsel Program, sponsored by the ABA Commission on Racial and Ethnic Diversity in the Profession, brings together minority firms and majority firms and corporate counsel. (The Commission does not function as a job placement service for individuals; minority firms participating must have at least two lawyers.) You can contact the Commission at (312) 988-5643 or **minorities@abanet.org** and visit their Web site at **http://www.abanet.org/minorities**. I personally have delivered many programs for the Commission designed for minority lawyers starting their own practices and have received recognition many times from the Commission for my work over many years.

Ethnic and Minority Bar Associations

There are dozens of ethnic and minority bar associations at the national, state, and local levels. I recommend supporting them and being active in their membership (if you qualify). They are excellent for networking with other lawyers. I'm proud of my three decades of service to minority bar groups.

The Hispanic National Bar Association, of which I am an honorary member, services Hispanic lawyers. The National Bar Association is a leading association for African-American lawyers. The National Asian Pacific American Bar Association was created to address the concerns of Asian lawyers. The National Native American

Bar Association serves Native-American lawyers and legal professionals. The ABA Commission can help you locate appropriate associations to support. See **http://www.abanet.org/minorities/ links/minoritybars.html**.

Women's Bar and Professional Groups

There are many groups of women lawyers on a state, local, national, and international level. There are also many women's professional and executive groups. Some of these groups exist to address social problems and some exist purely to network and send and receive business to and from each other, as well as sponsor educational and mentoring programs. The American Bar Association Law Practice Management Section's Women Rainmakers group is an example of the latter. At one time women and minorities worked together in groups to reach their goals, but in many cases have split apart. Many of these groups will welcome you and will be a source of clients. At the time of the writing of this fifth edition, I am not aware of any groups or associations that promote the interests and networking of male lawyers or majority lawyers (to answer two frequently asked questions).

How to Get More Legal Work from Existing Clients by Mining Your Closed Files

A satisfied client will produce more clients and generate more business for you than any other single source. There are two ways in which existing clients can generate business:

1. *They can bring in new clients.* A satisfied client is your most likely and probable source of new clients. Clients who have been well served have all of the zeal of missionaries. They can't wait to brag to friends and relatives and coworkers about what a great lawyer they have. They will recommend many clients to you over the years.

2. *They can bring you their own repeat business.* As a general rule, clients want more attention, not less attention, from their lawyers. They are willing to pay for legal work only if the lawyer is available to do it. The lawyer who shows a genuine interest in the welfare of a client will find that the client will want the lawyer to do "whatever is necessary" to keep the client's legal matters in order. The lawyer who stays in close touch with clients will get a telephone call from the client ("Before I sign this lease, I want you to look at it"), which will not happen if the lawyer is inaccessible to the client.

Mining Your Closed Files

After ten years in practice, I set up a twenty-year follow-up calendar. I wish I had started my first day. The following are examples of "follow-up" legal work, often required by clients, and commonly neglected by lawyers:

1. *Corporate Minutes.* Most corporations have periodic meetings of their governing bodies, at least annually, if not more often.

217

You should send a reminder letter about thirty days prior to meetings. There is nothing unethical in reminding the client of the meetings requirement. In most instances, the client will ask you for help in setting the agenda and preparing the minutes. The client will be happy to pay you and will be grateful to you for the reminder. In some instances, the client will ignore your letter. In my opinion, anything more than one letter starts bordering on solicitation.

2. *Lease Options.* Whether your client is the owner or the tenant, the lease may have options for renewal or for purchase. A letter to the client about ninety days before the option date will often lead to your doing legal work for the client.

3. *Contracts.* Any contract containing an option date, expiration date, renewal date, etc., or employment contracts, or buy-sell agreements: all these provide a source of legal work.

4. *Wills.* A letter should be sent to the client about five years after the will is drafted, reminding the client that five years have elapsed, and that a will review would be appropriate.

5. *Judgment Renewals.* A letter should be sent about a year before a judgment becomes unenforceable.

6. *Minors Becoming Adults.* Minors often are entitled to receive funds upon attaining majority. The funds may be from previous settlements, inheritances, trust terminations, etc. Modification of a driver's decree may be appropriate.

7. *Annual Statements of Officers for Corporations.* In most states, an annual statement of officers of a corporation must be filed with the Secretary of State, and a letter reminding the client of the deadline is appropriate. Send a copy to the client's CPA, who is in periodic contact with the client. Don't be upset if the client fills out the forms without your help. It's the reminder that will be appreciated and that may remind the client that you are available for other purposes. In some cases, the form may be sent directly to you, if you have formed the corporation for the client, in which case you will send the form to the client for signature, with a short note of explanation.

8. *Fictitious Name Statement.* A periodic letter to your business or corporate clients reminding them to file fictitious name statements for their various entities is often in order. Additionally, reminding clients that businesses that are no longer doing business should file an Abandonment of Fictitious Name could be an important reminder for the client, and additional legal work for you.

9. *Expungement of Prior Criminal Records.*

The above list is not intended to be exclusive. Depending upon your local practice situation, and your desire to be of service to your clients, there are many more possibilities.

The important things to remember are:

1. When you finish a particular assignment for a client and close the file, calendar future work that the client may need. (See closed file form in the chapter "Simple Hard-Copy Filing Systems for the New Lawyer.")

2. Remember that the client welcomes your reminders.

3. Don't send more than one or two reminders (thus avoiding the problem of appearing "pushy" or hungry for business).

4. Don't worry that your reminders may generate work for another lawyer; you'll get your share.

5. Never take a client off your mailing list(s) unless asked to. A client who doesn't need you when you contact them may need you later or may recommend you to a friend who needs you. I frequently receive client new business and client referrals from people I haven't seen or talked with in many years.

6. Always use high-quality engraved rag content stationery when communicating with clients. Avoid sending letters on copy paper. Communicate success, not poverty.

7. Remove headers and footers that make it appear that the client is receiving a form letter.

How to Recognize and Handle Conflicts of Interest

Foonberg's Rule of Conflicts

Anything that might impair your absolute obligation of total loyalty to a client is a conflict and must be dealt with. The impairment may arise out of your relationships with other clients, adverse parties, or your own interests.

New lawyers frequently fall into conflicts traps that experienced lawyers have learned about through sad experience. Experienced lawyers increasingly try to intimidate a new lawyer who didn't see the problem(s). The new lawyer may, out of panic, then cause detriment to the client or to himself or herself.

Any time you are representing more than one person in a matter, ask yourself if there is a conflict of interest. Remember that corporations, partnerships, trusts, estates, and other juridicial entities are "persons" for purposes of conflicts of interest. If there appears to be a conflict, explain the potential conflict to the client in writing and get permission in writing to continue the representation. If you can't do this, pick one prospective client at the beginning and tell the other prospective client to get another lawyer. Always ask yourself "Who is my client?" and "What is my client hiring me to do?"

When there are two people in your office, ask yourself, "Who is my client and why is the other person here?"

New lawyers are especially prone to problems involving conflicts of interest for the following reasons:

1. They don't recognize the problem when they see it.

2. They don't know how to handle the problem when they recognize it.

3. They are afraid to broach this subject for fear of frightening the client away and losing a fee.

4. They don't realize they can still do the work and gain a fee if the conflict problem is properly handled.

The importance of recognizing and solving conflicts of interests at the beginning has two aspects:

To you as the lawyer: If you don't recognize and solve the problem

1. You may have to withdraw from the case.

2. You may be the object of a motion to disqualify.

3. You may not be able to collect any fees due you.

4. You may have to refund any fees previously paid you.

5. Depending on the extent of the problem, you may be disciplined or disbarred for your stupidity.

To the client: The client will have to obtain a new lawyer and waste a lot of time and energy locating and educating the new lawyer. This delay might even prejudice the case.

How to Recognize a Conflict-of-Interest Problem

Simple Conflicts

These are conflicts between you and the client. To the extent that lawyers are compensated by clients and clients compensate them, there is always a theoretical conflict between the client and the lawyer. This theoretical conflict comes close to being actual when the lawyer is compensated by "a piece of the action." This problem, however, is normally treated by bar associations under the category of "unreasonable" or "excessive" fees rather than conflict of interests.

These simple conflicts also can arise when you have two clients unrelated to each other such as:

1. Client A wants you to collect $1,000 from X and Client B wants to collect $3,000 from the same X. X only has or is even likely to have $500. Who would get it? Client A or Client B or both A and B in some ratio?

2. Client A wants you to argue as a lawyer for a debtor that involuntary repossessions are unconstitutional and Client B wants you to argue to the same or a different court in a different matter that involuntary repossessions are constitutional. Do you take both cases on the theory that the court interprets the law and not the lawyer?

Complex Conflicts

These are the more common situations and arise out of the fact that multiple parties want to use only one lawyer, typically to save fees. The most common situations are

1. *Partnerships.* Each partner and the partnership are independent entities and there are conflicts and potential conflicts in the situation.

2. *Corporations.* Each incorporator, each director, each officer, each employee, and the corporation are independent and could have conflicting interests.

3. *Divorce.* Usually the husband and wife have conflicting interests in a divorce. In theory, the court represents the children. In some jurisdictions another lawyer is appointed to represent the children.

4. *Multiple Defendants or Potential Defendants in Criminal Cases.* The defendants may later wish to turn on each other or try to get immunity in exchange for testimony.

5. *Auto Accident Cases.*

   a. Insufficient insurance or assets. There may not be sufficient insurance or assets to cover all of the injured parties. For example, suppose the defendant has a $15,000 to $30,000 policy and there are four parties seriously injured in your client's car. Suppose that the claims of each are reasonably worth $20,000 or more. Suppose further that the defendant is an indigent who can successfully go bankrupt on personal-injury judgment debts. Suppose further that the insurance company is willing to pay in the entire $30,000. If you take all four cases, how do you divide up the insurance money? Can you take all four cases? Which client(s) do you keep or reject? If you advise one or more people to get independent counsel (probably the lesser value cases), should you explain why? Would an explanation be a conflict with the clients you keep?

   b. Passenger or driver. Can you represent both the driver and the passengers? Is there a possibility of suing the driver/owner for negligent operation or maintenance of the vehicle, or under a guest statute?

6. *Family Law and Probate Cases.* The "client" is often not the person paying the bill or giving you instructions. This is an extremely complex area of conflict and you should always seek help if you have two or more people in the matter.

7. *Other Conflict-of-Interest Situations.* Obviously, there is an infinite number of possible conflict-of-interest situations. Any time

you have or may have more than one client in a matter you should ask yourself, "Do I have a conflict-of-interest situation here?" If you are not sure, call another lawyer for an opinion or call the local bar association and get the name of a member of the ethics committee. (Some ethics committees will only answer requests of the bar association itself, however, as opposed to individual members of the bar association. And some ethics committee members will only respond to written questions for fear of misunderstanding of the facts.)

8. *General Conflict of Interest (Impairment of Loyalty).* Warning flag: Remember a lawyer is both an agent and a fiduciary. The lawyer has an absolute duty of total loyalty. Anything that impairs that loyalty or could impair that loyalty or appears to impair that loyalty is a conflict.

You should get another lawyer's opinion of the situation to protect both yourself and the client. The opinion of an older, more experienced lawyer can help you decide whether or not you have a conflict, and the fact that you were concerned over the possibility of a conflict and took steps to get another opinion or other opinions would probably be of help to you in the event of a subsequent problem.

How to Handle the Problem

Be honest, be forthright, put everything in writing, and get your client(s) to consent in writing! Face the problem as soon as you determine one exists. Keep in mind two "Foonbergisms":

1. You are better off not doing the work and not getting paid than you are doing the work and not getting paid.

2. If you have to eat crow, do it while the crow is young and tender rather than waiting until the crow is old and tough.

The Model Rules of Professional Conduct do not prohibit your representing clients when there is or might be a conflict of interests. The lawyer may represent more than one party provided the client understands the conflict and knowingly waives it. (In some states the waiver must be in writing, but it should always be in writing to protect you from a client's selective memory.) A form letter for conflict-of-interest problems follows. (I use the same or similar language in my oral discussions in the office. You may wish to modify it to conform to local rules.)

Name and address of Client
Re: [Matter involved]

Dear [_____]:

I am writing to you to repeat in writing what I told you earlier in the office. I cannot commence work on your case until you have returned the enclosed copy of this letter indicating your preference.

As I explained to you in the office, a lawyer cannot be on both sides of a fence; nor can a lawyer ethically represent people who may have conflicting interests unless they understand they may have conflicting interests and still wish to use the same lawyer to do the work by waiving the conflicts and consenting to the legal representations.

Partnerships, Corporations, Business Ventures

Each of you is a legal entity and in the eyes of the law, the partnership is a legal entity. Theoretically, each of the three of you should have a different lawyer to protect your respective interests.

I can draft your partnership agreement to conform to what you have agreed to and can raise additional problems that have to be solved by you, but I cannot take sides.

Alternative 1:

In the event of a dispute between you I shall have the right to withdraw from the case and not take either side.

Alternative 2:

In the event of a dispute between "A" and you, you must understand that I would have to represent "A" since "A" is actually my client.

Alternative 3:

In the event of a dispute between you, you have agreed that my client will be the partnership and you understand that I would not represent either of you personally.

Alternative 4:

In the event of a dispute between you, I will choose a client between you.

I would not intentionally favor one of you over the other but you may feel more comfortable with a lawyer who is actively representing your individual personal interest.

Divorces

You asked me to represent both of you in order to save legal fees and costs.

You told me how you wanted the assets and liabilities handled and the amounts you have agreed on for alimony and child support. I explained to you that if you wished to fight in court, a judge might give either of you more or less assets or more or less alimony. I explained that the issue of child support cannot be bargained solely between you and that the court keeps jurisdiction to decide child support and custody regardless of what you have agreed to. I have also cautioned you on the necessity of making full disclosure of all assets, liabilities, income, expenses, etc., and that the intentional or negligent omission of important facts might cause a court to overturn the whole agreement in future years.

I also explained to you that in later years it may be relevant who was the plaintiff and who was the defendant in the divorce action and that it was possible for each of you to sue the other for divorce.

You indicated that notwithstanding your rights, you wished to proceed with the divorce as a default proceeding and to make the provisions you have agreed upon.

Multiple Defendants in a Criminal Proceeding

You have indicated that you wish to be represented together and I indicated to you that you are each entitled to individual, separate counsel and that if you can't pay for separate counsel, a public defender may be available. I also informed you that you may wish to "finger point" at each other or that one of you may be able to receive immunity from prosecution for testifying against the other.

Multiple Plaintiffs in Auto Accident Cases

I explained to you that there may not be enough insurance or assets for all of you to recover what you are entitled to and you indicated that if this should happen you would divide the total proceeds between yourselves as you will agree and that if you can't agree, the funds will be held in my trust account while you arbitrate between yourselves to determine the share that each of you is entitled to. I would not represent either of you in any such arbitration, which would be at additional expense to each of you.

Additional Suggested Contract Considerations and Clauses

When there are multiple clients, some problems arise that are not common in single-client representation and that should be considered and covered in your fee agreement. Some possible guideline clauses are listed here, but should be considered in light of any applicable local rules.

1. Ownership of files and documents:

It is agreed by and between the clients that all files and documents pertaining to the matter shall be considered the joint property of all the clients and shall remain in the custody and possession of Mary Lawyer until conclusion of the case. At the conclusion of the case the files may be disposed of by Attorney Lawyer. Any client may have access to the files during normal business hours at a mutually convenient time and may make photocopies at the client's sole expense.

2. Joint client waiver of attorney-client privilege:

Client understands that in the event of a dispute between clients, the attorney-client privilege will not protect communications between you and the lawyers in the firm. Anything you disclose to us may be disclosed to the other clients.

3. Acceptance or rejection of global settlement offers:

Client understands that he or she may have a right to object to or veto acceptance of any global settlement offer by defendants (plaintiffs). Client understands that he or she is waiving that right and agreeing to accept and be bound by any settlement offer that is acceptable to one half the number of clients. (Any settlement offer in excess of $_____) (Any settlement offer that nets client $_____ before fees and costs) (Any settlement that nets client $____ after fees and costs)

4. Allocation of global settlement offer among clients:

Client agrees that any settlement offer accepted shall be divided equally among all clients regardless of the fact that one client may have suffered greater or lesser economic injuries than another client. (Or shall be divided in a ratio of 4:3:2:1)

In the event of a dispute among clients as to allocation or division of net proceeds of settlement, clients agree to binding arbitration and that lawyer may remove fees and costs and shall deposit clients' remaining portion into an interest-bearing trust account. Lawyer will not represent any client in such arbitration and such arbitration, and attorneys' fees and costs in connection with the arbitration, shall be at client's sole cost and expense.

5. Independent counsel (this clause to be initialled by client in addition to signing the agreement):

Client has been advised of his/her right to seek independent legal counsel to advise him/her of his/her rights and responsibilities prior to execution of this agreement. Client understands this advice and has been offered an opportunity to obtain and consult with independent legal counsel of his/her choosing prior to execution of this agreement.

6. Waiver and consent:

Clients waive any conflicts or potential conflicts and consent to representation by Mary Lawyer.

7. Delegation of decision-making authority:

The parties designate Mary Smith or any successor designated by a majority of the parties to make all decisions concerning conduct of the case and acceptance or rejection of settlement offers. Attorney may accept all instructions from Mary Smith and may communicate to Mary Smith all developments.

How to Keep Clients

What do clients want from you? There is often a difference between what people want and will pay for as opposed to what they need.

Often a person will happily pay for what is wanted, but resents paying for what is needed, if the two differ. Think of your own situation when you are sick. You'd pay anything within reason for a physician to make a house call. It is much more efficient and economical for you to go to the physician's office or to an emergency room of a hospital, but you'd still prefer a house call. You need a $75 office visit, but you want and would pay for a $200 house call. The supply-and-demand situation between new physicians and patients is such that new physicians can turn down business they used to welcome. Unfortunately for you, the supply-and-demand situation between new lawyers and the need for legal services is in a different balance, and you must give clients what they want.

The purpose of the comparison is solely to emphasize the difference between providing a client what is wanted and providing what is needed (these are not mutually exclusive).

Therefore, the gist of this chapter is to teach you the things that clients want in addition to your efforts and in addition to good results.

1. *Effort vs. Results.* New lawyers think that clients want results more than they want effort. Believe it or not, the reverse is true. Clients need favorable results; they want effort. Don't misinterpret what I am saying. I am not saying that clients don't care whether

they win or lose. They care very much. I am saying that whether they come back to you when a matter is over with, or whether they recommend other clients to you or pay your fee willingly, or not at all, is determined more by their opinion of your efforts and how you treated them than their opinion of the results.

2. *How to Project Efforts.* Listed below are things you can do to let the client know you are putting forth effort. It is not true that the practice of law is like the proverbial iceberg, with 90 percent hidden. It is true that there are lazy lawyers and lawyers who really don't care about their clients, and who obscure under a basket 90 percent of what they are doing.

a. Send your client a copy of EVERY document you produce, by e-mail or regular mail, including correspondence, pleadings, briefs, etc., as you produce it.

b. Send your client a copy of all incoming documents as they are received, including pleadings, correspondence, etc.

c. Return your client's calls immediately (within two hours), or have someone else return them. Remember this:

(1) I needed a lawyer;

(2) I couldn't get in touch with you;

(3) I got another lawyer;

(4) I don't need you anymore . . .

d. If you work on your client's case in the evening or on a weekend, call him or her at home to ask some questions, so that he or she knows you are devoting your "personal" time to the matter.

e. Bill monthly.

f. Make "house calls."

g. One of the most effective techniques I employ is to visit clients at their places of business.

(1) Visit your client's place of business to understand that business. Don't charge for the time you spend going through the factory, but do charge for the conference at the place of business to the same extent as you would have charged for the same conference in your office.

(2) Go with your client to the scene of the accident in personal injury and workers' compensation cases. This will really impress your client as to your effort.

(3) Go to the medical examination with your client when the defense doctor makes an examination.

h. Inform clients of new cases or statutes that come to your attention and that could affect their affairs. They will appreciate your concern. They will feel you care about them and are putting forth effort for them. Send the information both by regular mail and e-mail. Indicate on the e-mail copy that the client can forward the information to others who may be interested.

i. Return telephone calls within two hours or have someone return them for you within two hours, if possible.

j. Be careful about creating expectations about fees, time intevals, or results. Clients will accept what your fee will be and what you feel are the likely results of the case and the amount of time required, and will then hold you accountable to meet the expectations you created. If you fail to meet the expectations you created, they may not come back or refer others to you.

How to Satisfy a Client

The American Bar Association funded Temple University to conduct a study of the differences between satisfied and dissatisfied clients.[1] The results were totally predictable and proved that things really don't change.

While the study used the classification of Satisfied and Dissatisfied clients, I prefer to use the classifications of Happy vs. Unhappy clients. The difference between Happy and Unhappy clients is also predictable and there are obvious distinctions.

Happy Clients

1. Pay their bill as agreed.

2. Say nice things about you.

3. Refer more clients to you.

4. Make you feel good about being a lawyer.

5. Don't file nonmeritorious ethics or malpractice complaints against you.

Unhappy Clients

1. Do not pay the bill as agreed, especially the final bill.

2. Bad mouth you to anyone who will listen.

3. Do not refer clients to you.

4. Make you wonder why you ever became a lawyer.

5. Are quick to file nonmeritorious ethics and/or malpractice complaints against you to "get even" for real or imagined mistreatment and to avoid paying the bill.

---

1. "Report on the Legal Needs of the Low- and Moderate-Income Public," Study conducted by the Institute for Survey Research at Temple University for the Consortium on Legal Services and the Public (ABA, 1995)

As I indicated, the results of the survey simply confirmed what any practicing lawyer already knew, although the survey more precisely quantified what practicing lawyers already knew.

The results are as follows:	Satisfied Clients	Dissatisfied Clients
1. Explaining the legal process and the client's legal position.	95	50
2. Listening to the client and paying attention to what the client says.	93	47
3. Demonstrating interest and concern for the client.	91	47
4. Honesty in financial dealing with the client.	95	51
5. Keeping the client informed of what was happening on the legal matter.	84	34
6. Promptness in returning telephone calls.	83	42
7. Promptness in doing the work.	83	41

Each of these seven factors is repeatedly referred to either directly or indirectly throughout this book.

How to Lose Clients

Why Do Clients Leave?

According to one national survey,

1 percent die;

3 percent move;

5 percent dislike the product;

24 percent have some dispute that does not get adjusted;

67 percent leave because they feel they were treated discourteously, indifferently, or simply were not given good service.

Cases and Clients That Should Be Turned Down

Abraham Lincoln reputedly advised a new lawyer on passing the bar, "Young man, it's more important to know what cases not to take than it is to know the law."

As a new lawyer with relatively little caseload, you'll want to take almost any case from almost any client. The more experienced lawyer knows better. It is most crucial that you recognize that you need cash, as well as satisfaction in helping the downtrodden, if you intend to be in practice the second or third year. Therefore, I am going to list cases and clients that you should turn down during your first year or two. After you're established and can afford the luxury of laying out your time and money to be a "nice person," or to gamble on profitability, then you might wish to take these cases.

This list is based upon my personal experiences and you may wish to expand or contract it as time goes by. This list has changed very little since the first edition of this book in 1976 and is not likely to change much in the future.

When You Are the Second or Third Lawyer on the Case

Be very careful. There may be honest personality differences between the client and prior lawyers, but multiple lawyers often indicate:

A nonmeritorious case;

An uncooperative client;

A nonpaying client.

Check with the prior lawyers before accepting the case. Ask the prior lawyers if there is an unpaid bill or lien for his or her fees involved. If, after checking, you believe in the client and the merits of prosecution, then by all means accept the case if you want to.

If you do take the case, you should, whenever possible, communicate with the adverse lawyer or party to make clear the reasons for multiple lawyers, if you can do so without violating attorney-client privilege and without further damaging the case. The other side may, and probably will, equate multiple lawyers with the three problems stated, and your coming in as lawyer number three may harm your client's case and your economics. If you can't explain the multiple lawyer problem to the other side, then keep in mind that you'll have a more difficult and perhaps impossible task reaching a fair settlement without a trial to judgment.

"Hurt Feelings" Cases

This type of case usually has wrongful conduct by the defendant, but no provable special damages on the part of your client, or nominal damages at best. The case and your compensation are dependent on either presumed or punitive damages. Examples of this type of case are

1. Libel and slander;
2. Barroom brawls;
3. Most assault and battery cases.

Landlord-Tenant Cases (Unless You Are Paid in Full in Advance)

It makes no difference if you represent the landlord or the tenant, your client will never be happy and will never pay you after the case is over. Landlords greatly resent having to pay you money to evict someone who is already delinquent in rent or who is busting up the place, or driving other tenants away with such activities as drag racing in the driveway at 4:00 a.m., or having wild all-night parties. Tenants often want to leave, but want to blackmail the landlord into paying them something to leave. Sometimes tenants can't leave because they haven't got the first and last month's rent to move into another place. Sometimes tenants feel they are being unreasonably evicted because they made what to them is a reasonable request that the landlord ignored, such as fixing the leaky, noisy toilet.

Landlord-tenant disputes are often more vindictive than divorce suits, and each side wants to use the lawyer for revenge if they can use the lawyer for free.

Divorce Cases for People Heavily in Debt (Unless You Are Paid in Advance)

Please remember that poor people can get divorces through legal aid. In most—if not almost all—cases, divorce is an economic disaster for everyone involved. There is rarely enough money to support the parties and children living apart. I am not a qualified expert on the subject of causes of divorce cases, but I believe that economic insecurity is a major factor in divorce. In accepting or not accepting divorce cases it is safe to assume that the retainer money up front may be the only money you'll see. Be firm in getting the money up front. Court orders awarding you a fee of one-half of the fair amount at the rate of $25 a month if the breadwinner sticks around aren't worth much. Don't blame the court. Blame yourself for accepting a case legal aid would have taken.

A divorce court judge told me that the parties change lawyers during the case in more than half of the cases. The clients are difficult people for any number of reasons. You can be sure that the client will need money for the next lawyer and won't pay your last billing.

Criminal Cases (Unless You Get Paid in Advance)

A person in prison doesn't earn much more than cigarette money. Don't take clients who should be represented by the public defender.

Slip Falls (Unless There Are Substantial Damages)

Even the most meritorious slip fall is hard to settle for a fair amount short of trial. You'll spend huge amounts of time and have very little to show for your efforts.

Bankruptcies (Unless You Are Paid in Advance in Full)

It was embarrassing when my client amended his bankruptcy schedules to include the unpaid balance of the fee due me.

Clients Who Loudly Proclaim That You Can Have All the Money Recovered; They Are "Only Interested in the Principle"

These cases fall into the same category as the "Hurt Feelings" cases.

Clients Who Want to Use Your Telephones, Secretary, and Offices to Do Their Business

I don't know why, but this type of client always seems to end up being trouble. Be forewarned.

Clients Who Ask for a Loan of Money Against Their Case

You'd be surprised at how many new lawyers get stuck lending small amounts of money to clients. When clients say that if you don't lend them some money they'll have to go to another lawyer who will lend them money, then you're better off without those clients.

Cases Where "They'll Settle Right Away Because They Can't Afford the Publicity of Litigation"

When a prospective client makes this statement, I cringe. Usually the person honestly believes what is said. Unfortunately, it never happens this way. For some reason the adverse party in this type of case will consider discussing a possible settlement as soon as the United States Supreme Court denies certiorari. When you hear these magic words, convince the client that a noncontingency hourly rate payable in advance is best for him or her. Convince such a client that a contingency fee in such a case would overcompensate you as the lawyer in view of the early anticipated settlement of the case and that cash up front for hourly billings is more fair to the client.

Cases Totally Without Merit

If a case has no chance, be honest; tell the client you won't handle a case totally without merit.

I have included a chapter that will give you some techniques for saying "No" to the prospective client.

Keep in mind that you are not obligated to take cases that could and probably should be handled by publicly funded lawyers such as those in legal aid and public defender offices. Remember also that if your fee agreement is properly drafted, you can withdraw from the case. But don't forget that you cannot hold onto the client and stop working due to an unpaid fee.

Religious Fanatics

Be careful when the client says "God sent me to you." These people often expect God to pay the bill.

Clients Who Admit to Seeing Other Lawyers Before You but Who Won't Tell You the Names of the Previous Lawyer(s).

The prospective client may have been told they have no case and then lied to you by giving false facts to entice you into taking them as a client.

Clients Who Refuse to Give You Their Home Address and Want You to Accept Only a P.O. Box or E-mail Address.

They usually are concerned that you'll look for them if they don't pay.

The Prospective Client File

I recommend you open a file called "Prospective Clients."

This will be a file where you put your telephone, e-mail, and office conference notes concerning people and companies where you have listened to the facts of the case, but decided not to accept the case for whatever reason. (Case had no merit, inability to pay, conflict of interest, referred to another firm, client not interested in pursuing, etc.) Be sure to indicate the name of the prospective client and the date of your contact(s) with the potential client.

This file will become a repository of potential clients and contacts and potential conflicts.

Even though you did not represent the prospective clients on the matters for which you were consulted, you may be able to represent them on other matters in the future and they can still refer other clients to you.

In addition to storing the notes, you should add the names, addresses, and other names of people, companies, and industries to a computerized database. This database can become an invaluable asset for making contacts years later, long after you have forgotten all the names and facts of that brief interview.

This database can be added (if appropriate) to the list of those who will receive your announcements, greeting cards, newsletters, etc. These people now know you, they just didn't use you this one time. They can use you in the future.

This database should also be checked for conflicts as part of your regular conflicts search.

Record time devoted to prospective clients as a "Prospective Client" category. This will establish that you did not have professional responsibility on that matter and will avoid the problem of setting up a client file for everyone you see or talk to on the phone or from whom you receive an e-mail message, even though you did not undertake representation of the client.

How to Say "No"
to a Client or Case

For a new lawyer, cases and clients are hard to come by. You'll be afraid to say "No" when a case or client should be turned down. Lawyers by nature like to be "nice people." Lawyers also want as many clients as possible and don't like to get rid of clients or cases. The suggestions of this chapter may help you in a difficult situation.

Tell Your Client the Truth

Ninety-five percent of the problems will disappear when you tell your client the truth.

1. *No Merit to Case.* Tell your client that, in your opinion, the case is without merit. Tell the client that you'd like to take the case and make money, but there just isn't a case.

2. *Uneconomical Case.* Tell the client that although he or she is legally in the right, the economics of the case just don't warrant the use of a lawyer.

Suggest Alternatives

1. *Small Claims Court.* Suggest in the smaller cases that the client use the services of the Small Claims Court and keep all the money without sharing it with lawyers.

2. *Other Lawyers.* Suggest that the client seek the opinion of another lawyer who might disagree with your evaluation. Give the client the phone numbers of legal aid, public defenders, the bar association referral system, consumer advocate offices, etc., so that the client will know where to go for help.

3. *Suggest That Certain Clients Represent Themselves.* In some situations, such as landlord-tenant conflicts, you can teach landlord clients what they have to know to represent themselves. Let them know they are paying you for their education.

4. *Suggest Alternative Dispute Resolution (ADR).* Often a client can afford to pay for a mediation or arbitration in an otherwise uneconomical case. Always consider the possibility of ADR.

Put It in Writing

After you decline the case or client, send a follow-up letter confirming what you told the client, including the suggestion to contact another lawyer and repeating the phone numbers of the other lawyer or the bar association lawyer referral service. This will be of great help to you in protecting yourself if the client denies the conversation. (See sample nonengagement letter below for suggested wording.)

Ask Your Client for "Money Up Front" (Foonberg's First Rule)

Asking clients to put their money where their mouths are will help get rid of unwanted clients who know a case is nonmeritorious.

Believe it or not, the honest, legitimate client wants the truth. The client won't be angry with you for hearing bad news. You'll be respected and that client will come back in the future.

Nonengagement Letters

You must make it clear if, when after meeting the client or learning the facts, you decide not to accept a case. You should clearly decline engagement in writing, not leaving the person with nowhere to go, and still leaving the door open for the person to come back on another matter or to refer others to you.

Do not, under any circumstances, leave open the possibility of the potential client believing that you have accepted professional responsibility if you haven't.

A sample nonengagement letter might be as follows:

[1]   Mr. Arthur Smith
        1234 Main Street
        Anytown, USA 12345

[2] Re: Telephone Conversation of Jan. 3, 20xx
        Meeting at Jones Wedding on Jan. 3, 20xx
        Office meeting of Jan. 3, 20xx

Dear Mr. Smith:

[3] It was nice meeting you (talking to you) on Jan. 3, 20xx.

[4]   I am sorry that we cannot be of help to you in your boundary line dispute with Mrs. Peters. (Or whatever) As I related to you in the office (on the telephone) on Jan. 3, I do not feel it would be appropriate for me to undertake your case.

[5]   (optional/see comments) As I explained to you, based on the facts given to me, I do not think your case is economically feasible to pursue. I would not be willing to prosecute the matter on a contingency basis and cannot in good conscience recommend that you spend your time and money on this case. If you do not care that the case is not economically meritorious, but wish vindication, I would consider representing you on a noncontingency basis with payment of the fee in advance.

[6] Again, I do not recommend this expenditure of money, even though you may be legally right.
        (Optional/see comments) This is not an area of law in which I feel experienced enough to represent you.

[7]   (optional/see comments) I have expressed no professional opinion on the merits of your case.

[8]   I have given you no advice on any possible time limitations to your matter. There may or may not be a time limitation on your taking action.

[9]   I encourage you to immediately consult with as many other lawyers as you wish without delay. It is possible that another lawyer will disagree with me and will be willing to represent you on a fee basis agreeable to both of you.

[10]   If you cannot find another lawyer, I recommend that you immediately contact the Wilshire County Bar Association Lawyer Referral Service at 123-123-1234.

[11]   I have returned to you all of the documents that you showed me and have not kept any of your papers.

[12]   (alternative) I am returning herewith all of the documents you left at my office. I have not kept any of the documents you showed me.

[13]   I repeat again that we have not taken this case and we will not do any work on it and have not accepted any professional responsibility for the matter.

[14]   I would hope that at another time you would again give us the opportunity to be of service to you. We certainly would welcome your return on a different matter should the need arise. I am enclosing some general information about the firm and I will place you on our firm mailing list so that you can receive the information that we send to our clients from time to time.

Very truly yours,

I.M. Sorry
Attorney at Law

[15] bcc: Prospective Clients

Comments

[1]. Begin all initial contacts with asking the client for their card or for their name, e-mail and postal addresses, and phone number. Be extremely careful when the prospective client doesn't want to tell you. Ask why he or she won't tell you. If you have any funny feelings, hang up or walk away or ask the person to leave. Make a note of the event for your "Prospective Client" file. It is possible you are being set up for something.

[2]. Specify the contact(s) you had with this person. This person might at a later date confuse you with another lawyer and erroneously bring a complaint or claim against you.

[3]. Say something nice in the body of the letter. Refer again to the contact(s).

[4]. Try to refer to the nature of the matter in the letter to remind the person and yourself at a later time what the contact was all about.

[5]. I personally like to give the person an honest reason why I don't want to take the case. If the case is not meritorious for whatever reason, I like to tell the person why I feel that way and suggest they seek other counsel who may have a different opinion. I want

this person to come back in the future when he or she does have a meritorious case. Some malpractice insurance companies prefer that you give the person absolutely no opinion or assistance.

[6]. Surprisingly, many potential clients will respect your honesty and will hire you because you told the truth. They can accept losing the fight, but they cannot accept not even trying to win. I have earned many good fees and even won some of these losers and gained clients for life by simply telling the truth. This is why I disagree with the insurance company recommendation to give no advice or opinions.

[7]. I do not give any advice on the statute of limitations until I have a paying client. If you gave the wrong advice you can easily incur liability. You should not give any advice on the statute of limitations until the client signs the fee agreement and you have a paying client and you have made a thorough examination of the underlying facts.

[8]. Encourage the client to seek help from other lawyers. It is possible that you were wrong in your assessment of the facts.

[9]. Give the person the telephone number of the local Lawyer Referral Service. They will either try to find a lawyer to help or refer the person to the appropriate government social welfare office. This may protect you from the double claim of doing nothing and abandoning the client's case after you have taken it.

[10]. Keeping client papers may lead the client to think you have undertaken the case. Create a record that you kept nothing.

[11]. If the client left any papers, send them back.

[12]. Make it as clear as you can that you have not accepted the case and you are not going to be doing anything on it.

[13]. There's no harm in keeping the door open for business on another matter at another time or for a referral from the person. Additionally, getting his or her name into your database will make it easier for you to find the person at a future time and to do a conflicts search.

[14]. Create a file called "Prospective Clients" and put the copy of this letter and any handwritten notes you had and copies of any documents you copied into this file.

Accepting Cases With Doubtful Merit

Some clients will want to pursue a case with doubtful merit. They are often willing and able to pay to prosecute a case of doubtful merit for one or more of the following reasons:

1. They believe that discovery will prove that their belief as to the true facts will be substantiated.

2. They understand that they appear to have a losing case but are willing to pay to find out the truth of a matter or to find out what the truth is.

3. They understand they appear to have a losing case but they want to feel they have done everything that could have been done before closing the matter.

4. They know they will lose but need time to prepare for the loss.

5. They simply hate the other side and want to casue them to spend money on legal fees.

Situations 1, 2, and 3 are probably valid cases to accept and prosecute/defend.

The fourth situation is normally all right to accept. Insurance companies and others gladly pay lawyers to stall and delay in order to earn interest or profits on the money before they have to pay the money. Unreasonable, unjustifiable stalling can sometimes lead to sanctions against both the lawyer and the client. A lawyer accepting a stall and delay defense may want to advise the client of possible sanctions and might even want to provide for the client reimbursing the lawyer for sanctions if assessed.

The fifth situation is often referred to as representing "vexatious litigant" and can result in severe penalties and even civil liability against the lawyer. While a lawyer is almost never guilty of abuse of process for starting a vexatious litigation, the lawyer can be held responsible for abuse of process for maintaining the case after it is totally obvious that there is absolutely no merit to the client's reason for bringing or continuing litigation.

Damage Control If You Are Fired

Sooner or later, you will be fired by a client. The most usual form of notification is a letter from another lawyer asking for the files, accompanied by an authorization signed by the client.

If you handle the situation properly, you will protect the client's rights and you will protect your own rights.

While you normally will not feel good about being fired, you need not overreact by looking for a tall building from which to jump off. You cannot be all things to all people. Sometimes, no matter how hard you try and no matter how good a job you do, the chemistry just will not be there between you and the client (often the situation in divorce cases).

Remember, the client might still come back or refer others. Clients often regret changing lawyers and come back later.

There are several things you should do upon being fired.

1. Immediately call the new lawyer and confirm you have received the letter and will immediately send over the files. Offer to answer any questions the lawyer might have concerning the case or the client. (You do not want to make an enemy of the next lawyer. You may need his or her help if there is a balance due for fees or a subsequent fee dispute, malpractice claim, or disciplinary complaint.)

2. Confirm your call in writing and repeat your offer in the letter. Send a copy of the letter to the client in order to let the client know you are acting promptly to comply with their wishes and to give them a chance to say something if the new lawyer is not a lawyer they have selected.

3. Review the files before you send them over to be sure they do not contain any materials relevant to other clients' matters that got misfiled, or any other sensitive information that you feel does not belong there.

4. If you suspect that you will become the object of a fee dispute, malpractice claim, or other problem, photocopy the entire file to have your own copy to protect yourself at a later time.

5. Immediately send a letter to the client. Your letter should do the following:

(1) Identify legal matters covered.

(2) Indicate that you are acting immediately.

(3) Tell the client you still have some information about the case in the file in the event he or she wants to come back to you in the future in connection with this or other matters.

(4) Tell the client you have returned all original documents.

(5) Remind the client about search fees and time fees for digging out old files if you want to get rid of this client.

(6) Let clients know you are still trying to protect them even though they fired you.

(7) Ask for permission to destroy what you do not want to store.

(8) Establish the fact that you are not the lawyer.

(9) Establish the date from which to measure all possible statutes of limitation in case the client later wants to sue you for malpractice.

(10) Establish that if the next lawyer loses the case or gets a result unfavorable to the client, you are not accepting responsibility for what the next lawyer does.

(11) Set the record straight about what fee disputes, if any, arose after the person no longer was a client.

(12) Let the client know that you expect to be paid immediately.

(13) Offer arbitration or mediation. Many state bars require an offer of arbitration as a condition precedent to litigation. This letter can become the offer of arbitration.

(14) Let the client know you are willing to sue to get your fee, if necessary.

(15) Keep the door open for the client to return if you really want him or her to. I have had clients fire me and come back later

when they subsequently did not like the next lawyer(s). Some clients who have fired me have nonetheless later recommended me to other clients who had good cases and with whom I have had good professional relations.

(16) You may wish to send a survey to help you ascertain WHY the client left you. Remember, a former client who fired you is still part of your client base and can still return to you in the future or recommend new clients to you if you treat the former client properly when he or she leaves.

The following sample letter demonstrates the points listed above:

To: Disgruntled Client
123 Main Street
Anytown, USA
Re: *Files on Client v. Jones and Client adv. Smith*

Dear Mr. or Ms. Client:
As requested by Mr. Jones in his letter of January _____, 20xx, and your authorization of January _____, 20xx, we are in the process of immediately transferring your files to Mr. Jones. It will take a few days, as we must go through the files to be sure the file does not contain materials relevant to other clients that might have been accidentally placed in your file. We may also copy parts of your file for our insurance and tax needs.

We have telephoned and written to Mr. Jones to offer our immediate help should it be required. You have some other files from previous matters and we would appreciate hearing from you as to whether you want us to return them to you, send them to Mr. Jones, or destroy them. If you do not instruct us, we shall destroy them when we next periodically remove all files that have been inactive for five or more years.

I am sure that you understand we are no longer your lawyers in this case, and that as of _____, Mr. Jones is now responsible for the conduct of the case. If you have questions about the case, it would be appropriate for you to contact him and for him to contact us, if he wishes, rather than for us to discuss the case with you directly. It is possible that his office wants to treat certain aspects of the case differently from the way our office would treat them and we would not want to be in a position of giving you conflicting advice.

Until this point, you have never indicated any dissatisfaction with the fee arrangement or the amount of the fees and I assume that you have no disagreement over the fees.

Immediate payment of the outstanding balance of $_____ would be appropriate at this time as we are no longer the lawyers and there is no reason to defer closing the file.

In the event you do have a fee problem, our profession recognizes that honest, sincere people can have bonafide differences of opinion relative to fees and, accordingly, if you do have a fee dispute, I am hereby offering to arbitrate that fee dispute in accordance with the Rules of the State Bar of California and the procedures of the Beverly Hills Bar Association, which professional rules require us to notify you of the opportunity to arbitrate any fee dispute as an alternative to litigation. You can obtain information from the bar association directly, if you wish.

(Optional) In accordance with our fee agreement we are offering to mediate our problem prior to arbitration or litigation.

This letter may end up being Exhibit B in your complaint for fees (if your state requires proof of an offer to arbitrate as a condition to precedent to a suit). You may, therefore, be able to get all of the information that is in the letter into the court record and before the trier of fact as an exhibit.

To be ultra-safe, keep all new notes after being fired in a new file and code them with the date of the note and possibly the letter "L" (standing for litigation). You may wish to subsequently claim that you were anticipating possible litigation and for that reason began keeping your records in anticipation of possible litigation. Notes and records kept in anticipation of litigation may have some degree of privilege in subsequent litigation between you and the client. What you did during the representation probably won't be privileged, but what you did after the representation may be privileged if it was in anticipation of litigation. Most of the information contained in the letter is self-serving and will be of great help at a later time if the letter comes into evidence in court in a suit for fees or before the state bar on a client complaint.

It is important that you remain professional when you are fired. Be firm. Protect yourself and leave the door open for the client to come back or refer you to other clients. If you overreact or are uncooperative, you may not get paid what is owed you. You may get a disciplinary complaint filed against you by either the client or the next lawyer, and you will have lost possible future return work and referrals.

Part V
Setting Fees

The Fee and Representation Letter
(The Engagement Letter)

The importance of the fee-representation-engagement agreement cannot be overemphasized. It will help eliminate disputes between you and your client more effectively than any other procedure.

The fee letter can best be explained by using an all-inclusive example and then exploring the importance of the various parts:

John Jones
123 Main Street
Anytown, U.S.A.

[1]   RE: Jones vs. Smith; breach of contract
Dear Mr. Jones:

[2]   This letter will confirm our office discussion of Thursday, January 4.

[3]   It was a pleasure meeting with you in our office. As I explained to you, it is my opinion that you

[4] definitely need the assistance of a lawyer, whether it

[5] be our firm or another lawyer. In my opinion, the matter is too complex for you to represent yourself.

[6]   As I explained to you, if you wish us to repre-

[7][8] sent you, our fee will be $2,250 to prepare the complaint, do written interrogatories, take the deposition of Mr. Smith if necessary, and appear for the first day in

[9] court. If any additional work is required for such things as motions, additional depositions, or additional days in court, you will be charged at our hourly rate of

[10] $150 per hour. If the case is settled short of trial, the fee will still be a minimum of $2,250.

[11]   The above does not include any out-of-pocket costs that may be incurred, such as court filing fees, sheriff's fees, deposition costs, photocopying, etc. We estimate, but cannot guarantee, that these costs will run between $350 and $750, and, as explained, these costs are in addition to our fee and are not included in the $2,250 fee.

[12]   We shall have the right to engage other attorneys to assist us at our sole expense and at no additional cost to you.

[13]   You indicated that you wished to pay in installments of $750 fees and $250 costs to begin work, and $300 fees and $200 costs the first of each month until you are current, and then, additional fees and costs will be paid monthly, as billed.

[14]
[15]   This schedule is acceptable to us, so long as you understand that if you terminate payments, we may terminate our services and withdraw from the case.

[16]   You are also agreeing to cooperate and participate in the conduct of your case and to truthfully and immediately notify us as to anything that may occur that could affect the case. You understand we are relying on the facts as given to us by you.

[17]   As I indicated to you, based on the facts as you related them to me in the office, you should win, and you should be awarded a judgment of between $13,500 and $18,000, unless the case is settled at a different sum. Obviously, depending upon the facts as they are developed, our opinion could change and you could be awarded more or less, or even lose. You also understand that getting a judgment is not the same as getting cash and that you may have to expend additional costs and fees to collect the judgment.

[18]   Our State Bar Act requires that we advise you as to whether or not we maintain malpractice insurance for this type of matter. Please be advised that we are insured for this type of matter.

[19]   You asked me if spending money on legal fees in this case is throwing good money after bad, and I told you that at this point, I couldn't give you an answer, and that you should understand that there are no guarantees of winning or collecting.

[20]   It is my opinion, however, that whether you use our firm or other lawyers, you should proceed with

your case. Please do not delay. If you delay the commencement of your suit, you may at some point be barred from bringing it.

[21]   If the above properly sets forth our agreement, please sign and return the enclosed copy of this letter, along with a check in the amount of $1,000, payable to my trust account. I will draw $750 toward my fees,

[22]   and leave $250 toward costs as outlined above. Trust account funds are deposited to our Trust Account in accordance with the rules governing lawyers in our state including IOLTA (Interest On Lawyer Trust Accounts) rules as well as our fiduciary duty to you as a client. If the funds are significant enough to earn net interest for the period of time held, we will consult with you for instructions. A self-addressed, postage-paid envelope is enclosed for your convenience.

[23]   If we do not receive the signed copy of this letter, and your check, within 30 days, I shall assume that you have obtained other counsel, and shall mark my file "closed" and do nothing further.

If any of the above is not clear, or if you have any questions, please do not hesitate to call.

Very truly yours,

To be typed on the copy of the letter:

The above is understood and agreed to, and my check in the amount of $1,000, payable to Jane Attorney Client Trust Account is enclosed.

Dated: _____
John Jones _____

Essential Points to the Fee and Representation Letter

Obviously, the fee-representation letter must be tailor-made to the particular facts of the matter and the fee. Whatever form you decide to use, your letter should include the following:

[1] *The Matter Involved.* Perhaps your client has several legal matters, and has not told you about any of them except the Smith matter. This should prevent a later claim that you were responsible for more than this matter.

[2] *Your Interview Date.* This establishes when you had an interview to get the facts. This is for your protection in the event you are sued by your client or another party.

[3] *Whether or Not a Lawyer Is Required.* This avoids the interviewee claiming that you said no lawyer was necessary and that he or she should "forget about it."

[4] *Suggesting Other Lawyers.* Suggest that the client may wish to see another lawyer. This relates to not representing the client until the agreement is returned. (See point 21 below.)

[5] *If You Wish Us to Represent You.* This reinforces that you are not yet the lawyer, and don't yet have responsibility.

[6] *The Amount of the Fee.* This establishes what I call the "Basic Fee."

[7] *Describing the Work the Fee Covers.* This discusses what you will do for the Basic Fee.

[8] *What the Basic Fee Does NOT Cover.* This describes what is not included in the Basic Fee.

[9] *Additional Work Fee Arrangement.* How you will charge for the work that is not included in this Basic Fee.

[10] *Minimum Fee.* What the minimum fee will be.

[11] *Out-of-Pocket Costs.* The client will not understand the difference between costs and fees, unless you explain it. This reinforces your explanation.

[12] *Addition to Fees.* Reinforce that out-of-pocket costs are in addition to fees.

[13] *Engaging Other Attorneys to Assist.* This allows you to get help at your expense if you are in over your head and need help.

[14] *Payment Schedule.* Set forth the cash flow that you have agreed upon, to avoid later misunderstandings.

[15] *Right to Terminate Services.* It is important that the client understands your right to terminate services for nonpayment. In some jurisdictions there may be ethical considerations in domestic relations and criminal matters. This portion should satisfy the requirements of DR 2-110(C)(1)(e) so that you can withdraw when the client stops paying.

[16] *Agreeing to Cooperate and Be Truthful.* This may be the basis of your motion to be relieved as counsel at a later time.

[17] *Your Opinion of the Merits of the Case.* Repeat in a letter what you told the client in the office, and that what you said was based upon the facts that were given you. (Obviously, you may use

this part of your letter to state that you are not yet in a position to express an opinion as to the outcome, or that you won't be able to express an opinion until research is done or until discovery is underway or completed.) In some types of work, you can quote dollar amounts. In some types, such as personal injury, you should not. Always repeat in writing what you did or did not say in the office to prevent later problems when the client claims you quoted a large recovery.

[18] *Existence of Malpractice Insurance.* Some states require that you disclose to the client whether you do or do not have malpractice insurance in certain types of matters.

[19] *Explain Judgments.* Be sure the client is aware that winning a case and getting a judgment for fees and costs is not the same as getting cash, and that many judgments are uncollectible.

[20] *No Guarantees.* The client should understand that you have not guaranteed the outcome, and that it is possible that the funds expended on legal fees won't guarantee results.

[21] *Tell Client Not to Delay.* Warn the prospective client in lay language not to delay. Warn the prospective client that laches or a statute of limitations can prejudice the case if there are delays. Do not express an opinion on the statute date, unless you are engaged to do so. If you gave the client the wrong date, you could have malpractice liability.

[22] *Signing and Returning Copy of Letter.* Obviously, the signed copy in effect becomes a fee contract when returned to you.

[23] *Trust Account Rules—Explain IOLTA.* IOLTA rules may vary from state to state. You have to comply with your IOLTA rules and also comply with your fiduciary duties to your client. In some states IOLTA is mandatory. In some states it is optional or "opt out." Be careful when the amount of net interest that could be earned on your client's funds might exceed bank charges. Refer to your local IOLTA rules and *The ABA Guide to Lawyer Trust Accounts*, which I wrote.

[24] *Repeat that both letter and check should be returned.*

[25] *Set Date for Return of Engagement Letter.* Clearly indicate that you will assume the "client" has obtained other help to prevent the "client" coming in two years later claiming you undertook the case even though you never heard from the client again. Let there be no misunderstanding that you are doing nothing further until you receive the signed fee agreement and the check.

[26] *Clarify Any Loose Ends.* Give the client an opportunity to ask if anything is not clear.

[27] *Have the Client Sign the Fee Agreement, and Get Your Retainer for Fees and Costs.* Upon execution and return of the fee agreement, you have a client, and the client has a lawyer.

Other items to consider in your fee agreement:

1. Existence or nonexistence of malpractice insurance. This disclosure may be required in some states.

2. Possibly include a schedule of anticipated fees and costs, including faxes, photo reproduction, possible experts, depositions, and charges for file retrieval and copying after the case is closed.

3. Special provisions for potential conflict waivers.

4. Special provisions for multiple client representation.

5. Late payment penalties.

6. Who does or does not get copies of correspondence.

7. Where and how communications can be sent.

8. Requirement that fee disputes be arbitrated if allowed or required by local rules.

9. Relationship to third parties who guarantee or pay fees.

Referral Fees or Division of Fees

The payment or expectation of referral fees or division of fees to lawyers outside of your firm is a subject of heavy regulation.

Payment

Paying money to a partner or associate lawyer inside your firm as "client origination" is normally permitted even though the lawyer getting part of the fee did nothing beyond introducing the client to another lawyer. Payment of referral fees or division of fees with nonlawyers outside the firm is always prohibited. In some cases, a lawyer not licensed in your jurisdiction is considered a nonlawyer. Payment of referral fees or a division of fees with nonlawyers inside the firm is usually permitted at year end under the guise or disguise of a "bonus" or profit sharing. In some jurisdictions a contract lawyer or of counsel may be subject to the division of fees rules.

In some jurisdictions division of fees is permitted if there is a sharing of work and responsibility. In some jurisdictions it is permitted if there is a sharing of work or responsibility. In some jurisdictions there needn't be any sharing of work or responsibility if the fee is purely a forwarding fee.

In these circumstances where a division of fees is allowed two additional conditions normally must be met:

1. The fee must be no higher than if only one lawyer were being compensated.

2. The client must either be notified in writing or consent in writing.

Again, this area is subject to heavy regulation.

Engagement Letters, Nonengagement Letters, and Disengagement Letters

In your first contact with a potential client, immediately get the client's name, residence address (not just a P.O. Box), e-mail address, and fax. You will need that information to send one of these letters. Do not accept any client without this basic information.

In addition to the engagement letter, lawyers need nonengagement letters (not undertaking the case or client) and disengagement letters (closing the file).

When this book was published in its first edition in 1976, it was considered controversial and even unethical because I advocated discussing the terms of the engagement and the fees with the client and memorializing the agreement in writing at the beginning of the relationship. What I recommended in the 1976 first edition of this book is no longer controversial or unethical, and it is now considered unethical not to have your agreement in writing.

Unfortunately, consumer expectations generally, and malpractice claims and ethics complaints specifically, now require just about everything to be in writing. The need for writings is especially high to protect the lawyer from nonmeritorious claims and complaints. Accordingly, I now recommend three types of engagement letters. The terminology is mine but has been picked up by most writers so that my definitions reflect mainstream practice, but others may use the terms differently or use different terms.

These letters protect both the client and the lawyer. Sample form letters for use as modified by you are included. They are

1. *The engagement letter*. (See pages 255–260.) This is the letter that establishes an attorney-client relationship and defines the work to be done and the financial relationship.

2. *The nonengagement letter*. This is the letter that says you have not accepted the case, the client, or any professional responsibility. I

have included an optional "Come back later when you have another matter" clause, as well as a "Don't call us, we'll call you" clause. This is especially important where there has been an e-mail inquiry.

3. *The disengagement letter.* (See pages 477–481.) This is the letter that attempts to end the attorney-client relationship for a given matter. This letter is important to establish the statute of limitations for malpractice claims and ethics complaints (where statutes exist). The letter also covers file and document retention and destruction and solicits client comment and criticism for improving the relationship.

Each of the letters is written in simple English because the test is not what you thought you said, but rather what a reasonable person, under the circumstances, would understand to have been said.

Each of these letters is a generic letter to be modified to fit the facts.

Nonengagement Letter

New lawyers will usually talk to anyone who will talk to them. New lawyers are often eager to demonstrate their great expertise and knowledge. New lawyers are often accosted by friends and relatives at social and civic events and are often the victims of people who call claiming to have gotten the name and number from the Yellow Pages, their Web site or some person totally unfamiliar to the lawyer.

The purpose of a nonengagement letter is to protect both the lawyer and the nonclient. It is important for the nonclient to understand that you have not undertaken professional responsibility for the matter and the nonclient is still without counsel. It is important for the lawyer to be protected from the claim of someone who claims the lawyer undertook to represent the person.

You can still be held professionally responsible both with respect to malpractice and ethics in the following circumstances:

1. You never asked for or received any fee.

2. You only talked with the person by telephone one time and had no further contact until the malpractice claim.

3. The person is a friend or relative with whom you casually talked at a wedding or social event and never saw again.

4. You met with the person as a *pro bono* or public service gesture.

5. You met with or talked to the person as the result of a court or bar association project.

6. You responded to an e-mail inquiry without making it clear the response did not commit you to do anything.

Nonengagement Letter

[1] Mr. Arthur Smith
1234 Main Street
Anytown, USA 12345
VIA US MAIL AND E-MAIL

[2] Re: Telephone Conversation of Jan. 3, 20xx
Meeting at Jones Wedding on Jan. 3, 20xx
Office Meeting of Jan. 3, 20xx

Dear Mr. Smith:

[3] It was nice meeting you (talking to you) on Jan.
[4] 3, 20xx. I am sorry that we cannot be of help to you in your boundary line dispute with Mrs. Peters. (Or whatever) As I related to you in the office (on the telephone) on Jan. 3, I do not feel it would be appropriate for me to undertake your case.

[5] [optional/see comments] As I explained to you, based on the facts given to me, I do not think your case is economically feasible to pursue. I would not be willing to prosecute the matter on a contingency basis and cannot in good conscience recommend that you spend your time and money on this case. If you do not care that the case is not economically meritorious, but wish vindication, I would consider representing you on

[6] a noncontingency basis with payment of the fee in advance. Again, I do not recommend this expenditure of money, even though you may be legally right.

[optional/see comments] This is not an area of law in which I feel competent enough to represent you.

[7] [optional/see comments] I have expressed no professional opinion on the merits of your case.

[8] I have given you no advice on any possible time limitations to your matter. There may or may not be a time limitation on your taking action.

[9] I encourage you to immediately consult with as many other lawyers as you wish without delay. It is possible that another lawyer will disagree with me and will be willing to represent you on a fee basis agreeable to both of you.

[10] If you cannot find another lawyer, I recommend that you immediately contact the Wilshire County Bar Association Lawyer Referral Service at 123-123-1234.

[11] I have returned to you all of the documents that you showed me and have not kept any of your papers.

[12}   [alternative] I am returning herewith all of the documents you left at my office. I have not kept any of the documents you showed me.

[13}   I repeat again that we have not taken this case and we will not do any work on it and have not accepted any professional responsibility for the matter.

[14}   I would hope that at another time you would again give us the opportunity to be of service to you. We certainly would welcome your return on a different matter should the need arise. I am enclosing some general information about the firm and I will place you on our firm mailing list so that you can receive the information that we send to our clients from time to time.

        Very truly yours,

        I.M. Sorry
        Attorney-at-Law

[15}   bcc: Prospective Clients

Comments

[1] Begin all initial contacts with asking the client for a card or for a name, address, and phone number. Be extremely careful when the prospective client doesn't want to tell you. Ask why he or she won't tell you. If you have any funny feelings hang up or walk away or ask the person to leave. Make a note of the event for your "Prospective Client" file. It is possible you are being set up for something. Don't accept further information without this information. If a potential client balks at giving the information, tell the potential client that e-mail provides the fastest way to send written communication and you need a street address, not a P.O. Box, when documents have to be signed and returned immediately.

[2] Specify the contact(s) you had with this person. This person might at a later date confuse you with another lawyer and erroneously bring a complaint or claim against you.

[3] Say something nice in the body of the letter. Refer again to the contact(s).

[4] Try to refer to the nature of the matter in the letter to remind the person and yourself at a later time what the contact was all about.

[5] I like to give the person an honest reason why I don't want to take the case. If the case is not meritorious for whatever reason I

like to tell the person why I feel that way. I want this person to come back in the future when he or she does have a meritorious case. Some malpractice insurance companies prefer that you give the person absolutely no opinion or assistance.

[6] Surprisingly, many potential clients will respect your honesty and will hire you because you told the truth. They can accept losing the fight, but they cannot accept not even trying to win. I have earned many good fees and even won some of these losers and gained clients for life by simply telling the truth. This is why I disagree with the insurance company recommendation to give no advice or opinions.

[7] I do not give any advice on the statute of limitations until I have a paying client. If you gave the wrong advice you can easily incur liability. You should not give any advice on the statute of limitations until the client signs the fee agreement and you have a paying client and you have made a thorough examination of the underlying facts.

[8] Encourage the client to seek help from other lawyers. It is possible that you were wrong in your assessment of the facts.

[9] Give the person the telephone number of the local Lawyer Referral Service. They will either try to find a lawyer to help or refer the person to the appropriate government social welfare office. This may protect you from the double claim of doing nothing and abandoning the client's case after you have taken it.

[10] Keeping client papers may lead the client to think you have undertaken the case. Create a record that you kept nothing.

[11] If the client left any papers, send them back.

[12] Make it as clear as you can that you have not accepted the case and you are not going to be doing anything on it.

[13] There's no harm in keeping the door open for business on another matter at another time or for a referral from the person. Additionally, getting his or her name into your database will make it easier for you to find the person at a future time and to do a conflicts search.

[14] Create a file called "Prospective clients" and put the copy of this letter and any handwritten notes you had and copies of any documents you copied into this file.

Balancing the Public's Need for Legal Services and the New Lawyer's Need to Eat

Foonberg's Rule: You must limit the amount of *pro bono* work you do. If you do enough *pro bono*, you become *pro bono*.

Society as a whole has an obligation to provide legal services to those who need them. Lawyers as a part of society should bear their proportionate share of this burden.

There are some ignorant, misguided people (including some new lawyers) who feel that lawyers alone are obligated to bear the entire burden of society. This is not now, and never has been, the case.

The lawyer who feels that each lawyer is obligated to do free legal work for anyone who wants it should not go into private practice unless he or she can get a subsidy from some organization.

Ethical Considerations 2-16 and 2-26 from the Model Code of Professional Responsibility state the situation as fairly as possible and are submitted here for your consideration.

Financial Ability to Employ Counsel: Generally

EC2-16 The legal profession cannot remain a viable force in fulfilling its role in our society unless its members receive adequate compensation for services rendered, and reasonable fees should be charged in appropriate cases to clients able to pay them. Nevertheless, persons unable to pay all or a portion of a reasonable fee should be able to obtain necessary legal services, and lawyers should support and participate in ethical activities designed to achieve that objective.

Acceptance and Retention of Employment

EC 2-26 A lawyer is under no obligation to act as adviser or advocate for every person who may wish to become his client; but in furtherance of the objective of the bar to make legal services fully available, a lawyer should not lightly decline proffered employment. The fulfillment of this objective requires acceptance by a lawyer of his share of tendered employment that may be unattractive both to him and the bar generally.

Keep in mind that when a private-practice lawyer does free legal work, another lawyer may be deprived of a job in a publicly funded agency.

I submit that private-practice lawyers should earn a good income and then devote some portion of that income to activities that simultaneously provide work for other lawyers and provide lawyers for people who can't afford them.

I also believe that during the first few years the new lawyer should concentrate on building a solid financial basis for a practice so that in later years there will be resources available for charitable enterprises. If the new lawyer does not first build up a practice, there never will be a later time or later resources to devote to society as a whole.

You may be tempted to take nonpaying cases "for experience" or for a combination of experience and *pro bono* motives. If you do so, try to limit this type of work to about 5 percent of your time or about two and one-half hours per week at most.

If you are doing nonpaying work as part of your marketing activity (getting to meet paying clients and referrers of paying clients), you may wish to devote up to four hours per week.

As much as you want to help those who need your help, you have to limit your giveaway time or you'll be out of business and unable to help clients or yourself or your family.

How to Set Your Fees

No matter how long you practice law you'll make a lot of mistakes when you set fees. As a new lawyer you are obviously more vulnerable to making mistakes in fee setting than the more experienced lawyers.

There are no simple formulas for fee setting. Platitudes are plentiful and concrete advice is hard to come by. Acknowledging in advance my inability to give you a simple panacea, I'll try in this chapter to give you general rules for fee setting, emphasizing the problems you'll encounter in the early part of your career. Hopefully you won't quote $3,000 for a fee when you should have quoted a $300 fee, or vice versa.

Fee Surveys

The Law Practice Management committee or section of your state or local bar association probably conducts periodic surveys of prevailing fees being charged by firms for given types of work. These fee surveys are typically done by firm size. Bar associations don't like to disseminate these survey results for fear they will be equated with the old minimum fee schedules, which are generally not used anymore. You may have to ask the Practice Management Committee or your Bar Practice Management Advisor Chair of your bar association to get this information.

Other Lawyers

In my opinion the smartest thing you can do to get a handle on fee setting is to ask another lawyer. The other experienced lawyer will be able to give you some help in ascertaining the important factors that will affect fees and costs. If you explain to the other lawyer that you don't know what you are doing he or she will help you. Obviously you will get only generalizations. These generalizations are much better than nothing.

Contingency Fees

Contingency fees are common in some types of work such as personal injury and are absolutely prohibited in other areas such as criminal matters or domestic relations.

1. *Personal Injury/Auto Accident.* Fees are commonly quoted by formulas such as "one-third if no lawsuit is necessary or 40 percent if a lawsuit is necessary" or "one-fourth if settled before filing of suit or 40 percent if settled after suit is filed but before 30 days of trial date and 50 percent if tried or settled within 30 days of trial."

2. *Personal Injury/Assault and Battery.* Fees of 40 percent to 50 percent with a cash minimum fee of $300 to $600 or more paid in advance are common. Collection of judgments is difficult as there is often no insurance.

3. *Personal Injury/Slip Fall.* Fees of 45 percent to 50 percent are common due to difficulty of establishing liability.

4. *Personal Injury/Medical Negligence.* Usually slightly higher than personal injury auto accident due to high cost of preparation of case and difficulty of settlement until you are "on the courthouse steps."

5. *Workers' Compensation.* Depends on local practice. Private fee contracts not permitted or valid in some jurisdictions. A private fee agreement may even be illegal.

6. *Commercial Collections.* Usually 25 percent to one-third of collections, based upon amount involved.

Lump Sum Fees

This involves setting a lump sum fee regardless of how little or how much work is involved. This is very common in criminal matters and domestic relations. Although this method has the greatest potential for being grossly unfair to either the client or the lawyer, it seems to be the most desired by clients who prefer a fixed fee. Since both you and the client will be relatively unsophisticated, this method is probably best for both of you.

A word of advice. If you grossly underestimated the fee, that's your mistake, not the client's. Continue doing the very best job you can on the case. When you finish the case tell the client what you should have charged. About one time in twenty-five a client will offer to pay the difference to bring the fee to the proper amount. Be careful not to suggest that the difference be paid. As with friends and relatives, the client has no way of knowing the value of the services unless you tell him or her. If you did $4,000 of work for $1,500, tell the client. The client should know the value of what has been received and that you're a person of your word. The client will respect you and use you again.

Minimum-Maximum Lump Sum Fees

For the new lawyer this method is also good when you can't get an accurate handle on the exact amount. Give the client a range of minimum to maximum. For example: "I cannot give you an exact fee quotation at this time since the amount of work required will depend upon how aggressively the other side fights. The minimum fee will be $500 and the maximum, to and including trial, will be $5,000." Minimum fees must be "reasonable" or they will be refundable.

Hourly Rates

I don't recommend the use of hourly rates in the first several months for new lawyers for two reasons:

1. The time you devote to a matter in many instances will be inordinate due to your inexperience. It's not unusual for something to take you twelve hours the first time, including research and drafting, because you are starting from ground zero. The second time, using your form file as an aid, it may only take six hours; the third time perhaps only three hours and the fourth time one hour or less. There are many things I can do now in an hour that took me from ten to thirty hours the first time I did it. Based on purely hourly rates the inexperienced lawyer will be more highly compensated than the more experienced lawyer.

2. You'll frighten the client away. It is difficult if not impossible to quote an hourly rate of $150 per hour to someone who earns $85 per day. There simply is no communication between you. If you estimate that the work should reasonably take ten to fifteen hours and you want $100 per hour, then tell the client the cost will be between $1,000 and $1,500 and don't mention time.

Sophisticated business executives are used to being charged on an hourly rate; lower- and middle-class people are not used to paying on an hourly rate.

After you've been in practice six months or so you'll have enough background to be able to quote hourly rates where appropriate.

Fee by Stages

There will be cases where you simply cannot quote lump sum fees and where you don't want to quote hourly rates. You should try to break the work into "stages," estimating the work for each stage and then setting a fee for each stage as you go. An example would be as follows:

1. Research as to merits of case and written opinion: $350.

2. If I believe the case is meritorious and collectible, our fee will be one-third of recovery, giving you credit for $350 paid.

3. If I believe the case has uncertain merit or uncertain collectibility, you may use other counsel with no further obligation to us or you may proceed further as set forth.

4. Drafting of complaint: $350.

5. Law and motion appearances (prior to answer): $750 (includes two appearances if necessary; additional preparation and appearances $300 each if required).

6. Propounding or answering written interrogatories (four sets anticipated): each $100.

7. Deposition preparation and attendance: $300 per deposition of less than four hours, or $650 if more than four hours and less than ten hours.

8. Trial estimated (five days): $750 per day.

9. All other services not covered above: $100 per hour.

10. You may stop using our services at any stage simply by so notifying us. If we accept the case on a contingency basis and you

subsequently discharge us, our fee will be the greater of one-third of any offers received prior to or within five days of being terminated or $100 per hour. If we decide not to proceed further after taking the case on a contingency, then you will have no further obligation past the $350 and out-of-pocket costs advanced.

Bonuses

I personally believe that fees should be related to results. I pay substantial bonuses to employees based upon money they earn for the firm or money they save the firm with management suggestions and secretarial productivity. I also believe in billing clients over and above the agreed hourly rate when we accomplish unusually good results for the client. On the other hand I sometimes reduce a fee below the agreed hourly rate when the results are poor for the client. I have rejected substantial fees based upon purely hourly compensation where the client was not agreeable to a bonus. I have refused to accept a case based on a purely hourly basis, where I would have earned between $25,000 and $50,000, because the client was not agreeable to a bonus of 10 percent of the amount saved. The amount in the case was in excess of $1.2 million, with another $300,000 in interest and penalties involved. I was not about to accept professional responsibility for $1.5 million for 2 percent to 3 percent of the amount involved. I would have been happy to accept the fee arrangement if the amount involved had been about $500,000.

While the numbers involved here may be beyond what you can reasonably expect in your first year or two, the concept is the same for smaller amounts.

It goes without saying that the "bonus" must be agreed to in concept if not in exact amount as soon as possible in the case. The concept of a fee predicated in part upon the results obtained and the amount involved is recognized by most existing state bar rules.

Setting Fees after the First Year or Two

After you've been in practice a year or two, much of the mystery in the fee-setting process will be removed, although some will always remain. You may wish to use different methods, examples of which follow (these methods are not necessarily recommended):

1. *Supply and Demand.* Charge all you can get in each case, subject to the fee not being unconscionable or "clearly excessive."

2. *Follow the Leader.* Charge what your contemporaries charge on the theory that they know what they are doing (a premise of doubtful reliability).

3. *Take What the Client Pays and Be Grateful.* This is a sure way to bankruptcy court (your personal bankruptcy). Remember that even churches doing the work of God have to close when their parishioners don't give enough.

4. *Decide Your Own Value:*

    a. Estimate the number of chargeable hours you work per year (Factor CH).

    b. Set the net dollar profit you wish to earn per year (Factor P).

    c. Estimate your overhead per year (Factor O).

    d. Hourly rate = (P + O) divided by CH.

5. *The Big Mac Formula of Fee Charging.* McDonald's is one of the world's most sophisticated marketing companies. They operate thousands of stores all over the world. Their prices in any given store reflect local labor, food, and other operating costs. Their prices also reflect the economic abilities of local buyers to pay for their products. The product is uniform; it is the price that changes depending on local costs and the local economy.

It has been suggested that a law firm in a community could base their hourly rates on the price that McDonald's charges for a Big Mac in the community.

Guidelines might be as follows:

	Price of a Big Mac/$ 1.50
Clerk Not Yet Admitted:	50 times price = $ 75 per hour
Brand New Lawyer:	100 times price = $150 per hour
After One Year:	110 times price = $165 per hour
After Two Years:	120 times price = $180 per hour
After Three Years:	130 times price = $195 per hour
After Four Years:	140 times price = $210 per hour
Five to Ten Years:	150 times price = $225 per hour

It goes without saying that prices of many goods and services including lawyers are probably going to be higher in Manhattan than in a small community in Montana or North Dakota. Many large multinational companies get much of their legal work done in smaller communities throughout the United States and outsource to vendors outside the United States where hourly rates and operating costs are lower than in their headquarters city.

The new lawyer should also not be afraid to raise his or her hourly rate to reflect experience levels.

You might wish to play with the numbers based on local hourly rates, but this method may be of help to you.

Legal Fees and the Code of Professional Responsibility

The ABA Model Rules of Professional Conduct cover fees in Model Rules 1.15(a) and (d). Unfortunately, the code is of limited help to the new lawyer. It is very helpful in analyzing a situation in retrospect, but isn't very helpful to the new lawyer who wants to quote a fee to the client sitting across a desk.

I suggest you read Model Rule 1.15 and try to apply it within the context of the suggestions in this chapter.

Should You Charge for the Initial Consultation?

Our firm does not charge separately for the first consultation. We feel that the public should not be afraid to see a lawyer when they want to find out if they need professional help. After we have gotten the facts we advise them that they do or that they don't require professional help. (See points 3 and 4 in sample fee representation letter in "The Fee and Representation Letter" chapter.) We include the initial consultation services in the first bill if we do further services for the client.

Other lawyers tell the prospective client to bring a check to the initial interview. I feel that demanding a fee in advance for the first consultation leaves the public and potential clients with the impression that the lawyer is more interested in making money than in helping the client.

I have no proof, but I feel that our method gives the clients respect and confidence and encourages candor in relating the facts. I also feel that the client understands that we are sincerely trying to help. I also feel this establishes our professional concern that the public can get access to a lawyer rather than appear to be a money-grubbing slick business.

In many cases, the free initial consultation is a form of pro bono in that the client receives very limited legal advice when there is no source of payment.

Costs

Be sure to cover the subject of out-of-pocket costs. Filing fees, medical reports, depositions, expert witnesses, jury fees, etc., can cost more than a potential recovery. To the client, fees and costs may be indistinguishable. Be sure you look up your local ethics rules on advancing litigation-related costs such as filing fees and non-litigation-related costs such as car rental. If you advertise "No Recovery No Fee," you may be required to warn a client about costs if the case is lost.

Making Yourself Affordable Without Lowering Your Fee
(Alternative Billing Arrangements)

A client may honestly believe they can't afford to pay for the legal services they need. In some cases they are right, and it is better not to start something that won't be finished. A client rarely benefits from only half the legal services they need, and a lawyer rarely benefits when there is a large fee that will never be paid.

On the other hand, there are many situations where the client could afford the fee if there were a method or plan to get the fee paid within the economic ability of the client to pay the fee.

The lawyer and the client must work together and be creative in order to benefit both the lawyer and the client.

In this chapter, I will touch upon some of the methods that might work. I also wish to recommend a book on this subject I have co-authored with J. Harris Morgan entitled *How to Draft Bills Clients Rush to Pay*, Second Edition, which is available from the American Bar Association. I have no economic or financial interest in the book (nor this book either). I recommend the book as an expansion of this chapter.

Attitude

Begin with an attitude that you and the client are a team working together for mutual benefit, not an adversarial situation with each interested only in his or her own economic situation.

Listed here are some of the methods of alternative fee arrangements that might work in a given situation. An extremely short description of each is given. For more information, see the book *How to Draft Bills Clients Rush to Pay*.

1. *Credit Card Financing.* Clients can often easily obtain additional credit cards or additional credit that allows them to make low monthly payments.

2. *Borrowing.* A client may be able to borrow funds from a relative, friend, employer, credit union, bank, etc., or other person who will accept repayment within the client's ability.

3. *Wholly Contingent Fee Payable from the Proceeds of the Matter.* The client will often end up paying more than an hourly rate would have been, but shares the risk and the profit (or loss) with the lawyer.

4. *Partially Contingent Fee.* You work for break-even or small profit work plus a bonus based on results obtained.

5. *Reverse Contingency.* Like contingency, you work at break-even or low profit with bonus if client pays less than anticipated.

6. *Sale of Assets.* Often a client is in the process of selling an asset or hadn't thought about selling an unneeded asset and is willing to use part of the proceeds toward legal fees.

7. *Refinancing an Asset.* When interest rates go down, a client may be able to obtain cash from a refinancing with no increase in the amount of each monthly payment.

8. *Sharing Work to be Done.* Client or client's employees do work under your general supervision and direction that you or people in your firm might have done.

9. *Flat Fee (Also called Fixed Fee).* Client only pays the specific amount he or she can afford. You decide if you are efficient enough to make a reasonable profit at that fee.

10. *"Farming Out" Work.* Outsource some of the work to lower-priced people and companies. Using law students, newly admitted unemployed lawyers, foreign lawyers who will work for free, retired lawyers and judges are simply examples. Be careful about application of the division of fees rules.

11. *Matching Payments to the Client's Cash Flow.* Clients often receive cash at regular or irregular intervals. Time payments to you to coincide with their receipt of cash.

12. *Lower fees for routine repetitive client work after your learning curve has been met and you can establish systems and technology to reduce per unit cost.*

13. *Spreading Your Work Out Over a Period of Time to allow lower payments.* Be sure you are not prejudicing client's matter if

you and client are agreeable and understand pluses and minuses of delay.

14. *Taking a "Piece of the Action."* This is common in some industries (entertainment, high tech) where the client is sophisticated and has their own lawyers to advise them of the agreement's benefits and detriments. This can be a dangerous way to go and requires a giant case.

15. *Suggesting Alternative Legal Action.* Mediation or arbitration may be more affordable than litigation.

16. *Other Methods.* In many situations there are an appropriate number of ways to make legal services affordable if the client and the lawyer work together to reach a common goal, which is "affordable legal services at reasonable fees."

Unbundling of Legal Work

This is a newly developing concept with many serious ethical concerns. One lawyer defined it as doing half the work for half the fee. As a new lawyer, be careful about trying to use this concept unless you truly understand the ethical and malpractice concerns and the client will know what you are doing and, more importantly, what you are not doing. It is not being discussed further here.

In summary, with some homework and discussion on your part, you may be able to make yourself affordable without lowering your fee.

Don't Quote Fees or Give Legal Advice over the Telephone or by E-mail to New Clients

In discussing charging for the initial consultation in the last chapter, I said that some lawyers do ask the client to bring a check in advance of the initial interview, and that others don't require a check in advance of the initial interview. Both schools of thought have one thing in common, which is: *Get the client into the office for the interview.*

Don't be seduced into the trap of quoting fees or giving legal advice over the phone or by e-mail. As a new lawyer you'll want to talk to a prospective client all you can to impress him or her with your legal knowledge and ability to handle the case.

Be wary of the "client" who won't come into the office for an appointment and who is trying to pump you for legal advice by telephone. In addition to pumping you for legal advice, these clients will continually try to get a price quotation over the telephone. When you ask these people how they got your name they'll typically be very vague. They'll say that someone whose name they don't know at a bank or at a party recommended you. They may claim they were referred by the bar association, but they'll never be recommended by any client you know of.

This type of person will absolutely refuse to come into the office even when you say there's no charge for the consultation. You'll get some story about being in town for a few hours or some other crazy excuse. When you ask for a phone number or address to contact him or her, you'll get another long story, giving neither address nor phone number.

This type of person has absolutely no interest in using you for a lawyer. He or she may have gotten your name from a phone book or some client who owes you money. In most instances this person already has a lawyer and is trying to use your advice and fee quotation to get the other lawyer to reduce a fee.

You are a fool if you give legal advice to this unknown person over the telephone or by e-mail. When you get sued for malpractice two years later by this "voice," you'll have only yourself to blame.

Be firm. Tell the "voice" that you can't quote fees or give legal advice until after you've interviewed the client to be sure you have all the relevant facts and have examined the relevant documents. Don't waver. You'll be better off. If this person never comes, you won't have lost a client; you'll have lost a freeloading problem. It's hard to say "No" when you're a new lawyer who wants all the clients possible, but believe me, it's the best thing.

Be wary of clients who claim they found your name in the Yellow Pages if you don't advertise in the Yellow Pages, or in your Web site if you don't have a Web site.

"Cash Up Front"—
Shelly's Rule and Foonberg's Rule

Tens of thousands of lawyers have heard me correlate Foonberg's Rule and Shelly's Rule in my programs, but this is the first time I am doing so in writing.

You might remember Shelly's Rule or The Rule in Shelly's Case or perhaps it sounds familiar but you can't remember it.

Shelly's Rule is: If A makes a conveyance to B for life, remainder to the heirs of B, A has not created a life estate and remainder. The conveyance will be treated as though B gets a Fee Simple.

My reason for discussing Shelly's Rule is that we are discussing fees, and it's simple (you may have to read the foregoing sentence 3 or 4 times until you understand it).

The client who can't or won't pay cash up front is usually the same client who can't or won't pay cash during the case or at the end of the case.

If you didn't remember Shelly's Rule or the Rule in Shelly's Case, perhaps you can remember the Rule in Foonberg's Case or Foonberg's Rule, which is:

You will then normally be left with one of two choices:

1. Do the work and not get paid or
2. Don't do the work and not get paid.

Foonberg's Rule is that it is better not doing the work and not getting paid, than doing the work and not getting paid, and you'll only learn whether or not you'll get paid when you ask for "cash up front."

Getting Money Up Front
from New Clients

Abraham Lincoln is reputed to have said, "The lawyer should always get some part of his fee in advance from the client. In this way the client knows he has a lawyer and the lawyer knows he has a client."

Whether you call it a deposit or an advance, or a retainer, or any other name, the concept is still the same. Before doing a significant amount of work for a new client, the lawyer should always obtain part, if not all, of the fee in advance. It is not fair to the client or the lawyer for the client to undertake legal services that he or she cannot afford. I advocate that it is better for the lawyer not to do the work and not get paid than to do the work and not get paid.

Most people who seek the services of a lawyer expect to pay. A responsible client will not start expensive litigation if it is known that you will have to stop work if the fee is not paid as agreed. The client who cannot afford to pay for the services is not likely to pay the retainer fee in advance, thus saving the lawyer a lot of unpaid work. The prospective client who asks, "Don't you trust me?" should be answered, "No, why should I? I don't know you yet. If I can't protect my own legal interests, then what kind of job could I do protecting yours?" The same client who would be angry or insulted over paying some money in advance is usually the one who will be angry and insulted over your bill after you have done the work.

I am not advocating that you not do *pro bono* public legal work or just plain free legal work for experience. I am saying that you and not the client should decide when you are going to do nonpaying legal work. Being the most-loved lawyer in town won't help when you are evicted from your home and have to list your secretary's salary on a bankruptcy. We are dealing with an economic issue.

How to Handle "Cash Up Front"

"Cash Up Front" is commonly known as Foonberg's First Rule.

Cash up front is an essential litmus test to find out where you will stand when it comes time to get paid.

When you get the cash up front, you have to know how to handle it. The starting point is to review your fee agreement. If the cash is intended to be simply a deposit against future work to be done then it must go into the trust account until earned at which time it must come out of the trust account. If the cash is a "minimum fee," then it is your money when received and cannot go to the trust account. "Minimum fees" are looked upon with extreme disfavor, because in most cases the fee is not reasonable when little or no work has yet been done. The fee would likely be considered unreasonable or not reasonable or possibly unconscionable.

When a client contests the amount of a fee that has been received and put into trust as required, the contested amount must be returned to the trust account until the matter is resolved.

Avoid using the term "retainer fee" unless you and the client both understand what it is for. A true retainer fee (as opposed to a deposit) is earned the moment it is received and cannot go into the trust account. A true retainer fee is normally paid and accepted for the sole purpose of being conflicted out and not being able to take the other side in the case.

In a true retainer situation any work done would cause additional fees to be charged and paid. When what you mislabel as a "retainer" is in reality a prepayment of fees providing for a certain amount of work to be performed, the "retainer" must be deposited to the trust account until earned. When earned, or after a specific time period passes, the "retainer" can be withdrawn from the account and deposited to the office account.

In some states the word "retainer" is defined in accordance with local practices. Such fees are not uncommon in the world of corporate takeovers. In most other cases, the retainer fee would be deemed unreasonable and would have to be returned to the client on demand.

Cash Fees

When a client offers you cash fees, call in a secretary or another person to count the money and to give a receipt to the client. Deposit the cash intact in the bank with the deposit ticket indicating the source of the fee. Be very careful about the client who makes some sort of remark to the effect that the cash is "hot" or that he or she is not keeping any record of payment of the fee. When the client says that only two people will know, the two of you, tell the client that that's one too many, namely, him or her. This type of client is a good candidate to try to blackmail you at a later date. He or she will threaten to turn you in to the IRS if you press for a unpaid fee. Such a client may also threaten to turn you in to the IRS unless you "lend" him or her money. When you get cash fees, go out of your way to let the client know that you've recorded the fees in your books and will report them in your income tax return. (As a new lawyer you won't have the problem of being in too high a tax bracket.)

If you do receive a large cash fee, remember you may have to make a special report to the IRS ($10,000 in a single transaction or series of transactions). You may also have to concern yourself as to the source of the fee, because one or more government agencies may try to seize or forfeit your fee for themselves.

If you ignore the rules, you and the client may both be "investigated" for money laundering. The government may then try to disqualify you from representing the client. One government agency may claim "money laundering" to get otherwise privileged information about the client's activities, and then give what they find to other government agencies that could not otherwise have obtained the evidence. In short, be extremely careful when cash fees are involved. Ask an experienced lawyer for help.

Client Costs

The subject of cost advancement is subject to debate and disagreement in many jurisdictions. The purpose of this chapter is not to take any position, but to caution the new lawyer that you can go broke advancing costs. Costs should always be considered and handled from a cash flow point of view, keeping in mind your economic survival from a profit or loss point of view and also from a case acceptance or rejection point of view.

Never be afraid to ask an experienced lawyer what out-of-pocket costs and fees should be anticipated in a given type of case and at what stage of the proceeding they will have to be paid.

If at all possible, you should not have to finance client costs. You are not a bank or financial company. You should always ask the client for estimated costs in advance to place in your trust account to be used as needed and replenished as used. You should ask for costs in advance even in contingency fee cases.

The reality of life, however, is that you will be financing client costs for a number of reasons, such as:

1. Indigent client with meritorious case.

2. Convenience. You "lay out" the money for the client because it is more convenient, especially with smaller amounts such as long-distance telephone calls, court fees, etc.

3. The competition. Other lawyers in your community don't ask for or get costs up front and you're afraid of losing the client if you insist. In some cases you should ask the client for costs up front, but indicate to the client that if necessary or convenient, you can advance them subject to monthly reimbursement or reimbursement at the end of the case (meritorious accident cases, corporate formation, etc.).

In some cases you shouldn't take the case unless the client puts the costs "up front" (slip falls, doubtful recovery cases, etc.).

In some cases the amount of costs required on a meritorious case is so large that neither you nor the client can afford the costs, in which case you should associate in a well-financed law firm that can advance the costs for cases that require large amounts of investigation or outside experts (antitrust, medical malpractice, etc.) and cases where the pretrial, the trial, and the appeals will take years.

There are companies and groups of lawyers who finance legal matters, but I have never used them and don't know much about them.

Be careful about "lending" money directly to a client for living expenses, medical expenses, or other purposes. Loans to clients are absolutely prohibited in some jurisdictions and allowed under certain circumstances in other jurisdictions.

Don't forget to put all advanced costs into your trust account for later disbursement. You may deposit cost reimbursements (you already spent the money from your general or office account) directly to the office account, but it is the better practice to deposit the cost money directly into your trust account and then reimburse your office account from the trust account after the costs have been advanced by you.

The Importance of Cash Up Front
for Survival
(Also Known as "Foonberg's Rule")

The concept of "cash up front" is a critical one for two reasons:

1. The case selection process for all lawyers, new and experienced.

2. Economic survival for new lawyers.

Foonberg's Rule of "cash up front" can also be stated in three additional ways:

1. The client who can't or won't pay you cash up front at the beginning of the case is the same client who can't or won't pay you cash during the case, and is the same client who can't or won't pay you cash at the end of the case.

2. As I said earlier, if you choose between doing the legal work and not getting paid or not doing the legal work and not getting paid, you are better off not doing the work and not getting paid.

3. A bona fide client who seriously cares about his or her case will give you a cash advance for costs and/or fees to the best of his or her ability. Flaky clients or those who are holding back on telling you everything will not advance cash on their own cases because they know things either about the case or themselves that would affect your accepting or rejecting the case. (There will be some exceptions in criminal cases.)

Getting Paid by Client Credit Card

At one time, accepting credit cards was considered unprofessional. Doctors, dentists, CPAs, architects, and other professionals not only accepted them but prominently displayed signs indicating acceptance of credit cards. Lawyers finally joined the others in accepting credit cards.

New lawyers should be eager to accept credit card payment instead of chasing clients for monthly payments.

The discount you pay is a cheap price compared to the costs of bookkeeping and bad debts.

Banks are better equipped than you to grant credit and do the bookkeeping for monthly payments.

If you become a "merchant" you will be able to accept credit cards from your clients to pay their fees instantly by mail, by fax, in person, or by telephone. Your ability to accept credit card payments can open up new vistas of fee-paying clients.

Your bank will set you up as one of its merchants if it really wants your total banking business. If your bank doesn't want to set you up as a merchant, try other banks. If no local bank wants you as a merchant, you may end up going to an Independent Service Organization (ISO). ISO is a middleman between you and the bank. The ISO represents a bank, often in another state. The ISO guarantees your account with the bank against forgeries and frauds.

There are about 1,500 ISOs in the United States at the time of writing this chapter. There are all sorts of monthly and transaction fees to pay for being a credit card merchant. You should shop around among ISOs to get the best deal you can. Some bar associations now have deals with ISOs for their members. Check it out.

During the writing of this chapter, I am working with the American Bar Association to offer merchant status to every ABA member as a member benefit. If this program is in place when you read this book, it will be worthwhile for you to join the ABA just to get merchant status and be able to make credit card payment available to almost every client. (Certain types of cases such as bankruptcy may be excluded.) What you collect on otherwise uncollectible fees will more than pay your membership dues. Be sure you replace the discount with your own money if the credit card payment is going to your trust account. If the ABA does not offer this member benefit check out other geographic and specialty bar groups.

At one time, there was indecision concerning getting legal fees paid by credit card. This indecision is long since history and there is no valid reason not to accept credit card payment. (Many clients want to use credit cards to get airline mileage.) If you intend to use the clients' authorization to submit credit card charges without getting the client's signature each time, be sure to cover it in the fee agreement.

If you take a credit card for a payment that belongs in the trust account, you should immediately issue an office check or make other arrangements with your bank to reimburse the credit card discount so that the trust account balance reflects the full amount paid by credit card before the merchant discount.

Your doctor and dentist and the rest of the world accept credit cards and so should you.

Financing Your Practice with Bank Credit Cards

Credit is like medicine; properly used when and where appropriate, it can alleviate pain and discomfort and/or cure a temporary ailment. Improperly used credit, like improperly used medicine, can become addictive and even dangerous, to the point of doing permanent damage.

Financing your new practice for short periods with credit cards, in whole or in part, can be done, but it must be done very carefully and only as a last resort when you have no alternative.

The secret of financing yourself successfully with credit cards is to get as many credit cards as possible that allow cash advances or equivalent traveler's check purchases. The cash advances can be used just as loans from the bank to pay office bills that must be paid in cash. The cash advances also can be used to make payments on other credit card accounts to keep them current when you previously have used them for cash advances or for purchases.

Shop Around for Merchants Who Accept Credit Cards

Merchants accept major credit cards to give them a competitive advantage over those merchants who do not accept them. It is a form of promotion. It often is cheaper for the merchants to pay a bank a small percentage of a sale than to maintain their own credit departments.

When ordering merchandise or services, or when establishing relations with a vendor, always ask, "May I pay by credit card?" Often, although a company will accept credit card payment, it does not advertise it, preferring to ship C.O.D. or prepaid.

You may have to be imaginative or creative. For example, a book publisher may not take a credit card for payment, but you may be able to special order the same book at the same price through a bookstore that will accept credit cards. Your insurance company or agent may sell you insurance with monthly payments. When the company or agent offers you this payment schedule, it is called "premium financing" if it charges interest. You may wish to accept its financing and use credit card cash advances for the monthly payments, although this could cost you double interest, once to the insurance company and again to the bank. On the other hand, you should shop around. You may find you can buy an identical insurance policy or coverage through an agent or company that does accept credit cards for payment. If you can find such an agent, you can bypass the insurance company's financing. If prices, quality, and service are otherwise about the same, always use a vendor who accepts credit cards so you can use that vendor when it suits you.

Getting Bank Credit Cards

It is much easier to get credit cards than to get equivalent bank credit. The same bank that will give you $5,000 to $20,000 credit on a credit card might turn you down if you asked for a $10,000 loan. The bank's credit requirements on credit cards are more liberal than the credit requirements for a loan. You can check out the various bank card fees and rates on the Internet. When interest rates are low you will be deluged with credit card offers.

Go for "mileage" and "points" or cash rebates. Many credit cards will earn you points or mileage making vacations possible that are otherwise unaffordable. Some credit cards offer a cash rebate of up to 5 percent. Look for the best deal.

How Banks Earn Huge Profit on Credit Cards

(You either can take my word for it that credit cards can be an extremely profitable business for a bank, or you can read the rest of this paragraph to understand the mechanics.) When you buy a $1 item from a seller and pay with a bank credit card, you technically are signing a sales draft, which is something like a check. The merchant deposits your draft the same day and receives instant credit for the $1, less a discount that can run from 1 to 8 percent, but which is normally about 3 percent. The bank gives the merchant cash or credit to an account when it deposits your draft. Assuming a 3 percent discount, the merchant gets $.97 cash. You are expected to pay the bank the $1 within thirty days. Therefore, when you pay as agreed, within thirty days, the bank has earned $.03 interest from you on a $.97 advance to the merchant. Thus, the bank will earn about 37.11 percent interest on an annual basis. If you pay the bank over a period of time, you will pay an interest charge of about 15 to 19 percent per year on the $1 you signed for, even though the bank gave the merchant only $.97. Assuming you pay 18 percent on the $1, this is actually 18.56 percent on the $.97. Accordingly, the bank will earn from 37.11 percent (if you pay your credit card bills within the interest-free period) to 55.67 percent (if you pay the bill in installments). The bank could charge you only about 16 percent on a normal loan of cash based on prime-rate loans. (All prices are based on current information.) To protect this high-interest income and to push credit card use, merchants sometimes are prohibited by law or by contract from giving cash discounts to non-credit-card users.

Why Banks Give Out Cards Readily

Banks, as demonstrated, earn very high interest rates on their bank credit card business, whether you pay within the time limits without interest (euphemistically called "service charges") or over a period with interest. In a recent *Wall Street Journal* article, it was estimated that 94 percent of all Americans who want a bank credit card already have one. Accordingly, banks must push their cards onto the few people who do not already have one, using very low, if any, credit standards. Alternatively, the soliciting bank must try to get you to accept and use a second or third or fourth card when you already have one or two from another bank. If you had to go through a difficult procedure to obtain a card, you would not bother if you already had a good card. This is why banks send out unsolicited preapproved credit card applications. You may receive these applications from banks you have never heard of, in places you may never have been. To get help "pushing" the cards, the bank will give a kickback to bar and other associations, airlines, or other groups for help and recommendations in the marketing of the cards. Often, a charity or bar association gets a rebate or kickback when you use one of its "affinity cards."

Get All the Cards You Can

Consider the annual credit card membership fees as a form of "standby credit" expense. Large corporations often pay a bank a "standby fee" for unused credit. If you have to pay $50 per year to get a $3,500 line of credit, you are paying a 1.4 percent standby fee. If you pay no annual fees the first year, you are paying a seven-tenths of 1 percent standby fee the first two years. You ultimately may want a large number of credit cards, depending on the credit limit of each and the amount you eventually will need.

If you buy supplies or equipment using credit cards, from a large variety of vendors, you actually may have an offsetting savings through the reduction in the number of checks you have to write each month and you may save bookkeeping time, costs, and bank service charges, based on the number of checks written.

Paying Your Credit Card Debt

Banks don't want you to pay off your credit card purchases on receipt of the bill. They want you to be in debt in order to earn interest. In general, a bank makes maximum profits on credit cards (in addition to the annual fees you pay and the discounts the merchants pay) when you owe them about $3,000 or more. Some banks will want to charge you higher annual fees if you pay the bill on receipt.

If you are going to pay all your bills on receipt, you should seriously consider getting and using credit cards that give you airline mileage or some sort of rebate, either in the form of cash or trade. Almost all airlines have some form of credit card affiliation where they give you mileage when you charge. If it weren't for the mileage, the annual fees and finance charges on some of the cards would be ridiculous. On the other hand, if you pay the bill on receipt, the mileage can be an extremely valuable rebate and well worth the annual fee. Since most mileage tickets start at 25,000 miles, and the mileage is sometimes only good for three years, in most cases these cards are only worthwhile if you can charge at least $15,000 per year. Assuming you pay your bills on receipt and assuming you will charge about $15,000 per year, you will have bought an airplane ticket for the annual fee, which typically runs about $50 to $85 per year. Many lawyers finance their hotel and airfare for vacations using only credit card points.

Try to pay your credit card bill on receipt. You can authorize direct charge to your bank account by the credit card company but run the risk of paying unauthorized and fraudulent charges. Some credit card companies delay billing for several days after the cutoff date to shorten the period you can pay without finance charges. Be wary when the credit card bills never bear a postmark showing the true date of mailing.

Other rebates are available toward automobile purchases, cash credit on travel, gasoline, etc. It's worth thinking about.

Never Go into Default

Whether you pay in full on a current basis, without interest charges, or whether you pay in installments, never miss a monthly payment. As long as you pay on a timely basis, whether it be in full, within the no-interest period, or monthly with interest, the computer will show you are paying "as agreed." Paying "as agreed" will enable you to increase your line of credit and will result in a favorable credit rating when you seek additional cards and use the existing cards as a reference. Always use each card each month. Although it may be a nuisance to use all those cards and to write a lot of checks, use of the card creates an active status, which further improves your credit.

Seek the Maximum Line of Credit on Each Card

After you have received the card and used it for a period of time, call the bank (usually a toll-free number) and ask what is involved in getting a slightly larger line of credit. In some cases, you can obtain additional credit simply by asking for it by telephone. In other cases, you will have to request it in writing. Sometimes, the bank will treat your request for additional credit as a brand-new credit application and ask for references, financial statements, etc. Surprisingly enough, the same bank that gave you an unsolicited $3,500 line of credit without checking you out when it wanted you to take a card might consider you an unworthy credit risk when you submit financial information requesting $1,000 more on your line of credit. Once you have a higher limit, you have what amounts to a line of credit and don't need to reapply for a loan every time you need cash.

Never Use Any Card to Its Maximum Credit

Always leave a margin of unused credit on each card. Your payment check could get lost in the U.S. mails, lost in the mailroom of the bank, or applied to the wrong account. If this happens, you could make a subsequent purchase that, unbeknownst to you, brings your total debt beyond your credit limit. The bank's computers will be alerted and you'll be placed on a special list that could cause forfeiture of the card and negative or derogatory comments on your credit standing.

Understand the Interest Rates You Are Paying

When using credit cards, you should understand that you may be paying an interest rate of from 15 to 36 percent, that you are paying an annual fee that may be considered as just more interest, and that you may be foregoing cash discounts or lower prices that might be available if you do not use a credit card. When you add up all of these costs, you will see that credit card interest can be very expensive.

On the other hand, when you learn the true interest rates you pay on an automobile loan, a second mortgage, or a small personal loan from your friendly finance company, you may be surprised to learn you are not paying much more for credit card interest than for the other forms of interest.

The difference in rates between credit card interest and that of alternative forms of financing (if you can get the alternative financing) is not so great as to make the difference between success and failure as a lawyer. A lawyer pays rent for the use of an office and pays a rent called interest for the use of money. There are high-rent districts and low-rent districts, both for money and for offices.

Don't Mix Personal and Business Charges on the Same Credit Card

By using a separate card for the practice you'll make your life easier when you have to prepare your income taxes.

Never, Never Use a Credit Card Without a Clear Plan on How You Are Going to Pay for What You Purchase

Before you use the card, decide how you are going to pay for the projected purchase, even if you have to plan on getting a cash advance from that card or another card into your checking account to write the check to make the minimum monthly payment(s). Using a credit card with the intention of not paying the resulting debt is obtaining money or credit under false pretenses (fraud), and can result in jail or denial of discharge in bankruptcy. A criminal conviction or bankruptcy can cost you your license to practice law.

Improper credit card usage is a common factor in bankruptcy. Debt counselors often have an advisee symbolically cut all credit cards in half with a pair of scissors as the first step toward financial stability. By overuse of credit cards, at some point you simply will overextend your credit and end up in serious financial difficulty. As I said at the beginning of this chapter, credit is like medicine and must be used properly.

In conclusion, when planning your cash flow for the first year, you might wish to consider credit card financing if you can't get sufficient financing from a relative or bank at no interest or at low interest. In the final analysis, although credit card interest rates are high, the difference between credit card interest rates and other interest rates available to you is not going to make the difference between your making it and not making it as a lawyer. You must discipline yourself to use the cards properly and never to abuse your credit. Properly used, credit card financing enables you to get your practice off and running and to keep it running.

At the time of writing this edition, interest rates are at historic lows. Many people are refinancing their homes to pay off their credit card debt. Home interest debt is usually tax-deductible while credit card interest is usually deductible only in specific situations. If you are fortunate enough to own a home, consider the possibility of refinancing your home if credit card debt gets out of control.

Do Not Get or Use Debit Cards

You should neither apply for nor use a debit card unless you truly understand the differences between a credit card and a debit card. Many banks blur the applications to make you think you are applying for a credit card when you in fact are applying for a debit card.

Most credit cards have limits on liability for lost or stolen cards. These limits may be as low as $50. Some debit cards "limit" your liability to all the money you have in the bank. Many new lawyers have thanked me for this advice. Again, only apply for or use debit cards (or credit cards) if you truly understand the terms of the deal.

How to Get Cash Up Front to Reduce Bad Debts and Increase Cash Flow and Avoid Going Under

As a practicing CPA, I quickly learned that the most common cause of new business failure is undercapitalization. Over the years, the statistics put out by the Small Business Administration bear this out. In other parts of this book, I have emphasized the importance of minimizing overhead and cash outlay in the beginning of your practice. I have also dwelled heavily on how to borrow money. I have also indicated the importance of the concept of cash up front (Foonberg's Rule) in the case selection process.

In this chapter, I will cover how to use the cash-up-front concept. Perhaps you will be able to modify these examples to fit your own situations. First, things you can say at the interview:

1. "Mr. Jones, it is office policy to ask new clients for a cash retainer. This retainer will be placed in a trust account and used for payment of fees and costs to other people. Each month we will send you a statement and will simultaneously draw upon the trust account for payment of these fees and costs." The amount of the fee will be fixed ten days after sending the statement unless objected to in writing within the ten days. (This may allow you to keep the money without returning it in the event of a fee dispute.)

Alternative a. "When we have used up the funds in the trust account, we will then bill you monthly and will expect you to pay upon receipt of the bill."

Alternative b. "Each month we will expect you to send a check payable to the trust account to replenish the funds used." (This type of trust account arrangement is often called an "evergreen account." As the account is ever green, the color of money.)

2. "You can discharge me at any time and I will simply refund the unearned funds to you." (This reassures the client who is afraid you won't do the work after the funds are paid.)

Other things you can say and do:

1. "I tried to pay my secretary with accounts receivable, but the supermarket wanted cash from my secretary."

2. "Mr. Smith, you appear to have a meritorious case and I am willing to invest my time and overhead in your case and get paid my fee when the case closes, but I'm not a banker. I don't lend money to clients or anybody else. I expect you to advance $_____ to my trust account to be used for out-of-pocket costs. None of the money will go to me for fees, but I expect you to advance your own costs."

3. For some reason that I am at a loss to explain, clients react favorably and understandingly when I say, "Cars need gasoline, and my car is no different. I can't buy gasoline with accounts receivable." Clients invariably say "I understand," and either write out a check or send in a check.

Ask for a third-party guarantor or cosigner. Don't be ashamed to ask your client for a third party to guarantee the bill. The client's employer or a relative are common choices. Depending on the technical definition of "guarantee" or "guarantor," you may wish to have the third person be "jointly and severally liable" rather than a guarantor.

4. "Mr. Smith, neither you nor I want you to start the case, then have to abandon it or postpone it in the middle because you can't pay your bill. It's better for both of us for you to pay the legal fees in advance so you won't have to worry about it if you run out of money one or two years from now during the case."

There is no substitute for simply asking for the cash up front in a simple, forthright manner.

When to Discuss Fees During the Initial Interview

Clients want you to discuss fees. They don't know how or when to bring up the subject. It's up to you to bring up the subject. Your initial interview should be limited to one hour. Interviews of more than one hour may exhaust you or the client. At about forty minutes into the interview you should ask, "Would this be a good time to discuss fees?" You want to discuss fees before agreeing to do any work. You may want to modify the work to be done based on the client's ability or willingness to pay fees.

How to Word Invoices That Clients Are Happy to Pay

The basic secret in invoicing is to tell the client everything you did. There is no such thing as an invoice that is too long. If you do a good job of preparing invoices, clients will think they're getting a bargain and will be glad to pay them before you reconsider how little you seem to be charging.

When you keep the client happy by informing them of what you do, the invoice reminds them of what you did.

Source of Information for Invoices

The source of information for invoices is your time records. If you recorded everything you did, then preparing the invoice will simply be a matter of transferring the services-rendered record from your time records to the invoices.

Remember Kipling

To paraphrase Rudyard Kipling:

I met six honest serving-men
(They taught me all I knew);
Their names are What and Why and When
And How and Where and Who.

How to Word the Invoice

The most important thing in invoicing is to list every single document you prepared or reviewed. Clients often think that lawyers are in the stationery business. They ask, "How much for a will . . .

or a partnership agreement . . . or a lease . . . or a lawsuit?" List every single letter, court form, document (including the number of drafts or revisions) that you worked on. Also indicate whether you reviewed the document or prepared it or revised it. Also list the forms your secretary prepared, including such documents as summonses, declarations or returns of service, and instructions to the clerk of court. Examples of three invoices are included at the end of this section.

Be careful about repeating descriptions in your invoices. A common cause of client complaint arises when the client thinks that you have double charged or triple charged for the same thing. If you worked on drafting a contract several times during the week or month, you must vary or change the wording or at least use words like "further" or "continued" in describing the work.

Example:

Feb. 2, 2004: Draft contract 1.50 hours
Feb. 6, 2004: Draft contract 3.00 hours
Feb. 7, 2004: Draft contract 1.00 hours
Feb. 9, 2004: Draft contract 3.00 hours

The client may think you are charging erroneously for work you already did. The client will probably question or doubt the bill. It would be better at the very least to say "continued" drafting of contract or "further" drafting of contract.

The best invoice that a client would be happier to pay might read something like this (taken from your time records):

Begin drafting of contract. Outline major provisions. Discuss names and identities of contracting parties with client.

Continue drafting of Smith contract. Discuss arbitration vs. litigation with client. Use arbitration clauses. Analyze percentages referred to in contract. Telephone conference with client about application of percentages.

Continued work on contract. Assemble miscellaneous provisions as required and applicable.

Further drafting of contract. Verify signatures needed. Assemble documents with references to exhibits to be attached. Prepare index of page references. Prepare cover letter to client asking client to review and comment and enclosing first draft.

Services rendered Feb. 2, 6, 7,9, 2004;
total services rendered, 8.5 hours.

You easily get the idea. The more you can vary the descriptions of what you did, the more the client will appreciate that you did a lot of things and didn't make a mistake by repeating a bill for what you already had done.

Billing for Telephone Calls

Clients despise paying for telephone calls. Even our most-sophisticated clients grit their teeth and mumble when charged for telephone calls. However, the same clients gladly and willingly pay for correspondence or other tangible "stationery."

When clients call and ask a question about legal rights in a given fact situation, they balk at paying for that advice. ("All I did was ask a simple question about mechanics' liens that didn't require any work" is a typical response to the bill.)

On the other hand, if you immediately sent a letter repeating the facts given you and your opinion, the client will gladly pay for "correspondence and telephone conference concerning Mechanics' Lien Law." As an added benefit, you decrease your malpractice exposure by repeating the given facts or questions in the event the client later claims he or she gave you different facts.

Show Dates of Services

Your invoice should show every single date you worked on the matter even if only a minor service was rendered on a particular date. A client will usually be impressed by the fact that you worked on his or her case on six or seven different dates during a month. This technique lets clients know you are giving their cases continual attention.

Do NOT list the date opposite the service rendered unless your client wants you to do so. List the dates at the end of the invoice. If you worked on a single document on two different dates, the client erroneously may think that you are double billing if you show the same or a similar description twice, and become a common cause for unnecessary nonmeritorious client complaints and concerns.

Ask Your Client

Ask your clients, especially business clients, if they have preferences in the wording or presentations of invoices to them. Whenever possible, do it their way. Simply following the herd and doing what some other lawyers do may unnecessarily irritate the client and cause lack of confidence in your efficiency or honesty.

Show Litigation

If there is a pending lawsuit, always show the name(s) of the case(s), the court(s) where the matter is pending, and the case number(s). Clients know that litigation is expensive (because you warned them at the inception of the matter), and by listing the court information you remind them monthly that the matter is expensive because litigation is expensive and not because you are expensive.

Your client may wish you to use the *Uniform Task-Based Management System Litigation Code Set* available from the ABA Section of Litigation. (See **http://www.abanet.org/litigation/utbms**)

Don't Show Number of Hours of Service

Unless your fee agreement requires you to spell out the time devoted to each part of the work, don't do it. Listing each and every service and time often upsets the client over some minor aspect of the invoice and is a common cause of unnecessary delay in paying the bill.

If your fee agreement requires showing the hours worked, show the hours at the end of the invoice after all services are set out. Do not show every time detail alongside the work done unless the client asks for it.

Sample Invoices

Which invoice do you think your client would be most willing to pay?

Invoice 1

Re: Professional Services Rendered $450.00

Invoice 2

Re: Professional Services Rendered. Motion for Change of Venue and Answer to Complaint $450.00

Invoice 3

Re: Professional Services Rendered. Jones vs. Smith, Los Angeles Superior Court Case No. 123456: Analysis of Complaint; office conference with Arthur Smith to obtain facts of case and to discuss strategy of defending; preparation of Motion for Change of Venue, including Notice of Motion for Change of Venue, Points and Authorities in Support of Motion, Declaration of Arthur Smith in Support of Motion, and Declaration of Attorney in Support of Motion; preparation of Proposed Answer to Complaint; preparation of Declaration of Service by Mail of various pleadings. Telephone conference with Arthur Smith and opposing counsel concerning no settlement of case. Telephone conference with clerk of court and opposing counsel to obtain hearing date for Motion; preparation of Order Granting Change of Venue. (Services rendered January 4, 5, 7, 9, 11, 13, 15, 16, 25, 26, and 28, 2004.) $450.00

Always read your invoices before they go out. On reading the invoice you may find work or costs being charged to the wrong client. The client will not have much faith in the integrity of your bills and may be concerned that by billing another client for his or her work, you are violating attorney-client confidences.

Ask your clients if they want or need their bills in any specific format or style. They may or may not have a special reason for wanting their bills in a certain manner because of their accounting systems or accounts payable system or for income tax reasons as indicated. The ABA and The National Association of Corporate Counsel have developed a standard task-based system for billing litigation matters that some clients may want used. The system is free for the asking, but generally is for larger litigation matters.

Ask your clients where they want the bills sent. Some clients will have very specific instructions to send or not to send the bill to their offices or to their homes or to post office boxes.

Some clients want the bill only to say "Professional Services Rendered," with some sort of description in a separate document. Lawyers' bills are often subject to discovery and you may not want anything in the bill that might inadvertently tip off the other side as to where your strategy is headed. Some clients don't want their accounts payable staff or others to know what's happening in the matter. If you do produce invoices in litigation, remember to redact (blacken out) the work description.

How to Draft Bills Clients Rush to Pay, Second Edition, is a book co-authored by J. Harris Morgan and myself and further expands this chapter. It is available from the ABA.

The Importance of Monthly Billing

Invoices should generally be sent out monthly. You pay secretaries and clerks two to four times a month. You pay rent, telephone bills and bank loans monthly. You need income on a monthly basis. You cannot pay payables with work in process or accounts receivable. Monthly billing lets you match your income against your expenses.

Monthly billing lets the client know you are constantly working on his or her matter. It is a status report.

Monthly billing is also a status report to the client reminding the client of all the things you did for the client during the month. Even if the client is not going to pay until the conclusion of the matter, the monthly billing with the words "payment not yet due" will remind the client of your efforts. Weekly or biweekly billing may be appropriate if you are concerned about your client's ability to pay.

Monthly billing allows you to determine when a client cannot or will not pay a bill.

Clients prefer to make progress payments as the case progresses rather than be shocked with a big bill at the end of the case or end of the month. You are not doing the client any favor by letting bills run up that can't be paid. If the client is not happy with the results of the case, there may be an unwillingness to pay the last bill.

If the client cannot pay legal fees "as you go," you should consider handling the case on a contingency fee basis. If you have a low opinion of the merits of the case or the collectibility and don't want to proceed on a contingency basis, then you should be fair to the client and try to dissuade him or her from the litigation. Encourage the client to seek other counsel who may disagree with you as to the merits or collectibility, and who will take the case on a contingency fee basis. If there is no possible recovery and a defense is necessary, the client should be directed toward an agency with publicly paid lawyers.

(See chapter on "Cases and Clients That Should Be Turned Down.")

Billing More Often Than Monthly.

From time to time I'll offer a client billing on the first and fifteenth of each month or, on a few rare occasions, even weekly. Sometimes the client will want this because he wants to slow down or stop a matter when the fees reach a certain point or when it becomes apparent they might reach that point. I don't mind doing it because I'll know much sooner if I have a problem developing, and I know the client will feel more in control of the costs.

Final Billing on Completion of a Matter

Even though you have been billing your client monthly, there will be a final bill. This bill is usually a fairly large one because of the work normally incident to the conclusion of a legal matter. You will have put in a lot of time in trying the matter or in negotiating the settlement and drafting the documents.

There are three basic reasons for getting in the final bill as soon as possible after the matter is concluded:

1. *The Client's Financial Condition.* Often the client is about to receive or pay a large amount of money as a result of the conclusion of the case. If the client is going to receive funds, you want to be paid before they are dissipated. If the client is going to pay the money (or go bankrupt) this may be your last chance to get paid.

2. *The Amount of the Bill.* Typically, the bill will be much larger than prior bills and the client may feel shocked at the size. (This will especially be true if you didn't call the client before sending the bill, to warn the client it will be big.)

If you have the courage to do so, and it's not in violation of your fee agreement, ask the client for an extra-large deposit for fees and costs or monthly deposits to be placed in your trust account. Ask for the money so that you are paid for the final trial two months before you start doing the final work. This will give the client an advance warning you will need the money and will give the client time to raise the money for you.

3. *The Client's "Curve of Gratitude."* I created the famous Client's Curve of Gratitude based on one of my cases when I was a new lawyer. It has often been copied, and is based on a concept in an article in *Medical Economics* and is found on page 309. Obvi-

ously, the time to send the bill is between points 8 and 9. Practicing lawyers have related to me that they actually show the graph to clients when a client is late on paying the final bill.

After studying the Client's Curve of Gratitude, you'll understand the importance of sending a final bill when the matter is concluded.

My client's curve of gratitude has been translated into many languages and is often found and placed on lawyers' desks (facing the lawyer).

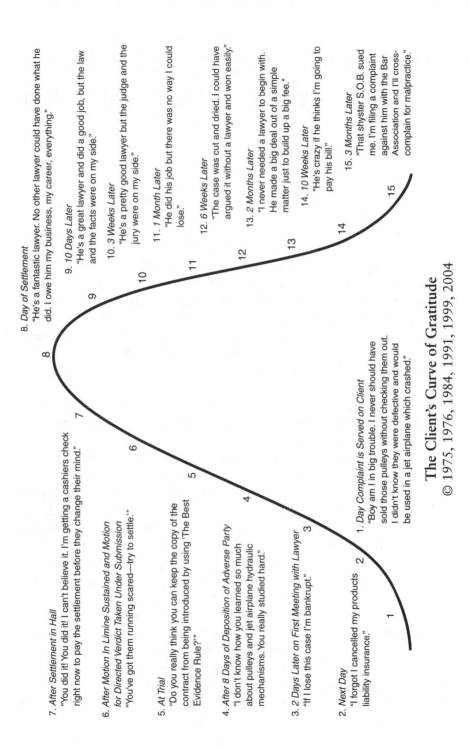

7. *After Settlement in Hall*
"You did it! You did it! I can't believe it. I'm getting a cashiers check right now to pay the settlement before they change their mind."

6. *After Motion In Limine Sustained and Motion for Directed Verdict Taken Under Submission*
"You've got them running scared—try to settle."

5. *At Trial*
"Do you really think you can keep the copy of the contract from being introduced by using 'The Best Evidence Rule?'"

4. *After 8 Days of Deposition of Adverse Party*
"I don't know how you learned so much about pulleys and jet airplane hydraulic mechanisms. You really studied hard."

3. *2 Days Later on First Meeting with Lawyer*
"If I lose this case I'm bankrupt."

2. *Next Day*
"I forgot I cancelled my products liability insurance."

1. *Day Complaint is Served on Client*
"Boy am I in big trouble. I never should have sold those pulleys without checking them out. I didn't know they were defective and would be used in a jet airplane which crashed."

8. *Day of Settlement*
"He's a fantastic lawyer. No other lawyer could have done what he did. I owe him my business, my career, everything."

9. *10 Days Later*
"He's a great lawyer and did a good job, but the law and the facts were on my side."

10. *3 Weeks Later*
"He's a pretty good lawyer but the judge and the jury were on my side."

11. *1 Month Later*
"He did his job but there was no way I could lose."

12. *6 Weeks Later*
"The case was cut and dried. I could have argued it without a lawyer and won easily."

13. *2 Months Later*
"I never needed a lawyer to begin with. He made a big deal out of a simple matter just to build up a big fee."

14. *10 Weeks Later*
"He's crazy if he thinks I'm going to pay his bill."

15. *3 Months Later*
"That shyster S.O.B. sued me. I'm filing a complaint against him with the Bar Association and I'll cross-complain for malpractice."

The Client's Curve of Gratitude

© 1975, 1976, 1984, 1991, 1999, 2004

How to Make Clients Happy to Pay Legal Fees by Selling Them Stationery

Foonberg's Rule #1: Bombard your clients with paper.

Foonberg's Rule #2: "cc" means "client copy."

Clients often have difficulty understanding that you are selling your professional advice. Professional advice is intangible. You can't see it or feel it; there is always a natural reluctance to pay for things that you can't see or feel. I have given this and similar advice in other parts of this book, because I feel the advice is important enough to be repeated.

Clients believe that lawyers are in the stationery business. They will ask you, "How much do you charge for a will . . . or a lease . . . or a lawyer's letter . . . or a lawsuit . . . or a partnership agreement?" Clients rarely ask you how much per hour you charge. Therefore, try whenever possible to convert your advice into stationery.

For example, a client calls and asks you a question about garage mechanics' liens. You tell the client that the mechanic at the garage has a lien on his or her car for up to $750 for parts and labor. If you send the client a bill for the telephone call for $35 you will get an angry response over being charged for a "telephone call." ("All I did was ask a simple question about mechanics' liens that didn't require any work," is a typical response to the bill.)

On the other hand, you should immediately send the client a letter repeating the facts given you, and your opinion. This protects both you and the client. Send the client a photocopy of the applicable statute. He or she will gladly pay $95 for "correspondence and telephone conference concerning mechanics' lien law." As an added benefit the lawyer decreases (or increases) malpractice exposure by immediately repeating the given facts or questions asked in the event the client later claims different facts were given.

According to a recent ABA study, 84 percent of satisfied clients reported that their lawyer had kept them informed of what was happening on their case while 66 percent of dissatisfied clients reported that their lawyer did not keep them informed of what was happening on their case.

Many clients save forever anything they receive from a lawyer. Make the client happy. Bombard him or her with copies of the paperwork. Clients can understand paying for paperwork. They often can't understand paying for "advice." Send copies of memos, statutes, cases, etc. Send them copies of pleadings and correspondence. Clients want the paperwork and stationery and will pay for it.

Keeping the client informed greatly increases client satisfaction and the probability of repeat business and referrals. Not keeping the client informed can easily result in an ethics or malpractice complaint that you have "abandoned" or "neglected" the client even though in truth you were working hard on the client's case.

I sometimes say to a client, "Mr. Jones, it is my office policy to send you a copy of everything that happens in your case. We do so automatically. In some cases, clients may know what's happening before I do because they will automatically get a copy while I'm in trial or out of the office."

Bombarding your clients with paper will eliminate or reduce wasteful client calls who want to know what's happening on their case. You may wish to get a big red rubber stamp "For your information—no reply necessary" or to put those words on a form cover letter to eliminate clients calling you to ask what the letter or document means.

E-Mail

This section is for the benefit of some foreign lawyers and some senior lawyers.

If you are familiar with e-mail, you can skip this section.

Many clients prefer e-mail to paper. "E-mail" means electronic mail. It can either go on telephone wire modem to modem or via the Internet. Information is sent electronically via a modem to a mailbox from which it is retrieved. E-mail is generally thirty times faster than fax. It can also be compressed for greater speed. E-mail allows the sender to send huge amounts of information in short periods of time at relatively low cost. There is no paper original or copy unless the sender or the recipient chooses to print out a hard copy. The recipient can print out only as much as he or she cares to print out. You can type or otherwise input (via scanning or voice recognition, for example) your data into a document. After cleaning up and perfecting the document into final form, you can send it as an "attachment" to an e-mail.

Many corporate counsel and corporate clients will not hire a lawyer unless the lawyer agrees to send and receive all information via e-mail. Some lawyers believe that faxes will be completely replaced by e-mail.

The speed at which e-mail can be transmitted and received depends on the speed of the sender's modem, the receiver's modem, and the intermediate transmission and compression system. Most communications packages can handle almost any modem speed commonly found in a PC.

An e-mail account (address and mailbox) can be obtained for free if you don't mind looking at advertising. Common sources are networks such as America Online, and CompuServe, and Internet services providers such as Netcom or Earthlink. Additionally you should check with what's available through your local telephone company. What is available changes frequently and companies go into and out of business or try to compete with each other to get subscribers.

Many organizations offer an e-mail address as part of ancillary services or member benefits.

With an appropriate notebook of e-mail addresses and appropriate software, you can simultaneously send the same message to hundreds of addresses with a single keystroke. You can send client news flashes relative to new laws or cases to any number of clients cheaply and easily.

It is false economy not to have and use e-mail. You can reach me by e-mail at **Jay@FoonbergLaw.com**, or you can reach me by the e-mail link on my Internet Web site, **www.FoonbergLaw.com**.

If you are concerned about privacy, various types and degrees of encryption are available. You should be aware, however, that telephone to telephone, e-mail, and fax are much more secure than using the Internet. It has been said that sending e-mail on the Internet is like sending a postcard; anyone who wishes to read it can do so and you might never know it has been read.

How to Make Money by Reading Advance Sheets, Technical Journals and E-mail Law Bulletins

I spend about an hour a day reading advance sheets, journals and e-mail law bulletins for the following reasons:

1. To be a good lawyer by keeping current on the law;
2. To make money;
3. To impress clients that I care about them and their legal matters. I read the journals with a red pen or highlighter in hand. When I find an article or new case that affects or may affect a case in the office, I circle or highlight it and write the case name and client name on the face of the journal as well as the page number where the materials can be found. If the information arrives by e-mail I print it and mail it with a cover letter rather than just forwarding it. I then dictate a letter. (You can do it the next day at the office or if, like me, you read advance sheets at home or on airplanes or during commuting, you can use a portable machine, as I do, to dictate it immediately.)

A sample letter would be as follows:

Ms. Mary Jones
123 Main Street
Hometown, USA
      Re: Jones vs. USA USDC Case No. _____
             Smith vs. USA decided June 1, 20____

Dear Ms. Jones:

     I am enclosing a copy of the decision of the Second Circuit Court of Appeals in the case of <u>Smith vs. USA</u>.

     This case was decided on May 15 and was just reported in the May 25, 20xx____ issue of the <u>Daily Journal</u>. A copy of the case is enclosed for your files.

The facts and legal issue of the <u>Smith</u> case may have an effect upon your case. The case was decided by the Second Circuit Court of Appeals in New York. We are in the Ninth Circuit here in Los Angeles, but nonetheless the Department of Justice (the trial lawyers for the government) will be aware of the case and it may affect the judge's decision in your case.

You will note that one of the principal issues in the <u>Smith</u> case is the principal issue in your case (deduction of travel expenses for spouses).

No response on your part is necessary. We thought you would appreciate receiving this information.

Very truly yours,

Enclosure: <u>Daily Journal</u> article

I prefer to print and mail an e-mail by snail mail as I believe it makes a better impression than receiving an e-mail with an attachment, or simply being forwarded. Clients like getting lawyer letters with useful information on fancy stationery.

Typical Client Costs

If you are handling a certain type of case for the first time or are not quite sure of yourself, ask an experienced lawyer for help in estimating the kinds of costs to be anticipated in a given case. The costs listed here are simply some of the typical or "classic" costs you are likely to encounter in any given type of case.

Litigation

Police reports, court reporter minimum appearance fees, transcript costs, deposition appearance fees, medical examinations, medical opinions and reports, medical testimony, investigations, photocopy costs, record-copying costs (employer and hospitals), expert opinion and testimony costs in addition to nonmedical, including accountants, actuaries, engineers, etc., sheriff's fees or other process fees, and travel expenses are typical litigation expenses. If the matter will require expert witnesses, be sure both you and the client understand their fees.

Business Formation and Businesses Generally

Advance payment of franchise or income taxes, filing fees for secretary of state or for county clerk, permit fees for stock issuance, transfer taxes, certified copies, recording costs (per page), newspaper notices and advertising, stock certificate, corporate seals and books, notarial fees, travel costs, long-distance telephone calls and express delivery costs, title searches and reports, and out-of-state lawyers are typical costs; there may be others.

You should always, when necessary, ask for help from other lawyers in estimating costs. Don't forget that advance costs go into the trust accounts.

Can You or Should You Pay or Receive "Forwarding Fees" or Referral Fees?

Can You Pay Such Fees?

To Lawyers?

This is a rapidly changing area and you must check your own local rules and get assurance from the other lawyer that all ethical requirements are being met.

As a general rule, you can pay or receive forwarding fees if you follow certain rules as set forth in Disciplinary Rule 2-107 and Model Rule 1.5(e). These rules are as follows:

1. The client knows there will be a division of fees and consents. This consent should be in writing. Local rules may require the consent to be in writing.

2. The total fee of the lawyers is no more than the reasonable value of what the client received. This is not usually a problem if the receiving lawyer charges a usual and customary fee and the lawyers share that fee. This restriction is intended to prevent overcharging the client to cover the fee splitting. For example, if a personal injury lawyer normally charges a contingency fee of 40 percent of recovery for a certain type of case, but increases the fee to 50 percent to cover the forwarding fee, then this fee conduct is probably improper.

3. There is a division in proportion to the services performed and the responsibility assumed by each. This is easier preached than practiced. I don't know how to divide responsibility proportionately. I suppose a written agreement between the two lawyers stating that they agree to divide responsibility proportionately is as close as you can come.

In some jurisdictions referral fee agreements must be filed with the court.

Read your local rules and ask more experienced lawyers what is the local practice. In some jurisdictions it is not necessary to share work or responsibility if a fee is purely a forwarding fee. The theory is that the referring lawyer earned his or her fee by selecting the correct lawyer for the client. The referring lawyer then can be liable for "negligent referral" if the wrong lawyer was referred the case.

In some jurisdictions payments to contract lawyers and to of counsels may be considered as a division of fees.

To Nonlawyers?

The world is changing. Increasingly, nonlawyers want "performance bonuses" for bringing in legal fees. Marketing directors, lawyers, staff, and others can be very creative in finding ways to get a "piece of the action" that hopefully does not appear to violate the rules. Remember, it's your license if they are wrong. In theory, fee splitting with nonlawyers is prohibited, yet some states seem to allow sophisticated systems of paying for referrals based on various factors. Improper fee splitting with nonlawyers is the second fastest way to get disbarred, running second after improper use of clients' funds. Improper fee splitting with nonlawyers is absolutely prohibited, and there are no ifs, ands, or buts. Indirect fee-splitting schemes might be just as wrong as direct payments. Sample fee-splitting devices that may or may not be prohibited include: paying "investigators" a percentage of fees; paying "landlords" or "business managers" a percentage of fees. Be very careful on paying nonlawyers amounts related to gross fees or net profits. The recipient risks losing a job. You risk losing your license. In some jurisdictions, an out-of-state lawyer is considered a nonlawyer.

Should You Pay or Receive Such Fees?

From a purely economic, short-range point of view, forwarding fees may be a very desirable policy for a new lawyer for the following reasons:

1. It encourages getting the client over to a qualified specialist rather than leaving the client with an inexperienced lawyer who is afraid to lose a fee.

2. On an hourly rate, both the sending and receiving lawyer get relatively well compensated at no increase in price to the client. This is particularly true in percentage and standard fee situations. The

specialist can accomplish the task in fewer hours and will get the fees more quickly.

From a long-range economic point of view, referring clients to others may be detrimental to the growth of your practice, since you've given up the major portion of your fee and since the client may refer other clients to the specialist rather than to you. Although a receiving lawyer should decline to accept employment on other matters from a previously referred client, this restriction does not apply to the people the client refers.

To illustrate: Suppose Ms. Client comes to you, Mr. Swellperson, with a case, and you refer Ms. Client to Mr. Specialist, who satisfactorily handles the matter. Two years later Ms. Client calls Mr. Specialist on an unrelated matter. Mr. Specialist should refer Ms. Client back to you rather than accepting the employment. In theory, this is simple. In practice, it often does not work. Ms. Client will usually say something along the line of, "I don't want to go back to Mr. Swellperson. It's you I have confidence in. If you won't accept my case, then I'm going to a third lawyer because I don't want to go back to Mr. Swellperson"; or the conversation may be to the effect, "I don't want Mr. Swellperson because he didn't want me." However you dress the package, the results are the same: Mr. Swellperson never sees the client again nor does he see the people referred by the client. On one hand, the referring lawyer may feel that the referred-to lawyer is stealing a client. On the other hand, the referred-to lawyer may assert the right of the client to choose lawyers without restrictions. Whether this result is good or bad or right or wrong is beyond the scope of this book.

Is There an Acceptable Middle Ground?

I believe there is an acceptable middle ground that is fair to the client and fair to you. I engage a specialist to work for me. I pay the specialist by the hour out of my own funds to get advice on how to handle the case and on the merits or value of the case. Often the specialist has no contact with the client at this point. The specialist should be paid a consultation fee up front by you (after clearing potential conflicts) and then be given the facts by you. The specialist will tell you if he or she thinks the case can be handled by you with assistance, or if the matter is so far over your head that both you and the client would suffer if you tried to handle the matter without the assistance of a specialist.

For example, products liability cases or aircraft crash cases may require tens of thousands of dollars for investigators and testing. A difficult medical malpractice case may require expertise possessed by few lawyers. A first-degree murder case is no place to get some experience before a criminal jury. There are many types of cases where you simply will not have the bankroll or expertise to handle a case simply because it's too big or too complicated.

On the other hand, if you can handle the case with the help of a paid specialist, you will have the best of all worlds in that you will still earn the major part of the fee, keep a well-served client and his or her referrals, and receive experience under expert tutelage. You may wish to put a sentence in your engagement letter giving you the right to engage or consult with other lawyers at no additional expense to the client.

In the Final Analysis, Should You Pay the Referral Fees?

On balance, during the first year of your practice, you should pay referral fees as asked for and permitted. Referrals from other lawyers can be a significant source of cases, experience, and fees in the beginning of your career. The case you get from the other lawyers will not be any bargain from a fee point of view, but if you play it straight and honest with the referring lawyer, he or she will gain confidence in your integrity and refer more cases to you. In most cases, the referring lawyers who send you the low-pay cases will not want a referral fee, but they might, and if so, pay it following the rules set forth in Model Rule 1.5(e).

Caveat

As a general rule, neither courts nor legislatures are concerned about fights between lawyers over fees.

Client Stealing

As indicated, the legal profession is divided on the issue of "client stealing" of referrals. It is my personal opinion that you should seek assurances from the referred-to lawyer that he or she will not accept new matters from the client unless and until clearing it with you. As a referred-to lawyer, or as a lawyer accepting over-flow work, you should not accept new matters from the referred client without clearing it with the referring lawyer. The short-term income advantage of accepting a matter may seriously damage your long-range prospects of receiving referrals in the future from the first lawyer and from other lawyers who find out what you did. As always, what you do may depend on current local rules.

The advice I have given here is general advice. It behooves you to make inquiry of local lawyers to modify this general advice to your local situation. The rules and law in this are changing rapidly, and you must be sure you are current. Some of this advice may be totally inapplicable to your local situation and, in fact, may even lead to unethical conduct, judged by local standards.

"Bedside Manner" in Setting Fees

1. *Be Firm.* No matter which method of setting fees you use, be firm. If you are uncertain or wishy-washy, clients will rapidly lose confidence in you as a potential lawyer to handle their cases. After all, if you can't set a value on your own services, perhaps they have no value.

2. *Use Words Like "Per My Standard Fee" or "The Standard Fee" or "In Cases Like This."* Instill confidence in the client.

3. *Don't Ask the Client What the Fee Should Be.* This is one way to guarantee the client's using another lawyer.

4. *Distinguish between Uncertainty in the Amount of the Fee and Uncertainty in the Manner of Setting the Fee.* When it is impossible because of the facts in the case to tell the client what the legal services will cost in total, you can still confidently set the method of computing the fee.

5. *Don't Back Down.* If you quote "one-third" or "$165/hour" or "$750" for the matter, don't back down when the client suggests one-fourth or $90/hour or $500 for the matter. If you back down, the client will think you were deliberately attempting to overcharge. The same client will again try to get a discount as a precondition to letting you close the case. What you look upon as an accommodation will be taken as a symbol of overcharging or dishonesty. If you are desperate for the fee or case, tell the client you will allow the client to pay some of the fee in monthly installments (a violation of my rule of Cash Up Front).

6. *Don't Be Swayed by What the Client Says Another Lawyer Charges.* Usually there is no other lawyer, or if there is or was an-

other lawyer, the client had no confidence in that person. Clients who really want to use another lawyer wouldn't be seeing you.

7. *Don't Be Tempted by the Client Who Wants You to Take a Case at a Reduced Fee with the Promise of More Cases Later at Reasonable Fees If You Do a Good Job on the First Case.* Take my word for it that there will be no later cases. Simply tell this client that in your office every piece of work has to stand on its own and pay its own way. Say that high-quality work can't be handled at low-quality fees, and if price is a principal consideration, you're wasting each other's time.

Put yourself in the position of a patient getting a filling. You ask the price. The dentist says, "My standard fee is $115." You state that you'll pay $95. The dentists says, "O.K." Aren't you going to be concerned about the quality of the filling you'll get?

8. *Be Sure You Bring up Fees at Your First Meeting.* (Note I said meeting/not phone call or letter.) Tell the client that you wish to discuss fees and that the client should never be embarrassed or ashamed to discuss fees with you. Don't leave the client wondering if you used a Ouija board to set fees. Try to limit your first meeting to one hour. After about 40 minutes, ask the client, "Would this be a good time to discuss fees?" Don't wait until the end of the interview. You may wish to modify the amount of work to be done based on the client's willingness or ability to pay a fee.

9. *Use the Number "5" in Quoting Fees.* Professional marketers have determined that people prefer odd numbers such as 3, 5, 7 and 9 to even numbers such as 2, 4, 6 and 8 when setting prices. $195/hour is more acceptable than $200/hour.

A lump sum of $2,500 is preferable to $2,400. Look at advertised prices in newspapers or TV ads to see how money prices end in the number 5. I'm not sure if the marketers are right or wrong, but I always try to include a 5 in setting a price.

10. *Suggest, When Appropriate, That the Client Borrow the Fees from a Credit Union or Relative.* When the client says he or she doesn't want to go to relatives, watch out. That person may not want to go to relatives because there is no intent to pay.

11. *Suggest, When Appropriate, That the Client Give You Collateral or Security for Payment of the Fees.* This is extremely important when the client may be defunct, bankrupt, or jailed if the case is lost.

12. *Suggest the Client Use a Credit Card or a Friend's or Relative's Credit Card.* Get written approval for future charges by your authorization.

Remember, you can't have all the legal business in your state. Don't be overly concerned when a client goes to another lawyer for no other reason than cheaper fees. In these cases it is your gain and the other lawyer's loss. Be pleased that a client who was more interested in price than quality went elsewhere.

In summary, when discussing legal fees, you should exude confidence at every stage and be firm. Remember, if you can't properly represent your interests, the client will not think much of you.

For a broader coverage of this area, read *How to Draft Bills Clients Rush to Pay*, Second Edition, by J. Harris Morgan and me. It is available from the ABA. I have no economic interest in that book (or this book either).

Alternative Dispute Resolution (ADR)

You would be wise to become "certified" as a mediator or arbitrator as soon as you can if certification is required by your state. Many courts and bar associations periodically have free or low-cost programs that lead to a certificate of some sort entitling you to receive assignments from that court as a mediator or arbitrator. In some states you must be a lawyer and receive a specific number of hours of training (typically forty). In other states, one need not be either a lawyer or trained to be a mediator or arbitrator if the parties are willing to use you. The rules for who may or may not be a mediator or arbitrator are not consistent.

In my opinion, ADR will eventually replace much, if not all, of litigation as now practiced, unless we can make the repairs the legal system desperately needs. The only real question is whether the mediators and arbitrators of the future will be lawyers or nonlawyers.

It is sad, but true, that our existing litigation system often does not provide litigants with an economical timely resolution of problems. The reasons for the shortcomings of the existing civil litigation system are beyond the scope of this book. My analysis of the reasons for the success of ADR is as follows:

1. People want to tell their story. Trial objections and motions in limine and the rules of evidence prevent people from expressing how they feel rather than what they observed firsthand.

2. People want conclusion. The delays and continuances of every stage of litigation are endless. Cases go on forever. People get their day in court, if, after the time has passed when the damage could be repaired. Appeals can be endless.

Abraham Lincoln is reported to have said, "A new inexperienced lawyer, never having handled anything can take on the simplest of all cases and it drags on for a year. An experienced lawyer can drag it out for three years."

It is commonly said that "Defense means Delay and Deny." Money is saved when claimants die or become desperate to settle for anything they can get when the case is delayed.

3. People want an economic resolution. Formal discovery rules and multiple continuances and delays drive up the costs of getting a day in court.

As a new lawyer, your clients may not be able to afford the economic costs and delays of the trial promised them by the U.S. Constitution. They may have to accept, as court ordered, mediators and arbitrators, people who have not been trained as judges and indeed are not even lawyers.

By suggesting ADR, your clients may be able to get an economic timely resolution of their problems otherwise unavailable in the litigation system, and you may be able to earn a fee that they can afford to pay.

Mediation works best when parties have a dispute where it is in the best interests of all concerned to continue some form of relationship on a basis acceptable to all concerned. Mediation works 85 percent of the time.

For a variety of reasons, many contracts and relationships require mediation and/or arbitration as a precondition to, or alternative to, litigation. You should determine if mediation or arbitration is required before beginning legal process. When a client has a litigation matter, your local rules may require that you discuss ADR with them.

You'll feel foolish trying to charge your client for all the work done in filing a complaint when you are faced with a motion to strike or demurrer because the agreement being sued upon required arbitration instead.

When and How to Withdraw from a Nonpaying Matter

In this chapter, I am limiting my discussion to the aspects of withdrawal due to payment factors. I recommend very highly to you Model Rules 1.7, 1.8, 1.9, 1.10, and 1.16(a) and your local rules, which cover withdrawals for other reasons such as conflict of interests, the lawyer's being a witness, etc.

To paraphrase a line from a popular play, "Poverty may not be a shame, but that doesn't mean it's necessarily a blessing." Don't let a client take you under, too. Get out when it is in the best interest of both you and the client.

As one lawyer from Canada told me, "If you're going to have to eat crow, it is better to do it when the crow is young and tender rather than waiting until the crow is old and tough."

Whether you call it "dropping the case" or "withdrawing from the matter," the end result is the same. The desired result is that you are no longer taking a financial bath and the client is free to make some other lawyer rich (or poor).

If you are unhappy with the economic arrangements for the case or the client, you are going to have difficulty psychologically observing the Model Rules that require you to *represent a client with zeal*. It should be obvious that if you like feeding your spouse and family, you may handle the paying cases and clients first, pushing the no-pay and poor-pay cases to the bottom of the pile where they may languish to the mutual detriment of both you and the client.

There are three possibilities with respect to withdrawing from a matter:

1. You cannot withdraw (you are stuck);
2. You must withdraw;
3. You should withdraw.

You Cannot Withdraw from a Matter

As a general rule, there are two instances when you cannot withdraw from a matter.

1. *The client has paid your agreed fee in full.* In this case, you have no recourse but to honor your fee agreement. You may not like the situation. If you erred in setting your fee, that's your problem. Chalk up your mistake as a learning experience. The next time a similar matter comes in, you'll have learned what a proper fee quotation should be.

You can sometimes get out of this mess by offering to refund 100 percent of the fees received. (Note: I said 100 percent, not some or part.) You should also offer to turn over your file to the client or to another lawyer.

Misunderstanding a fee arrangement is common with new lawyers because of their negligence in not putting the fee agreement in writing. I blame the lawyer, not the client, for misunderstandings. There is no excuse for misunderstandings.

2. *Your withdrawal would prejudice the client's case.* Although there are a few exceptions, you may not withdraw from a case unless you have taken appropriate steps to protect your client's rights. Oversimplified, you can't abandon your client on the courthouse steps a few hours before trial just because you haven't been paid. As above, if you allowed yourself to get stuck in this situation, you should grin and bear it. (See Disciplinary Rule 2-110(A)(2).)

You Must Withdraw

There are many times when you must withdraw from a case and these will be listed here. The problem from a financial point of view is whether or not you'll get paid for what you've done. As a very general oversimplification, you'll have a right to payment where the reason for the withdrawal is not your fault. If the reason for the withdrawal could have been, or should have been, foreseeable by you, then you probably won't get paid. In fact, DR 2-110(A)(3) may require you to refund what you've collected in fees.

The following is a "warning list" of situations where you may have to withdraw from the case after you've started working ("Forewarned is forearmed."):

1. *You intend to call yourself as a witness for your client's case or know you will be called as a witness in the case.*

2. *You will have a financial interest or loyalty to another client or person adverse to your client.* To a certain extent, all fee agreements are to some degree financially adverse to the client. This "adverse financial interest" problem is overcome if the client understands the situation and consents to it. You should protect yourself by getting the consent in writing when feasible.

3. *There is or may be a conflict between two or more clients.* This problem can be solved by the client consenting to the continued employment and waiving conflicts with a knowing waiver.

4. *You know, or should know, you are not competent to handle the matter and will not associate with a competent lawyer.* Under the old Canons, competence was not considered an ethical matter. Under the Model Code and Model Rules, a lawyer must associate with a competent lawyer when he or she is not competent to handle a matter.

5. *You know your client is offering forged or perjured testimony on material issues.* Clients do exaggerate and give their side of what they remember, but when the line is crossed and the lawyer knows the line is crossed, withdrawal may be mandatory.

6. *The client's case has no merit whatsoever and is being maintained for some ulterior motive such as delay or harassment.*

7. *Your conduct in handling the case would either be illegal or prohibited under the Model Rules.*

8. *You are fired.* The most obvious situation where you should withdraw is when you've been discharged as the lawyer. This raises the question of fees. In fixed-fee and hourly fee cases, you probably will be entitled to be paid in full for what you've done.

In cases where you've been paid in advance, you will have to refund some portion of the fee unless you and the client have properly agreed that the fee was a *minimum* retainer and that you earned it by accepting employment in the case.

In contingency cases, how much you're entitled to depends on the law in your jurisdiction. In some jurisdictions, you will be entitled only to *quantum meruit* recovery. In some jurisdictions, you'll be entitled to the contingency percentage on whatever offers you've already received on the case. In some jurisdictions, you'll be entitled to your contingency percentage on the final settlement obtained in the case, even though obtained by another lawyer or the client in "pro per."

Local Custom and Rules

In some jurisdictions and tribunals, you cannot be relieved as the lawyer for a corporation unless there is another lawyer willing to accept the case. This situation is created because corporations cannot represent themselves but can only be represented by a lawyer licensed to practice law. Keep this in mind when you undertake the representation of a corporation.

In some jurisdictions, you cannot be relieved in a criminal case once you have appeared. This is a throwback to the days before the extensive public defender system existed. In those days, private lawyers simply did work for free as a professional obligation that public defenders and other government-paid lawyers now do for salaries. Some judges, trying to avoid more work for overburdened public defenders, insist on a private lawyer continuing on the case for free. Fortunately, this practice is disappearing, and judges now let unpaid private lawyers "off the hook" and request the paid lawyers to take on the case.

Unfortunately, you are going to learn a lot of lessons the hard way. There are many areas of practice where you just can't get "off the hook" without your client's help. Divorce court, bankruptcy court, cases involving children or decedents or incompetents are typical situations. You will find that your client has disappeared, you haven't been paid, and you can't get out of the case. It's a real nightmare that will happen to you sooner or later in spite of the warnings of this book.

You Should Withdraw

In my opinion, you should withdraw from a case as soon as clients give you the indications that they're not going to live up to their fee agreement. Model Rule 1.16(b)(4) specifically allows a lawyer to withdraw from a case when the client "fails substantially" to live up to an obligation to the lawyer, such as a fee agreement (provided the lawyer can mitigate the consequences to the client of his or her withdrawal).

It is a basic rule of money management, reinforced by the famous "prudent person" dicta of your law school days, that losses should be cut short and not allowed to roll on. It is better for you (and your bank account) to lose out on three months' work on a nonpaying client than to lose out on six months' work. Cut your losses short. Take the time you would have spent on the nonpaying client and devote it instead to your paying clients.

How to Withdraw from a Case

The best way to withdraw from a case is to do so cleanly, honestly, and with as much advance notice in writing to the client as possible. A series of letters would set the stage for your subsequent motion to be relieved or substituted out. The letter should contain language to the following effect:

Letter No. 1

Dear Client:

      I cannot effectively represent a client when I have an overriding concern about being paid. In our written fee agreement, you promised to pay monthly as billed. My secretary has called twice to see if there is a problem or a mistake and you indicated that "a check is in the mail." You are now three months delinquent in paying your bill. Unless you pay the bill in full within the next ten days or make a new arrangement satisfactory to both of us, I shall have to terminate our professional relationship. I prefer to keep you as a client, but you will remember that when the case first arose, we discussed a fee agreement and put it in writing to make clear our arrangement. At that time, I was not willing to take the case on a contingency basis or on the basis of being paid at the end of the case. Nothing has happened to change that position. Please contact me within ten days.

Letter No. 2

Dear Client:

      You have not responded to my letter of _____, a copy of which is enclosed. We no longer wish to be professionally responsible for your case and request you seek other counsel. Please be assured that we will cooperate with your new lawyer. Your trial date is about one year away, and you and your new lawyer will have plenty of time to take reasonable measures to complete the trial preparation.

Letter No. 3

Dear Client:

We are enclosing a substitution-of-attorney form for you to sign where indicated by the red "X." We will file it with the court and will no longer be your lawyers in this matter. You will be your own lawyer until you select another lawyer. Upon receipt of the signed form, we will forward your files on to you.

Letter No. 4

Dear Client:

Enclosed is a copy of our motion to be relieved as lawyers in this matter. It will be heard on _____, 20__, at 10:00 A.M. in room 123 of tho courthouse located at 5th and Elm. If our relief is granted, we will no longer be your lawyers, and you will be representing yourself until you select another lawyer.

Letter No. 5

Dear Client:

Judge Jones granted our motion on _____, 20__ . A copy of the order is enclosed. Effective immediately, we are not your lawyers in this matter. Your files have been sent under separate cover, "return receipt requested." We caution you to obtain new counsel as rapidly as possible to prepare your case for trial.

Alternatives to Withdrawing from the Case for Nonpayment

Suggest mediation or arbitration.

Suggest getting a third party to pay or guarantee the payment. Offer credit card or financing.

Ask for collateral (check local rules).

What Not to Do

Disciplinary Rule 2-110(C)(1)(f) specifically gives you the right to withdraw from the case where you are not paid. You do not have the right to keep the case and the client and refuse to do the work the case requires until you are paid. Therefore, you cannot, for example, refuse to proceed with a case until you are paid. You must either do what is required even though you are not being paid or you must withdraw from the case.

Liens on the Case File

In general, you cannot hold on to a file just because the client owes you money. A very few states allow "charging liens" on the file, but this is a rare practice.

Part VI
Managing the
Law Office

Management of the Law Office—
General Comments

There are many gimmicks or tricks advocated by management experts for making the most effective use of your day. These suggestions run the gamut from that of training yourself to go to the restroom only during nonoffice hours to suggestions on how to dictate, where to place lighting, use of computers, etc.

Some of these suggestions are adaptable to law offices and some are not. I leave it to the reader to select his or her own management experts, books, consultants, etc.

The management suggestions I have made in this section and throughout this book are suggestions that I recommend to the new lawyer in practice based upon my experience.

Most of the suggestions are those that you will be able to use during your entire legal career, regardless of the size or nature of your practice or how long you've been in practice.

Overhead control and management of your office is to a great extent simply a matter of self-control and self-management in your first few years. Later you will have to control and manage others.

The difference between earning "a living" and earning "a good living" from the same practice will depend on how well you follow the lessons of this section on management.

Time Management 101—
Finding Time and the To-Do Lists

Good lawyers are extremely busy people and yet seem to be able to make time for family, clients, continuing legal education, keeping up with technology, practice management, exercise, vacations, volunteer legal work, community service, and self.

Parts of this chapter will be found in other chapters of this book and in any articles I have written and seminars I have given because it is so important for you that it is worthy of repetition in different settings.

"Time Management" is technically a misnomer. Time cannot be managed. The earth spins in its orbit and rotates and time goes on regardless of what you do or don't do. You cannot manage time and you cannot "find time," but you can manage what you do with your time.

Use of a to-do list puts you in charge of how you spend your time. Failure to use a to-do list puts others in charge of how you use your time.

Making and using a to-do list for your daily activities and even for your medium- and long-term planning is not difficult.

Some people keep one to-do list for their practice and another list for their personal life. I recommend integrating the two into a single list so you don't neglect your family or yourself by always giving priorities to clients and their problems. Integrating the two will help you to keep perspective and better balance your life.

By first handwriting the two lists, you will both review and rearrange everything on it. Writing it down is like making a contract with yourself. Crossing off finished items makes you feel good.

You can have two to-do lists, one encompassing all of your un-kept promises and obligations so you don't forget anything, and the second being for only a single day.

Prioritizing and Rearranging Your Lists

When you make and prioritize your to-do lists, you should list three to five things at the top of your daily list. The first thing should be the one thing you would do if you could only do one thing be-cause of interruptions, urgencies, new matters, etc. The second thing will obviously be the second thing that has to be or should be done that day, and the third item would be the third task to be done that day, and so on.

There may be days when there is only one urgent matters on the entire list and other days when you have seven or eight things, each of which will only take a few moments. A list of only three things gives you impetus to get them done and off the list. Having five to ten or more items on the list can be psychologically frustrating and debilitating and confusing with the result that nothing gets done.

If the first task requires uninterrupted time, immediately block out the line and let the office know you will be not be taking calls except for true urgencies that won't wait an hour or two and new clients who may go elsewhere if they can't talk to you immediately.

I personally prepare and update the list by hand and then enter it into a computer or give it to my secretary to enter into a computer for a daily printout.

By sharing it with your secretary (or a family member, if you wish) another person will be able to help you by reminding you of what needs to be done.

Your list can be preprinted on a legal pad, in a notebook, or on plain paper, or in a computer, as you wish.

Maintaining the To-Do Lists

As soon as you make another promise to someone or acknowl-edge an obligation, immediately put it on the daily list at the end of the list. If you are out of the office when the new task becomes known, you may wish to immediately jot things down on one of your cards or the other person's cards and stick the card in your shirt pocket, your money clip, or your purse.

If you are more comfortable immediately adding tasks with a personal digital assistant (PDA) or by immediately dictating into a tape or digital recorder, do it that way.

The important thing is not how you add to the list. The important thing is that you do it.

You should prepare and rearrange the list as the last thing you do after reviewing your daily time sheet and before going home. Your daily time sheet should reflect things you may have started that day but haven't finished or that require more work to be done. (See chapter on how to keep time records.)

By preparing the list before you leave the office, your subconscious will be working on your list even while you are sleeping.

Put your number one, two, and three priorities on your desk or photocopy the handwritten lists and give the originals to your secretary for his or her information and to type as the first task every morning so he or she will be aware of your priorities.

By disciplining yourself to maintain your to-do lists as a number-one priority (you could even put "Update to-do lists" as your number-one priority every day), you will find yourself in control of your time, better organized, and you'll make much more money and have much more free time than you ever imagined possible.

Organizing Your Day and Your Life to Make More Money by Planning and List-Making

List-making is the fundamental tool for professional and economic success. The winners in life are almost always compulsive list-makers.

The president of one of America's "Big Three" auto manufacturers supposedly comes into his office every morning and stares out the window for a few minutes. Then he turns around to his desk and begins a list of "Things to Do." He puts the most important thing at the top and the list continues with things of decreasing importance.

If he only does one thing all day, he does the first thing on the list. After days or weeks he may take that last thing off the list by either giving it to someone else to do or deciding not to do it at all. He may never get to the last item on the list.

I don't know if this story is true or false, but it makes sense.

In hospital emergency rooms, sometimes several people arrive at the same time. This often happens after a large accident such as a multiple-auto accident, building collapse, or train wreck. There often are only one or two doctors then on duty to handle a large number of emergencies. Decisions are made to rank the medical cases in order of priority. Red blankets are put on those who can be saved but require immediate attention, purple blankets are put on those who will be saved if they are taken care of later. White blankets are given to those who really don't need emergency medical care to begin with and also to those who are going to die anyway or who require so much attention that many others would die if they were taken care of. These cases are quietly wheeled out of the emergency room and given pain killers and ignored until the red blanket and purple blanket cases are taken care of. (The blanket color code differs from hospital to hospital, but the principle is the same.) Just as the auto executive and the hospital emergency room have to organize their workloads, you have to organize yours.

I have recommended starting each morning with a written list of "Things to Do." Whether you use a plain legal pad, a commercially prepared pad, or a computer to compile the list is immaterial. The important thing is to discipline yourself to make a list and use it. The examples that follow, along with an explanatory note, should convey the idea. You might wish to review your list at fixed intervals such as lunch time, end of day, etc.

You should make your daily to-do list the last thing before leaving the office for both you and your secretary. Your subconscious will be thinking about the list while you are out of the office. The next day you'll hit the deck running, immediately going to your first task without wasting ten or twenty minutes trying to decide what to do that day.

You may wish to review your short-term plans and goals and list quarterly. You may wish to review your long-term plans and goals and list annually over the New Year's holiday or over the last weekend before your birthday so you know what you want to do the coming year.

List-making is the fundamental tool for professional and economic success.

Planning and List-Making/The Keys to Management Success

The winners in life have plans and goals. They have a rough idea of where they want to go and when they want to get there.

You should have goals of where you want to be at the end of your first, second, third, fourth, and fifth years of practice. It is difficult to make plans beyond five years. Your goals can include type of practice, income level, etc.

If you have goals and a timetable and a to-do list, you may get to where you want to go sooner or later than you planned; you may have to detour, or you may even have to change your goals as things happen. The important thing is to have goals and a timetable. Your business plan is in effect your road map and your timetable.

The losers in life don't have specific goals or plans. They are simply pinballs in the pinball machine of life, continually being buffeted from side to side by flippers and forces controlled by other people.

Things to do TODAY

DATE December

		✓	☐
1	Call Bob Wilkins re program		
2	Call Tom Peters re overdue bill		
3	Answer attorney Smith's letter re Settlement		
4	Have Mary call re stationery delivery		
5	Start research on Jones case		
6	Get accident reports on Jones case		
7	Start research on Alaska statute re transfer probate		
8	transfer probate		
9	Work on 9th Circuit Brief (due Feb 13)		
10	Start research on Tax Article for Bar Journal		
11	(due Mar 1)		
12	Begin rust edition of How-To Start a Business		
13	Work on audio tapes for How-To Get a Keyboard Class		
14			
15	Get estimate on auto damage in Evans car		
16	Get # Lite on www.Fordbuglaw.com		
17	Get Conell re rate for new team on AOA		
18	Look @ Roberts file – Smith re problem with contest		
19	Save Summers on the letter		
20	Send Fee letter to Mr Thomas		
	Set Appo re Mr Fisk		
	Decide if Peters case governed by new statute		

1. Beginning of day

Things to do TODAY

DATE December

		✓	☐
1	Call Bob Wilkins re program		
2	Call Tom Peters re overdue bill		
3	Answer attorney Smith's letter re Settlement		
4	Have Mary call re stationery delivery		
5	Start research on Jones case		
6	Get accident reports on Jones case		
7	Start research on Alaska statute re transfer probate		
8	transfer probate		
9	Work on 9th Circuit Brief (due Feb 13)		
10	Start research on Tax Article for Bar Journal		
11	(due Mar 1)		
12	Begin rust edition of How-To Start a Business		
13	Work on audio tapes for How-To Get a Keyboard Class		
14			
15	Get estimate on auto damage in Evans car		
16	Get # Lite on www.Fordbuglaw.com		
17	Get Conell re rate for new team on AOA		
18	Look @ Roberts file – Smith re problem with contest		
19	Save Summers on the letter		
20	Send Fee letter to Mr Thomas		
	Set Appo re Mr Fisk		
	Decide if Peters case governed by new statute		

2 and 3. During the day

Things to do TODAY

DATE _December 2_

		✓ ☐
1	Get accident reports on Jones case	
2	Serve summons on Mr. Peters	
3	Send fee letter to Mr. Thomas	
4	Start research on Jones case	
5	Answer attorney Smith letter re settlement	
6	Set deposition of Mr. Fish	
7	Decide if Peters Case governed by new Statute	
8	Work on 9th Circuit brief (due Feb 15th)	
9	Start Research on Tax Article for Bar Journal (due Mar 1)	
10		
11	Ask Tom to help on Bar Tax Article	
12	Get dict. from ABA for How To Start a Bus...	
13	Call Bob re company wedding dinner for House	
14	Get 1 keep Good clients	
15	Look up probate file - Smith - re will contest	
16	Go to Cornell will note for new firm on 10A	
17		
18		
19		
20		

Explanation

1. Start with a list of things to do. Put the most important thing at the head of the list. This should be the only thing you want most to get done during the day or the next day. Continue the list in order of descending importance.

2 and 3. Cross off things as you do them. Add new things which came up during the day.

4. Rearrange the list for the next day before you leave the office at night.

4. End of day

They are drawn inexorably downward by gravity to a no-win ending. They don't have a business plan. They have no realistic goals or ways to accomplish what they want.

The fundamental tool of success that almost all successful people use to reach their goals is list-making. You must learn to be a compulsive list-maker. You must list every promise you have made. (I sometimes call my to-do list my list of unkept promises.) Put everything on the list and decide to do one of three things:

1. *Do it.* You will get great satisfaction crossing items off the list.

2. *Delegate it.* Give it to someone else to do.

3. *Decide not to do it.* Call the person to whom you made the promise and tell them you won't do it. That person will be disappointed, but they will be more disappointed if you never do the task or do it after it no longer helps the other person.

Almost all winners in life are compulsive list-makers. List-makers are almost always the winners.

Managing Telephone Communications—Never Let the Sun Set on an Unreturned Call

My writing style is to write books with stand-alone chapters, complete in themselves without reference to other chapters. Accordingly, some of the information found in this chapter may also be found in other chapters. This is intentional.

Good telephone communications are an excellent, low-cost way to develop and keep good clients. It's good business to have good telephone communications.

Eighty-two percent of people form an opinion of a business in whole or in part by the way telephones are handled.

According to an American Bar Association study 83 percent of satisfied clients reported that their lawyer promptly returned telephone calls. Of dissatisfied clients who would not recommend the lawyer to others nor use the lawyer again only 42 percent reported that their lawyer promptly returned calls.

Clients want their calls returned within two hours or they worry that you didn't receive their message or won't call them back.

Since you can't always return the call within two hours, have someone else return the call and reassure the caller that you will get the message as soon as possible.

When the phones are handled well, your clients and potential clients start off on a good level and can communicate easily with you. When the phones are badly handled, your clients and potential clients have chips on their shoulders before you even get to talk to them. They become distracted by poor telephone handling and forget to tell you important things. They become unresponsive to what you say and do because they have the telephone problem at the front of their minds. You get diverted from the ability to make a good impression on the client because you spend your time defending your poor system. People often equate poor or impersonal telephone communications with poor or impersonal professional skills. They worry that if you can't handle simple phone calls, perhaps you can't handle their problems.

On the other hand, if they love your receptionist and the way their calls are handled and returned, things start off on a great note.

Poor telephone communication is the single most common source of complaints about lawyers and law firms. It is estimated that alleged failure to promptly return calls is present in more than one-third of malpractice complaints and more than one-half of disciplinary complaints.

Clients frequently recommend lawyers and law firms and come back for more work based on the way they return calls. Reputation for promptly returning calls is often a factor when clients choose lawyers and firms. Conversely clients fire lawyers and firms and then file complaints when the client perceives telephone mistreatment.

Allegations of poor telephone communications are normally present in complaints by clients of neglect or failure to perform work. In many cases the lawyer has not failed to perform the work, but rather has failed to accept or return the client's calls when the client called to find out what was happening on the case.

It is easy for a client to accuse a lawyer or firm of failure to return calls. Poor telephone communications, including failure to return calls in a reasonable length of time, are sometimes so endemic among lawyers that people are quick to believe undocumented erroneous accusations and slow to believe the defense.

It requires a sincere desire implemented by good systems to maintain good telephone communications.

Fortunately, it does not require much money or equipment to maintain good systems. Often the best communications involve the least technology and equipment. In fact, excess technology and procedures are often the cause of poor telephone communications.

Establishing good telephone communications will require a very small amount of effort to implement, but will require ongoing teaching and supervision.

1. Adopt a "written firm statement of policy" concerning telephone calls. A sample starting point might be as follows:

It is the policy of this firm that telephone calls to and from clients will be given priority. No client call will be ignored. We will accept all client telephone calls if practicable, and we will return all client telephone calls as soon as possible. We will endeavor to return calls immediately and always within two hours.

Client calls received before 3:00 P.M. will be accepted or returned the same business day, preferably within two hours, if possible. Clients who call after 3:00 P.M. will be advised that unless it is an emergency the call might not be returned until the next business day. The client will then be asked if it is an emergency call, in which case someone in the office will immediately speak to the client and an attempt will be made to reach the lawyer by fax or by pager.

Telephone communications are an essential and critical part of the firm's dedication to quality service.

All lawyers and support staff are reminded that allegations of nonreturned telephone calls are commonly present in complaints to the state bar's disciplinary staff. The firm does not wish to dissipate its resources defending ethics complaints.

Lawyers or support staff who are not willing to support the firm's commitment to this policy are subject to immediate dismissal for cause.

All voice mail and e-mail messages are to be reviewed daily to determine if a response is necessary. E-mail is considered to be subject to inspection. Personal e-mail and voice mail should be handled outside the office.

2. If the ability to receive and return client telephone calls is part of the job requirements, be sure it is in the job description.

3. Document all incoming client calls and document all outgoing client calls, including unsuccessful attempts to return calls. It is especially important to document voice-mail calls and calls to answering machines where a record must be created because the original message (if it existed) will be erased.

Whether you use a predesigned form or simply a sheet of paper is not important. What is important is to have a hard-copy document showing the date and time of the incoming or outgoing call.

4. Only use letter-size (8 $^1/_2$ × 11) paper to record notes of incoming and outgoing calls. Small pieces of paper from telephone memo pads get lost in and out of the file. Use colored paper. You

might use blue for incoming and yellow for outgoing or the same color for all telephone communications. These colors will help you quickly find telephone notes and memos in the file when you need them.

5. Train yourself to dictate memos to the file on all calls, but especially client calls. These memos will be more accurate than your memory or the client's memory as to who said what when. Hand-written notes are often illegible or incomprehensible except to the person who made them. Even I sometimes cannot decipher my notes made many years previously. These memos will also make it easier for another person in the office to assist the client if you aren't available or for you to assist on a matter being currently or previously handled by another lawyer.

Resist the temptation to go immediately on to the next call when you finish one call. Dictate your memo and then go on to the next call. If you wait, you'll either forget to do the memo or forget some of the conversation.

6. Record your telephone call on your time sheet whether or not you spoke with the client. In addition to being able to review your time records for lost or forgotten work promised to clients, you will be able to charge where appropriate and you will have what amounts to an index of when and with whom calls took place.

Reviewing the suspense or pending copy of these memos at the end of the month helps you to be sure you didn't forget to charge for a chargeable call. The suspense memo can be part of your "to do" system until you can dispose of it as a finished task.

7. Three sample forms follow. Form 1 can be used for documenting telephone calls and conferences. Form 2 is a multipurpose form that can be used for documenting telephone calls, conferences, depositions, etc. Form 3 is suitable for documenting telephone calls and voice-mail messages. The form was designed by me based on a suggestion from Malvina Abbot of San Diego.

8. Hire and train the right people to answer telephones and talk with clients.

9. Screen applicants (including lawyers) by telephone as a standard part of the hiring process when a position requires telephone communication ability. Start the interview process by telephone. Ask five to ten simple questions such as name and address. Ask one open-ended question such as what the applicant knows about the firm, or about the areas of law the applicant likes best. Your secretary or personnel administrator or office manager will

TELEPHONE CALL RECORD
Form 1
For Telephone Calls and Conferences

File or Matter:

_____

Date:

_____

Spoke With:

_____

I Said	They Said

TELEPHONE CALL RECORD
Form 2
Usable for Multiple Purposes

		Client Name
A	Date _____/_____/_____	
B	__Call __From __To Time Started	File Name
C	__Conf __Analysis of Law	File #
D	__Memo __Depo __Ct Total Time	Attorney
E	__Call/Conf With	

	I SAID	THEY SAID
1		
2		
3		
4		
5		
6		
7		
8		
9		
10		
11		
12		
13		
14		
15		
16		
17		
18		
19		
20		
21		
22		
23		
24		

Follow-up Required __yes __no   Follow-up Done __yes __no   File in Client File __yes __no

TELEPHONE CALL RECORD
Form 3
Suitable for Voice Mails

Date this Memo Prepared: _____

Incoming Voice Mail: _____

Outgoing Voice Mail: _____

Voice Mail System: _____ Answering Machine: _____

Spoke With: _____

Will this call be followed up by fax or other writing? (Give reason if appropriate.)

Yes _____

No _____

OUTGOING TELEPHONE OR VOICE MAIL

Person or Firm Called: _____

Number Called: _____

Time and Date of Call: _____

Reason for Call:

Returning call(s) of: _____

To inform of: _____

Other: _____

Message Left:

Please Return Call: _____

Call not Successful because: _____

Message Left: _____

_____

Comments: _____

INCOMING TELEPHONE OR VOICE MAIL

Person Called: _____

Return Number or Address Left: _____

_____

Incoming Time and Date According to Caller: _____

Incoming Time and Date According to Machine: _____

Message Left: (Prepare more detailed memo repeating or summarizing message if appropriate.)

_____

_____

Person preparing this memo: _____

File this memo: _____

Route this memo to: _____

Copy of this memo to: _____

Client or case name: _____

350

waste some time on the telephone but will save even more time that would have been wasted in face-to-face interviews. Applicants who can't handle a simple telephone conversation and answer some simple questions when applying for a job aren't going to do any better after they're hired. If they mumble or are incomprehensible or have accents that make them difficult to understand, they are not likely to be the right person for the job and you can end the interview right there. If the person is understandable to the degree the job requires one to be understood on the telephone, then you can continue the interview process. Tell the applicants to call back at specific times (perhaps fifteen-minute intervals between calls). Applicants who can't return a call on time when their own career is involved are not likely to return a call on time when a client's problems are involved.

10. Train everyone in the office (including incoming lawyers regardless of level) the rudiments of handling telephone calls. The State Bar of Wisconsin has an excellent twenty-minute videotape that can be shown to all new employees. Even the most experienced lawyer can benefit from a refresher course.

Do not allow totally untrained people to answer telephones except in cases of dire emergency. An untrained person may not properly direct the call or may not properly arrange for a return call. Calls handled by untrained people are most likely to be the ones that get lost in the shuffle and never returned. It is the lesser of two evils to keep a client on hold until someone can be found who can properly handle a call.

11. Do not allow others to commit you to return a call. I've seen cases where clients and potential clients became angry and went to a different law firm because a receptionist promised that a call would be returned by a lawyer. The client or prospective client stayed by the telephone waiting for a call that never came, because the lawyer left the office or started a conference or deposition totally ignorant of the call. The message was in the lawyer's message box, but the lawyer never knew of the message or that the client was waiting for the return call. The client assumed the lawyer was "ducking" the call.

The receptionist or secretary should say, "I'll see to it that Mr. Foonberg gets the message." Or he or she should say, "I'll see to it that Mr. Foonberg gets the message as soon as possible," or "I'll see to it that he gets the message as soon as he checks for messages." The receptionist should NOT say "Mr. Foonberg will return your call."

12. Whenever possible, offer the client the opportunity to talk with a human being. If possible, a voice-mail system should begin with the offer of "Dial O to speak with an operator, or dial the star sign to speak with my secretary." A human being can document a call to protect the lawyer from the charge (often unfounded in fact) that the client made "repeated" calls that were never returned. In fact the client may have called three times in two months, but the distraught or unhappy client will remember that he or she called every day.

13. Tell the receptionist when you are leaving the office and when you will return. Receptionists won't have to keep people on the line looking for you when you aren't there.

14. Voice-mail systems are a major source of client dissatisfaction. New or prospective clients will often hang up and call a different lawyer.

15. The allegation of unreturned calls can affect a client's charge that a lawyer did not handle a case competently and that the failure to return calls prejudiced the client's case. I have had to deal with unethical lawyers who falsely have asserted in self-serving letters and affidavits that they made "numerous" or "repeated" calls that were not answered or returned. (The phantom calls often concerned *ex parte* notices and statutes of limitations.)

Although the number of these sleazy lawyers is fortunately low, it has become necessary for me to devise a form letter for these situations in order to protect both the client and the firm. A sample letter follows the text. The letter could also be used with noncooperative clients.

> Sleazy Lawyer
> Ketchem, Holdem & Skinum
> 123 Main Street
> Anytown, USA
>
> Re: No Telephone Contact
>
> Dear Sleazy Lawyer:
> In your correspondence of January 2, 20xx, you refer to several telephone calls with this office that, in fact, never occurred. In your affidavit of November 12, 20xx, you refer to a telephone call with this firm and quote us on what never was said.

You are instructed not to contact this office by telephone unless required to do so by the rules of court. You may communicate via U.S. Mail, express an bonded messenger services, or fax at (555) 123-1234. Do not call or "drop off" any documents. Use only third-party deliveries where receipt can be confirmed.

We regret that your flagrant references to nonexistent telephone calls and nonexistent conversations have created this necessity.

Very truly yours,

Noble Lawyer

16. The "Nonclient" Client. A malpractice claim or disciplinary complaint may claim that you have neglected a client you have no memory of or a case you never handled.

The scenario is all too common. A person calls your office, asking to speak to you. The person claims he or she was referred by some client or person or firm you never heard of. The person relates a few facts over the telephone to you. You tell the person to come in for an appointment. The person never comes in or promises to call for an appointment in a few days when the person will know his or her schedule. The person never calls.

One day after the statute of limitations runs out, that person calls you up and asks "How's my case coming?" You tell the person you don't know who he is or why he thinks you are his lawyer. The person claims you took all the facts over the telephone and agreed to represent him or said you would "take care of it." The next communication you get from the person is the malpractice or disciplinary complaint.

It is possible that the person is lying and it is also possible that being unsophisticated, he honestly believed you were in fact handling his case. Usually the person can prove the call with a telephone bill or with other evidence. Often the lawyer has absolutely no memory of the events.

The lawyer should be careful not to discuss the case until after the person gives a name, telephone number, mailing address, and the names of the probably adverse parties. The lawyer should immediately terminate the call unless the person gives this information, unless there is some very good reason for not giving it. If the call is terminated, the lawyer should record what happened on his or her time records under the category of "prospective clients." An entry might read, "Call from Mrs. Smith. Claimed to have been referred by a Mr. Jones. Refused to give me address. I told her I would not represent her and told her to call the County Bar Association Lawyer Referral Service."

If after getting the name and address, the lawyer does not want the case, a form letter should be sent declining representation and/or recommending the lawyer referral service or another lawyer. It should be remembered that the prospective client you turn down often comes back or refers someone at a later time.

Organizing Your Desk to Make More Money

You will spend many hours at your desk. Your desk is not just a place to put knickknacks. It is the place where you will earn much of your living. You can make money at it.

1. Get a picture of your loved one(s) and place it on your desk facing you, not facing the client. Look at the photo whenever you feel awkward about charging fees. This photo will make it much easier to discuss fees, or to refer the client with no funds to legal aid. Update the photo when appropriate (for example, when your children start to walk, to remind yourself that shoes cost money). Your family's growth will remind you of increased food needs. If you don't have a family, put up a picture of whatever is dependent on you, whether it be a boat or a plane or a pair of skis or your unpaid student loan coupon book. One husband-wife law partnership sent me a copy of the sonogram of their unborn child. They wrote, "Never too soon to start using Foonberg's Rule."

2. Put a clock on your desk facing you. A digital clock silently reminds you that time is a "wasting asset." Put the clock squarely in front of you. Get in the habit of looking at it and recording the time as soon as the phone is answered by you, or the client comes in. Don't depend on your computer clock. It is too small and easily overlooked.

3. Put your telephone on the left side of your desk (if you are right-handed), so that you'll be able to dial or hold the phone with your nonwriting hand. Use a speakerphone or headset so that you can use your hands to flip through a file when necessary. Be sure to use a headset and microphone if you are going to type onto your computer while talking to the caller. Callers may feel you are not listening to them if they know you are typing.

4. Put your pen set on the right. Pick up your pen the moment you begin a telephone call or conference.

5. Your dictating microphone or digital recorder and keyboard should be readily available on your desk.

6. Your time record book should be directly in front of you in the two o'clock position, in front of your pen so that you can jot down the client's name when you pick up the pen; and add the services rendered when you put the pen back at the conclusion of the call or conference.

7. Keep a "Things to Do" pad. You can either buy a preprinted pad entitled "Things to Do," or just keep a list on any lined tablet. Every morning (or evening if you prefer), make a list of "Things to Do" and number them in order of importance. During the day, add the new things to the list as they come in and cross things off as they get done.

Prepare the list so that if you only did one thing all day, it would be the number-one item. Don't be upset if it takes a long time to get to do the least important things, or if the least important things never get done (within limits of good sense and professional responsibility).

8. Files and papers neat on desk vs. cluttered desk: This is another area where five lawyers have at least ten opinions. I have seen articles prepared by psychologists that indicate that a cluttered desk is psychologically debilitating to the lawyer, creating a subconscious dread and resistance to the amount of undone work. Supposedly, according to these articles, the client will feel that you are "too busy" to give personal attention, and will not hire you.

On the other hand, my desk looks like a rummage sale. Once a client refused to trust me with documents for fear they would get lost in the piles on my desk. I have a sign that reads "A clean desk is the sign of a sick mind."

On some occasions, I have apologized to clients for my cluttered desk, and they have remarked that they want a lawyer who has lots of clients and work, and that they wouldn't want a lawyer who had very little work to do.

To me, a cluttered desk is a security blanket. When I see all the files, I don't worry that the phone won't ring that day.

Some lawyers only meet with clients in a conference room. This is a good idea for new lawyers with incomplete office furnishings.

This is an area where you should do whatever makes you feel comfortable.

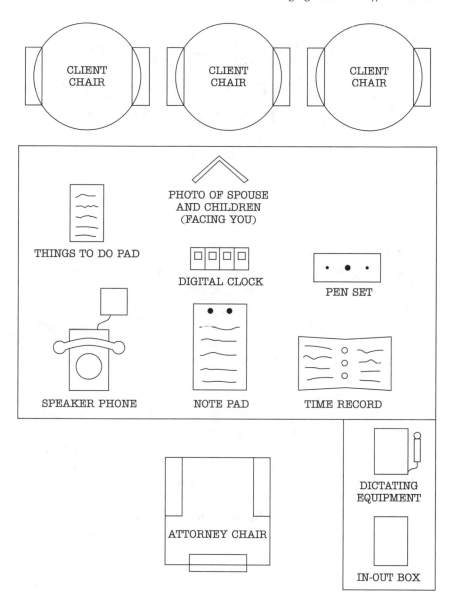

**ORGANIZING YOUR DESK TO MAKE MONEY
(DESIGNED FOR A RIGHT-HANDED LAWYER**
This configuration assumes computer, monitor, keyboard,
printer, fax, copier will be placed on desk or table behind you
and that attorney chair will swivel

How to Keep Time Records to Make More Money and to Preserve Evidence of Work Done

The famous Missouri Bar Survey shows that lawyers who keep time records earn 40 percent more than lawyers who don't. Later studies indicate that lawyers who keep good time records earn 15 percent more than lawyers who keep poor time records.

If you are concerned enough about earning a decent living to read this book, you are probably already keeping time records.

Whatever system or method you use, whether manual or computerized, be sure you keep the time book or time slips on your desk in front of you as a constant reminder. There are many systems on the market. The Day-Timer System is adequate for most sole practitioners. When I first started out, I used the Day-Timer Junior book. After a few years, I "moved up" to the Day-Timer Senior Sample Sheets. (Illustrations follow this chapter.)

Time records are not just billing records; they are, or can be, evidence for a claim in the estate when your client dies.

Time records can also be used to prove you have met your mandatory continuing education requirements and to support your application for specialty certification.

Record All Services

Record all telephone calls and all correspondence. If you decide later not to bill for a telephone call or letter, you can consider the services rendered as your contribution to the client. If you do not immediately record the services rendered, you will not be able to remember later to charge. It's simply not possible to remember what you did at the end of the month or the end of the week or even the end of the day.

Record out-of-office work done. When you work on a client matter out of the office, make a note on one of your cards and stick it in your shirt pocket or purse. When you return to the office, record the time and determine if there is something you should be doing on the matter. Alternatively, call your office and leave yourself a voice-mail message.

Allow No Exceptions

Even a nonbillable call or service may be important to you or to the client.

Record *all* services rendered. If you try to be selective, you will tend to err toward not recording enough.

Don't Wait/Start Your Time Record *Before* You Do Anything

Pick up your pen with your right hand or make an entry on your PC when you pick up the phone with your left hand. Write the name of the client when you start the call or letter or conference and record the service the instant you hang up the phone or finish dictating the letter or returning from an out-of-office meeting or court appearance. By writing the client's name or matter before you start working on the case, you can use the client's name with more description of services yet written as a reminder to do the work.

Time vs. Billing Records

You are keeping *time* records, not billing records. By recording all time, you will be able later to charge as appropriate, using hindsight. If you attempt to record only those services that at the time seem chargeable, you'll omit a lot of billable services. Remember, you are keeping time records, not billing records.

Review Your Time Records at the End of Each Day

Do not leave the office until you have added up your time for the day. If you come in at 9:00 A.M. and leave at 5:30 P.M. with an hour for lunch, you should have seven and one-half hours of time recorded.

Time Records as Evidence

We keep time records for all work, including personal injury and worker's compensation. We have asked for and received fees based on time and services from various administrative agencies such as Worker's Compensation Boards, as well as from courts when submitting minors' cases for approval. We do well in fee arbitrations because of good time records. We have quickly cut off nonmeritorious ethics complaints and nonmeritorious malpractice allegations with good time records. Our time records have served as evidence in disciplinary proceedings brought against other lawyers; our records of telephone conversations with the other lawyers saved them because their clients accused them of neglecting a case.

Time Records to Support Income Tax Deductions

You should record your out-of-pocket expenses immediately. Parking lot fees, public telephones, deductible meals, and promotional expenses should be immediately recorded as the contemporaneous records required by the Internal Revenue Service.

Computer Time Records vs. Handwritten Time Records

I recommend handwritten time records that can be subsequently entered into your computer program. Handwritten records are easy to review for omissions. Whether your original records are handwritten or keystroked, you should print and keep a copy of the original time sheet. With the passage of time, computer data may become impossible to read due to obsolescence or abandonment of the equipment or software needed to open and read the work. Companies often go out of existence or abandon supporting their hardware or applications in order to sell new products.

21 FRIDAY
NOVEMBER   40 Days Left

APPOINTMENTS & SCHEDULED EVENTS

ITEM NO.	TO BE DONE TODAY (NUMBER EACH ITEM)	NAME PLACE IN RE:	HOURS
			8 00 / 15 / 30 / 45
		MR CHAN @ 9ᵗʰ Cir 8:30 a.m.	
			9 00 / 15 / 30 / 45
		Conf John Cohen here @ 10:00 re Switchbread	**10** 00 / 15 / 30 / 45
			11 00 / 15 / 30 / 45
		Conf @ Lunch with Mr Big Bucks. Start here noon: Lunch at el Ripoff @ 12:30	**12** 00 / 15 / 30 / 45
			1 00 / 15 / 30 / 45
		Barber's appointment @ 1:00	
			2 00 / 15 / 30 / 45
			3 00 / 15 / 30 / 45

NOTES & MEMOS MADE TODAY

San Francisco Express Thur 11-20		Meeting @ North Coast with	**4** 00
Cab airport to Green	$18	VIC @ Delby SC @ 4:00 p.m.	15
Cab to District Court	6	(714-456-1234)	30
Photocopies Certificates	11		45
airport to airport	7		**5** 00
Park LAX	9		15
	$51		30 / 45
21 NOV			
Valet & Tip @ El Ripoff	3	7:30 UCLA LAW SCHOOL	**NIGHT HOURS**
Parking @ UCLA	5	PROGRAM	
Lunch @ El Ripoff	9+		
(on credit card)			

HOURS	File #	Our Client	Other Party	Description of Services	Hours
8		CARA INC	buis and Francisco	Conference with client re filing by stay with 9th Circuit in SF on Thursday 11-2	3/4
9		Bala vs Franchise Tax Board		Letter to client with explanation Reg 98.930 as applied to his case	28 / 1/2
		CARA INC		TC U.S. atty in SF re stay question	
10		Sweetbread Inc		Conf John Cohen, CPA re depreciation possibilities for trucks	3/4
		Bangkok Republics		memo to file re 30% withholding	
11				requirements for interested smelted	1/2
		Sweetbread Inc		memo to file re possible application	
		AB Inc		Section 269	1/2
12		Cohl Bank Thomas		Speed letter to client re renewing judgment	1/2
		Client Relations — ? administration		Lunch with Mr Bucks @ El Pippo Possianoy Representation for outwork	1
1		Bauvin	Trade assn.	Take phone call from Mr Jones re plans for meeting	1/4
2		JGF Personal Jones ads Smith	H Aircraft @ Barber Shop	Telephone call Mr Jones with preliminary facts and to set up meeting in office on Monday	1 / 1/4	4/c
3		Sweetbread Inc		Conference @ office of Lessor Northeast Co. with Sam Peters and William Smith of outside counsel for N.G. and R.H. Samuels Controller for NG and William attm President v or	2
4		and Tom Goodguy, President of Sweetbread re possibility of arranging do sales terms to create avoidance of 269 problem — Ltr Client summarizing results			1/2
5		Republic Pants ads Schlock Pants		of meeting — Conf client to get facts and do research on liability of company	1/8	4/c
NIGHT HOURS		Bar Association		TC Tom Goodguy re my nomination to serve on Board of Governors	
		Continuing Education		CEB program @ UCLA on Divorce	2

and adoption tax consequences and
Y2K compliance   TOTAL 10/3/4

Getting Ready for Your First Clients

As a lawyer with a new practice you don't know who will call or why they will call. If you were fired from a firm, your method of termination may have been to learn that your electronic hall pass was deactivated and you were locked out of the computers without an opportunity to take forms or client names and addresses with you.

In some cases, your first contact with a new client will be a telephone call from a prospective client. In some cases the prospective client will simply walk in and want to see you.

If possible, try to get basic facts over the telephone or at the first meeting. Try not to give advice or quote fees until after discussing what the case requires with another more-experienced lawyer.

Tell the client you simply want to have as much information as possible before your meeting with the client. Encourage the prospective client to fax you or photocopy and send you all documents so you can study them before the client comes in.

Use the time between the call and the office visit to look up the applicable law and/or discuss the legal issues and how to charge with another lawyer.

If you don't or can't find out what the case is about by phone and you meet with the client, tell the client you want to get an update on the most current state of the law before quoting a fee or advising the client. Again, use your time to look up the law and/or call another lawyer for guidance.

This chapter includes a Generic New Matter First Client Contract Intake Form that you can use to get some basic facts to push you in the right direction (Generic Form No.1).

I have also prepared a list of legal areas upon which you as a new lawyer might be consulted. I encourage you to get as many form files and court forms as you can before you open your doors. You may be able to get many of them off the Internet or from one or more mentors.

If you don't get forms *before* you open your doors, then review this list after getting facts from the client. The list may help *you* identify the legal problem area(s) involved.

You will find this list in the accompanying Generic Form No. 1.

A list of court forms also follows (see next chapter). These are simply typical court forms in California. Your courts will also have their own forms that have to be filled out. Get the forms off the Internet or directly from the court (typically five cents per form), or you could buy a CD-ROM with the forms. I suggest you not spend money for what you don't need. Get one set and then scan the forms into your word processor or print them as needed.

Simply as examples of the types of forms you can develop, I've included a Criminal Law Checklist, a Simple Will Interview Form, and a Durable Power of Attorney Checklist. (See page 378.)

Again, get all the information you can by telephone, and look up what you think are the applicable area(s) of law. Get the forms you'll need to interview the client. Get help from a more experienced lawyer if you feel you need it (you will probably need help in determining what a fair fee might be).

Then proceed to interview the client in the office with the forms and instructions you'll need.

Simple Generic Practice Forms

In the last four editions of this book, I deliberately avoided covering any substantive legal areas because law is both fact-specific and local-law-specific. In prior times, most new lawyers got some supervision in their early cases from their firms. If they didn't know the law, they would have a library of form books and "how to do it" Continuing Legal Education (CLE) books to turn to for help. In recent times, many firms give almost no training because the partners who used to train now must produce billable collectible hours and have no time available to train new lawyers. Law libraries have skyrocketed in costs as practices and the needs of the practices become more specialized, resulting in fewer book sales of any title.

In this new section of the book, I am including some generic forms to help the new lawyer ask some intelligent questions until the lawyer can learn what else he or she needs to know in order to help the client.

I encourage you to copy these forms into word-processing files and then modify them to fit the needs of your case and your jurisdiction.

You can then print up a new form every time you have a new matter in the office.

The basic client intake interview form really is the most universal form and is accordingly the longest. You may wish to modify it for your own preferences.

Generic New Matter First Client Contact Telephone Intake Form (Generic Form No. 1)

The explanations given in the parentheses can be given to the caller if he or she asks you why you need or want the information. When you are prepared to interview the client face-to-face, you can get additional information. Get as much of this information as possible in your telephone interview before the client comes in.

1. Name of person calling (spell it back to the person to be sure you have it correct.) _____

2. Telephone number from which person is calling you. (In the event the caller or you are cut off and you want to reestablish contact immediately.) _____

3. How did the caller get your name? Who recommended the caller to you? (Tell the caller you keep track of who recommended you so you can thank that person for the referral and also to be sure there does not appear to be a conflict of interest.) Be wary of people who say they don't know or remember who recommended you. They probably got your name out of the Yellow Pages. There is nothing wrong with getting your name from the Yellow Pages, but you want to know if the caller is forthright. The important thing is to discover what you can about the source and to determine if the caller appears to be lying or not cooperative, which may be the forerunner of problems in the future._____

4. Ask for the caller's home address. (Tell him or her that a city or place of residence is sometimes important in a case and you need a place to deliver documents for signature and immediate filing.) Do not accept a P.O. Box without an additional home address. (Explain to the client that the messenger services cannot deliver urgent documents to a P.O. Box and it is sometimes critical to get a client's sig-

nature on a document immediately.) Be wary of people who won't tell you where they live. _____

5. Ask for the caller's business and address. (Tell the person you may have to contact him or her in an emergency during work hours or get documents signed in an emergency.) _____

6. Ask for business and home and cellular telephone numbers. Ask if it's all right to call the person at work or at home. Ask if it's all right to leave confidential messages on voice mail ._____

7. Ask if the person has access to fax or e-mail for sending or receiving. Get the fax number(s) and e-mail address. Ask if it's all right to send confidential information by fax or e-mail. _____

8. Ask if the caller knows the names of other persons involved in the matter, either on the same side or on the other side of the dispute. Ask the names of anyone who may have been a witness or with whom they have discussed the case. (Tell the caller you have to be sure there is no conflict of interest before you begin listening to the facts of the matter.) _____

9. Ask the caller to give you what he or she feels are the important facts and to tell you what he or she hopes to obtain with the help of a lawyer. (Tell the caller you may have to get current information to be ready when he or she comes in for an interview. Explain that you want to be sure that you can handle the matter or, if not, possibly try to find a specialist for the person if needed.) _____

_____

10. Ask the caller what documents or other writings he or she has or can get before the meeting. Ask if the person can fax or e-mail you copies of the documents before the meeting. Explain that you do not want to sit there and read documents while the person looks at you, and by sending you the documents before your meeting, you will be better prepared for them. _____

11. Get as much information as possible from the caller. Remember Kipling's verse:

> "I keep six honest serving-men.
> They taught me all I knew.
> Their names are What and Where and When
> And Why and How and Who."

_____
_____
_____
_____

12. Claims against governmental entities or agencies (federal, state, local, school districts, special districts, etc.). Are any governmental agencies involved? Are there time periods within which claims must be made? Must claims or notifications be on specified forms or contain specified information to be valid?

13. Insurance policies, employers, principals, or other third-party protection or assistance available to client. Is the client entitled to protection or assistance from a third-party source to pay or reimburse legal fees or prosecute or defend the matter?

14. Insurance coverage. Ask if there might be insurance coverage for the loss or to provide a defense. If the answer is "yes," "maybe," or "I don't know" have the client bring policies with him.

15. Have you advised the caller that you have not yet agreed to accept the case or represent the caller, nor will you do so or quote a fee until after you have interviewed the caller? _____

16. Based on what the caller has related to you on the telephone, try to classify the problem into one or more of the following areas and select or create a generic interview form for each area of law and get as much additional information by telephone as possible to enable you to do research or get assistance from another lawyer if necessary before the client comes in. These are typical areas of law where you may be contacted for legal work.

16.1 Starting a new business and choosing form of doing business. (Sole proprietorship, corporation, limited liability company, partnership, etc.)

16.2 Starting or incorporating or advising a nonprofit or tax-exempt organization.

16.3 Independent contractor agreement. (Create, modify, review, or negotiate agreement. Advise on independent contractor or employee status.)

16.4 Getting a copyright or a patent or protecting an idea.

16.5 Internet and list-serve agreements.

16.6 Technology. (Create, modify, review, or negotiate software or other technology agreement.)

16.7 Employment agreement. (Create, modify, review, or negotiate employment agreement.)

16.8 Employer-employee disputes.

16.9 Civil rights and discrimination claims.

16.10 Tax disputes.

16.11 Criminal law. (Getting out of jail after arrest.)

16.12 Criminal law. (Representation of adult.)

16.13 Criminal law. (Representation of juvenile.)

16.14 Family law. (Modify previous order; financial, visitation, custody, etc.)

16.15 Family law—no previous proceeding.

16.16 Job-related injuries.

16.17 Automobile accidents.

16.18 Slip/fall accidents.

16.19 Automobile repair and purchase disputes (Lemon law cases).

16.20 Defective product and repairs disputes.

16.21 Rental of real property—commercial. (Create, modify, review, or negotiate lease or occupancy agreement.)

16.22 Rental of real property—residential. (Create, modify, review or negotiate lease agreement.)

16.23 General civil litigation representation.

16.24 Administrative law or agency representation.

16.25 Landlord-tenant disputes.

16.26 Medical malpractice claims.

16.27 Legal malpractice claims.

16.28 Other professional malpractice claims. (Engineers, architects, stockbrokers, real estate agents, etc.)

16.29 Environmental law. (Civil disputes, criminal or administrative investigations.)

16.30 Claims against government entities or agencies.

16.31 Claims against insurance companies.

16.32 Representation of client in arbitration.

16.33 Representation of client in mediation.

16.34 Representing heirs and claimants and contestants in probates, will contests, and disputes over decedents' estates.

16.35 Representing the estate in probates and conservatorships and guardianships.

16.36 Will or trust preparation where testator or settler is feeble, very elderly, or where capacity or mental condition may be a factor if will or trust is challenged.

16.37 Trust litigation.

16.38 Health-care provisions with or without will. (Durable powers of attorney, living wills, nomination of conservator, organ donation, general powers of attorney.)

16.39 Elder abuse.

16.40 Elder law—conservatorship.

16.41 Simple wills. (No taxes or trusts involved.)

16.42 Estate planning. (Trusts or taxes probably involved.)

16.43 Estate planning to protect assets for spouse or children in the event of long-term medical care or possibly devastating medical expenses.

16.44 Asset protection trusts to protect assets from litigants, creditors, or others who may claim property.

16.45 Appeals.

16.46 International other than immigration.

16.47 Immigration.

16.48 Bankruptcy—Chapter 13 debt consolidation or Chapter 7.

16.49 Student loan repayment problems.

16.50 Credit reporting and denial problems.

16.51 Client does not wish to discuss over telephone.

16.52 Witness list.

16.53 Document list.

16.54 List of people, including lawyers and investigators, with whom caller has discussed the case prior to contacting you.

As indicated, this is a list of typical areas of law where you may be called upon for advice. Try to get all the information you can by telephone before your first client interview including dates of events and names of potentially adverse parties. Get more information when the client comes in. Based on the information you get by telephone or in person, do research to determine if you can prepare yourself to handle the case without assistance or whether you will need the help of a more experienced lawyer. Do not be afraid to call another lawyer(s) to relate the questions asked and the answers given, and to determine what to do next. The other lawyer(s) may also give you help in how to quote and charge and collect a reasonable fee.

You can build up a list of "mentors" in various areas of law. You typically can find these mentors through your local bar association. They may be part of a formal or informal mentoring program. They normally will help you because they remember when they were inexperienced and needed help. Some will help you hoping for referrals where there is a conflict. Some will help you hoping you will refer them clients or associate them into the case or joint venture or representation when the matter is simply over your head and needs a more experienced lawyer. Different lawyers may have different reasons for offering to help you, but no lawyer will turn you down for a limited amount of help when you explain you are a new lawyer and want to be sure you are not prejudicing a potential client by accepting a case.

You may need forms from more than one area of law. Be sure to select and complete as many as you think might be applicable. It is better to have too much information than too little information. Additionally the client might not realize that he or she may have more than one legal problem.

Remember that these will be generic forms to get you started in your first telephone interview or your first office interview. As you develop experience you should modify the forms to fit your needs and the needs of your particular jurisdiction. The lawyer you call for help may be willing to e-mail or fax you one of his or her intake or interview forms, which will, of course, be on point to the needs of your jurisdiction and areas of practice.

Typical Court Forms

This chapter and list of forms is included as a reference to help the new lawyer ask the proper questions when a client calls and the lawyer is not sure what fields of law are involved or what questions to ask or where to look to be better able to interview the client and render legal advice or other assistance.

Unlike other parts of this book, this chapter is not intended for easy reading. This chapter should be read carefully. The information can be invaluable in a specific case.

The court forms can help you get a handle or "feeling" for what the procedure in a given area might be and what facts you have to obtain to get started. The forms also often include form interrogatories designed for the particular area of law. These form interrogatories will be helpful to you in being careful to have asked all the important questions so that you have made an adequate minimum investigation of the facts.

It is very probable that your state has a similar list and assortment of court forms in various areas of law that you can obtain for free or at a low nominal cost. You may be able to get the forms directly from the court or from your state bar or state bar library or local law library. In some cases they are available on word processing disk and in some cases online. In many cases court forms and instructions for usage can be downloaded from the Internet.

This list has been prepared by me on a selective basis from a collection of approximately 800 California court forms. I have selected court forms and areas of law that are likely to be of help to a new or inexperienced lawyer.

By scanning this list you might get a better handle on classifying a client or prospective client's legal problem. The forms themselves are replete with applicable statutes, controlling cases, regulatory authority, and cross-references to secondary authorities and to other areas of law.

These court forms are often complete with the law and instructions, written in simple English. In some cases the simplified court forms and instructions were designed and promoted by various interest groups to encourage people to litigate their legal rights without use of lawyers. The forms are often completed by checking off boxes or filling in blanks and often include detailed explanations of the law and procedure and instructions in simple English.

The courts of your state probably have similar forms available from the court or on the Internet. You can get a quick education or refresher in the law of the subject matter before your client interview so you'll better know what specific questions to ask. You may also find the list of value in setting up your own form file system and in preparing your own interview questionnaires.

Your client may already have gotten the forms and you will want to know at least as much about the area of law as the client does.

If you are in fact going to litigate a matter, you will need the forms to prepare the appropriate pleadings and other documents required by the court in your jurisdiction.

Although I have only listed state court forms, almost every state and federal administrative agency also has a collection of forms and instructions that can be of value to you in preparing for an interview with your client.

The mere fact that you have the forms available in your office will help reassure the client (and possibly yourself) that you know what you are doing in the area of law involved.

I have in many cases paraphrased the title of the form and added my own description and comments about what the form asks or what the process is, to give the new lawyer an idea of the type of information the lawyer will need for an interview and a little refresher on the law.

I must repeat that every form you use must eventually be modified to fit both the law and procedure of your jurisdiction and the types of cases and clients you will have.

It is worth your time to peruse this list to see if the descriptions seem to be what you might need and to encourage you to obtain the counterpart form from your courts for use in your office. Many of these forms will not be found in other places and many of the forms in your jurisdiction will not be listed here.

List of Some Typical Court Forms with Description and Comments

1. *Facsimile Transmission Cover Sheet.* Used for filing pleadings and service by fax. Provides for payment by credit card or lawyer deposit account. Provides for processing instructions to be given to court clerk and other officials. Filings after 5:00 P.M. deemed filed the next day.

2. *Small Claims Court Form.* Extensive instructions on how and when to use small claims court, including jurisdiction, venue, and service of court process. Checklist and fill-in-the-blank forms for the claim, the order to the defendant to appear, proof of service, information on substituted service, motion to continue, request to pay a judgment in installments, request for *subpoena duces tecum* with preprinted descriptions of documents commonly sought, defendant's cross-complaint, how to enforce judgment including writs of execution and debtor examination, judgment debtor's lists of assets, motion to vacate, request to pay judgment to court, information on how to appeal.

Using these Small Claims forms, a new lawyer could easily and properly ask the client all the right questions, give the client good advice on what evidence to present, advise the client on the probability of success, and give the client a set of forms to fill out, or fill out the forms for the client. The client should be happy to pay for the lawyer setting up the case so that all the client has to do is tell his or her story to the judge supported by the evidentiary materials you have helped the client obtain. The client will pay for an office consultation and the form processing and save the expense of the lawyer sitting around a courthouse waiting to present the case. If the client wins you *may* have further work in enforcing the judgment, and if the client loses you may have additional work for the appeal, which is sometimes a trial *de novo* with a lawyer.

3. *Request to Conduct Film and Electronic Media Coverage and Order.* Request for television, movie, still camera, or audio coverage of a hearing, witness, sentencing, bail, or when no official recorder is available.

4. *Petition to Determine If Dog Is Potentially Dangerous, Vicious, Menacing, etc.* Contains appropriate allegations and citations concerning liability for acts of dogs.

5. *Petition for Probate.* Several pages of forms containing everything you have to allege and prove to get a will admitted to probate, or to allege that the decedent died intestate, and to receive appointment as the personal representative of the estate.

6. *Probate Citation.* The equivalent of a summons or a subpoena in a non-probate proceeding.

7. *Proof of a Subscribing Witness.* What the witnesses to a will must testify to in person or by affidavit.

8. *Proof of a Holographic Instrument.* How you prove a will that is handwritten with no witnesses.

9. *Duties and Liabilities of Personal Representative.* Tells the personal representative what he or she must to do as personal representative.

10. *Request for Special Notice.* Requires the personal representative to send you copies of pleadings and proceedings so you can monitor what is happening in the estate.

11. *Waiver of Notice.* Waiving the notices a person might otherwise be entitled to in an estate.

12. *Notice to Creditors, Inventory and Appraisement, Creditor's Claim, Allowance of Creditor's Claim, Rejection of Creditor's Claim.* Various forms and instructions concerning specific steps that must be taken in probating a decedent's estate.

13. *Spousal Property Petition.* Petition to include in or exclude from the probate proceeding property claimed to be spousal. Can affect amount of bond, calculation of fees, and have significant tax implications.

14. *Petition to Sell Securities, or Personal or Real Property.* Various procedures with explanations for selling estate property with or without notices.

15. *Petitions to Avoid Full Probate.* Used in specific circumstances involving small estates to avoid full probate.

16. *Attachments: Application for Writ of Attachment.* Delineates between *ex parte* and noticed applications. Sets forth the minimum jurisdictional grounds and includes proposed temporary protective order.

17. *Notice of Attachments with Instructions for Garnishee on How to Respond.* Bond instructions.

18. *Application to Set Aside Writ of Attachment or Temporary Protective Order.*

19. *Claim and Delivery-Application to obtain possession of personal property.* Includes proposed order and procedure for *ex parte* and on hearing writs and instructions on bonds and application to quash *ex parte* writ.

20. *Petition for Injunction to Prohibit Civil Harassment When Family Law or Domestic Violence Is Not Involved.* Also includes instructions on what to do if there is domestic violence or family law violence is involved. Includes order to show cause and proposed temporary restraining order.

21. *Petition for Guardianship, Conservator, or Limited Conservatorship.* Sets forth the grounds, the notices required to be given to the various family members and state agencies, the inventory and appraisement of assets, and the procedure for selling assets when necessary.

22. *Petition for Temporary Guardianship or Conservator of the Person or of the Estate of a Proposed Ward.* Similar to general petitions.

23. *Forms for Authority to Give Consent for Medical Treatment of Minor or Other.*

24. *Miscellaneous General Legal Forms.* Abstract of judgment. Request for dismissal of civil action with and without prejudice to refile and as to entire complaint or part of complaint or cross-complaint. Summons. Joint debtor summons. Unlawful detainer (eviction) complaint and answer. Subpoena. Subpoena for deposition. Subpoena for production of business records. Subpoena for criminal or juvenile matter. Proof of service of process.

25. *Personal Injury Pleadings.* Form for personal injury complaints and cross-complaints and answers for personal injury, property damage, and wrongful death. Covers actions arising out of motor vehicle accidents, general negligence, intentional torts, premises liability, products liability, and procedures for exemplary damages. Use of these forms with their instructions may help you be sure you have covered what you have to need an adequate pleading.

26. *Wage Garnishment Forms.* Including application, claim of exemption, opposition to claim of exemption, form of financial statements and information necessary, earnings withholding order, earnings withholding order for support. Return of employer, formulas for garnishment, earning withholdings order for taxes, em-

ployer's return. Everything you need to know about wage garnishments.

27. *Family Law Forms and Checklists.* It is estimated that family law constitutes about 60 percent of all civil litigation. It is not surprising that the Superior Court system in California has more than fifty forms and checklists to be used in family law disputes. As opposed to many other areas of law, family law and procedure is generally very state-specific. The listing of these forms and their descriptions is only intended to prompt you to see if similar forms and checklists and instructions exist in your jurisdiction, which, of course, would reflect your laws and procedures. New lawyers get a lot of family law work because their contemporaries have family and divorce problems.

28. *Family Law.* Petition for dissolution of marriage, legal separation, nullity of marriage, and declaration under Uniform Child Custody Act. Form contains check-off grounds for each type of action. Form response to petition.

29. *Family Law.* Conservatorship for adults, guardianships for minors. Commencement, modification, termination.

30. *Family Law.* Summons with standard restraining orders. Confidential marriage counseling statement.

31. *Motion for Order to Show Cause Form for Child Custody, Child Support, Visitation, Spousal Support, Injunctive Order, and Attorney Fees and Costs.* Contains explanations of rights and calculation formulas for child and spousal support depending on who has custody of children.

32. *Notice of Hearing and Opposition to Request to Change Support Order.* Ex parte application for wage assignment for support, wage, and earnings assignment order, application and order for health insurance coverage, request for final judgment of dissolution of marriage.

33. *Form Interrogatories for Family Law Matters.* Schedule of assets and debts, request for production of income, and expense declaration.

34. *Joint Petition for Summary Dissolution of Marriage.* Can sometimes be used if no children, no real estate, limited debts, short marriage. Detailed instruction and information booklet accompanies the petition form. Instructions tell litigants that they needn't see a lawyer, but if they want to, they can find one who will charge a

small fee by looking in the Yellow Pages. Booklet also available in Spanish.

35. *Domestic Violence Prevention.* Contains a series of forms and information to restrain violence and to obtain support. Forms for emergency protective orders, booklets in Spanish and English containing instructions and enforcement advice.

36. *Parentage Complaint.* Complaint to establish parentage and to seek support. Forms for expedited hearing and expedited support.

I would advise you to get all the court forms you can from the court or the Internet and to be familiar with the existence and general context of each form.

Sample Generic Checklists and Forms

Durable Power of Attorney Checklist
(Sometimes Called a Living Will or Health Care Directive)

A living will in general is a document by which a person gives instructions concerning prolonging or ending his or her life when that person is not able to make that decision.

The person also appoints another person(s) as a health care agent to make the health care decisions under certain conditions and within certain guidelines.

There are serious legal, moral, and ethical issues involved in the process. In those jurisdictions where these instructions are recognized in whole or in part, there are usually very strict conditions imposed by the legislature that reflect the political and moral positions of the legislators and their constituencies.

Forms and instructions are often provided or sold by your local medical association.

This questionnaire will enable you to ask some relevant questions, but you should not attempt to prepare the final document without researching the current status of the law in your state and determining if there is a current form that has been promulgated or approved by the legislature or medical association.

There are often strict limitations on who may be a witness and who may be designated as a health care agent.

Courts will generally respect the wishes of people expressed during their life when they are healthy and fully competent and informed. Courts may be reluctant to assist if there is any question of the competency of the person when the document was executed. Hospitals or physicians may not be willing to honor the person's instructions without a court order to protect them from liability. Accordingly, you may assume that the document must be perfectly prepared and executed and be current or it may not be honored.

1. Name of client.

2. Address of client.

3. Names and addresses of current physician(s) and health care provider(s).

4. Names and addresses of others whom the client will designate as his or her health care agent(s) to help make decisions if the client is unable.

5. Have the persons designated as health care agents been notified of their appointment(s) and have they agreed to serve?

6. Does the client wish to be kept alive even if in a permanent vegetative state and terminally ill with no reasonable medical hope of recovery?

7. Does the client wish life-saving treatment to be instituted or continued when such treatment artificially prolongs "life" and the benefits of prolonging life are outweighed by the burdens?

8. Does the client wish to be kept alive if in great pain and life-sustaining procedures will only prolong life a few hours or a few days?

9. Does the client want life-prolonging procedures to be discontinued if it is determined that the client is in a permanent irreversible vegetative state?

10. What specific instructions does the client wish to make as to unwanted treatment or procedures?

11. Does the client wish to authorize the health care agent to allow an autopsy and/or donation of body parts? (Note there may be severe religious implications.)

12. Does the client wish to allow the health care agent to make burial or other disposition-of-remains decisions?

13. Does the client wish the document to be for unlimited duration or for a specific length of time?

14. Who are client's first, second, and third choices to be designated as health care agent?

15. When and where will the document be signed and who will witness the execution?

16. Has the client been advised that this document is not a general power of attorney nor a designation of conservator nor a will (if such is the case)?

17. Does the client wish a will or designation of conservator or to execute a general power of attorney?

This questionnaire will cover many of the relevant questions, but you must research the law to determine limitations and appropriate execution of the document.

Health care directives, designation of conservation, and similar forms are often state specific. Sample forms can usually be obtained free from state medical or hospital associations.

Criminal Law Interview Checklist

1. Date.
2. Full name of accused or arrested person. (Include middle names, nicknames, aliases, and maiden names.)
3. Social Security number and date of birth of accused or arrested person. (To find their location by computer-Internet search.)
4. Is the client in jail or in custody? If so, complete next section.

    4.1 Name and address of facility where client is, or was last known to be.

    4.2 Where client can be interviewed if different facility or if client will be released or moved.

    4.3 Phone number and name of jailer where client is believed to be.

    4.4 Booking number or other numbers given to client for identification in the jail system. (Date of birth and Social Security number.)

5. Normal home address and phone number of client.
6. Normal work address and phone number of client.
7. Other persons and means of communication with client.
8. Name, badge number, and location of arresting officer(s).
9. Time and place of arrest.
10. Does jail allow unannounced client-attorney interviews?
11. Has the client been charged with a crime? If so, indicate crimes charged or indicated.
12. Is there an indicated bail or has bail been set?
13. Can client afford bail?
14. If client cannot afford bail, who will pay bail premium or post bail?
15. Is it necessary to have a bail hearing?

16. If a bail hearing is necessary, who will appear? Bonding company lawyer or our law office or other lawyer?

17. When will the accused be able to come to the office to discuss the case?

18. Have you instructed the receptionist and all who handle phones to accept collect telephone calls from the jail if the client calls?

19. Who will pay the fees to visit the client in jail?

20. Has either a prosecutor or a public defender been assigned to the case? If so, indicate name and phone number of these people.

21. Can client afford private counsel or should this case go into the public defender system?

22. When and where is next scheduled court appearance?

23. Has client given any relevant written or oral statements to police or to others? If so, indicate to whom and under what circumstances.

24. Other defendants and their counsel.

25. Witnesses known.

26. Client's version of facts.

27. Additional notes and comments.

Develop a relationship with a bail agency or a criminal lawyer. You will be judged by how quickly you can get the client out of jail. This also protects the client from making admissions while in custody.

Simple Will Interview Form

(Simple wills do not have trust provisions.)

You may wish to convert this form into a do-it-yourself questionnaire for the testator to fill out before coming in, or you may wish to use the form as an interview sheet, spending the time to do the interview and getting to know the client.

Note: Many state bar organizations sell or provide forms for simple wills with instructions at a very low price. You may wish to obtain a supply of them or to follow the format in those simple wills.

This form is a simple will. It is not an estate plan. For all clients, especially elderly clients, it should be prepared after an interview in which the client is explained his or her rights, limitations, and options are explained.

Other documents should be considered at the same time, including a nomination of conservator, durable power of attorney, living will, burial instructions, etc. Often the client does not want to pay for counsel and insists on a simple will according to his or her wishes without consideration of options.

I personally will not prepare a will without the minimum counseling described above even if the client can't or won't pay for the help. This checklist covers the offering of those services.

Much of the information asked in this interview form will not be necessary for actually preparing a will, but will be of great help in probating the will, locating assets after death, and notifying the appropriate people after death.

Additionally, getting information about pedigree and assets will help establish the minimum requisites of testamentary capacity, which is to know the general nature and extent of one's property and the natural objects of one's bounty. Clients who are hesitant to disclose the nature and extent of their assets are often afraid that you will charge more if you know what they have. When you explain to them that you are trying to protect their desires and ensure that the will is not successfully challenged, they become more candid and trusting.

It is also important for you to determine if the amount of the testator's wealth suggests the need for more sophisticated estate planning, taking into consideration death taxes. Even if you cannot provide this help, you have protected yourself from malpractice by suggesting calling in a tax or probate specialist.

1. Name of client as used by client in everyday life, such as on driver's license or payroll records.

2. Residence address of client. Be sure to include city and county.

3. Mailing address if different from above.

4. Home and work phone and fax numbers.

5. City and date of birth.

6. Name as shown on birth certificate.

7. Other names used during life.

8. Social Security number of self and of spouse.

9. Name and address of father. If deceased, indicate city and year of death and whether a probate proceeding was held.

10. Maiden name of mother.

11. Current name of mother.

12. Name and address of mother. If deceased, indicate city and year of death and whether a probate proceeding was held.

13. Names of deceased brothers and sisters, including half-brothers and half-sisters. Indicate whether deceased brothers and sisters left living children and their names and addresses and approximate ages.

14. Names and addresses of living siblings, including half-brothers and half-sisters. Indicate names and approximate ages of their children.

15. Name of spouse and date and place of marriage.

16. Names and dates of birth of children of marriage with spouse.

17. Names of prior spouses and date of divorce or death of prior spouse.

18. Names and ages and addresses of children of prior marriages.

19. Names of aunts, uncles, and first cousins if included in testamentary plan as "heirs at law."

20. If military service, indicate date and place of enlistment and discharge, branch of service, highest rank attained, and serial number.

21. If any of the testator's children are minors, indicate whom the testator wishes to be guardian of his or her person, if there is a need for a guardian. (The spouse may indicate a different person than the testator wishes to appoint.)

22. If any of the testator's children are minors, indicate whom the testator wishes to appoint as guardian of his or her property if there is a need for a guardian. (The spouse may indicate a different person than the testator wishes to appoint.)

23. Designate alternative guardians if originally named guardian is unwilling or unable to serve as guardian.

24. Designate personal representative (executor) to gather assets, pay bills, and distribute property in accordance with the will.

25. Designate first and second choice of alternate personal representative if originally named personal representative is unable or unwilling to serve as personal representative.

26. Does testator wish to notify personal representative of appointment as personal representative in will?

27. Does testator wish to send a copy of will in sealed or open envelope to personal representative to enable personal representative to move rapidly if necessary?

28. Does testator wish to leave the entire estate to one person? If so, to whom? Include full name and address unless described above.

29. Who is to inherit if the primary beneficiary predeceases the testator? (Who are the alternative takers?)

30. Are there any specific monetary bequests? If so, how much and to whom? Is the amount indicated to be free and clear of expenses and taxes or should that person pay some portion of taxes and expenses?

31. Who is to receive the specific monetary bequests if the previously indicated beneficiaries predecease the testator?

32. Are there any specific bequests of personal or real property? Who is to receive the personal or real property if the indicated beneficiaries predecease the testator?

33. Have funeral and burial arrangements been made? If so, where?

34. Any special requests as to funeral and burial arrangements? Modest, expensive, in accordance with religious and/or fraternal or military ceremonies?

35. Provide a no-contest clause? (Anyone contesting the will gets nothing.)

36. Any anticipated special problems?

37. Any special requests in the will? (Remember, simple wills do not contain trust provisions.)

38. List all real estate owned along with description of how title is held and original cost and current value.

39. List all life insurance policies with numbers and amount of insurance and beneficiary provisions.

40. List all pensions and retirement plans along with beneficiary provisions.

41. List all stocks and bonds and other securities along with description of how title is held and cost and current value.

42. List all savings and checking accounts and how title is held and approximate balances.

43. List valuable personal property such as jewelry and collections and location and approximate value.

44. Was any of the property of either spouse inherited? If so, give details.

45. Does either spouse expect to inherit property in the future? Should that property be treated any differently?

46. Does either spouse wish asset protection planning to keep the assets from doctors and hospitals and the state in the event of long-term or expensive medical care needs?

47. List all medical insurance coverage.

48. Does testator wish to take possession of original will or to leave it with firm to prevent accidental or intentional loss or destruction?

49. Have you explained to testator(s) that you are not accepting any responsibility for tax planning or asset protection and that such assistance is available? (If true.)

50. Did testator appear to be under the dominance or control of another person during the will interview or the will signing?

51. In your opinion did testator possess adequate testamentary capacity?

52. Would a medical opinion or videotape be of value in probating the will if testator's capacity were attacked?

53. Any special questions or concerns expressed by testator?

54. Comments on your part.

Note: This is a generic questionnaire that must be adapted to your jurisdiction. It can be used orally as an interview questionnaire to be filled in by the lawyer or as a form to be filled in by the client. In either case, the client should be provided a copy in advance, so the client can be prepared for the interview.

If your client is a senior, review the chapter on representing seniors.

Your First Court Appearances

This chapter is intended to help you the first time you go to court. Volumes have been written about trial and appellate advocacy. This short chapter is not intended to replace the multivolume works on advocacy. This chapter is intended to take a little bit of the fear element out of your first few appearances in a court or adversarial hearing.

A world-famous trial lawyer once told me, "Jay, ninety percent of being a trial lawyer is just feeling comfortable in the courtroom." In retrospect, I don't agree with him, but I see now that he made it easier for me to go to court when I was a new lawyer with no one to navigate me through the courthouse or a trial.

I hope that this short chapter makes you feel just a little less nervous about your first few court appearances.

Remember, there is no substitute for getting mentoring or help from other lawyers, who in most cases will be more than happy to give advice and tips to a new lawyer. In addition to the mentoring, I believe what follows will help you feel more comfortable in the courtroom.

A. Before the Trial or Hearing Starts.

1. If your local bar association or court system offers a walk-through tour of the courthouse, either for lawyers or for the general public, take it. Call the court administrator (a common title) or the public information or public relations office of the court to find out when and where these walk-throughs take place.

2. If the court publishes its own "Rules of Court" in addition to the state rules or instead of the state rules, get a copy and peruse or read it. It may be available on the Internet.

3. Find out where to park and how to get there by public transportation. List alternatives in case your first-choice parking lot is full or closed. Make a map of the courthouse location and the parking locations, and the traffic flow for one-way streets and public transportation routes. List parking lot prices so your client will know how much money he or she needs to get there. Send a copy of the map and information to your client in addition to keeping one for yourself. The client will feel more comfortable knowing that you know where the courthouse is and how to get there.

4. If the court publishes forms that it wants used with instructions for using those forms, get the information and read it. The forms may be available on the Internet.

5. For your first filing in any courthouse, I recommend you do it in person, even though it may be faster and cheaper to use an alternative method. Doing it yourself will make you feel more comfortable about the process.

Find out the location and hours of the filing window(s). Find out if they will take your check or credit card or a client's check or credit card, or if you can open an account of some nature to pay filing fees. Get a copy of the current fee schedule of the court. Filing clerks often refuse to accept papers unless accompanied by the exact proper payment. This can cause severe problems if a statute of limitations is involved. Find out if the court accepts filing by messengers, lawyer services, FedEx, U.S. mail, fax, or e-mail. This information may save you unnecessary trips to the courthouse or may enable you to file papers by a deadline.

6. Never, never be haughty or arrogant with a court clerk or any court personnel. These people can make your life pleasant or miserable almost at their whim. Their displeasure may end up prejudicing your client's case. They know you are a lawyer and went to law school and that time costs your client money. Your emphasizing these matters won't get you any merit points.

If a court clerk doesn't like you, he or she may mention it to the judge over coffee. If the judge is angry over what you did, he or she may mention it to other judges at their coffee breaks or over their internal e-mail systems or when they get together. You can find that you have a bad reputation with every judge in the courthouse, and you were accused and convicted without notice. You can have a bad reputation before judges you never even heard of. These judges can belittle you in front of your clients and even prejudice your client's case without consciously realizing why.

7. Find out which judge or department or division will hear the matter. Call that judge's clerk or court clerk to ask if that particular judge or court has its own set of instructions for lawyers, and if they do, get a copy and read it before you go. It may be on the Internet.

8. Find out the location for filing last-minute documents. You may have to file them with the main filing window or with the court hearing the matter, or you may have to file them in one place and hand-carry them somewhere else.

9. Ask the court clerk or the judges' clerk about the court's policy on accepting late filed papers. Some judges are loose and others demand strict compliance with all time deadlines. It's embarrassing when a judge announces from the bench, in front of your client, that he or she will not read your sixty-eight-page points and authorities and trial brief because they were late filed. It's humbling when the judge calls you up to the bench, hands you your brief, and tells you to give it to the clerk to cancel the filing stamp, and that it has not been read or considered. If the matter is ultimately lost, you may have great difficulty billing your client for the effort work and convincing your client that your late filing was not the cause of the loss. Holding back on a filing until the last moment in order to give opposing counsel less time or no time to prepare a response is a dangerous tactic, which can easily backfire.

10. Get to the courtroom early or even a day before to learn the physical setup of the courtroom. Find out where you sit while waiting for the case to be called and where your client sits while waiting for the case to be called. Don't allow your clients to sit somewhere where the judge or bailiff will order them to leave.

11. Ask the clerk if you are supposed to be on the left or on the right side of the counsel table or lectern. Most judges have a system. Some judges want plaintiffs, or movants, or appellants to sit on their right (your left) so they will know where to direct their questions or comments. If you are on the wrong side, the court may get angry.

12. The local rules on where you sit and whether or not you may stand or move around may be based on local security needs. In

some courts, a misstep in the wrong direction will result in a pistol being aimed at you to protect the judge or a witness or a party.

13. Ask the clerk if the court prefers you to sit or stand when addressing the court or making objections or asking questions and whether you should speak from counsel table or from the lectern if there is one. Unless the court admonishes you to remain seated, it is best to stand whenever you speak or when the judge arrives or leaves.

14. Find out how the case file gets to the judge or courtroom. Are you supposed to get the file from a central filing area and bring it to the court, or will it be there automatically waiting for you?

15. Ask the court clerk if the clerk or judge normally administers an oath or swears in either the lawyers or the parties or the witnesses en masse at the beginning of the calendar call or at the beginning of the case. You want to let your client know in advance of their expected participation in the "opening ceremonies."

16. I have always prepared a short, one-sided trial brief for every matter, no matter how simple the matter or how complete the pleadings. I personally believe the trial brief is invaluable in reviewing to prepare yourself, and it convinces the court that you and your client are serious about the case and in the client's opinion, should win. Judges are often extremely busy people with no time to read a file before taking the bench to hear the case and the judge may carefully read your short trial brief and only skim or glance at the voluminous pleadings in the file. Often trial briefs are not subject to the pleading time deadlines and can be filed at the last second, thus depriving the other side of an opportunity to be prepared for you (unless they also prepared a trial brief). After you have handled several matters before a specific judge or court, you may not want to use trial briefs where the matter is small or short, but at the beginning of your career, I recommend it.

17. Different judges have different systems for offering a document into evidence, receiving it, marking it, and moving it from clerk to judge to witness, etc. Ask the clerk or bailiff how the judge wants it done.

18. Pass out one of your cards to the sheriff or bailiff, the court clerk, the reporter, the judge's clerk and any other official in the courtroom. Jot down the case name and calendar number on the card. Tell the person how you pronounce your name. Tell the person that this is your first time in that courtroom or before that judge and

that you want to do everything correctly. Ask them if they can make any suggestions to avoid your making any stupid mistakes or if they are aware of any idiosyncracies of the judge or clerk. These people will try to help you if you are polite and sincere. I used to say to each of them "I'm a new lawyer (if true). This is my first case before Judge Jones (if true). This is the first time I've handled this type of case (if true). If I do something wrong or stupid, please don't hold it against my client."

Often one or more of these people will inform the judge that you are a new lawyer and this is your first case. I've had judges welcome me to their court from the bench. I've had judges take a few moments to call me and opposing counsel into chambers and welcome me. One time, when a judge took an uncontested matter under submission, the clerk called me to tell me that the judge had ruled in my favor even though I had presented the case incorrectly, and the only reason the judge had done so in this very borderline case was that it was my first time in his courtroom.

I would not make these comments to the court directly, as that contact could be interpreted as *ex parte* contact with a judge outside the presence of opposing counsel.

B. During the Hearing or Trial

19. Address the court by saying "Good morning, your Honor. My name is Jay Foonberg." Turn toward the reporter or clerk and say "That's j-a-y f-o-o-n-b-e-r-g of the offices of X, Y, and Z." Turn back toward the judge and say, "This morning, I'm representing the plaintiff and moving party, Aardvark Widgets Incorporated and its president, Mr. Jones, and Mr. Jones is present in the courtroom and has been sworn.

"I have here a short trial brief in addition to the pleadings on file, and with your permission, I'd like to give a copy to Mr. Smith, opposing counsel, and offer the original to Your Honor. May I approach the clerk to receive the trial brief?"

The judge will say yes or no or whatever. Always call the judge "Your Honor," not "sir" or "ma'am" or judge. Then state, "I am prepared with an opening statement if the court wishes to hear it."

20. You are now in trial and what happens from this point forward will depend on the case, but you will be off to a comfortable

start and your client will feel comfortable that you are heading in the right direction.

21. Be courteous but firm in your presentation. Do not interrupt opposing counsel with speech or facial or other gestures, no matter how outrageous the statement of opposing counsel. If opposing counsel interrupts you and the court does nothing, ask the court for an admonition to opposing counsel not to interrupt you. If the court refuses to give it, you may have a shouting match on your hands. Speak to the judge, not opposing counsel

22. Do not be afraid to object to a judge's questions if the objection is appropriate. More often than not, judges will respect you and rule properly on an appropriate objection to their own questions. You may wish to ask the court clerk if the judge respects counsel who objects or gets angry with them.

23. If the court asks you a question, answer it honestly and directly. Nonresponsive "waltzing around" answers simply tell the judge you don't have a meritorious answer to the question.

24. Be respectful to the judge, even if the judge is arrogant, demeaning, insulting, and in a bad frame of mind generally. Ignore the judge's tone of voice and respond firmly to the words used by the judge, not the tone of voice. Judges are experts in speaking so that the transcript will reflect their words, and not their tone of voice.

25. Be polite, but not friendly, to opposing counsel in the presence of your client. Clients may be paranoid and believe that friendliness is a sign of a "deal" or "sell-out" harmful to their case. Save the questions about opposing counsel's family and personal life for when the client is not present.

26. Don't antagonize or insult a judge, no matter how wrong you think the judge may be on a ruling.

27. Know when to shut up. A judge once admonished me, "Mr. Foonberg, I'm inclined to rule in favor of your client, but keep talking and I may change my mind."

The trial is not over when the judge announces a decision. Ask who gives notice of ruling or if notice is waived.

Times for appeal and ability to get an order signed by the court may be measured from formal notice of the result.

Call your client from the courthouse with the result.

The above won't replace a course in advocacy and is not as good as having someone in the courtroom to help you and evaluate your representation, but these few pages may give you just the amount of confidence you need for your first few matters.

Lastly, let me remind you of my analysis of most of my trials:

1. There's the way I intended to try the case. (What I rehearsed.)

2. There's the way I actually tried the case. (What I did when faced with on-the-spot decisions.)

3. There's the way I should have tried the case. (What went through my mind as I was driving back from the courthouse.)

A surgeon who has never lost a patient hasn't had many patients. A lawyer who has never lost a case hasn't had many cases. Many of your early trial cases will be small cases or losing cases to begin with. It is not likely you will get any multimillion-dollar six-month trial cases in your first few years. If you do the best you can with the case you've got, no one can or will expect more of you. Don't forget that even "small" cases and losing cases are important to the client. It's often the only case they've ever had. They can and do come back to you again and recommend you to others, even if the case is lost.

Don't be afraid of the courthouse.

Trial work, like all legal work, is professional and not a science. It must be learned and improved upon through experience. Your client is entitled to a fair trial with competent representation, not a perfect trial with perfect representation. Perfection is only realizable after the trial is over. Don't be afraid to get in there and do your job and don't be too proud to ask for help if you feel you need it.

You may wish to list yourself with various agencies which provide lawyers for making "one-shot" or administrative appearances where knowledge of the facts and the case is not necessary. Be careful about malpractice coverage and be careful that you do not become the attorney of record in the case.

How to Interview a Client

The way you conduct your interview will have a profound effect on whether or not the client has confidence in you and whether or not you will be engaged. Often the interview is the only face-to-face contact you have with your client unless you go to court. In this age of good electronic communication, subsequent client contact is often not face-to-face.

The initial interview is often your opportunity to show a prospective client how you would help, even if a case or a client is a turndown. You can encourage the turndown to return at a later time when he or she has a meritorious matter or to refer others to you.

In the Reception Room

1. Be sure there are some straight-back chairs. Injured or elderly clients can't get into or out of plush or overstuffed sofas and chairs.

2. If the client is early, have the receptionist offer the client coffee or a soft drink. As an international lawyer, I have met with clients and lawyers in Paris, Buenos Aires, and from all over the world, in such places as Beijing, Rio, Tokyo, Cairo, Nairobi, Hong Kong, Istanbul, Geneva, and London, among other places. It is an international custom appreciated by clients to offer them something to drink to "wet the whistle." Your client will be put in a relaxed mood by the beverage.

Be Prompt

Don't be early or late. If you have a 10:00 A.M. appointment, go in to get the client at 10:00 A.M., not 9:55 or 10:05. The client may take tardiness as a sign of disrespect (I do), or earliness as a sign of nothing to do.

Greet the Client

Ask, "Ms. Smith?" Don't assume that the only person in the reception room is your client. Your client may have gone to the restroom or back to move the car. If the person says, "Yes," then introduce yourself. Offer your hand in a handshake and say, "I'm John Jones." Don't introduce yourself as Mr. Jones, or Attorney Jones, unless this is the custom in your community. Calling oneself "Mister" or "Ms." is often taken as a sign of lack of self-confidence. The client knows you're a lawyer or he or she wouldn't be there.

Shake Hands with the Client When You Say Hello

Touching is a basic human trait of friendship. Shake hands when you say hello. The touching should be appropriate for the client's gender, age, and position. Cheek to cheek air kissing, touching shoulders or arms may be more appropriate. In some religions, male-female touching in public is forbidden.

Help the Client

If the client has a purse or coat or envelopes or documents, take it upon yourself to help carry the burdens.

Take Command of the Situation

From this point on, you must take command of the situation. You must be firm in voice and mannerisms. The client wants to lean on you, not vice versa.

Give the Client Directions

Tell the client "Follow me, please" to direct the client from the reception room to your office or the conference room. When you get to your office door (which you should have left open when you went to the reception room), stop at the door and say, "This is my office" (especially if there is more than one room that could be your office). "Please go in."

Tell the Client Where to Sit

Tell the client, "Please, sit down," indicating with a hand gesture the chair you wish the client to occupy. Help the client, if the client is injured or elderly. Ask the client if he or she is comfortable.

Ensure Privacy

Call your secretary or the receptionist to say, "I'm in conference with Ms. Smith. No calls, please." Tell the client that when you're in conference you don't take calls, except from judges and family members and for emergencies, because the client who is in your office is entitled to all your attention, and because you don't like to discuss one client's legal matters in front of another client.

Start Your Interview

Actually, the client started the interview with you when you came into the reception room. Now you are starting your interview of the client.

Learn to Take Good Notes

In law school you probably took extensive notes looking down at your notebook. In practice you must look at your client to establish trust and confidence and the client's demeanor while you take notes, and you must look at witnesses while you take notes.

Unfortunately, you must keep good notes to protect both yourself and your client. You must balance between looking at your client and looking at your notes. Observe your doctor the next time she or he examines you. Note how the doctor both takes notes and looks at you.

The following tips may help you take notes while listening to your client and looking at your client.

1. Learn to use initials, symbols, and abbreviations. Some might be "Cl" for "client," "Atty" for "attorney," "H&W" for "husband and wife." Develop your own shorthand to fit your particular needs as you go along.

2. If the client or witness says something important, put it in quotes, quoting exactly what is said.

3. If you don't want to interrupt the client but want to ask more questions about what a client said or did, put a big circle or question mark or F/U (for "follow up") next to the comment.

4. Don't focus on your notebook, focus on the client or witness, breaking eye contact only when necessary to make a note.

5. Practice note taking. Turn on the television set and tape-record a news program. Look at the newscaster and make notes of what is important. Later play back the tape and see how complete or incomplete your notes are.

6. Taking notes on a keyboard or using a tape recorder while interviewing a client may distract or irritate the client. The client may feel you really aren't listening or paying attention to what he or she is saying. Clients want to be listened to.

7. When the client leaves, dictate into the tape or digital recorder or type out your handwritten notes, embellishing the notes with additional information you still remember.

8. Put a mark such as a star or a big "X" next to critical or important information.

9. Sample interview forms and checklists can be found throughout this book and should be used whenever possible. Use of checklists and interview forms give the client confidence that you know what you are doing.

10. When you take notes, the client will know you are listening to him or her and paying attention. From time to time, repeat or paraphrase what the client just said.

Ask Simple Questions

Start with simple questions such as name, home address, mailing address, home telephone, work telephone, etc. Establish the format immediately whereby you will ask the questions and the client will answer them. Repeat the answers so the client will know you are listening. Clients want to tell their stories and they want you to listen to them tell their stories.

Keep Control of the Situation

If the client is verbose and will not stop talking, tell the client that he or she must learn to answer questions and not to answer more than the question asked. Tell the client that each question and answer may have legal significance and that the client must listen carefully to the question and answer it carefully. Tell clients that you are listening to them and that you won't let them leave until they have an opportunity to ask you anything they want to ask you or tell you anything they want to tell you. The easiest and fastest way to stop a client from talking is to show them the palms of your hands. I don't know why this works but it does; try it.

Make Tissues, Candy, and Soft Drinks Available

If the client cries, offer tissues and ask if he or she would like a drink of water. Ask the client if he or she would rather finish the interview another time. (The client never says yes, but appreciates the offer.)

Toys for Children

Have toys for children to play with. Children like toys that are colorful, have moving parts, and make sounds. I use a plastic model of a gear box and kids love it. If the children don't have toys, they'll turn your knickknacks into toys and will distract you preventing good attorney-client communication.

Give the Client Something in Writing with Your Name on It

Give clients or turndowns a pamphlet, brochure, legal pad, ball-point pen, or multi-year calendar, or legal information with your name on it. The clients or turndowns may keep the pamphlet for years or give it to a friend or share it with a friend. Give them information about you or what you do or about their legal problem areas. Pamphlets can be obtained from your local bar association with space for you to add your name.

Tell Clients What Their Legal Position Is and What Lies Ahead

Clients want an honest, truthful legal opinion of the merits or weaknesses in their matter. They want a road map of what's going to happen, when it's going to happen, what it's going to cost, and what will be the likely results. Give clients your best estimates (if you can) or explain that you need to do some research as to the current state of the law before answering, and then try to answer their questions after you've discussed the case with other lawyers.

In an American Bar Association study, 95 percent of satisfied clients said their lawyer explained the legal process and their legal position. Only 50 percent of dissatisfied clients said their lawyer explained the legal process and their legal position. Satisfied clients come back for more work and refer others to you. Dissatisfied clients don't.

Limit Your Interview to Between One and One and a Half Hours

Interviews longer than this are physically and mentally exhausting and should be avoided if possible.

How to Discuss Fees

Clients want you to discuss fees at the first meeting and sometimes before the first interview. At about forty minutes into the interview, ask the client, "Would you like to discuss fees?" The client will always say "yes." It is important to discuss fees after you have a good feeling for what's involved; forty minutes should be adequate in most situations. You want to leave time to discuss the client's ability to pay fees. Based on the ability of the client to pay the fees and the time period needed for the client to pay the fee, you may wish to modify either the amount of work you will do or the timing of when you will do it.

Discuss Fees During the Interview

If the client tries to bring up fees at the beginning of the interview or before you are ready, tell the client that you don't want to discuss fees until you've gotten all the facts and have a better idea of what's involved. Tell the client that your first concern is to hear the facts, so you can tell the client what kind of help is needed. At the end of the interview, discuss the fees and then dictate the fee engagement letter in the presence of the client.

Always Ask the Client What He or She Wants to Add or Ask

Tell the client that sometimes in the interviewing process facts get overlooked. Before ending the interview always say to the client, "Is there anything else you want to tell me or anything you want to ask me? I don't want you to leave here feeling that I didn't give you a chance to tell me anything you want to tell me or ask me anything you want to ask me." If you've done a good job with the interview there won't be anything else. You'd be surprised at some of the things clients ask you or want to tell you. You have an obligation to make a complete and full investigation of the facts to avoid malpractice liability. By routinely asking "Is there anything else you want to tell me or ask me?" you may be protecting both yourself and the client. Additionally, the client will like you because you gave them an opportunity to tell you or ask you everything they wanted to tell you or ask you.

End the Interview

The client is dependent on you to say when the interview is over. The easiest way to end the interview is simply to stand up and walk over to the door. Tell the client when you want to see or talk to him or her again, or say that you'll begin work as soon as the fee engagement letter with the retainer fee is returned.

Walk the Client Back to the Reception Room and Stay with Them Until They Leave Your Offices

Don't leave them wandering about confused or able to see other client's information on monitor screens.

Don't assume the client knows the way out. Shake hands with the client and say you are happy to have met him or her and look forward to working on the case.

What Clients Want: Learn How to Listen to Clients When They Talk
(Foonberg's Rules of Listening)

Every client who comes into your office wants four things from you:

1. They want to tell their story.

2. They want you to listen to them tell their story and pay attention to what they say.

3. They want you to reassure them that they did the right thing by calling you rather than ignore the problem.

4. They want closure. They want to get on with their lives. Their legal problem is an interference with their life.

Knowing how to listen to a client is easily more important than knowing how to talk to a client. Many volumes and treatises have been written on how to manage client relations. In this short chapter I am only covering a few simple points for the new lawyer to learn and apply in their practice.

In a recent American Bar Association study, it was learned that 95 percent of satisfied clients (they would use you again and recommend others to you) reported their lawyer listened to them and paid attention to what they said. Among dissatisfied clients, only 42 percent of them said the lawyer listened to them and paid attention to what they said. To use these numbers in perspective:

Set the stage for listening to the client. Just before starting the interview pick up your phone and say to your secretary or receptionist, "Hold my calls, I'm in conference with Ms. Smith." Turn to Ms. Smith and explain, "Ms. Smith, I'm all yours and I won't take any calls, with three exceptions:

1. If any member of my family calls, I'll take that call. They rarely call, but nothing is more important to me than my family.

2. If a judge calls, I'll take the call. Judges are on the bench and can't make or take calls during court. They have to call when they can and I must take the call. (This may also impress the client that you are an important lawyer with legal matters in court.)

3. A true client urgency. If there is an urgency I must take the call. But you as a client have the same privilege. Simply tell the receptionist that you are a client and this is urgent and he will put the call through to me even though I am in conference with another client."

Allow no telephone calls or walk ins. Hang a hotel "Do Not Disturb" on your door knob. Look at the client while they talk. Take notes (they'll know you're listening because you are taking notes).

About every three minutes, repeat or paraphrase what they said.

At the end of the interview ask "Is there anything you want to tell me or anything you want to ask me? I don't want you to leave upset that I didn't give you a chance to ask me what you wanted to ask me or tell me what you wanted to tell me." Wait about thirty seconds or a minute for the client to respond. The client will feel you listened to their story and paid attention to them.

Foonberg's Rules of Listening are actually named after my father, who taught me two rules of listening:

1. You can either talk or you can listen to what people are saying so you can learn, but you can't do both at the same time.

2. The Lord gave us ears and one mouth. It is intended that we are supposed to listen 2/3rds of the time and talk only 1/3rd of the time, or else we would have two mouths and one ear.

The result of Foonberg's Rule is that any time you are talking more than 1/3rd of the time, you are talking too much and not listening enough.

How to Conduct a Meeting
(Foonberg's Ten Rules)

Lawyers spend a lot of time in meetings. You will be in meetings with clients, staff, other lawyers on your side of the matter, other lawyers on the other side of the matter, judges, insurance adjusters, vendors, etc.

A well-run meeting results in confidence in you as a leader. You will be recognized as a person in charge upon whom clients and others can rely and look to for leadership and counseling. A poorly run meeting will result in everyone being angry or frustrated and blaming you for wasting their time when they had more important things to do.

While this chapter is intended primarily for face-to-face meetings, it can apply equally to telephone conferences and video conferences with others.

These rules can help you save your time and money.

1. Have a written agenda even if there is only one item being discussed. Do not assume that people know the purpose of the meeting. The purpose of the agenda is to be sure that everyone understands why they are there and the purpose of the meeting. Unless you have a written agenda, Mr. A. will think he is there to discuss one thing, Ms. B. may think she is there to discuss another thing, and you may think the purpose of the meeting is to attend to a third matter. There may be no communication between you. Each will be discussing a different subject, unaware of the fact that you are not communicating with one another. Do not allow "surprises" that you are not prepared to discuss. Tell the person, "I am sorry, that is not on the agenda. I will be glad to put it on the agenda for the next meeting." You must be firm. If necessary, call for a new meeting

after the present meeting, at which time you will discuss the new subject. Do not allow you or your client to be booby-trapped with last-minute agenda items.

The person who habitually comes late to meetings is challenging you and your ability to lead. Stop them with public statements the others can hear. You may wish to ask them to see you privately after the meeting. You can then relate the total hourly dollar value of the people in the meeting as your reason for starting on time and progressing without going back over previously discussed items.

2. If there is no written agenda because of time urgency or because the meeting is an unscheduled meeting, announce at the beginning of the meeting; "The purpose of this meeting is. . . ." Again, unless the purpose of the meeting is clearly set forth, people will not be communicating with one another. If someone else has called the meeting and has not provided a written agenda or made an announcement of purpose, you should make the statement. You could say something like, "Pardon me, Mr. Jones, I want to be sure I understand what we will be discussing today. Am I correct in saying the purpose of this meeting is . . . ?" By making this statement, you will be saving everyone's time, including your own, and you will be establishing yourself as a leader rather than a follower on the team. You might even state, "Let me write this down. The purpose of this meeting is. . . ."

3. Try to set a beginning and ending time before the meeting so that people can plan their activities around the meeting. Without an ending time, you risk people getting up and walking out because of other commitments, real or contrived. They will blame you for not completing their daily work assignments. Try to end all meetings on schedule or earlier. It is better to continue a meeting to another mutually agreeable time and place than to go on and on. The amount of time devoted should normally depend on the importance of the subject.

If someone comes in late (normally announcing they had something more important to do in order to establish how important they are), embarrass them by stating, "I'm sorry you're late. Come see me later or read the minutes to find out what you missed." If they go into the reasons they missed, stop them immediately. State, "I'm sorry, we've already discussed this." If they are habitually late in order to establish self-importance, tell them you won't bother them with the meetings, and will not invite them in the future, and decisions will be made without their input. Try not to go beyond ninety minutes without a break or an ending.

4. Announce in the written agenda, or orally, whether the purpose of the particular meeting is merely to discuss a problem, exchange input, or to take some action that may be influenced by what happens at the meeting. People will become angry when meetings take place and nothing happens when they are expecting something to happen.

5. Limit the amount of time any one person can speak, at any one time. Richard Ferguson of Alberta, Canada, who was chair of the Canadian Bar Association's Law Practice Management and Technology Section, actually gives a small egg timer to each person at the meeting and announces the person either has three or six minutes to say what they want to say.

6. Do not let people ramble beyond the three- or six-minute limit. Show them the palms of your hands and tell them, "I'm sorry, your time is up. We'll come back to you if there is time after everyone else has had their say. Perhaps next time you would like to prepare a written handout in advance so we can give your thoughts more attention." Alternatively, you may wish to repeat the Foonberg Rule of knowing when to stop talking. I often relate the following, mentioned earlier: Once, during a trial, the judge said to me, "Mr. Foonberg, I'm inclined to rule in favor of your clients, but keep talking and you may convince me to change my mind." This tells the person, "You've made your point. We all understand you. You are beginning to anger us by unnecessarily going on."

7. End the meeting on time with an announcement of personal responsibilities and decision making. "We only have five minutes left. Let's be sure we understand our next steps. John, you are going to. . . . Mary, you are going to. . . ." You might state, "We have decided to change our system," or "We have decided not to change our system." "We have not decided what to do about the X problem." Be sure each person (including yourself) has a clear understanding of what they are expected to do and of what was or was not decided.

8. Set time limits for accomplishing next steps. "John, you'll have your report by the 15th." "Mary, you'll send a memo to each of us (or to me) by the 20th." "Sam, you'll contact Mr. Jones by Friday and let us all know the response." Record these time limits and remind people in writing immediately after the meeting of what they are expected to do.

9. Thank each person orally for their input. Try to say something about what each person has said, done, or contributed. Praise them in front of the others as a reward for attending and participating. If appropriate, thank them in writing. Be flexible. Every meeting develops its own dynamics. There's nothing wrong with ending a meeting in half the scheduled time when there's nothing left to discuss or decide or if the meeting is out of control. It's all right to extend a meeting just a little if the goals of the meeting are being met in an orderly manner. A well-run meeting leaves all those who attend with a sense of empowerment and control over their lives, and establishes you as a leader.

10. Pay attention to both motive and motif. Try to hold the meeting in a clean, well-lit room. Place a new legal pad and a new pencil at each seat. Some big Wall Street firms and European law firms put out new legal pads with the firm's name, city and telephone number across the top of the legal pad and on the new pencils, hoping the attendees will take them as a form of marketing. Some firms also provide napkins with the firm name. Provide liquids, but try to avoid caffeinated or alcoholic drinks, which may cause people to leave frequently to go to the restroom. Cookies, which can be eaten without making a mess, are preferable to sticky cakes or candies. Tell the receptionist the names of those expected to be in attendance at the meeting so he or she will know what to do with their incoming calls. Assure the attendees that the receptionist knows the attendees are in the meeting and will take messages.

Preceptors and Internships

It is an unfortunate fact of life that many new lawyers are turned out of law school and into practice with absolutely no real-life experience relevant to running a law practice.

They may have had no courses or training as undergraduates on client relations. If they have had any training it may only be a single clinical course. They may never have had any contact with a real, live client or a court or drafted a document or dealt with another lawyer. It is possible that there may someday be an internship requirement.

Delaware has long had a preceptor program. As the program now stands, an applicant for admission (called a "clerk") must work with or for another lawyer (called a "preceptor") for a minimum of five months of full-time practical experience.

More and more states are requiring some form of course instruction in the practical aspects of being a lawyer, but only Delaware, to the best of my knowledge, requires hands-on experience.

It is of value to review the Delaware requirements as well as proposed content of courses in Georgia and Tennessee and other states in order to give some advance planning to what your own bar association or law school might require of you in an internship program. These requirements may also indicate the most common types of practice in the area.

These lists from these three states are valuable because they represent the opinions of many lawyers as to what a lawyer has to know to practice law in that state.

The lawyer starting a practice might expect to have a client call or walk in with a problem in any of the possible areas listed. The new lawyer in practice should use these lists of topics as a springboard to find lawyers or other resources to whom the new lawyer can turn for help in the areas described when a client has one of these problems for the first time in the lawyer's career.

Included in the various Delaware requirements are the following:

Attend civil trial sessions in Justice of the Peace Court, Municipal Court, Divorce Court, Court of Common Pleas, U.S. District Court, etc.

Attend criminal trials in Court of Common Pleas, U.S. District Court, etc.

Attend a sheriff's sale.

Attend a pretrial conference.

Attend a judicial arbitration.

Attend a deposition.

Attend civil and criminal jury trials.

Attend an arraignment and a sentencing.

Review the court record and pleadings and briefs of a case on appeal and attend the appellate hearing.

Attend an administrative agency hearing.

Review the completed probate files of three wills that were probated.

Review the file and attend a motion hearing.

Prepare a draft will and trust agreement.

Attend the interview of a client, witness, or litigant.

Complete a title search.

Tennessee's proposed course materials include workshops in motion practice, personal injury practice, adoptions, guardianships, conservatorship, appellate practice, collections practice, handling a divorce, alternative dispute resolution, negotiation skills, juvenile appointments, criminal appointments, wills and probate practice, deposition strategies, commercial real estate, and banking practice.

Among Tennessee's required courses would be maintaining client relations, maintaining professional relations, malpractice prevention, building and maintaining a practice, client interviewing and counseling, time management, stress management, and civil and criminal practice tips.

Georgia is considering requiring courses in professionalism, legal ethics, law office management, ADR (Alternate Dispute Resolutions), negotiations, counseling, billing, escrow accounts, resolving conflicts of interest, engagement letters, civil and criminal litigation, business practice, real estate practice, family law, and other areas.

The legal subjects from any of these three states may change from time to time before or after implementation. Nonetheless, the new lawyer should try to get ready for any of these client problems when they arise.

The 1992 ABA MacCrate report addressed the relationship between the law school and the world of practice. This book meets many if not all of the requirements of the MacCrate report. The MacCrate report is discussed in the following chapter.

The MacCrate Report

The ABA section of Legal Education and Admissions to the Bar issued a report in 1992 entitled "Task Force on Law Schools and The Profession: Narrowing the Gap," commonly called the "Mac-Crate Report" after Robert MacCrate, the Chair of the Task Force.

That report identifies ten fundamental lawyering skills and four fundamental values of the profession that the commission felt were essential to competent representation. Those skills and values are acquired by a lawyer before, during, and after law school.

To the best of my knowledge the 1992 MacCrate report is the only "official" ABA publication—except for this book—that attempts to deal with the real-world problems of real-world clients and real-world new lawyers.

I believe *How to Start and Build a Law Practice* continues to help the law student and new lawyer by providing the materials and information necessary to acquire and utilize those skills and values.

The skills and values identified in the MacCrate report are
Fundamental Lawyering Skills
1. Problem Solving
2. Legal Analysis and Reasoning
3. Legal Research
4. Factual Investigation
5. Communication
6. Counselling
7. Negotiation
8. Litigation and Alternative Dispute Resolution Procedures
9. Organizations and Management of Legal Work
10. Recognizing and Resolving Ethical Dilemmas

The four fundamental values of the profession included in that report are providing competent representation; promoting justice, fairness and morality; improving the profession; and professional self-development.

This book addressed those skills and values fifteen years before the MacCrate Report, and continues to address them. I am proud that this book is used as the book for courses in law schools.

Negotiating Skills

The ability to negotiate is an important part of being a good lawyer. You will negotiate with adversaries, their lawyers, their representatives, judges, your office staff and your own client. Unfortunately, negotiation is not a skill currently taught in most law schools. It would be worth your time and trouble to take a course somewhere on how to effectively negotiate.

In this chapter, I'll simply pass on a few basic pointers which may help you in your first negotiations.

1. Try to start a negotiation with a win-win attitude rather than a win-lose attitude. Ask yourself the question, "Is there some way both sides could get what they really want?" If you start with an attitude that one side must win and one side must lose, you will have created a hostile environment within which a settlement, which is good for your client, may not be possible.

It is a mistake to treat an interest in possible settlement as a sign of weakness. Immovable positions invite immovable positions to no one's benefit.

I have no problem with picking up the phone, calling the other lawyer, and saying:

> "Ms. Smith, my name is Jay Foonberg. I never start any matter without picking up the phone, calling opposing counsel and asking the five-word question, 'Can this case be settled?' If the answer is 'no,' or you can't control your client, I'll respect that, but, I don't consider it a sign of weakness to simply inquire if expensive, nonbeneficial, conflicting positions are really necessary."

Usually, the other lawyer will respect you for doing this and your client is less likely to object to your fees if you make it clear that the work required is not your fault and indeed you tried to avoid spending the time and money.

2. Try to separate legal rights, legal positions, and interests. Your client (and the other client) has an interest they want to achieve. The interest may be to receive more or pay less money, or to do or not do a certain act, or to get the other side to do or not do a certain act. Try to keep clearly in mind, at all times, your clients' and the other clients' interests. When you discuss legal rights and legal positions you are communicating an attitude of "I prefer to fight" rather than "what's best for our clients."

3. Listen very carefully to your client, the other clients' lawyer, or the other party. Try to understand what they really need or want. Often, what they need or want may not be money or may not be obvious.

I remember what my father taught me; either you can talk or you can learn, but, you can't do both at the same time. The Lord gave us two ears and one mouth. It's obvious we are supposed to listen 2/3 of the time, and talk 1/3 of the time. If the Lord intended us to talk 2/3rds of the time, we would have two mouths and one ear.

A good rule of thumb is to try to listen carefully 2/3rds of the time. If you are talking more than 1/3 of the time, you are probably talking too much.

4. Look to alternatives to money as a means of settlement. Judges, Juries, and Arbitrators can only award money to the claimant. Often, a party will take a significantly smaller sum of money, or no money at all if it's accompanied by a letter of apology, or a forum in which to tell their story. Mediators may offer a solution to an impasse. Try to satisfy a party with a letter that summarizes the events and expresses regret rather than apologizing (a client is often willing to sign a letter regretting what happened rather than apologizing for what happened).

5. Don't make ridiculous demands or offers. Ridiculous demands or offers often engender anger and immovable positions. Ask another lawyer for help when you don't know where to start.

6. Never forget that money always has a time value. Most people will accept less dollars if they can get it immediately. Most people will pay more dollars if they can pay over a period of time. People who buy and sell businesses are keenly aware of the time value

of money. Individuals don't normally calculate time values, but, they will accept time of payment delay to pay more money, or delay of payment to pay less money.

Look to see if there is a tax angle which can be utilized. Deals can often be done by structuring the transaction to give the other side some tax deduction or advantage that costs your client nothing. Prior to negotiating you may wish to ask a tax lawyer or a CPA if there are any tax features that can be negotiated or offered. (As an example, payments for pain and suffering are normally not taxable income, but, payments for lost earnings are taxable income.) The payer might have no tax consequences or care less how the payments are allocated or labeled.

7. Never negotiate without first refreshing your memory with the facts or the file. If an insurance adjuster or opposing counsel calls you unexpectedly, tell them you have to get the file and you'll call them back in a few minutes. Use the interviewing time to review the file before returning the call.

8. Be sure you prepare your client with reasonable expectations. Negotiations are a waste of time if the clients' expectations are totally unreasonable.

9. Involve your client in the negotiation process. Keep them informed of where you are in the process. Ask for their input and suggestions. Set time limits for your keeping them informed and for them to respond to your communications.

10. Lastly, always be courteous, dignified, and professional when dealing with opposing counsel. Remember, it's the client's case, not your case. A client once told me, "Jay, opposing counsel is my best friend. He's going to hammer his client to settle rather than face a possible seriously adverse alternative."

If you act like a jerk toward opposing counsel, you can expect to be treated like a jerk by opposing counsel. Your conduct might prevent a settlement that benefits all; your conduct could cause unnecessary expense, delay, and possibly bad results. You don't have to be humble. (Although a new lawyer often would benefit and get better results by being humble and respectful with the other lawyer.) You can be firm and resolute, but be professional.

Negotiation is both an art and a skill. You must always be flexible and keep the clients' best interests and expectations clearly in mind.

How to Maintain Bank Accounts

The day you open your office, you should open three checking accounts, as follows:

Personal Account

The checks, checkbook, and deposit slips should be printed "Personal Account" or other title clearly indicating it is not a trust account or office operating account. Use this account for nonoffice-related, personal, or family matters, such as food, clothing, etc. Your spouse may be a signator on the account to write checks if you desire.

Office Account

The checks, checkbook, and deposit slips should be printed "Office Account." This account should be used for all items that are, or that might be, related to the practice income and expenses. Your spouse or your secretary can sign on this account but should only do so if authorized by you in clearly defined situations.

Client Trust Account

The checks, checkbook, and deposit slips should be printed "Client Trust Account." This account is for client money. You should never use it for your money. No person other than you should be able to sign on this account. You should not allow your spouse or a secretary or even another lawyer to sign on this account.

You should not use a check-writing machine signature or rubber-stamp signature. In some states the rules of trust account maintenance are set by the state bar in order to get the interest income. A more-detailed discussion of the client trust account will follow later.

You may wish to get a copy of *The ABA Guide to Lawyer Trust Accounts*, which I wrote, or a free copy of an hour-long videotape on trust account management (while supplies last). Your CPA and office staff would benefit from the book and the videotape.

Other Accounts

1. *Savings Accounts.* It is rare that you would have any use for a savings account in your firm name insofar as your practice is concerned. Any interest income on trust accounts would belong to the client, not to you. (In some countries the lawyer can keep the interest, but not in the United States.) It is possible that when you will keep a large sum of client money for a significant time, an interest-bearing account in your name, as trustee for the client, should be used, but this is an exceptional situation, and generally you should not keep trust account funds in an interest-bearing account, unless it is for a client or to comply with IOLTA rules (Interest on Lawyer Trust Accounts).

2. *Payroll Account.* I recommend maintaining a separate checking account for payroll and payroll taxes, even though it is not required. As a practicing CPA, I learned to have a healthy respect for payroll taxes. When I hired my first secretary, I immediately opened a payroll account, and used the special payroll checks with appropriate spaces on the check and the stub to indicate the computation of the net pay. In some states, an employee is entitled by law to a statement of computation of the net pay, and the check with the computation will usually satisfy that requirement.

I also recommend transferring to the payroll account from the office account an amount equal to the gross pay, plus a flat percent allowance (12 percent to 15 percent is usually sufficient) to cover the employer share of the various payroll taxes, and workers' compensation, etc. In this manner, you set aside most or all payroll money as you go along, and don't have to worry about coming up with the payroll taxes monthly or quarterly.

It is foolish, in my opinion, to attempt to use or spend the difference between the employees' gross pay and the employees' net pay.

This practice has led to serious problems for employers, including lawyers, when they couldn't come up with the taxes withheld.

For example, assume a secretary is entitled to $500 gross pay, and the employer taxes are 6 percent Social Security, 1 percent workers' compensation insurance, 3 percent unemployment insurance; assume 1 percent state disability, and another 1 percent state withholding and 20 percent federal withholding. (These rates and taxes are for this example only. The rates change continually):

Gross Pay		$300.00
Employer Taxes:		
Social Security	$18.00	
Workers' Compensation	3.00	
Unemployment	<u>9.00</u>	
Total Employer Taxes	$30.00	<u>$30.00</u>
Amount to be transferred from		
Office Account to Payroll Account:		<u>$330.00</u>
		$330.00
Gross Pay		
Less Deduction:		
State Disability	$ 3.00	
State Withholding	3.00	
Federal Withholding	<u>60.00</u>	
Total Deductions:		<u>$66.00</u>
Net to Secretary:		$234.00

It is very tempting to set aside only $234 and to hope to have the balance of $66 employee taxes and $30 employer taxes when the time comes to pay the taxes. It will give you great peace of mind to set aside the entire payroll cost of $330 at the time of paying the payroll, and then not have to be concerned about coming up with the balance.

Failure to make withholding deposits can be criminal.

"Laundering Money"

Be very careful when a client or prospective client asks you to deposit a check or cash or accept a wire transfer to one of your accounts in exchange for one of your checks; or when you purchase a cashier's check for the client often payable to a third party. Banks shouldn't practice law, and lawyers shouldn't engage in banking.

There is sometimes a valid reason for your handling a "secret" transaction for a client (such as sealed bids); however, be careful. You may be required to file a report with the IRS when you are paid more than $10,000 in a single transaction or series of transactions.

When cash is involved, various federal agencies may knock on your door and accuse you of being a coconspirator or aiding and abetting. You may be disqualified from representing the client and have to hire your own lawyer to defend you. These agencies are sometimes instructed to ignore attorney-client confidences.

Picking a Bank or Banker

As a new lawyer in practice, some banks or bankers will go out of their way to accommodate you. Others will not want your business until you are more firmly established. Often the reason a bank wants your business is to get some of your checking and trust account deposits. You may have anywhere from a few hundred dollars to hundreds of thousands in your checking or trust account for days, weeks, or months. Since your office checking account doesn't draw interest or draws low interest, the bank will want these deposits. IOLTA trust accounts can be very profitable for both the bank and for the IOLTA agencies. Start with the bank or branch closest to your office (for convenience), and tell the manager that you are starting your practice and want to establish a banking relationship. Do the same thing with two or three banks. See which bank or banker seems more interested in you, and open your accounts with that bank or banker. A good relationship will give you access to loan funds as you need them for temporary cash flow problems, as well as equipment financing and other personal banking needs.

Go to the bank personally to make deposits. Say "Hello" or wave to the branch manager every time you go in. Be sure the manager knows your name and your face. You are more likely to get credit if you need it and possibly referrals if the manager actually knows you.

What to expect from the bank you select:
1. No service charges on any of your accounts;
2. Free check printing (within limits);
3. Lunch with the banker, at bank expense;
4. Wills and trusts form books;
5. Favored treatment on your banking needs.

Reporting Financial Fraud

A few states and most prosecutors want an attorney to turn in a client if the attorney suspects financial fraud, especially if the client has funds sent to the attorney's trust account. This, to me, is a "killing flies with a cannon" reaction to the financial fraud of Enron and other similar debacles. This type of financial fraud is usually perpetrated by large corporations who have large law firms and CPA firms representing them. Solos, new lawyers, and small firms rarely are involved in these high-level frauds, yet the solos, the new lawyers, and the small firms are likely to be prosecuted or disciplined because they don't have the resources to resist.

Getting Business from Banks and Bankers

Banks and bankers are excellent sources of business for a lawyer. They are frequently asked to recommend a lawyer to a customer.

Unfortunately, the new lawyer will rarely get any of these referrals, which usually will go to the bank's general counsel, or to lawyers who give the bank a lot of business. The bank's general counsel is often represented on the board or key committees of the bank. A branch manager may not wish to place his or her own position at risk by referring business to lawyers.

Occasionally, a bank customer will specifically ask the bank manager to recommend a new lawyer, or a young lawyer, to handle a case that other lawyers have already declined to handle.

Look upon these referrals as a golden opportunity to demonstrate how hard you can work. Don't make unrealistic promises to the client. Be honest as to the merit or lack of merit of the case. If you handle it, work as hard as you can. The banker may learn of the customer's satisfaction from the customer, and you may get a referral on a good client or good matter.

Sign All Checks Personally and Do All Bank Reconciliations Personally

As a new lawyer you can get a better handle on expenses if you personally sign the checks and personally reconcile the bank statements. When you reconcile the bank statement, you can again look at the check(s) you previously wrote and ask yourself if you made a wise or unwise investment of your limited funds.

How to Maintain a Trust Account to Avoid Disbarment

When I read the disciplinary reports that say "and shall be disbarred effective January 1, 20__ , and his/her name shall forever be removed from the roll of attorneys of the state," a chill goes through me. I think of the years of study gone to waste; I think of the shame and tears of parents, the dashed hopes of the spouse; the fears of wondering how to provide for children and of having to explain to the children years later about their disbarred parent. I think of the high degree of suicide among disbarred lawyers. Most of all, I think about the client or clients who may have gone under with the unfortunate lawyer.

There are many ways to get yourself disbarred. The surest, fastest way to lose your license is to ignore the rules for handling client funds.

If you are going to get involved with "close practices" with client funds, remember that in this game every rule in the book is written against you. The referees (your state disciplinary board) will not look for extenuating circumstances, and ignorance on your part is no defense.

If you ignore this section of my book, you are not only a fool, you are a damned fool. I cannot emphasize strongly enough the importance to you of understanding and applying the rules of trust funds. For a more comprehensive guide for yourself, your CPA, and your office staff, I strongly recommend the book *The ABA Guide to Lawyer Trust Accounts,* which I wrote.

Many lawyers are disciplined for various matters, ranging from failure to return telephone calls to fee disputes. Lawyers are sometimes thrown out of bar associations for violating ethical rules. However, most disbarments result from mishandling of client funds.

Get it in writing as to whether or not your malpractice insurance covers trust account violations by you or a staff person. You may be shocked to learn that you are uninsured due to the exceptions and exclusions not covering "willful acts."

You can still practice law after being kicked out of the local bar associations. You can still practice law after your period of discipline is over. You can usually never, never practice law again if you are disbarred. With this background in mind, let's examine the basic rules and some practical examples of how to apply it in your everyday situations.

Model Rule 1.15 and Disciplinary Rule 9-102 are carry-forwards of ABA Canon 11 and will be found in the law of your state, either as part of the Rules of Court or codified in your Business and Professional Code or in your general laws. I recommend highly that you read the exact wording of the law in your state as well as some of the annotations to get a sense of how easy it is to get disbarred.

Opening a Trust Checking Account

1. Title the account "Client Trust Account" or a similar wording. Although the word "Trust" is not required *per se*, I recommend it.

2. Use a red checkbook cover. The color red obviously indicates "Danger."

3. Use checks of a color different from your office or payroll checks.

4. Yours should be the only authorized signature. Do not allow your spouse, secretary, or office manager to sign the checks. Do not use or authorize a rubber-stamp or computer-generated signature.

5. Reconcile the account monthly.

Don't use savings accounts unless there are very exceptional circumstances. I am continually confronted by new lawyers who get the bright idea of putting trust funds into savings accounts to get interest on the "float." I have to deflate the egos of these financial wizards by pointing out two basic fallacies in the scheme:

1. The funds are the clients' and the interest on the clients' funds belongs to the clients whose money earned the interest. In cases where you decide the "net interest" (interest income less costs of maintaining the account) is "not significant" or is "not substantial," the interest may go to IOLTA, but it never goes to you, the lawyer.

2. DR 9-102(B)(1) and Model Rule 1.15(b) require the funds to be promptly paid to the client. Delaying the payment to the client in order to earn interest is not proper in any event, in my opinion, even if you did eventually send the interest to the client. I have been told, but have not independently verified, that lawyers in some countries can ethically and legally keep the interest earned on client funds. This may explain in part the delay I have experienced in getting client money from overseas lawyers.

In any event, if you have several clients' money in a savings account, you would have to bookkeep on a daily basis which client had earned the interest. The amount of work involved for the amount of interest involved for a particular client usually will not justify your going through all the work of computing the interest. This complex bookkeeping problem is one of the reasons interest on the entire account will be paid to IOLTA. Typically, the IOLTA authorities in effect "own" your account. They pay a negotiated amount per month for your account and receive a negotiated rate of interest on the money in "your" account.

1. *Don't pay personal bills from the account.* If you have a fee in the trust account that you are entitled to, don't just spend the money from the trust account. Transfer the fee from the trust account to the office account, then transfer your draw from the office account to your personal account. Thus, you will have a clean record, and no explanations will be necessary at a later time.

2. *Don't make any disbursements without notifying the client and obtaining the client's written authorization.* Ordinarily, your fee agreement contains your written authorization to reimburse yourself any costs and fees you're entitled to.

3. *Suppose client Jim Jones whom you are representing on a good accident case has an unrelated problem such as a criminal or domestic relations matter. He wants you to work on the unrelated case with you getting your fee from his share of the proceeds of the accident case.*

a. *Can you ethically do this?* Yes. A client may engage you on an unrelated matter and you may agree to defer the time of payment until the accident case closes.

b. *Can you take the money from the trust account when the case closes?* Yes, providing you have the authorization to pay the fees in writing. You must understand that when you have client funds in your trust account, you are a fiduciary. When the client owes you a fee, you are a creditor. You must act as a fiduciary with the trust fund, even though your client acts as a debtor with the unpaid fee.

c. *Suppose your client disputes part of your fee; can you take the undisputed portion out of the trust account?* Yes. You must withdraw from the trust account your funds and you must forward to the client his or her funds.

4. *Suppose your client engages you and gives you a retainer check of $725, representing a $250 minimum fee, $350 toward additional fees (if your fee exceeds $250) and $125 in costs. What do you do?*

a. Deposit the check to your trust account.

b. Wait three to five banking days for the check to clear (unless you want to take a chance on your client's credit).

c. Withdraw your $250 minimum fee immediately because it is yours in any event and must be withdrawn (unless your fee agreement specifies otherwise).

d. Pay for costs out of the trust account as incurred. Stop when costs reach $125. At this point, either get more money from your client or advance costs from your office account. Do not use the "excess" fee funds. You may be obligated to return them if not used.

e. When you and the client have agreed in writing to your "excess fee," you may withdraw it from the trust account.

5. *Suppose client Jane Jones owes you $125 for a loan or for fees or costs on an unrelated matter. You then settle a case for her and have $35,000 in your trust account that belongs to her.*

a. *Can you simply send her a check for $34,875?* No. Again, you are a fiduciary with respect to the $35,000 and a creditor with respect to the $125. Therefore, you must send her the $35,000 and ask for your $125.

b. *Is there some way you can withhold the $125 from the trust funds?* Yes. Simply get her permission in writing to pay yourself the $125 from her trust funds.

6. *How do you get clients to agree in writing to your taking the fees from the trust funds?* The simplest way is to send a letter explaining what you wish to do and ask the client to sign the copy indicating permission and to send the signed copy back to you by mail. If you simply stick a piece of paper in front of the client and tell him or her to sign it, there may be a later claim that the letter

wasn't understood when it was signed. By getting the letter mailed back to you, the client presumably had time to consider what was being agreed to.

7. *Is it required that the permission be given in writing?* There is nothing in the rules that requires the permission to be in writing. However, you will be in a difficult situation two or three years later when the client simultaneously sues you, alleging a breach of fiduciary duty, and files a complaint with the state bar for unauthorized use of trust funds. Clients (and some lawyers) have a tendency to remember only what they want to remember, and it will be a matter of your word versus the client's word.

Reminder: The book *The ABA Guide to Lawyer Trust Accounts* is much more comprehensive and covers many more situations commonly encountered by practicing lawyers in the real world.

A free hour-long videotape on managing your trust account can be obtained from me while supplies last.

No Insurance

Keep in mind that money stolen from the trust account by you or an employee is probably not insured. Be careful who has access to the account.

Financial Fraud

There is a movement underway to compel lawyers to turn in their clients and ignore attorney-client confidences if the lawyer thinks the client might be committing a financial crime. This movement is a "using a cannon to kill flies" reaction to high-profile financial collapses like Enron. Prosecutors want to pierce attorney-client confidences. You should be aware that someone might be using your trust account for this purpose.

Endorsing Clients' Names on Settlement Checks

Many lawyers build a limited power of attorney into the fee agreement empowering the lawyer to endorse the client's name and deposit settlement or other checks made payable to the client or to both the lawyer and the client. This procedure can prevent the client forging the lawyer's name to the check or forgetting to return the en-

dorsed check or holding back on the endorsed check to try to negotiate a lower-than-agreed-upon fee. This procedure also lessens the
likelihood of the check getting lost in transmission and return. This
procedure also makes it possible for the client to get his or her
money earlier since there won't be the delay of the mail going back
and forth.

Some lawyers have the client come into the office to endorse the
check in the office.

Generally it is permissible for the lawyer to obtain the power of
attorney and to endorse and negotiate the check, but you should
check if there is any local prohibition on this common practice.

Insurance Needs of the New Lawyer

Insurance is an expense that new lawyers hate to pay since there is a cash disbursement with no probability of profit. However painful it might be, accept the fact that you are a complete and total fool if you are not adequately insured.

Malpractice Insurance

Accept two basic facts:

1. You are responsible for malpractice, even if you did someone "a favor," and did not charge or collect a fee;

2. At some time during your career, you will be sued for malpractice. Whether you want to call it "errors and omissions" or "malpractice" or "professional negligence," it is the insurance that protects you, your clients, and third parties when you get sued. Often the costs of defense alone will be many, many times what you paid in premiums.

Your local rules may require you to disclose the existence or nonexistence of malpractice insurance in you fee agreement.

As a general rule, your local bar association will have gotten the best "deal" available for you. Sometimes a private agent or broker can get you a better "deal." Be careful. From time to time, insurance companies simply go out of the malpractice insurance business, and you may find yourself stranded without coverage. As a member of your local bar association, you will be part of a larger economic unit in a better bargaining position.

There is no substitute for working with a good insurance agent or broker who has your interests at heart. The purpose of this section is not to replace the broker, but rather to educate both you and the broker in the peculiarities of insurance as it affects a new lawyer in practice. Keep in mind that the terminology for insurance coverage changes from time to time and from place to place.

There are some points you should be careful about.

1. *"Gaps" in Coverage.* Some policies are "claims" policies and some are "occurrence" policies. In general, most policies currently being written are "claims" policies and not "occurrence" policies, but you must understand the differences. The difference can best be illustrated by a hypothetical example. Suppose Company "A" insured you for 2002 on a "claim" basis, and Company "B" insures you on an "occurrence" basis for 2003. Suppose you commit a negligent act in 2002, and a claim is made against you in 2003. Company "A" will not cover you because the "claim" wasn't made during the policy period 2002, and Company "B" will not cover you because the "occurrence" didn't occur during its policy period, 2003. Therefore, even though you had policies in effect at all times, you have no coverage.

Another important thing to remember is that any time you change carriers, be sure that you don't have any gaps in your coverage.

2. *Settlement Approval.* If possible, try to get a policy that gives you the right to approve settlements being made. The problem here is to avoid the stigma or rating problem in the future when a settlement is made of a nonmeritorious claim without your approval.

3. *Deductible.* Many policies now provide for significant deductibility of $10,000 or more, including costs of defense and investigation. In other words, you must pay the first $10,000 of defense costs incurred.

4. *Exclusions.* There is a tendency for insurance companies to reduce risk by excluding certain areas of practice from coverage, such as securities or being an officer or director of a client who has a claim. Be sure you read and understand your policy. Your carrier may exclude trust accounts from coverage.

5. *Sufficient Coverage.* From time to time, you may have a very significant case matter, involving large amounts of money, and large exposure if you are negligent. Give consideration to buying more insurance to cover that matter, and don't be afraid to raise your fee so that you are adequately compensated, giving effect to the

cost of the premium. Remember that insurance protects both you and your client.

6. *Cheap Insurance for New Lawyers.* Practicing without malpractice insurance (commonly called "going bare") is not only risky, but may not be necessary. The new lawyer should double-check whether or not malpractice insurance is mandatory and whether or not lack of malpractice insurance must be disclosed to clients before accepting work.

Malpractice insurance for a new lawyer may be dirt cheap for two reasons:

First, the company wants to get you as a regular customer early in your career so that you will know its name even if you later temporarily use a different carrier.

Second, the chances of a claim against a new lawyer are minimal. Most malpractice policies are currently being written on a claims-made basis. A new lawyer hasn't been in practice long enough for claims to start showing up and a new lawyer doesn't have as many clients and matters as a more experienced lawyer. Accordingly there is relatively little or no risk in insuring a brand new lawyer on a claims-made basis.

A lawyer leaving a firm and starting a practice may be able to obtain "new lawyer" insurance by excluding prior acts from coverage.

If you do contract work you may be able to get malpractice insurance by the hour.

Accordingly, a new lawyer should not consider going bare without at least first finding out the cost of malpractice insurance.

7. *Fee Arbitration and Mediation Clauses in Fee Agreements.* Fee arbitration and mediation reduces the risk of a malpractice claim and the need for malpractice insurance. Many malpractice claims are brought by clients or their successors-in-interest where there is no malpractice simply as a tactic to stall a fee collection suit. Arbitration and mediation often reveal to both the lawyer and the client the strengths or weaknesses in their positions without the expenses of litigation including the discovery aspects. You have to check your local rules to determine if mandatory binding or nonbinding fee arbitration or mediation clauses are permissible or required in your jurisdiction. I recommend the fee arbitration and mediation clauses both to reduce exposure and expenses where there is no malpractice insurance and as a practical device where there is malpractice insurance.

8. *Self-Consuming Policies—Cost of Defense.* You should understand that many policies currently being written reduce the amount of insurance available to pay claims by the costs of defending the claim. Accordingly, if you think you have $100,000 of coverage (for example), that $100,000 may be reduced by the company's costs of defending the claim. Some companies begin to charge expenses against the policy the moment you notify them of a potential claim even before they use a lawyer on the claim. This self-consuming feature is intended to encourage you to settle claims as early as possible before you find that the costs of defense have eroded the coverage you thought you were buying.

9. *Practicing with or Near Other Lawyers.* When you practice with other lawyers or other people, whether in a firm, a law suite, a business incubator, in a counsel position, with a contract lawyer, or any other relationship, you must consider the risk of being sued for their acts and omissions. This is a new trend in the law. Clients claim they thought there was a partnership or other joint-venture relationship. A trier of fact looks at the facts to decide whether the client's perception is reasonable, and, if so, you find yourself a defendant who must spend time and money defending yourself, even if you ultimately prevail. A carrier may or may not be willing to defend you, with or without a reservation of rights. Be sure you explain to your insurance agent or broker in writing what you are doing so you know what protection you do or don't have. Put a clause in your fee agreement and insist that all the other lawyers in the suite put a clause in their fee agreements acknowledging that you are not in partnership or otherwise responsible for the professional work of the other lawyers.

10. *Tail Coverage.* If you decide to stop practicing law for a short or extended period of time, you should consider "tail" coverage. You pay a single premium which covers you for all prior acts. The tail will not cover you for future acts and, depending on the policy, when you start practicing again the policy is cancelled.

Umbrella Coverage

"Umbrella" or excess coverage, in my opinion, is the best insurance value available, considering premium cost and coverage. Oversimplified, it picks up coverage where your underlying policies do not. For example, it normally would be cheaper for you to have a $300,000 malpractice policy and a $1 million umbrella (in effect, a $1.3 million policy with a $300,000 deductible) than to have a $1 million malpractice policy. Additionally, the umbrella will often pick up the "excess" coverage in other areas of insurance besides malpractice. Any time your broker or agent quotes you rates for malpractice or other liability insurance, ask for quotes on rates for the same coverage using a smaller "underlying policy" with an umbrella coverage.

Nonowned Autos

Be sure you and your office help are covered if there is an auto accident when an employee is running an errand for you, such as going to the post office to mail that rush, rush letter.

Nonowned Assets

Your employees may bring in or use their own computers or other equipment. Determine if there is insurance on the computers if they are stolen from your office. You may also be temporarily in possession of something that belongs to a client (for example, a document, jewelry, or whatever), which should have been kept by you in a safe or safe-deposit box.

Office Furniture, Etc.

Be sure that you are insured for "replacement value." In inflationary times, insurance that pays claims based on cost less depreciation is close to having no insurance at all. Don't assume that just because the insurance company takes your premium based on present-day replacement costs they will pay claims based on present-day replacement cost. Here again, either read your policy or get a good broker.

File Replacement and Cost of Insurance for Valuable Papers

For the first year or two, you will not have much concern over this problem, but ultimately, this type of coverage will be extremely important to you. This coverage includes the cost of replacing your files, rather than the value of the paper in the files. In the event of fire, it could cost you thousands of dollars to buy photocopies of documents, letters, etc., from the courts and clients and other lawyers to reconstruct your files. Determine if you are insured for the cost(s) of installing backup files or reinputting data from paper to computer.

Insurance for Computers and Data Processors

Insurance for computers and data in computers is very limited. You may need a special policy or endorsement to get this coverage. You might not be insured in your general insurance policies. You may think you are insured and find you are not. You may have extremely limited or no coverage for the following: the cost of duplicating information; any computer off the premises of the office (in an auto or house not covered); computers lent to others; business interruptions due to computers being inoperable; equipment operated or controlled by your computer(s). This is a new and extremely complex area. A knowledgeable broker may be difficult to find, but can be invaluable in helping you get what you need. The difficulties encountered in this area are another good reason to maintain a good backup system.

Employment Practices Liability

A new type of insurance covering violation of employment laws.

Workers' Compensation

Remember to get this coverage when you hire your first secretary. That person may be real clumsy and push a computer off the desk onto a foot the first day of employment. Your first secretary's first task should be to call your broker to be sure of insurance coverage. If your state has a state fund or state policy, you should check its rates during your first year or two of coverage. With only one secretary or clerk you may fall within the "minimum premium" cost category. The minimum is often substantially lower with state-owned companies or funds than privately owned companies.

Fiduciary Liability

This is coverage for when you act as a trustee or fiduciary. You may need a rider.

Office Block Insurance

This is a "package" available in some areas that combines several types of insurance a law office needs into a single "block" or package. It is similar to the concept of "homeowners" package insurance. Here again, you need the help of a good broker.

Trust Account Theft

Thefts of funds from a trust account by an employee may not be insurable under malpractice or other insurance and may require employee bonding.

Other Types of Insurance

The other types of insurance are not peculiar to new lawyers in practice and will be simply listed as a checklist here.

1. *Disability Insurance or Office Overhead Insurance or Business Income*. Buy all you can afford. In my opinion, this type of insurance is more necessary than life insurance. Life insurance protects others if you die. Disability insurance protects you if you live. If you get sick or disabled and can't work, both your office overhead and your home overhead will continue. In some states, you are eligible for state coverage.

It is my opinion that, as a general rule, you should purchase this insurance through your bar association during your early years. It is not unknown for some insurance companies in this area to be very eager to accept premiums for coverage and later threaten you with cancellation and refusal to pay if you have a claim.

Unfortunately, when you need this coverage you need it badly and cannot afford the luxury of collecting your money with 7 percent interest three years later when you win your lawsuit against the insurance company. Possibly you will not be able to wait even the three to six months involved for the insurance company doctor to examine you and send a report to the insurance company. As part of the larger bar group, you and your claim will be in a better position to get faster payment of just claims. Insurance companies have been known to act rapidly when faced with the loss of hundreds or thousands of policies. On the other hand, if the insurance company drops the entire bar association (or vice versa), you'll have lost the bargaining position and might have been better off with your own broker.

Given all factors, I repeat my recommendation that you buy this coverage through your bar association for the first few years of your practice.

2. *Life Insurance.* Don't be pressured by arguments of how cheaply you can buy a six-figure policy "at your age." Remember that in your early years, cash flow and conservation are your biggest problems. Although premiums will be higher five years later, you'll be in a better position to pay for the higher coverage when you have the income. I suggest you investigate one-year renewable term insurance with your broker or bar association.

3. *Public Liability, Fire, Employee Bonding, ERISA, Health, Comprehensive, Medical, Long Term Care, Notary Bond, etc.* These are general insurance problems not peculiar to new lawyers in practice and a competent broker or agent should be able to help you.

Arbitrator or Mediator Insurance

You may need special coverage or a rider to your malpractice policy if you will be acting as a mediator or arbitrator.

Checklist on Insurance Coverage

Contact or obtain an insurance broker or agent who is likely to refer you business (old family broker, if possible), or buy from different brokers:

1. Malpractice insurance (errors and omissions). Get occurrence rather than claims-made coverage, if possible.
2. General liability insurance for office.
3. Workers' Compensation.
4. Nonowned automobile insurance.
5. Nonowned assets.
6. File replacement and valuable papers coverage.
7. Electronic data processing policy.

8. Fire and theft (get replacement value).

9. Get "umbrella" coverage, if available.

10. Check with broker or bank for "premium financing" (monthly payments).

11. Check if "office block" policy is available.

New Lawyer, Part-time Lawyer, and Retiring Lawyer

Many malpractice carriers offer a reduced premium for policies based on the number of chargeable hours of the lawyer. This is a new area of marketing to lawyers who are not full time.

Don't Forget Taxes and Licenses

Many new lawyers (and others as well) get into serious trouble because they didn't know they had an obligation to pay a particular tax or file a particular return. Often the amount of tax involved is very small, but the penalties for not filing the requisite returns is high and is cumulative for each year the tax is not paid or the return not filed.

City license inspectors regularly go from office to office and door to door and building directory to building directory looking for new names that are not yet licensed. When they find these names they sometimes tell every state, county, and city agency on their list. Often one agency will notify others immediately of your application. In most cases each agency will notify the others of the date(s) you submitted as being your first day of business. These other agencies may not get around to you for a year or two, by which time you can have serious problems.

A good CPA can be an invaluable helper in making sure you stay out of trouble. He or she is likely to initially charge you small or no fees to get you as a referrer of clients or as a worthwhile client in your own right.

You may be able to purchase a guide to the required relevant local taxes and licenses from your state or local Chamber of Commerce. They frequently sell "start-up" kits for new businesses with applicable application forms and mailing addresses. In addition to the tax and license information, the Chamber of Commerce start-up kits often include references to various employment laws. Joining the local chamber may get you a discount on the publications in addition to introducing you to the local movers and shakers. Chamber meetings and activities are worthwhile promotional activities.

Some states require posters and other materials to be displayed. The Chamber may sell them or direct you to a source.

Some of the information you need to know includes:

1. Federal and state payroll tax reports required;
2. Sales tax permits and licenses (where required);
3. City licenses and fees;
4. Personal federal and state income tax filings required;
5. Unemployment, disability, and workers' compensation insurance requirements;
6. Permissible and impermissible employment questions;
7. Required health notices and sexual harassment notices;
8. Immigration law requirements;
9. Minimum wage and overtime laws;
10. Independent contractor requirements and information;
11. Required withholding and other tax deposits required;
12. Property taxes.

Many new lawyers get themselves into tax and license trouble early in their practices because they didn't get help from a CPA or other source.

Why You Need a Personnel Manual

As strange as it may seem, you should have a personnel manual before you hire your first employee. As a general rule, lawyers are softhearted and don't like to do unpleasant tasks, such as docking or firing employees who are habitually sick or late, or who abuse common rules of good office systems and decorum. Additionally, you, as a new lawyer, have had little or no experience or ability in personnel management. If you doubt this, figure out how you would handle the following factual situations:

1. For the third time in two weeks, your clerk Jack calls in at 10:05 a.m. to say he's late because of car trouble.

2. Your secretary comes to work in jeans, T-shirt, and no bra, and torn tennis shoes. She calls you a male chauvinist pig for asking her to dress more conventionally and says she'll file a civil rights suit against you based on sex discrimination if you fire her or discipline her.

3. Your secretary is into Zen Buddhism and claims the right to a paid holiday for Buddha's birthday, equating it to Christmas for Christians and Rosh Hashana for Jews. Again, the threat of a civil rights suit.

4. Cigarette smoke annoys you, and your secretary insists on smoking on the job (or vice versa).

5. Your secretary takes home expensive legal pads for a spouse's night-school note taking.

6. Your secretary claims time-and-a-half for dropping the mail into a mailbox on the way home.

7. After two months on the job, your clerk tells you a grand-mother died, and he has to take one month off, and expects his job to be waiting for him.

Believe it or not, the above situations, and some even more bizarre, are factual and have happened to me over a period of years. It is not satisfactory to wait for problems to occur and then try to handle them on an ad hoc basis. You should have an employee office manual ready for your first employee. As a final step in the hiring process, you should hand the manual to the employee, getting a signed receipt in which it is acknowledged that it was read and understood and the employee agrees to be bound by it. Such things as tardiness, absences, sickness, holidays, overtime, dress, office supplies, etc., would ordinarily be covered in the office personnel manual.

Given that you now understand the need for a manual, where do you get one?

1. Create your own manual. You could write one, but it might not conform to what is or is not permissible by current state and federal law.

2. Copy the manual of another law firm. This is better than writing your own but is still risky for the reasons stated above.

3. Buy a manual from the ABA (or state bar) Law Practice Management Section. The ABA Law Practice Management Section has published *Law Office Policy & Procedures Manual, Fourth Edition,* edited by Robert Wert and Howard Hatoff, as well as *Law Office Procedures Manual for Solos and Small Law Firms,* Second Edition, by Demetrios Dimitriou.

4. Ask your local practice management advisor (if there is one) to recommend a manual for use in your state.

Subjects for Office Personnel Policy

Following is an alphabetical list of some of the elements that should be considered for inclusion in an office personnel policy:

Absences	Clothing
Accidents	Coffee breaks
Attitude	Complaints
Bonding of employers	Compliance with various
Bulletin boards	state and federal
Cleanliness	employment laws

Confidential nature of work
Contracts
Decorum
Deductions
Disability insurance
Discounts
Discrimination
Dismissal
Dress
Economy
E-mail usage
Emergencies
Emergency leave
Employee addresses
Employee lounge
Employee personality
Employee roster
Employee-client relations
Family leave
File retention and destruction
  policy
Fire
Funeral pay
Garnishments
Gossip
Grievances
Health insurance
Holidays
Housekeeping
Internet usage policy
Intoxication
Introduction
Jury duty
Labor laws
Leaves of absence
Liability and malpractice in-
  surance
Loyalty
Lunches
Magazines

Marriage and pregnancy
Maternity
Meal schedules
Medical care
Meetings
Merit review
Military service
Misconduct
Moonlighting
New employees
Noise
Office supplies
Overtime
Parental leave policies
Parking
Pay day
Pay period
Pension plan
Personal mail and e-mail
Personal phone calls and
  voice mail
Personal visitors
Personnel counseling
Privileged communications
Privileged information
Probationary period
Professional ethics
Promotions
Re-employment
Resignations
Retirement
Safety
Salary
Salary calculation
Salary increases
Schedules
Sexual harassment
Sick leave
Smoking
Social Security

Soliciting of employees
Suggestions
Supervisors
Tardiness
Telephone courtesy
Temporary employment
Terminal vacation pay
Termination of employment
Time cards
Trial period

Unemployment insurance
Use of facilities for personal
   use
Vacations
Work evaluations
Work habits
Work periods
Workers' compensation
Working hours

Bookkeeping and Accounting Systems

Get a CPA.

Unless you have some accounting knowledge or bookkeeping experience, you really shouldn't try to maintain your own books or prepare your own income tax return. Even with my background as a Board-Certified Specialist in Taxation and as a Certified Public Accountant, I don't maintain my own books or prepare my own tax returns. I am simply applying the old maxim, "The lawyer who represents himself has a fool for a client."

1. A CPA can be an excellent source of clients for a lawyer. CPAs normally are in periodic close contact with their clients. These clients frequently ask the CPA to recommend a lawyer for the problems of the business, and the employees of the business.

2. Try to select a CPA in a small or medium-sized CPA firm. A large firm rarely can refer anything to a new lawyer and may not have the same interest in you as a client as a small or medium-sized firm.

3. Unfortunately, you probably won't be able to send much business to the CPA. CPAs send many more clients to lawyers than vice versa. As a new lawyer, the kind of work you can generate for a CPA (other than your own accounting) is called "special engagement" work, such as looking for assets in marital cases. In any event you need some simple accounting procedures and systems for your day-to-day financial transactions.

Keep It Simple

You won't have many transactions your first year or two, so you really don't need a national CPA firm with an IBM or Cray mainframe. A simple checkbook for your office expense checks should be adequate. If you want to use a four-part snapout checkbook for client costs, you can.

Your accountant will probably recommend a "write-it-once" system for you.

Read the chapter on bank accounts and the simplified "chart of accounts" that starts below. Note that the trust account does not appear on your statements since the money in that account is not yours. Your accountant may wish to show the account with a "contra" or offset. This is an area of theoretical debate among accountants. The important thing is that you do not include the trust account on your financial statements.

Leave Tracks

An accountant can easily reconstruct transactions if you leave tracks. Put explanations on your duplicate bank deposit slips and explain in detail what you are writing checks for.

Use Cash Basis Books

For income tax purposes you'll want to be on the cash basis. After you're in practice a few years you can get sophisticated with accounts receivable and accounting accruals, but not at the beginning. You may wish to examine Quicken or whatever bookkeeping applications your CPA recommends.

Buy the ABA Publications

The American Bar Association Law Practice Management Section (**http://www.abanet.org/lpm**) publishes several publications on law office accounting. You should buy one of each that is available and keep them as part of your permanent library for your CPA to use. Let your CPA firm buy its own set, including the book *The ABA Guide to Lawyer Trust Accounts*. Don't let it remove yours from your office. I contributed to several of the publications in various capacities and recommend them highly.

Chart of Accounts for the New Lawyer

Assets	*Expenses*
1. Cash in Bank/Office	Accounting
2. Cash in Bank/Payroll	Associate Fees

Assets (cont'd.)
3. Client Costs Receivable
4. Deposits/Lease, Utilities, etc.
5. Deposit Account/Sheriff and Marshal
6. Desks and Chairs (accumulated depreciation)
7. Dictating Equipment (accumulated depreciation)
8. Lease Hold Improvements (accumulated depreciation)
9. Library (accumulated depreciation)
10. Other Office Equipment (accumulated depreciation)
11. Prepaid Expenses
12. Computers (accumulated depreciation)

Liabilities
1. Bank Loans Payable
2. Equipment Contracts Payable
3. Withheld Payroll Taxes Payable
4. Other Liabilities

Capital
1. John Lawyer Capital
2. John Lawyer Draw (deductible)
3. John Lawyer Draw (nondeductible)

Income
1. Business
2. Criminal
3. Domestic Relations
4. Fees Received
5 Personal Injury
6. Probate
7. Other

Expenses (cont'd.)
Attorney Service
Auto
Bank Charges
Business Promotion
Computer Consulting and Maintenance
Continuing Education
Depreciation
Dues, Professional
Employee Meals and Incentives
Employee Procurement
Equipment Rental
Insurance
Interest
Investigation, Investigators (nonreceivable)
Medical Insurance
Meetings and Seminars
Office Supplies
Outside Secretarial
Payroll Taxes
Photocopier Rental and Supplies
Postage
Postage Equipment Rental
Professional Periodicals
Rent/Office
Rent/Parking
Repairs and Maintenance
Salaries/Secretaries
Salaries/Office
Salaries/Clerks
Stationery and Printing
Taxes and Licenses
Telephone
Travel and Conventions
Trust Account Maintenance

I recommend *The ABA Guide to Lawyer Trust Accounts* (which I wrote), also available from the ABA's Law Practice Management Section.

Software Applications

I don't like to recommend specific software because new programs and products are always coming out. Quicken seems to be a financial program of choice for new lawyers. You can do your check writing and simple bookkeeping on Quicken and Quickbooks..

Even with software applications that you feel you can maintain, you should still use a CPA to check how you are using your systems.

Although you may be able to print your checks with your software, I nonetheless recommend hand writing your checks for the first year of your practice. You will have a better understanding of where the money goes and you will be better prepared to use a software system that will meet your needs.

Hard Copies of Computer Data

Financial records should be printed and stored in printed format. Keeping data only on computer is risky due to rapid changes in technology and applications that may make it impossible to later recall data stored in obsolete systems that are not supported by the manufacturer or publisher.

The Office Cash Flow Survival Budget

You must have a positive cash flow if your practice is to survive. The incoming cash must equal or exceed the outgoing cash or you soon will be out of business. Do not confuse a cash-flow budget with profit and loss since the latter involves depreciation, amortization, accruals, and other noncash items.

By budgeting your cash income and your cash outgo, you will be able to prioritize where you do and do not spend your funds. The budgeting process will force you to think about what it will cost to run your practice. Monthly, you should compare your actual cash in and cash out to the cash-flow budget to take stock of where you are. Revise your estimates monthly so you will be prepared for cash-poor periods.

Monthly revisions will enable you to change directions and be prepared to meet your anticipated needs when events do not occur exactly as you anticipated.

Learning to make budgets both on a cash-flow basis and on a profit-and-loss basis will help you set goals and targets during your entire professional career. If you do not have the foggiest idea of what your operating costs or income will be, then ask a CPA, another lawyer, or an office manager to help you with your first budget. Subsequent budgets will be much easier to prepare and revise.

Making and monitoring your cash-flow budget can make the difference between success and failure. It takes effort to make your first and subsequent cash-flow budgets, but it is a wise investment of time and effort in starting and maintaining your practice.

The following categories of cash in and cash out may help you accumulate your figures and estimates.

Anticipated Cash Requirements for the New Lawyer for First Twelve Months of Practice

	Budgeted	*Actual*
Income: Fees from clients; overflow work from other lawyers; part-time practice; working spouse; parent loans; other loans to your business, etc.	$_____	$_____
Total Income	$_____	$_____
Expenditures: *Occupancy*: Rent, parking, landlord "pass throughs," security deposit.	$_____	$_____
Payroll: Secretary, paralegal, receptionist, word processor, law clerks, others (add 20 percent for payroll taxes).	$_____	$_____
Taxes and Professional Associations: City license fee, state bar dues, fees for admission to courts and for certificates of admission, sales tax permit, bar association dues (American, state, county, city), law specialty associations.	$_____	$_____
Insurance: Malpractice, auto, general liability, fire, workers' compensation, medical insurance health plan, disability, valuable papers, EDP for computer and software, umbrella, other.	$_____	$_____
Court Service: Messengers.	$_____	$_____
Communications Equipment: Deposit, telephone equipment, Yellow and White Pages, monthly service charge, e-mail, fax, Internet service provider, telex, postage, messenger services, other service providers.	$_____	$_____
Periodicals: Legal journals, specialty journals, periodicals for reception room.	$_____	$_____
Furniture: Down payment and monthly payments for lawyer, staff, and reception furniture, down payment and monthly payments for other furniture.	$_____	$_____
Office Equipment: Down payment and monthly payments for computer and printer, dictating equipment, fax machine, photocopy machine, postage meter, file cabinets or filing shelves, and bookshelves.	$_____	$_____

Library: Purchase and installment payments on books not available to you from lawyers' libraries. (Electronic libraries through WESTLAW or LEXIS Internet Web sites are more economical than hard-copy libraries if you are proficient and new electronic libraries are increasingly available.) Don't be afraid to negotiate with the vendor to get only what you need.　$_____　$_____

Stationery: Letterhead, second sheets, envelopes, professional cards, pleading paper, photocopy paper, fax and computer paper.　$_____　$_____

Promotion: Tickets for athletic and cultural events, business lunches, seasonal greeting cards, announcements, firm newsletter or brochures, dues for service organizations.　$_____　$_____

Automobile: Monthly loan or lease payments, gas, oil, repairs.　$_____　$_____

Travel: State bar, national bar, or specialty bar meetings and conventions.　$_____　$_____

Client Costs: Medical reports, depositions, filing fees, investigators' fees, witness fees, etc.　$_____　$_____

Accountant: Bookkeeping and payroll and income tax return fees.　$_____　$_____

Banks: Check printing, safe-deposit box, bank charges.　$_____　$_____

Loan Payments: Student loans, parent loans, bank loans, etc.　$_____　$_____

Miscellaneous: Online subscription services, equipment maintenance contracts, software updates.　$_____　$_____

Office Supplies: Small office equipment, pens, pencils, paper clips, staplers, legal and note pads, scissors, rubber stamps, postage, etc.　$_____　$_____

Insurance:　$_____　$_____

Other:　$_____　$_____

Total Cash Expenditures　$_____　$_____

Estimated Total Cash Surplus or Shortage
for First Year (Income Less Expenditures) $_____ $_____

Making and measuring budgets is time-consuming and not very exciting, but you will learn how to plan your career and growth if you will simply learn a skill that you didn't learn prior to going into practice.

The Paperless Office vs.
The Less Paper Office

The goal of having a virtual or paperless office may be admirable but unfortunately is like the goal of inventing a perpetual-motion machine.

There must always be paper in a law office. As technology moves forward, existing systems and equipment rapidly become obsolete and worthless. Data stored on old systems is often not readable because the manufacturer went out of business or simply stopped supporting the necessary software or necessary hardware.

The mag cards and magnetic tapes were replaced with 8" floppies and 5" floppies and 3" floppies and then memory sticks. Information stored on these media cannot be reproduced.

A "less paper" office is good. Paper is scanned and stored and the information available at the desk without getting the paper from which the data was obtained.

However, even though the information from this paper is stored and moved inside and outside the office in electronic form, the paper from which the data was taken must be filed away somewhere to be used if needed as evidence or for other purposes.

Documents produced must be stored somewhere in paper form to be available if needed in the future.

The "paperless" or virtual office can only be possible if statutes of limitations eliminate the obligation of producing data after it is created or read.

There may be no statute of limitations in ethics matters. The statute may not run on a minor's matter until the minor reaches age 21. Tax data for basis may be necessary decades into the future.

The lawyer who tries to maintain a "paperless" rather than a "less paper" office is taking a serious calculated risk.

I advise new lawyers to be "less paper" oriented, but not "paperless" oriented.

Paper and Computer Document Management

Skim or skip this chapter. If you already know what's here, read some other chapter. This chapter is intended to help lawyers who know very little about doing their own word processing on a computer. It is also intended to help lawyers going into practice from corporate or military backgrounds where client identification was not an issue. It will also be of help to lawyers not accustomed to creating or working with multiple versions of a "tailormade" document depending on the facts of the particular matter.

Starting the Document

1. *Paper.* Start with yellow pad and pen or dictating equipment.
   Computer. Start with a computer screen and a keyboard.

Inputting New Information

2. *Paper.* Input by writing with pen onto paper or by transcribing dictation.
   Computer. Input by typing onto the keyboard or by transcribing dictation.

Copying from Previous Documents

3. *Paper.* Copy parts of previous similar documents (yours or others') by manually cutting paper with a scissors and taping or pasting the desired words where wanted in new document.

Computer. Copy parts of previous similar documents (yours or others') by blocking old text from original and moving the copied text into the new document electronically.

Adding New Text

4. *Paper.* Create new text by interlineating or adding by handwriting.

Computer. Create new text by adding or interlineating new wording into new text by typing on keyboard.

Naming the Document

5. *Paper.* No need to give the new document a name. You may wish to do so when you are ready to send it somewhere or when you want to file the paper copy.

Computer. The new document should immediately be given a name at the time of starting it. (See separate chapter on naming of documents.)

Making Revisions

6. *Paper.* Cross out the unwanted text. Interlineate or add new text. Mark and save copies of old superseded paper versions for tracing and "redline" purposes.

Computer. Modify or change name of new version. Your software package may or may not allow you to show version number or time and date of creation of new version as part of the naming system or separate from the naming system. Delete or remove unwanted text. Type in new text. New version will have new name. Old version will have old name. You should keep (electronically at least) old versions for tracing and "redline" purposes.

Comparing Revisions and Different Versions

7. *Paper.* This is done to determine the history of a document, including changes and revisions authorized to be made and changes and revisions not authorized to be made. In a pure paper system, the best way to compare revision and versions of documents is to use

the "knee-to-knee" method. You simply sit opposite another person who reads aloud to you (or vice versa). You follow along with the other person until you find a discrepancy. Alternatively you hope and trust that no unauthorized changes were made to the earlier version and that all changes that should have been made were in fact made by your personally glancing back and forth from one version to the other version.

Computer. It is often important to determine what changes have been made to a prior version of a document in arriving at the current version. You may also wish to be sure that no changes have been made to the document that you are unaware of. Software applications exist that automatically "redline" a document to highlight how it is different from another version of the same document. The "redlining" or comparison of the two documents is accomplished by simply scanning the previous document (with OCR) into your computer or using your own prior version and then comparing the new version to the old version electronically. Both intentional and accidental changes will be emphasized by underlining or cross-outs or highlighting.

Using Documents Prepared by Others

8. *Paper.* Cut and paste the other person's document (or copy of the original) and rewrite it into your document.

Computer. Scan the other person's documents with a scanner into your computer. Do not use OCR (optical character recognition) if all you want is a "photo" or picture of the document. Simply scan the document into your computer. Do use OCR if you wish to use and modify the wording contained in the other person's document. You will then be able to use the other person's text as he or she composed it and use and change those words in your document(s). Name the scanned document whether or not you simply scanned or used OCR so you can find it later. You should also name the newly created document.

Storing the Document

9. *Paper.* The paper document is stored into a file folder using the system found in another part of this book. In all probability you

will have to maintain a paper file even though you also have a computer file.

 Computer. The newly created document will ordinarily be stored electronically on a hard drive simply by saving it after it is created.

Retrieving the Document from the File

 10. *Paper.* You will first have to get the paper file from wherever it is stored. You will then have to look through the paper file for the document you are seeking, hoping it has not been misfiled within the client file or into someone else's file.

 Computer. The process of looking for the document in the computer is commonly called "searching." When the document is found by the search process it is then "retrieved" onto the screen for modification or is then printed. The document can be retrieved for production or modification by using the applicable naming or indexing system, or by a text search engine that can search a subdirectory, a directory, an entire hard disk, or a series of hard disks in a single computer.

Retrieving the Entire File

 11. *Paper.* As indicated, you will have to get the paper file or that part that you want from wherever it is stored or have someone else get it and bring it to your desk.

 Computer. If you have created your own documents and have scanned into your system the documents received from others, you do not have to leave your desk to retrieve the entire file. It's all there in your computer without you or anyone else having to get up and find the paper file to bring it to your desk. You can print out whatever you wish to print, including color photos stored in the file.

Archiving Documents

 12. *Paper.* To store documents into a paper form file for later use, you will have to file the documents into a system that allows you to find the forms you need when you need them. To make a copy for revision purposes, you will have to make a photocopy of

the form or be able to print it out from the archived electronic storage. If you make a photocopy, you will have to replace the original form into the form file. (Over a period of time, the best forms are often removed and inadvertently not replaced.) You can use the system of creating paper forms described elsewhere in this book.

Computer. At some point almost any document produced in a computer will have to be removed from the computer when the computer is simply overloaded with too much data, when the information relates to a closed case, or at periodic "purges" of the computer files. This process is commonly referred to as "archiving." At the same time you decide to remove the document from the computer, you should create an electronic version that you can store with a paper file or independently of the paper version. A common way of archiving the computer's documents is to remove (copy and then delete) the document onto a floppy disk, which you store with the paper file. Do not forget the document is still in the computer and can be restored by law enforcement agencies or third parties seeking information about your client. As many lawyers and clients and others sadly learned, "delete" does not mean "erase." It just means to move the information to a different part of the computer.

Organizing Your Computer Files

If you already know Word Perfect, Word, or another word-processing system you may wish to skip this chapter.

Naming Your Documents

The system you use for naming the documents you create and copy can be extremely important. You should give serious thought to how you name documents and you should have a written system that you can provide to office assistants and others with whom you work or interact.

The system you use will be important in finding and retrieving a specific document after you create it, or a form file document after you have created one for the form files. A document misfiled in a computer is just as misfiled as a paper document misfiled in the wrong file. You may not be able to find it when you need it. Your system can help you build a good file of forms for future use. You will be much more efficient and you will make more money more quickly if you can simply modify an appropriate previously created form than if you have to start from scratch every time you prepare a form.

Most naming systems are client-oriented. I recommend you use a system that starts with the client's name. As a new lawyer, you will be able to remember the names of your clients and what you did for them with relative ease. As your practice grows over the years or if you merge with another lawyer, or if you become a corporate lawyer, you may wish to become document-oriented rather than client-oriented for ease in integrating systems, but you should start with a client-oriented system of naming.

I recommend a distinct file designation for every matter that has a distinct billing designation. You should also use distinct file names for each litigation matter to avoid misfiling documents into the wrong file for the right client.

What you might call separate files in a paper system are called separate directories and subdirectories and sub-subdirectories in a computer-naming system of naming. You can use the same simple system of filing I recommend for paper filing for your computer naming and filing.

For example:

1. Client name in paper system: Jones. Client name in computer system: C:\Jones. If you are handling more than one matter for Jones you may need an extension or subdirectory for each matter. You may also wish to include a billing number or file number in some part of the document-naming system.

2. Storing correspondence sent and received in paper system: place in upper-left side of paper folder. Storing correspondence in computer system: C:\Jones\corres\. Putting letters in chronological order in paper system: place most recent one on top of others. Placing letters in chronological order in computer system: C:\Jones\corres\204 (February 2004) or C:\Jones\corres\22304 (February 23, 2004). The word-processing software system you use may restrict the number of characters and extension characters you use or may give you virtually unlimited ability to describe the letter. The important point is to be able to identify correspondence by date sent for the letters you send, and to identify the date you received letters for the letters you receive from others that you scan into your system for computer retrieval at your desk without a paper file.

3. Storing disbursements and bills received and sent in the paper system: place in the lower-left side of the paper folder. Storing disbursements and bills received and sent in a computer system: you can create a subdirectory for financial data. You may wish to include copies of invoices sent and scanned copies of bills received.

Pleadings are normally kept in a separate subdirectory just for pleadings. You will soon develop a way of describing a pleading to correlate to the particular pleading. In an unlimited-number-of-characters system, you can be as long-winded as you wish in describing the pleading in exquisite detail. In a restricted system (eight characters and a three-letter extension), you may have to be imaginative. Common examples might include: Afsupmot.001 or Afoppmot.002.

This could represent an affidavit in support of (or in opposition to) a motion draft/version 1 or draft/version 2 of the document. With pleadings, as with correspondence, you may wish to scan the documents of an opposing counsel for your own use at a later time on a different matter as well as for the case file.

Memos to the file, copies of research, articles from periodicals, contracts, and other miscellaneous documents can be lumped together in a subdirectory called "miscellaneous" (the directory being the client name or case file) or can be grouped into a subdirectory with documents of a similar nature.

You may wish to save documents used in a file for other future similar cases that may require similar forms. You may wish to store them and retrieve them independent of any client designation. After completing a document for use by a client, the document can be copied and renamed in your personal form file.

Finding or retrieving a document from the electronic form file after it has been created can either be accomplished by your naming system or by a text search system that is part of your word-processing software program or a stand-alone text search program.

Naming the File

I recommend starting every file with the name of the client and with a separate file for every matter that requires time-keeping or accounting for disbursements.

Start with the client name followed by a description of the matter (*Jones, Real Estate; Jones, Partnership; Jones, Divorce; and Jones, 4/2/04 Accident* are examples). In litigation put the client name first whether the client is plaintiff or defendant, alone or with others. If the client's name is Jones use *Jones vs Smith* when Jones is plaintiff and *Jones advs Smith* when Jones is defendant. Use *Jones, et al.* when Jones the client has more than one person in the caption. If more than one client is included in the matter, list the multiple clients in alphabetical order and cross-reference the multiple client names. If there is a statute of limitations involved you might wish to include the date of the accident or triggering date in the file name.

When you close the file, give the file a new number so that you will know when a closed file is three years old or five years old for destruction purposes.

Simple Hard-Copy Filing Systems for the New Lawyer

File Cabinets

If a well-meaning relative bought you an old-fashioned two- or four-drawer file cabinet, throw it out or give it to charity; but don't use it. Use vertical files. (See sample on exhibit following this chapter.)

Using vertical files, you can store two-and-a-half times as many files in the same space or, to put it another way, your rental cost for floor space when using vertical files is 25 percent of that when using horizontal files.

A file cabinet will usually occupy about six square feet (including drawer pull-out space). At $1 per month per square foot (a nominal rent), you'll pay $6 per month or $72 per year for that file cabinet. The cost per file is four times the cost of using vertical files. Use low-cost shelving instead.

Ask your stationery store for samples of each type.

Organizing the File

Keep it simple. There are dozens of systems for organizing files. Some are good for personal injury plaintiffs, some are good for personal injury defendants, some are good for probate, some are good for wills and estate planning. Some systems appear to have been invented by geniuses, some appear to have been invented by idiots. My advice to the new lawyer is to ignore all these fancy file folder systems until you are somewhat established and can appreciate and understand what you actually need in a filing system. I suggest a simple file folder as illustrated in the exhibit at the end of this chapter.

Keep everything in chronological order. Don't open multiple files for the same matter. After a couple of years, this system will probably become inadequate for you. At that time you can make changes depending upon your specific needs.

Use a Numerical Filing System

The simplest and best system for you is to use a year-matter system. Each year start a new series. For example, 04/1, 04/2, 04/3, etc., then 05/1, 05/2, 05/3, etc. If you are embarrassed over the small number of files you have, then cheat on the numbering system. About February 1 of each year simply add 200 or 300 to the last number so that in February your numbering system would start with 04/202, 04/203, etc. Other lawyers will think you're doing a lot of business.

Make an alphabetical cross-index system, putting the client names on index cards cross-referenced to the file number.

Use a different numbering system for closed files. Be sure the file number indicates the year the file is closed so you can find it easily when you later want to destroy it.

When and How to Open a File

1. *Opening files.* Open a file when you have a client and a case and are professionally responsible for the matter. Until then, keep the copies of the documents, letters, etc., in twenty-six alphabetical, miscellaneous files, each in chronological order. When you open the file, remove the documents from the miscellaneous file and put them in the separate numerical file for the client matter. If you never open a file, simply leave the documents in the miscellaneous file for that alphabetical letter.

2. *Open a new file for each matter.* Believe me, it will make your life much easier to keep each matter in a totally different file with its own file number.

3. *Closing files.* After you've been in practice a few years you can get involved with microfilming or scanning. Until then, stick with my simple system.

a. Fill out a closed-file sheet. It will replace the bulky file and become the basis of future work the client will need. This closed-file sheet can be kept in a three-ring notebook in your office.

The filling out of this form will serve as a "last chance" to clean up any loose ends or errors you spot. A sample closed-file information sheet follows the next, "When and How to Close a File."

b. Remove duplicate copies of documents that you know will never be needed. (Remember pleadings can always be obtained from the court.)

c. Send valuable original documents back to the client with a cover letter (unless you enjoy being a bailee-insurer of the item).

d. Get the file folder out of your high-rent office to a low-rent or no-rent storage area and file it in numerical order.

e. Remove the alpha-numeric cross-index card from the active index and put it in the closed-file card index.

4. *When to close a file.* Close the file when there is nothing more for you to do on the case and when you've informed the client in writing that you are doing nothing further and are closing your file. (Also see the next chapter on when and how to close a file.)

5. *When to destroy a file.* I'm a coward and have rarely destroyed files. Other more-courageous lawyers than I close them after three-year or five-year intervals. I don't recommend file destruction. Microfilm, image, or scan them before destruction.

Color Filing to Prevent Lost and Misplaced Files

During your first year or two, lost or misplaced or misfiled files will not be a problem. As time goes on and you accumulate a large number of folders, misplaced files can be a serious problem. I invented a color filing system that virtually eliminates misfiled files. Simply get your file folders in different colors. When I last counted, thirteen different colors were commercially available. Change colors every hundred files or every letter. For example, all file folders for matter 04/1 through 04/99 are blue; from 04/100 through 04/199 red; from 04/200 through 04/299 green; from 05/1 through 05/99 orange; etc. Or use "As," "Bs," "Cs," etc., and have a different color folder for each letter.

The theory is simple. You can misfile a red folder in the section with the other red folders, but you can't misfile it in the green-folder section or the brown-folder section. Believe me, the system works.

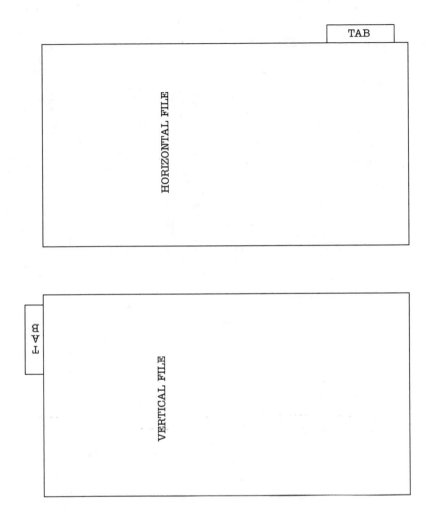

TAB

HORIZONTAL FILE

VERTICAL FILE

TAB

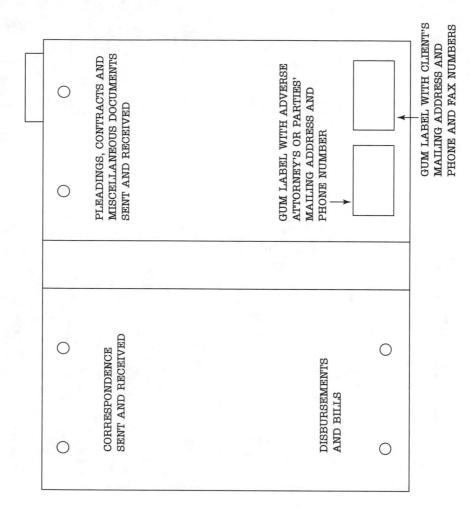

PLEADINGS, CONTRACTS AND MISCELLANEOUS DOCUMENTS SENT AND RECEIVED

GUM LABEL WITH ADVERSE ATTORNEY'S OR PARTIES' MAILING ADDRESS AND PHONE NUMBER

GUM LABEL WITH CLIENT'S MAILING ADDRESS AND PHONE AND FAX NUMBERS

CORRESPONDENCE SENT AND RECEIVED

DISBURSEMENTS AND BILLS

Distinguishing Between "Prospective," "Active," "Closed" and "Dead" Files

As your practice grows, file maintenance, storage, and destruction can become a serious problem if not anticipated.

In this chapter I simply want to create and use terminology that will make your life easier in deciding what to do with a file and where to keep it. In another chapter I deal with the process and system of closing and disposing of files.

Prospective Client File

These are accumulations of information for prospective clients. You have no fee agreement and you have not undertaken to do anything for which you might be professionally responsible. Letters rejecting the client or matter will be kept in this file. Number or name the file with the letter P.

Active Client File

These files contain the information on matters on which you are currently working. Work has been done and/or work needs to be done in the future in accordance with your written fee agreement and/or you have not been paid in full

Inactive Client File

Inactive client files contain information on matters for which you have done everything you were hired to do and have been paid in full, but for some reason decided to keep the file active hoping for future work involving the file. For example if you just completed a will and living trust and have been paid in full for a 96-year-old person, you might want to keep this Inactive file where you can easily access it. You may have formed a corporation for a client and have been paid in full but hope to get future work for annual minutes or employment agreements, etc. You have to get modification work after a family law matter is completed. Paid Inactive files also include files where you have done all the work but have not yet been paid in full. You must keep tabs on clients who owe you money for past work and therefore the file is inactive but not closed.

Closed Files

Closed files contain information on matters for which you have fully performed all the work required by your written fee agreement and have been paid in full, and for which you have no reasonable expectation of future work in connection with the matter. You have notified the client that the matter is closed, that you will do no further work, and that the file will be destroyed without further notification after a certain number of years.

Destroyed Files

As the name indicates, the file is gone and no longer exists. You might or might not wish to scan the file before destroying the paper file. If you scan it, be sure you keep hardware and software to be able to print the file at a later time. There's a strong probability that your existing system will become obsolete and that new systems will be unable to read or reproduce the information. Additionally, magnetic information can deteriorate over a period of time.

Create Destroyed File and Closed File lists to be kept in your office to replace the bulky files that have been moved or destroyed.

Closing and Disposing of Files

At some point in your practice, you will have to deal with the closing of files and the disposing of files. File storage is a nonproductive expense. A lot of nonchargeable time is wasted getting information out of closed files for clients and others who don't want to pay for the time involved. Public warehouses are filled with boxes of old client files with rent being paid month after month and year after year. The disposal of files becomes a serious problem to be cleaned up when a lawyer dies or wants to join with another firm or retire. Complying with the ethical restrictions on file disposal can be a nightmare.

A lot of wasted time and money can be avoided with a good ongoing file closing and file destruction system. Your system should be part of your fee agreement or policies of which the client is aware. There are three basic rules involved.

1. Client property must be given to the client.
2. You must preserve confidentiality.
3. You must protect yourself and the client.

Closed files should have a different file number system than open files. When a file is closed it should be given a different number that identifies the year in which it was closed. The numbering system will help you identify files which are "ripe" for destruction. The closed file should be removed from the open files and stored in a different place until it is destroyed or otherwise disposed of. By removing a closed file from the files you reduce the chances of misfiling something into a closed file where you might never find it again. You also can tell at a glance how much file space you need for open files and how much you need for closed files.

465

A simple system of renumbering would be to keep the old file number and add the letter and year of closing as a prefix or suffix. Alternatively, you could create a new numbering system but would need to create and maintain some sort of cross reference table between the two lists. When you destroy or dispose of the file, you can add the letter D and the year of destruction to the original file number. Thus the original file number never changes, but additional information is added to show the year of closing and the year of destruction.

Create a closed file sheet which will replace the bulky file when the file is closed.

Destroying Old Files

Some of this chapter can be found in other chapters in this book. This chapter recaps essential information from other chapters and consolidates file destruction into a single chapter.

Many books and articles have been written about inactive file maintenance, yet most lawyers are not really interested in file maintenance but rather in file destruction.

There are several different situations where a new lawyer will want to destroy files rather than pay for storage or worry about needing information in later years or worrying about file integration if he or she should join up with another lawyer or firm.

1. You never represented the "Client." You may have notes or copies of documents made during or after an interview that did not result in employment.

Be sure you have nothing that was given to you by the client. If you do, send it back. I often ask potential clients to fax me or e-mail me copies of any documents or photocopy them and mail them to me before the interview. Thus I do not have any documents that belong to the client, but only copies made expressly for me.

Assuming you never undertook to represent this person, send them a nonengagement letter and put the various information into a file called "Prospective Clients." Trash this file when the statute of limitations runs out on professional malpractice (one year, three years, or whatever the rule in your state).

You should not have given this information an "open file" number and it won't need a "closed file" or "destroyed file" number.

2. You did represent the client. You have done all the work. There is nothing more to do but you are owed fees. This file should not be

considered a "closed file" until you have given up all hope of ever getting paid. I once received $85,000 fourteen years after doing the work from a bankruptcy where I had filed a claim, but had to prove my case twelve or thirteen years after filing the claim. Had I destroyed the file, I would have received nothing. You may have to prove your case many, many years after the work was done. This is especially true any time a court approval is involved (bankruptcies, class actions, probates, conservatorships, etc., are common examples).

Don't give up and destroy the file if there is any chance you will be paid.

3. You have done all the work required and have been paid in full. When the work is finished and you have been paid in full, you should do the following:

A. Carefully go through the file piece of paper by piece of paper and remove anything that belongs to the client. Your work papers, research memos, comments, strategies, and drafts of documents normally would not belong to the client in most states when the work is finished.

B. Send the client these items belonging to the client: Mortgages, original evidence, wills, share certificates, leases, and other items that bear signatures or seals normally belong to the client. Make photocopies or scan them if you wish, but send those items that belong to the client to the client along with a cover letter that makes it clear

1. The case is closed.

2. You will do nothing further.

3. You may destroy the file in the future without any further notice to the client.

4. The client should immediately contact you if there is any information that the client wants. If the client responds, send them what they asked for (if you have it), making and keeping a photocopy or scan for yourself.

5. A client satisfaction survey form is enclosed. (Return of the form by the client will establish that the client received the letter and items sent.) Put that card into the closed file.

6. Renumber the file with a new closed file number and cross-reference the open file number to the closed file number.

How to Destroy the File

The manner of destruction may be one of local custom and you may need an opinion for what you have to do. Simply shredding is normally sufficient even though shredded files can be painstakingly reconstructed by hand or with computer programs used by police and intelligence agencies. Processing the paper into pulp is normally not necessary, although the companies that shred paper files might sell that paper to paper recycling companies.

Simply dumping the file into your trash may not be adequate if you don't know what happens to it after you have dumped it. Although everything in the file is your property, you still have a duty to preserve client confidences. You have no way of knowing whether government agencies or private investigators or others are going to be able to use this information to your detriment or the detriment of your client.

When to Destroy the File
(Assuming Everything in the File Belong to You)

This must be determined by local custom and typically depends on the nature of the work done and applicable limitations of actions against you. Common time limitations might be the longest of the following types of actions:

1. Professional negligence (malpractice)
2. Breach of Contract
3. Conversion of client property (civil & criminal)
4. Fraud
5. Bailment Law

Local law, rules and practice may dictate specific applications to specific types of cases (criminal, minors, trusts, wills, etc.). Hopefully your local bar association or practice management advisor can give you guidance or point you in the right direction to get an answer.

What to Give the Client When "The File" is Demanded.

In some states the file consists of EVERYTHING in connection with the case, whether on paper or electronically stored.

In some states the lawyer is not obligated to turn over personal work product or information not connected to the legal matter itself. (The client's credit report, for example.)

In some states you don't have to recreate what the client has previously been given, such as copies of correspondence and pleadings and other items that the client previously received. (Another reason to give your clients copies of everything as the case progresses.)

Destroying Old Files When the Client Has Disappeared or You Did Not Follow Proper File-Closing Procedures

Like many things in law, a few ounces of precaution are better than several pounds of repair. Had the file been properly closed, you could simply destroy everything with no further notice to the client.

Basically you are going to have to do the same things you would have done had you properly closed the file:

1. Remove and send to the client everything belonging to the client along with a disengagement letter.

2. Wait for client response (if you had a good address).

3. Destroy whatever you can destroy without exposing yourself to litigation or disciplinary risk.

You now must deal with locating the former client who may be dead or may have disappeared.

You must use "reasonable" means to locate the client; Internet search engines, telephone directories, voter registration lists, and other resources may be helpful. With increasing anti-identity theft procedures, locating information on individuals is becoming more and more difficult. You may be wise to hire a credit reporting agency or insurance claim investigating agency to make a search. They often seem to have access to information that in theory is not public. Here again, life would be less difficult if you had acted earlier on closing the file.

If you can not find this client or their heirs, you may have to locate whatever branch of your state government accepts unclaimed credits and unclaimed property under your state laws. Communicate with them and send the former client's property to them.

Malpractice and Ethics

When you have developed a file closing and destruction procedure or policy (possibly based in part on my suggestions), you would communicate them to your malpractice carrier and your local ethics committee. They may or may not assist you or refuse to assist you, but at least you will have left a trail of reasonable attempts to comply.

What to Do With Electronic File Data

No matter what I write in this chapter, it is likely to be obsolete before the book gets printed.

Accordingly, you might end up being on your own and five years later hoping you guessed correctly.

Hopefully you will be able to apply the concepts set forth in this chapter within the context of available technology when you read this chapter.

The Nonexistent Paperless Office

New lawyers are tempted NOT to make paper copies, but rather to rely on computer files and memories.

Unfortunately, it is a fact of life that paper files are here to stay for the foreseeable future.

Paper files are necessary for at least three reasons:

1. Computers can and do crash without adequate backup storage.

2. Many clients and third parties do not have the necessary skills and technology to operate without hard-copy paper.

3. It is only a question of time until your files will not be readable due to software or hardware being obsolete. Backup tapes and discs will be of no value if they are not readable. The highway of word-processing equipment and software is littered with the corpses of systems that leave a lawyer unable to read the data so carefully stored and backed up.

Even if you only store your printouts in files in boxes in storage, you will at least have them when and if you need them until you destroy them.

We all fantasize about the paperless office with everything stored electronically on some form of disk or tape, but you shouldn't try to run a law practice without hard copies of what you create or use.

I personally have seen the evolution of storage of data as follows:

1. Punch Cards
2. Papertape
3. Magnetic Tape
4. Mag Cards
5. 8" Floppy
6. 5.25" Floppy
7. 3.5" Diskettes
8. CD-ROM

As of the writing of this chapter, 3.5" diskettes are becoming obsolete in favor of memory sticks.

Each of the above eight required different hardware and different software, and some of the vendors have gone out of existence leaving me with unreadable data.

Until recently we purged the hard disk of the file and kept the hard disk information on a back-up tape.

We made floppies of the client files involved and filed a floppy with the paper file in closed files or in a separate closed file location.

As floppies go out of usage, I do not know how the electronic data will be filed with the client file in the future; perhaps on CD.

You will have to make your decision(s) based on existing and proposed technology.

Closed File Sheet

Closed File No. _____   Original File No. _____

INFORMATION FOR CLOSED FILES

Court Case No. _____

1. Title of case as it appears on file _____
2. Nature or type of case _____
3. Names of our clients _____
4. Last known business and residence addresses and phone numbers of our clients _____
5. Date file closed _____
6. Reason file closed _____
7. Who authorized closing of file? _____
8. Letter in file advising client file has been closed?
   Yes_____ No_____

9. Letter in file advising client we will do nothing further and file will be destroyed?
Yes_____ No_____ If so, date of letter _____
10. Any statutes of limitations involved? Yes_____ No_____
If so, is statute of limitations indicated in either of above letters? Yes_____ No_____
11. Any original documents of client in file?
Yes_____ No_____
If so, specify _____
12. At time of closing file, any unpaid fees or costs due?
Yes_____ No_____ If so, amount: $ _____
13. List all plaintiffs in case _____
14. List of all defendants in case _____
15. Description of last document or pleading in file (include date) _____
16. Date and nature of last contact (letter, call, meeting, etc.) _____
17. Number of file folders and estimated thickness in inches
No. _____ Thickness _____
18. Is party a minor? Yes_____ No_____ If yes, date of birth and indicated activity required upon majority _____
_____
Has client been advised as to what must be done upon majority? Yes_____ No_____
19. Dismissals filed? Yes _____ No_____ If yes, against whom? _____
With prejudice_____ Without prejudice _____
20. Abstract of judgment in file? Yes _____ No_____ If yes, recorded? Date of recording_____
Released? Date of release_____
21. Satisfaction of judgment in file? Yes _____ No_____ If yes, recorded?_____
Date of recording_____ Amount of Satisfaction _____
_____
If partial satisfaction, indicate amount, date, if recorded
_____
22. Date judgment entered _____
23. What is there to do in the future? _____
A. Review judgment after 10 years _____
B. Disburse money (to whom?) _____
C. Need renewal or notice because of lease _____
D. Need renewal or notice because of provision in contract _____

E. Trust involved? Yes_____ No_____If so, need to notify client when trust terminates or other reason
for notifying client? Yes_____ No_____

24. Anything requiring us to notify client in the future?
Yes_____ No_____ If so, what? When? _____

25. Has there been a request made on the twenty-year
calendar for future work? Yes___ No___ If so, nature
of request _____

26. Have all applicable files been copied from the hard
disk to a floppy for inclusion? _____

27. Have all applicable files been copied on a backup disk?
_____

28. Date set for file destruction_____
_____

Fondling the Files

There is no substitute for periodically taking the file off the shelf and physically examining the contents to be sure a file hasn't gotten lost and forgotten in the system.

A periodic review of the status of every case is critical to avoid malpractice and to keep clients happy with an observed processing of the matter. Clients won't be afraid that their matters have been overlooked or abandoned or lost in the shuffle or feel that they or their cases are not important to you.

You (or another lawyer) should physically remove the file from the shelf at least once every sixty days and physically go through it.

Among other things, you should look for the following:

1. *Loose papers in the file.* Loose papers may indicate that someone stuck the paper in the file without you or another lawyer properly looking at the paper before filing it. The paper may call for some action on your part. The action might have gotten overlooked.

2. *No written contact with the client in sixty days.* The client should receive something in writing from you at least every sixty days. If nothing else, send the client a letter that explains that you haven't communicated because you have nothing to tell him or her, but that the case is being properly handled by you and that all is normal and under control.

3. *Inactivity in the file.* If nothing is happening on the file, ask yourself why not. Activate the case or close it.

4. *Files that should be closed.* If the file should be closed, do so. Closing the file with appropriate notice to the client may start the statute of limitations on a malpractice or ethics complaint.

5. *Files that someone in the office is trying to hide or cover up.* Someone in your office may have done something wrong or something he or she is ashamed of or embarrassed about.

6. *Misfiled documents that belong in some other file.* You don't want to inadvertently give one client information about another client's matter. A misfiled document may be the symptom of a problem in your filing system or your filing personnel.

7. *Documents in the right file, but in the wrong place in the file.* You will then understand the value of using different-colored papers for different purposes. (Research on green, telephone conference memos on yellow, sensitive on red [hard to photocopy], etc.)

In theory, a good case management software system could pull up everything onto a computer screen and save you from going into the file room and into the paper file, but the online system only knows what you tell it and information does not always get entered or entered correctly. If you do have an online case management system, examine the file physically and compare it with a printout of what the computer system says is in the file. This will help you find defects in the management system or in the use of the management system.

The largest firms in the world periodically do physical inventory observations to compare what's on the books with what actually exists. No system is perfect and you have to compare what's actually happening and what's actually in the file with what your printout says is actually in the file.

You could delegate this task of "fondling the files" to a paralegal or assistant, but you really should do it yourself, especially when you are starting a practice and want to catch the bugs and problems while you have a smaller number of files to fondle.

Form Letter for Closing a File, The Disengagement Letter

The primary purpose of a disengagement letter is to let the client know that you consider the legal matter closed.

There are at least three important reasons to be able to determine the end of the active attorney-client relationship on a given matter.

1. You want to let the client know what is going to happen to the file and its contents, for the benefit of the client and possibly to

relieve yourself of the responsibility of being a free perpetual ware-
housing and record storage service for the client.

2. It may also be important, for ethics and conflicts reasons, to
be able to determine whether a client is an active client or a former
client. For example, the rules for representing a client adverse to a
present client in a litigation matter may be different from the rules
for representing a client adverse to a former client.

3. Perhaps most importantly, a disengagement letter may start
the statute of limitations on a malpractice claim or ethics complaint.

Many states have an exception to the statute of limitations that
parallels California CCP section 340.6 (a) (2), which creates the following exception to the statute:

> ". . . Except that the period shall be tolled during the time
> that the lawyer continues to represent the plaintiff regarding
> the specific subject matter in which the alleged wrongful act
> or omission occurred."

In litigation matters, there normally is some sort of final pleading indicating the matter is over, but often the client does not understand the pleading document, even when the client has signed the
document. In nonlitigation matters, the lawyer has to create a document to tell the client the matter is over and closed.

The following form letter may be of help to you:

      Ms. Mary Client, President
      ABC Manufacturing
[1]   Last Known Address
      Anytown, U.S.A.
[2]   Re: Jones vs. Smith
        Our File No. 97-890
        Superior Court Case No.123456
[3]   Via U.S. Mail and Fax (555) 652-5019

      Dear Ms. Client:
[4]   We are honored and pleased to have served you
[5]   in connection with the Smith matter. The matter is now
      closed. We suggest that you keep all your copies of the
      file and the various documents in a place where you can
[6]   easily find them if necessary. We are closing our files
[7]   for this matter and are removing the case from the ac-
[8]   tive-files list as we have completed our legal work in the
      matter.

[9]   We believe that we have returned all original documents to you and that we are not in possession of any
[10]   original documents or papers of yours. If you believe we
are still in possession of an original document or document you provided us, please let us know immediately so
that we may look for it before we put the file in the
[11]   closed files. If we have to retrieve the file or research it
for documents or information after it is placed in closed
files there may be a closed-file retrieval charge depend-
[12]   ing on the prevailing charges at the time. Accordingly it
may save you time and money to double-check your files
and to let us know if there is a problem within 30 days,
at which time the file will be formally closed.

[13]   After five years, your file may be destroyed with-
[14]   out further notice to you. It is important that you pick
up anything you want or need from the file or immediately direct us in writing where you want documents
sent.

[15]   We are honored to have served you on this matter and want you to know that you will always be welcome for any other matters that you may have now or
in the future, in which we may help you.

         We are always concerned that we meet the expec-
tations of our clients on each individual matter that we
[16]   handle for them. Since this matter is now closed, and
[17]   our work is finished, we would appreciate your taking a
[18]   few moments to fill out and return the enclosed short
questionnaire by fax or in the enclosed postage-paid
envelope.

         Please feel free to call with any questions or
comments you may have.

         Very truly yours,

         Better, Faster, and Cheaper, Attorneys at Law

Enclosures:
[19]   1. Client Short Form Survey
[20]   2. Postage-Paid Return Envelope (U.S. Mail only)

Comments:

   [1] Send to last known address and other addresses where client
might be.

   [2] Identify the completed matter as fully as you can.

[3] I do not recommend certified or registered mail because the client may be worried or suspicious. Use your judgment about certified mail if you don't trust the client or don't feel comfortable. A fax confirmation slip and your telephone bill will be proof that the letter was sent and received if you send a fax reminder follow-up.

[4] Identify the matter again to avoid confusion if you have ever handled another matter for the client.

[5] This clearly tells the client matter is closed.

[6] This tells the client a second time the file is closed.

[7] This tells the client you are taking the case off your active-file list.

[8] This tells the client you are finished doing the work and you are not doing any more work.

[9] This tells the client you don't have possession of any of his or her property and should start the statute of limitations on a conversion case against you.

[10] This gives the client the responsibility of helping himself/herself and may create a defense of contributory or comparative negligence if you didn't give everything back.

[11] Many firms now charge for this service but you are emphasizing that the charge will be a charge for retrieving a closed file. You may wish to put this information about charging to retrieve closed files in your initial engagement or in your "billing policy memoranda."

[12] You are giving a certain time limit to respond. You may wish to send a fax follow-up or mail "final reminder" if you don't get a response.

[13] If you are permitted to do so, you can trash the file without trying to locate and notify a client who has disappeared. Check the ethics and malpractice rules carefully before doing this. Check also the chapter in this book on closing a file.

[14] Give the client the burden of doing something affirmative if he or she wants the records back. The client must either pick them up or direct you in writing where to send what the client wants. If you get no response, the client may be considered negligent or contributorily negligent or put in a bad light for doing nothing to protect his or her own interests if there is a subsequent problem.

[15] This tells the client he or she is welcome back.

[16] You are telling the client again the matter is closed.

[17] You are telling the client again the work is finished.

[18] The survey tells the client you care about his or her opinion.

[19] The short form survey should be a form used only when you close a file to help establish that it came from this client. You may wish to use a special form or mark or identify the form.

[20] The envelope should be coded or keyed so it can be identified as containing the survey sent to that client. The returned survey or the fax confirmation is proof of receipt of the letter from you.

[21] There's no harm in sending an e-mail or fax duplicate of the letter as additional proof of actual receipt. Your phone bill will show the fax sending and you may wish to print out a copy of the "sent" e-mail.

How to Build a Good Form File

Your electronic or paper form file will be one of your most valuable assets. During the first few years you'll be doing a lot of things for the first time. You'll be copying from books, from other lawyers, from the Internet, and from shareware, and you'll be doing a lot of drafting of forms. If you are like most lawyers, you'll want to copy prior work whenever possible, changing the names and adding or subtracting a few paragraphs. This practice is to be commended, provided you know what you are doing. Blindly copying pages of "boilerplate" language that is neither intelligible nor applicable will eventually get you or your client into trouble. Remember that many of the forms in form books appear as they do because the language incorporated in them has been decided in litigation. Thus, the wording of the form has been judicially tested, whereas new language is subject to being challenged, and the intent of the drafter defeated, or, if not reviewed by the courts, left uncertain.

Keep in mind that during your first few years, the work of other more experienced lawyers is likely to be somewhat better than yours. Therefore it makes good sense to take the work of another lawyer *as a starting point* and improve from there.

In the final analysis there are only two things you need for a good form file. These two things are: (1) Good Forms, and (2) A Good Index to the Forms.

Good Forms

The best way to get good forms is to start with electronic or paper form books and resources. Keep a healthy respect for the copyright laws, but don't forget the doctrine of "Fair Use," which allows you to copy most forms that are not copyrighted, and to a certain extent some that are copyrighted. Normally, form books and pleadings and Internet shareware are copyable for your own use without difficulty.

Save and hard copy everything that you feel is or may be useful to you. Put it into a permanent form file. Get the forms bound by a commercial bookbinder with your name engraved in gold on the outside. Don't use loose-leaf files, as over a period of time the best forms tend to disappear as you remove them and forget to replace them. The theory underscoring saving everything is that the latest form on a subject should be the best and you can put several together to develop what you need.

Save electronically produced forms both on paper and on your hard disk and in a format where they can be easily located and reproduced.

A Good Index to the Forms

You can either invent your own subject matter index starting from scratch, which is a gross waste of time, or you can use a system developed by experts at a cost of millions of dollars. The West Key Number System used in this chapter is a good one. A copy of the basic index form follows this chapter. You may wish to obtain a list of subjects that is more current and more closely follows the kind of practice you have or expect to have.

If your state has another index system that you feel is superior, then use it, but don't try to create your own (subject to a penchant for masochism on your part).

I recommend that you index everything that goes into your form file along the following classifications:

1. Subject matter (using the commercial index developed by someone else);
2. Client's name;
3. Adverse party's name;
4. Statutes involved;
5. Court or tribunal in which you appeared;
6. Judge or administrative person who heard the matter;
7. Adverse lawyer involved.

You cannot over-index a document; you can only under-index it. Using this index system (which I invented and which you can copy), you'll be able to recall almost anything you've done or seen if it's in your form file. Admittedly, this form file will be of more value to you the longer you're in practice, but start it with the first document or pleading you prepare. This system will more than service your needs for the first few years of your practice.

Text search software can be of immense help in finding forms, data, etc., in your computer files. Text search software functions by seeking specific words or combinations of words (sometimes called "strings") on your hard drive. You can find documents using the client's name or using words or key cases found in the document. Unfortunately, documents that get purged from the file usually get "lost" unless they are specifically copied onto a disk devoted to form storage.

You may also use forms prepared by opposing counsel, using OCR (optical character recognition) equipment to copy other lawyers' hard copy into your word-processing system.

A good "search" feature on your computer will also help you get to the right form more quickly.

WEST KEY NUMBERS AND TOPICS

1	Abandoned and Lost Property	17	Adoption	41	Associations
2	Abatement and Revival	18	Adulteration	42	Assumpsit, Action of
		19	Adultery		
3	Abduction	20	Adverse Possession	43	Asylums
4	Abortion and Birth Control	21	Affidavits	44	Attachment
		22	Affray	45	Attorney and Client
5	Absentees	23	Agriculture	46	Attorney General
6	Abstracts of Title	24	Aliens	47	Auctions and Auctioneers
7	Accession	25	Alteration of Instruments		
8	Accord and Satisfaction	26	Ambassadors and Consuls	48	Audita Querela
				48A	Automobiles
9	Account			48B	Aviation
10	Account, Action on	27	Amicus Curiae	49	Bail
11	Account Stated	28	Animals	50	Bailment
11A	Accountants	29	Annuities	51	Bankruptcy
12	Acknowledgment	30	Appeal and Error	52	Banks and Banking
13	Action	31	Appearance		
14	Action on the Case	33	Arbitration	54	Beneficial Associations
		34	Armed Services		
15	Adjoining Landowners	35	Arrest	55	Bigamy
		36	Arson	56	Bills and Notes
15A	Administrative Law and Procedure	37	Assault and Battery	57	Blasphemy
				58	Bonds
		38	Assignments	59	Boundaries
16	Admiralty	40	Assistance, Writ of	60	Bounties

Library Needs and Costs

A 1998 study conducted by Catherine Paunov, Esq., came to the following shocking conclusion concerning the three-year library needs of a new lawyer opening a practice in California:

	Initial Purchase	Annual Upkeep
Hard Copy	$29,000	$12,000
CD-ROM	$7,000	$12,000
Online	$-0-	$6,000
Internet	$-0-	$-0-

Since the study was done, the differences have become even more pronounced.

It must be emphasized that these figures *do not* include rental space required for books, property taxes, insurance, labor of inserting supplements, lawyer's time in walking back and forth to the books, time spent looking for lost or misplaced books, etc.

The message is clear. Do not buy any book unless you have to. Do not buy online services or CD-ROMs to get what you can get for free on the Internet.

The Internet as a Library Resource

It is only a matter of time until almost any library resource you might need will be available for free or low cost if used on the Internet. There are thousands of law-related Internet sites and the number is growing astronomically.

One or more law schools will place all or most of their library on the Internet. Internet sources are limited only by copyright restrictions. Law schools are aggressively using the Internet as a form of marketing and advertising the school to practicing lawyers as well as to law students. Various legal publications make current cases and information available to get you to subscribe to or buy their publications. Private law firms provide free information on various areas of law in order to convince you of their expertise in the area or to generally familiarize you with their names and abilities.

You may wish to check out my Web site at **http://www.Foonberg Law.com** or **www.willcontests.com**, **www.fractionaljetownership .com**, **www.HowtoStartandBuild.com**, and **www.Gettingclients.com** to get an idea of how private law firms give away legal information to attract lawyers and nonlawyers. You will find information at my Web site in areas I wish to practice and various publications I have written that are sold by the ABA. (Currently I am in the process of providing information on estate contests, will contests, trust contests, fractional jet ownerships, and legal ethics on my Web site in order to attract that type of work.) You may wish to create your own Web site on some new or developing area of law in order to establish a reputation and to attract clients.

As of the writing of this book, I consider Greg Siskind of Memphis to be one of the most knowledgeable people on marketing law firms on the Internet, and I recommend his presentations and his written publications on the topic, including *The Lawyer's Guide to Marketing on the Internet*, Second Edition, which he co-authored with Deborah McMurray and Richard P. Klau (ABA, 2002).

In addition to the law schools and law firms and legal publications, governments at every level make materials and information available on the Internet. Governments encourage use of Web sites to provide information including forms and instructions. People who use the Web site to get information and download the forms save the government the time and postage expense of providing paper information to those to need it.

Many of the providers of legal information link their sites to other related sites, creating an endless trail to be followed.

As with any library, electronic or paper, much of the information is permanent and historical and will not change. On the other hand, there is always new information that must be used to update the permanent part. Some Web sites are updated daily. Some Web sites have not been updated for years. The multiple search engines can also be of help to see what current information exists in periodicals, etc., but using search engines every time you want to do research can be very time-consuming.

You will have to invest some time finding and getting familiar with those Web sites you feel are helpful to you and your practice. You should "bookmark" those Web sites. There are multiple online and paper publications containing information on new or specialty Web sites. One I recommend is *The Lawyer's Guide to Fact Finding on the Internet*, Second Edition, by Carole A. Levitt and Mark E. Rosch (ABA, 2004), which has many chapters of value to a new lawyer, especially the chapter on "Accessing Public Records" and the chapters on specific industries. Carole Levitt is a dynamic and interesting speaker who knows more about the practical and real world of using the Internet, especially for free, than any other person I know. The book she has coauthored with Mark Rosch on using the Internet would be of value to any lawyer. Web sites come and Web sites go, yet some of the basic information will be there in a new Web site, or in a Web site that would seem to be an unlikely place to look. This book goes way beyond being a list of useful Web sites, because it teaches you WHAT can be found rather than getting involved in the minutiae of how to find something on a specific Web site.

I recommend you begin working with the Web by becoming familiar with the law schools' sites first, followed by the government Web sites. As a new lawyer, it is important for you not to spend cash on books or periodicals when you can get the information for free.

Get one or more domain names for yourself even if you don't intend to use them for a while. Currently it costs $35 a year or less to get and keep a domain name. By having your own domain name you'll be able to receive e-mail from clients and others without having to notify clients if you change office location or service provider. You can always reach me at **Jay@FoonbergLaw.com** because my domain name is **www.FoonbergLaw.com**.

Some sources will allow you to subscribe to e-mail updates for free or for a fee.

Library expenses for books and periodicals can be a bottomless pit. The gradual growth of your library and the corresponding increase in monthly payments can deprive you of cash when you need it most. Before ordering any book or periodical, put the order form in your desk drawer for twenty-four hours; then take it out and examine it again. Put it back in the desk drawer for another twenty-four hours and if you still feel you need the book, then sign the order form.

Free and Low-Cost Publications and Information

These books and forms and information sources are usually available from several sources: government, commercial, and the Internet.

Compose a form letter that you can have printed along the following lines:

Dear _____:

    I am a newly admitted lawyer about to open my own practice. I anticipate that I may have contact with your agency in the near future.

    I would appreciate being placed on your electronic or paper mailing list for publications and forms that you make available to lawyers. If there is a charge for the publication or forms either on a periodic or other basis, I would appreciate your informing me of the cost by return e-mail.

    Thank you for your courtesy and cooperation.

Very truly yours,

J. Novice

Government Sources

Many government agencies distribute materials, via e-mail or mail on their Web sites, for free or at nominal cost (less than a few dollars). Don't worry about getting or buying useless information. Any library contains some information that will never be used. The cost is so low that you can afford to make a few mistakes.

There is an element of surprise or grab bag involved. You'll be surprised to find which agencies administer which laws. In California, the corporation checklist with invaluable information for forming corporations comes from the Secretary of State rather than the Department of Corporations. I got an adoption manual from the Department of Social Welfare for about $2. Within a few weeks I had my first adoption matter and every form and procedure was spelled out in detail. I also got a free subscription for all Security and Exchange Commission releases. After more than thirty years, I'm still waiting for my first Security and Exchange Commission case.

You should get the local phone books (from the phone company or public library) for your state capital, the largest commercial city in the state, and your hometown. Write to every agency listed under the state, county, city, and federal governments. If you are really ambitious you can get the Washington, D.C. phone book and write to every federal agency listed. Internet telephone directories are often dated and inaccurate.

In the first few years get everything free and everything that is available at nominal cost. After a few years you can cancel the unnecessary subscriptions if you don't want them. If you subscribe to e-mail services, be sure to create mailboxes for the e-mail messages to avoid being inundated every day.

The forms and accompanying instructions as to when and how to use them that you will receive are exceptionally valuable, particularly those that you receive from courts and administrative agencies. You will soon learn that when an agency or court makes a form available you'll be acting at your peril to use a different form or to make up your own form. Some civil service clerks are very definite in their opinion that there are two ways to do things, their way and the wrong way. In most cases you'll end up using their forms and recommended procedures, so you might just as well start that way and save yourself and your clients delay, expense, aggravation, and embarrassment.

Court Forms

I have recommended asking to be placed on the mailing list of every court, administrative agency, and government office. I have suggested a form letter for you to use and pointed you to where to write.

I am now addressing only the matter of court forms.

You should obtain court forms whether or not you intend to litigate matters.

There is a trend among the courts throughout the United States to promulgate checklists and fill-in-the-blank forms that ask for specific information given in a specific way. The courts have their own reasons for doing so, including to make it easier for litigants to not use lawyers, and to make it easier for information to be put into computers by court administrative personnel so they and the judges can more easily find and use data without having to read custom-made documents.

The forms actually are excellent checklists for you to use to be sure you have asked your client for all the relevant data you will need for the case. Certainly, the court may bounce a form back with prejudicial consequences to you and your client if you didn't give the court what it wanted, in the manner the court wanted it.

The forms are often accompanied by instructions that spell out exactly what the applicable cases and statutes are and what has to be proved and how it has to be proved.

Even if you do not intend to be a litigator or litigate a matter, the forms can sometimes be invaluable in helping you interview a client and in creating good transactional documents.

You should obtain one of every form published by each court with which you are likely to have contact. Be sure to include all trial courts, including federal and small claims.

The forms may be available one at a time or the court may sell or provide a bound or assembled collection, one containing each of every form. In some cases the forms are available online electronically and in some cases the forms are available on CD-ROM disks published by the court or the local legal newspaper or a commercial vendor.

The State of California alone uses more than 700 court forms. Almost every form sets forth the pleading information needed, and many also make reference to the applicable cases and statutory law and cross-references to other applicable laws, and contain instructions for using the forms and proving the case. (It should be taken into account that the forms were designed to help people get to court without lawyers.)

A selection of these forms repeating some of what is said here is in another chapter of this book.

I highly recommend you scan my list and that you get your own set(s) of court forms. These forms are often obtainable off the Internet and can be used by you to learn or familiarize yourself with the area of law involved and provide you with questions to ask the client.

Commercial Sources

Free books, publications, and forms are usually available from banks, insurance companies, title or escrow companies, trust companies, form printing companies, etc. Not only will you get free publications but you will also get some free lunches when the business development or sales representative calls on you to deliver the forms and books and wants to take you to lunch. As a new lawyer with forty or fifty years of practice ahead of you, you are a very important potential source of business for these companies. The representatives know that as a new lawyer you can't send much business to them so there won't be any "hard sell." As you might expect, the banks' and trust companies' form books contain will forms and trust forms naming the sponsoring bank or trust companies as executor and trustees in the wills.

The life insurance companies' form books contain business buy/sell agreements for partnerships and corporations (funded with life insurance), pension and profit-sharing and retirement plans (also funded with life insurance), and question-and-answer questions about insurance taxation.

The title insurance companies and escrow companies have good forms for deeds and mortgages as well as good publications with highlights of real estate law.

You must be aware, however, that the form provided may not be the right one for your specific client or matter.

The form printing companies will usually send a "sample kit" of forms available from them. Some of the companies charge for these sample kits. There are many CD-ROM and online vendors who provide various forms of varying quality and of varying value in a particular jurisdiction.

Law Firm Sources

Many law firms will gladly send you their paper or e-mail newsletters and place information on their Web sites (look at mine, for example, at **www.FoonbergLaw.com**) in order to market their availability in their practice, geographic, or legal area.

Some law firms give away good, immediately useful information, and many give away just barely enough information to impress you and to solicit your business. Some information is dated and some is current. You may need to experiment by trial and error to find what is helpful to you.

Legal Association Sources

Many specialty bar groups and some state and local bar groups provide current information, forms, and links to other databases.

More Expensive Books

When in doubt, don't. Law books are very expensive, as is the maintenance. You should not buy one book that costs more than a few dollars during your first few years unless you know exactly what you are getting and unless you have a need for it. Use the law libraries of the courthouses, the law schools, and other lawyers whenever you can. Save your cash—use the Internet and online services whenever possible.

The materials available vary from state to state. Depending on your state, and recognizing that lawyers differ as to what is best, I recommended obtaining your books in the following sequence:

1. Law dictionary;
2. Unannotated codes or statutes (most recent edition);
3. Annotated codes or statutes;
4. Legal encyclopedia (if available in your state);
5. Digests;
6. Reporters; and
7. Specialized works
   a. continuing education
   b. pleading books
   c. tax services
   d. bankruptcy services
   e. others

Electronic Databases

Electronic databases, including CD-ROM alone or as part of an online service, are infinitely cheaper than paper and should be used where possible to conserve cash. Most electronic databases are more current than paper book publications. Many booksellers have low-cost programs for new lawyers.

Book Advertising

Don't trash book ads before skimming them. Most book ads have a table of contents and some description of the special features of the book. The ads can alert you to changes in the law since you studied the course in law school or last handled a case in the area.

Use the Resources of Other Paper Law Libraries

During your first few years of practice you'll have the time to go to the nearby law libraries including the libraries of nearby established law firms. These nearby firms will gladly make their paper libraries available when you explain that you are a new lawyer. In my opinion a good library is essential to doing complete, thorough, professional legal work. Most, if not all, lawyers with good law libraries feel the same way and will respect you for trying to do a thorough job. Using their libraries will enhance your reputation in the community—but don't abuse your privileges.

Follow these simple rules:

1. Never "drop in" to do research. Call first to ask if it's all right to come over "for a few minutes" (libraries are often in use as conference rooms, collating rooms, evidence rooms, etc.).

2. Be unobtrusive; remember you are a guest.

3. Don't interfere with other lawyers doing research. Be polite. Exchange a few pleasantries (introducing yourself to whomever is using the library at the same time). Ask if that person can suggest one or more works in the library that may help you, but don't let him or her do your research and don't let a friendly lawyer spend more than a few moments with you. Remember, that person is being compensated by a client to do the client's work, not to do your work. It won't do you or the associate any good if a senior partner who has clients in the office and who is waiting for the research comes into the library and finds you and the associates in a "bull session" discussing college football teams.

4. Copying and photographing of books: If you must get a form or case or statute photocopied, offer to pay for the cost. If there is a reluctance to accept your money, ask the reproduction operator to take the money and to use it for the employees' coffee room. If the firm doesn't want the funds, offer to pay at the same rate charged by the local library. Your few dollars won't be needed by a firm that has a six-figure monthly overhead, but your desire not to be even a

slight burden on your host will make a favorable impression and keep the doors open to you.

5. Electronic copying: Bring your own diskettes or other memory devices to download or copy information.

6. Clean up your mess before you leave. Put all books back.

Subscriptions

In my opinion, money spent on subscriptions to periodicals during your first few years of practice is a better investment than money spent on hardbound books. Generally speaking, such works fall into three categories:

1. What's new in the law;
2. How-to-do-it articles;
3. Scholarly research and writing.

1. *What's New in the Law.* These are the most important periodicals for you.

a. In law school you learned general legal theories, sometimes using cases 300 years old as teaching guides. You now must apply the principles to a specific factual situation in a modern context. Reading these periodicals will give you a good feeling for what is happening currently.

b. Clients and potential clients will be very impressed when you tell them about new laws and new cases that apply to them. They will be grateful that you are thinking of them.

c. Several of my cases in my early years were cases where another lawyer had told the clients that their case had no merit. In some of these cases the first lawyer simply didn't know the current state of the law. By being aware of recent changes, I helped the clients and got devoted clients who many years later still brag to their friends and anyone who will listen about the "miracle lawyer" who helped them when the other lawyers said the case was hopeless. This kind of client will send you new clients as long as you live. (Wouldn't you if you were the client?)

d. You have no choice. If you don't keep up, you will soon be skilled in what the law used to be.

2. *How-To-Do-It Articles.* These articles are usually valuable to you for the current forms and procedures they contain. If you have a problem in any area covered by the article you will save valuable

time. Use of these articles is on a hit-and-miss basis. The best article on zoning won't be of much help if you never get a zoning matter. Unless you have a particular interest in a particular field it is my opinion that this type of publication should be deferred until you have been in practice two or three years.

3. *Scholarly Research and Writing.* If you have an interest in keeping up with the law reviews or journals of your particular law school and you want to subscribe and continue your subscription, then do so. Absent this motivation, I recommend against these types of periodicals. The cost simply isn't warranted in view of the probable uselessness early in a law career. This type of publication can be of great value in appellate briefs, but you probably won't have many cases going to appeal in your first few years. After you are established three or four years and can afford the luxury, you can subscribe to all those you care to; for example, textbooks with annual supplements.

Specific Types of Periodicals

1. *What's New in the Law.* The local legal newspaper for your community is a must. Advance sheets are also excellent. Bar journals of the American, state, and local bars and specialty associations also contain excellent critiques on what is new in the law. If you wish to keep current in specific specialty areas such as taxation, there are innumerable journals available such as the *Journal of Taxation.* Both Prentice-Hall and Commerce Clearing House have excellent weekly reports. Other areas of the law have similar journals. Many Web sites will have e-mail subscriptions to provide you with current major changes in given areas of law.

2. *How-to-Do-It Articles.* Here again, bar journals and legal newspapers are excellent investments.

3. *Special Prices.* Most legal newspapers and bar associations have free or reduced prices for new admittees or for a trial period.

4. *Section Publications of the American Bar Association and Others.* Bar association sections have excellent publications; however, they often are of limited value to a new practitioner with a "local" rather than national type of practice. It is difficult to generalize on these publications; the new lawyer should carefully consider, however, which sections are likely to be of any use early in a career.

5. *Infomercials*. Many presentations and publications are simply information on promoting commercial enterprises. It is difficult to generalize; however, the new lawyer should carefully consider whether or not to spend money on what appears to be informational but is, in fact, a commercial.

Information Overload

It is easy to become overwhelmed with e-mail and paper mail. Don't be afraid to unsubscribe from e-mail and subscription lists.

How to Buy Law Books (If You Buy Them at All)

Book salespeople are sometimes less than candid in telling you how much law books cost. Keep in mind that most law books have four elements of cost:

1. Initial cost;
2. Annual or more frequent upkeep for pocket parts or supplements;
3. New volumes;
4. Hidden costs.

1. *Initial Cost*. When you ask a book sales representative how much a set of books cost, you may hear double-talk about "monthly payments" being small. Be insistent on knowing what the set costs.

2. *Annual Upkeep*. Insist on knowing what the annual cost of pocket parts or supplements is, based upon the most recent year's cost. Don't be put off by the sales rep answering your question by referring to the fact that this is "free" for one or two years. Remember, it won't be free after the first year or two.

3. *New Volumes*. Book publishers periodically replace old volumes with new volumes. They often do this when the pocket parts become too thick. Sometimes you'll still be paying off the old volumes when the new volumes get added to the bill. Perhaps you remember one or more instances in college of not being able to sell a used book at the end of the course due to a "new edition" (often with nondetectable changes except for the edition year); this is similar to new volume problems. Here again, the sales rep wants to talk about "low monthly payments." Try to negotiate a written guarantee that if a volume is replaced within a certain number of years, then you won't have to pay for the replacement volume.

4. *Hidden Costs.* Law books have hidden costs including property taxes, rent for the space needed to house the books, insurance, obsolescence, depreciation, and labor for supplement upkeep.

How to Save Money Buying Used Law Books (If You Buy Them at All)

1. *Law Schools and Law Libraries.* Let the librarian know you are interested in buying law books. These institutions are frequently the beneficiaries of intervivos and testamentary gifts from lawyers or their widows. Often the set is a duplicate or triplicate of a set the law library already has. The library may be willing to sell you a set to use the cash for other purposes.

2. *Widows or Widowers.* The estate of a deceased lawyer will usually want to sell the library.

3. *Mergers and Dissolutions.* When you receive notice or read about two firms merging, you can call to see if there is an extra library for sale.

How Much to Pay for Used Books

You should be able to buy used books for almost nothing. Nobody wants them. You may get them for just paying for having them taken away. Obviously you may be willing to pay more or less depending upon the condition of the books and the urgency to sell or buy. Before buying be sure to check the age of the pocket parts, especially if the books have been around awhile. If you're not careful, the cost of your "bargain" and the cost of bringing the books up-to-date may be more than the cost of buying a new set.

Financing the Purchase

Although the book companies claim to sell you the books "interest-free," you might do better borrowing money from the bank to buy the used books. Ask how much the cash price is to determine whether to use bank or publisher financing.

The Cost of a Library (Hard Copy)

A very modest one- or two-lawyer paper library for an established firm costs more than $10,000 per year and therefore should not be purchased by the new lawyer.

How to Avoid Library Costs

1. Try to avoid library costs totally by affiliating with lawyers where there is already an existing library.

2. Use courthouse law libraries. Judges have libraries and usually share with local lawyers.

3. Use electronic law libraries.

4. Use the Internet. (See materials on "The Internet as a Library Resource.")

Go with what you know. Learning one or more new methods of doing research is costly in terms of learning time. Is some cases (especially senior lawyers starting a practice) it may be more economical to continue using old ways, although one cannot expect clients to pay inflated costs caused by extra time and inefficiency.

Negotiating with Vendors and Sharing Electronic Research Expense

New lawyers and lawyers newly opening an office have an advantage in negotiating with vendors. The vendors want you for life. They'll do almost anything to get you to become accustomed to and dependent on their products. This began in college and law school with "free" and reduced cost services.

A vendor will "mix and match" the library services in a combination package (sometimes called a suite) to provide exactly what you want at a "suite" price.

A vendor may allow several new lawyers (typically two to five) to share and divide the cost of a service if one agrees to be financially responsible in the event of default by the other.

Don't be afraid to ask for what you want and don't be afraid to negotiate price. They want you.

How to Buy Law Books
(If You Buy Them at All)

Before spending your hard-to-come-by dollars on a law book that you think you do need or will need, ask the following questions at a minimum:

1. *When was the book originally published and when was it last revised?* Is the book a 2004 reprint of a 1982 book with no updating? Be careful about books with copyrights from several years ago. It is difficult, if not impossible, to ascertain if the book is really current or is just the 1982 original with a few chapters modified to allow the publisher to claim it is a 2004 edition.

2. Understand that "Tenth Printing" of a book does not mean Tenth Edition. The publisher may have little or no confidence in the long-term viability of the book and is simply printing the book 100 at a time.

3. *Does the publisher plan a substantial revision or replacement within a year or so, and if so, will you get some credit or refund for your nearly obsolete book?*

4. *Does the title really reflect the contents?* Often titles are chosen with a view in mind to selling the book rather than accurately describing the contents.

5. *Are supplements intended, and if so, what will they cost?* Be careful when a publisher won't commit to a maximum price on supplements in progress.

6. *What is the total price?*
   a. For cash.
   b. For installments. Don't waste your time with a company that won't give you an honest answer to an honest question. When the advertisements or the sales reps insist on talking about monthly

503

payments instead of total price, you can assume they have something to hide.

7. *Are you sure you ordered or received the book?* You'll be surprised at how many bills you will receive for books you never ordered or never received. I suppose there is a thin line between "bookkeeping mistakes" and attempting to obtain money under false pretenses in some instances. Be very careful about paying for books.

8. *Do you understand the bill?* As you expand your library and online services and incur a lot of monthly payments (it's unbelievable how fast they add up), your monthly bill will become very complex. The opportunities for "bookkeeping mistakes" are immense with large companies and their complex internal computer systems. If you don't understand the bill, don't pay it until you get a satisfactory explanation. Be sure that the bill conforms to your "deal" with the sales rep.

Saving Money by Eliminating Postage and Express Delivery Services

Postage and express delivery service expenses can be reduced to almost zero with appropriate use of e-mail and fax.

You may think that postage and delivery expense is beyond your control. This is not so. There are several things you can do to reduce expense. Postage and express delivery service costs can be reduced or eliminated with fax and e-mail. In many cases your clients won't pay for postage or express delivery service. Some clients insist on e-mail to help keep expenses low.

Eliminate Postage Stamps

Postage stamps are commonly lost or stolen by employees, cleaning crews, etc.

1. *Outgoing mail.* Get the cheapest postage meter available. The meter will save you money. Postage meters can be rented on a monthly basis. Postage can be bought online.

2. *Incoming mail.* Get a reply permit from the post office. (See following details.)

Get a Small Postage Scale

If you put too much postage on a letter, you'll waste the excess. On the other hand, if you don't put enough on, you may waste whatever you've used, if the recipient refuses to pay postage due and the letter is returned. Governmental agencies such as courts and sheriffs' departments ordinarily won't pay postage due. The delay in getting the mail back to you and out again may be detrimental and even fatal to your client's case and your malpractice liability.

You'll have many occasions to send out packages of documents. It is easy to waste money on excess and insufficient postage. Break the package into segments that can be weighed individually with the totals added together for the total cost of the package.

1. Go in person to the post office to fill out a form for a "Permit No."

2. Have envelopes printed (post office will give you samples).

3. For two or three months the letter carrier will collect postage due when mail is delivered.

4. Your cost is regular postage plus an add-on per item delivered to you (you pay regular postage and postage-due postage).

5. Remember that the postage for the first ounce of a letter costs more than additional ounces.

6. Be sure that all foreign mail contains adequate postage and is clearly marked "air mail" or "via avion." A letter that is not marked "air mail" may go by surface mail regardless of the amount of postage affixed.

7. After two or three months you can open a "Postage Due Account" with the post office and the postage due will be charged to your account without daily collection by a letter carrier. The principal advantage to this system is that you only pay for postage actually used. You don't spend money on stamps that clients never use and you don't risk employee theft or loss of postage. Although this seems expensive, it actually will save you money. Also, your clients can immediately return their documents or payment checks to you.

Use Fax Instead of Postage

As of the time of writing the fourth edition in 1999, it was estimated that 65 to 70 percent of all lawyer-to-lawyer and lawyer-to-client correspondence was by fax, with regular mail backup increasingly being ignored. A fax costed the same as a telephone call and less than a postage stamp. Additionally, expensive firm stationery and envelopes are not needed to fax a letter.

Currently, e-mail has almost completely replaced fax, especially among educated clients.

Use E-Mail

Use e-mail whenever possible. E-mail sent over the Internet is basically free after you pay the Internet service provider. E-mail is especially valuable for sending long documents. Even if you are sending e-mail on a direct phone-to-phone connection instead of via the Internet, you have a lesser cost and faster delivery than snail mail or express package service. Caution: E-mail can and does get lost in cyberspace without ever arriving. If possible, ask the recipient to call you or e-mail you to confirm receipt.

Just about every bar association and alumni group to which you belong will provide you with a free e-mail forwarding address so that you can receive e-mail from clients and others no matter how many times you change your physical office location during your first few years of practice.

Ask the Client

Always ask the client if they have a preferred way of sending or receiving information and do it their way unless there is a good reason not to.

Squeezing Extra Hours into the Day to Make More Money

If you can squeeze an extra fifteen minutes a day into your billable day, this would translate into one and one-fourth hours per week or about sixty hours per year, allowing for vacations, etc. At $100 per hour, this multiplies out to $6,000 per year at fifteen minutes per day, or $12,000 per year at thirty minutes a day.

Here are some "tips" for squeezing extra time into the day:

1. *Keep a portable tape recorder or digital recorder in your car, in your home, and in your briefcase.* Whenever you get a "brilliant" idea concerning a case or a client, dictate it immediately and enter it into your time records when you get back to the office.

2. *Keep small notepads near your home telephone.* When a client calls you at home, make a note of the call on the pad, and enter the call on your time records when you get to the office. People sometimes call you at home, hoping to get free legal advice. When they see "telephone conference at home on Sunday re: mechanic's liens' on the bill" they will respect you for accuracy of your records. These notes may also protect you in a malpractice claim.

3. *Live as close as possible to your office.* In my entire professional career, I have never lived farther than fifteen minutes from my office. The difference between a fifteen-minute commute and a forty-five-minute commute is obviously five hours of chargeable time a week. In my early years, I frequently went home for dinner to see my children, and then returned to the office for an hour or two to work or for a meeting with clients.

4. *Don't waste your commuting time.* If you commute by public transportation, use the time for reading advance sheets and jour-

nals or listening to continuing education tapes. (I recommend my tape series on "How to Get & Keep Good Clients" and "How to Practice Profitability and Stay Out of Trouble.")

5. *Leave messages for yourself.* When you get a bright idea while out of the office, call and leave a voice-mail message for yourself. Transcribe your voice mail and record the time and content of the voice mail when you get back to the office.

Should You Hire a Secretary?

A "secretary" can refer to a person of either gender who does many of the tasks that a "secretary" used to do, but who also acts as an assistant to a lawyer, doing many varied tasks ranging from being a paralegal to being a photocopier or messenger or an Information Technology (IT) specialist.

Get help. Don't waste your high-value time doing low-value tasks. Survey after survey proves conclusively that lawyers make more money and give better service when they have help. You are wrong if you think you are increasing your net profit by doing everything yourself.

By getting help, even low-skill level help, you will increase your productivity and profit by allowing someone else to do some or all of the following tasks:

Open mail.

Stuff outgoing envelopes.

File copies of documents.

Run errands.

Do court and administrative filings.

Photocopying.

Go to post office to receive or deliver mail.

Do personal chores. (Cleaning, shopping, etc.)

Answer phones.

Word processing.

Return telephone calls when you can't.

Download and print out e-mail.

Back you up in maintaining your tickler system to remind you of undone tasks.

Proofread your work for obvious errors, misspellings, and omissions.

The list is endless.

Use this time saved to practice law, market to clients, and go to bar association meetings to network with lawyers who can refer clients. Go to CLE programs. Spend time with your family.

One of the consequences of "doing everything yourself" is to undervalue your time and charges. You feel (correctly) that it is not appropriate to charge a lawyer's rate for nonlegal work, and then you start charging lower rates for your legal work. Getting help reduces this problem.

Having a secretary on either a full-time or a part-time basis immediately available for your work is a luxury that you may not need initially. If you are in a suite with other lawyers, you may be able to borrow or buy a small amount of secretarial time from one of the lawyers who does not use a secretary's time fully.

I strongly recommend, however, that the new lawyer in practice contact the various secretarial services in the immediate neighborhood. You will find that these secretarial services will offer to the lawyer one or more of the following features:

1. Dictating equipment or access to an 800 or other toll-free number for telephone voice dictation;

2. Daily pick-up and delivery by messenger, fax, or e-mail of finished work;

3. A reasonable, minimum cost;

4. A cost per word, or per line, over and above the minimum, based on actual usage;

5. General familiarity with legal terminology.

Basically, the concept of a legal secretarial service is that you give the secretarial service a supply of your stationery. You then dictate all of your work into a tape recorder or digital recorder or via telephone. (You could handwrite, if you wish, but this is not a good habit to get into.) The secretarial service will pick up your tapes at the end of the day. The next morning your dictated material has been typed and is ready for you on disk or paper to be delivered by messenger or by e-mail.

For the first several months of your practice, when you have very little need for secretarial service, this is probably the most efficient and economical way for you to generate and handle secretarial work. Depending upon the particular secretarial service, you may be able to walk over there for a rush-rush emergency, and have the service do it while you wait.

A variation on this theme is to call the toll-free number and dictate the information. It will then be transcribed and e-mailed to you allowing you to modify it on your computer and put out the final version with which you are satisfied.

An additional side benefit of the use of a secretarial service is the self-disciplining and good dictating habits that can be formed early in your career.

Due to the fact that you do not know who will be typing your particular work at the time, you must develop the habit of giving full and complete instructions when you dictate. In other words, you will not simply be able to say, "Send a letter to Mr. Jones." You will have to give specific instructions regarding name, address, how many carbon copies or photocopies have to be made, etc. This giving of complete instructions for the secretarial service will be of invaluable assistance to you later in your professional career, when you dictate letters and documents for your own secretary, or for a secretarial pool.

Dictating and Digital Recording Equipment

Don't make any investment in dictating or digital recording equipment until you have to. Use the equipment supplied free by your outside secretarial service. Don't buy used equipment unless it's been under warranty or maintenance contract. After you buy equipment, be sure to keep it under maintenance contract if it is expensive. Use only equipment that has a thumb-operated stop, dictate, and reverse on the microphone handle. When you open your doors, get cheap portables for your car and briefcase. Get them cheap enough so that you can throw them away after a year or two and not feel badly. Footage meters are not necessary. Don't dictate for more than five minutes' duration if you can help it. Word processing people get psychologically depressed by a twenty- or thirty-minute tape or recording, but don't seem to mind five- or more five-minute tapes or recordings.

Electronic voice recorders may be adequate to record something you don't want to forget, but aren't a substitute for dictating equipment.

Typing Your Letters and Documents

A new lawyer can be faced with a bewildering number of ways to type letters and documents. What works best for you will depend both on your prior background and your willingness to try and learn different methods. In a given situation you may combine multiple methods. Your prior background may be law school, or a law firm or corporate or government work and you will want to keep on doing what you already know how to do, but try to be flexible.

Some of your options include the following:

1. Self-production of documents doing your own typing on a computer.

2. Dictating into a recorder with someone else transcribing first or second drafts onto a disk for you and/or a secretary to clean up.

3. Dictating into a telephone connection at a secretarial service with the service sending you a rough draft via modem for cleanup by you or a secretary.

4. Dictating into a voice recognition system.

5. Writing in longhand for typing by another person.

Most people can only write longhand at about ten words per minute, type about fifty words per minute, and speak clearly at about one hundred twenty words to one hundred sixty per minute. Accordingly, it should be obvious to you that speaking is preferable to typing, which is preferable to writing longhand.

If you can train yourself to prepare first drafts by speaking into either a voice recognition system or a tape recorder, you can produce your first drafts at least twice as fast as doing your own typing. Writing longhand is generally the worst way to do first drafts.

Beyond the Typing and Printing of Documents

New lawyers often think they are saving money by doing everything themselves. The new lawyer should get some assistance from another person to do the following:

1. Proofread the document for obvious spelling and structural errors and possible omissions.

2. Make the appropriate number of copies for clients, courts, files, other lawyers, etc.

3. Be sure the correct enclosures go with each copy.

4. Be sure that the letter goes out via mail, fax, e-mail, express service, or other form of transmission with correct payment of charges.

5. Get the appropriate copies to the appropriate office files (client file, chron file, suspense file) or whatever number of copies needed.

Sending Letters to Clients

No matter how much e-mail you send to clients and no matter how many faxes you send to clients, clients and others still love to receive letters via either U.S. mail or a messenger service.

A few tips may help you with your written communications.

1. You must read everything that goes out of your office to a client for accuracy and for spelling. Clients do not appreciate obvious errors. They may equate your errors in your letters with errors in practicing law.

2. Do not depend on your spell checker. The word "spell checker" may not even be in your spell checker.

3. List all enclosures at the end of the letter even though the enclosures are referred to in the letter. The list can serve as a double check to be sure nothing was left out that was supposed to be included.

4. Be careful about using headers and footers on correspondence. You may inadvertently be revealing client identity or other sensitive confidential matter in the header or footer of a letter. I have seen motions for disqualification where an individual was erroneously listed in a footer.

5. Be careful when sending copies of documents and faxes to third parties, especially other lawyers. Lazy lawyers often program fax machines to send copies of client faxes or e-mail to third parties, often erroneously including opposing counsel. I have received many faxes and e-mail I should never have received.

6. Use high-quality engraved stationery. As I have often preached, using cheap stationery is like wrapping a diamond bracelet in an old newspaper. Your stationery is part of your image to people you have never met. To me, schlock stationery equates to a schlock lawyer, which equates to a schlock case and schlock client.

7. As always, never fail to send clients copies of all incoming documents and all outgoing documents. Keeping your client informed is a good way of keeping clients happy and preventing unnecessary ethics and malpractice complaints.

8. Clients get angry when they see their name misspelled and they begin to doubt your competency to do a job correctly (wouldn't you?). Put the client's name into the spell checker and assume personal responsibility for reviewing the letters and envelopes for proper spelling of the client's name.

Voice Recognition Systems.

Fifteen years ago I predicted that voice recognition would someday be a major way of preparing documents. I am still waiting. As of 2004, it is my opinion, based on surveys I have done, that about 70 percent of practicing lawyers have tried voice recognition systems and about 2 percent are actually using it. I tried it and quit. In my opinion the amount of time needed to be proficient in using voice recognition is not justified. Perhaps in the future the software and hardware will improve to make voice recognition feasible.

Timely Delivery of Work

I am including this chapter on timely delivery of work because it is a major factor in the creation of client satisfaction.

When you tell a client how long it will take for you to accomplish a matter, you are creating an expectation in that client. When you don't fulfill that expectation, you will then have an angry or unhappy client.

Procrastination and failure to deliver work in a timely fashion is a strong negative among clients. If you have a reputation for being consistently late in delivering work, clients will not use you again and they will not recommend you to others. Late delivery and last-minute delivery creates quality-control problems and the embarrassment of cleaning up mistakes, as well as uneconomical utilization of staff.

Procrastination generally is a time management problem curable by using a to-do list. Only on a few rare occasions is late delivery of work due to unforeseen intervening emergencies. In many cases procrastination is caused when you don't know how to do the job and avoid it by ignoring it. If this is the case, get help from another lawyer on an informal basis.

A good tickler system with at least five advance reminders is the best way to get a job done in a timely way. I am continually amazed by the large number of lawyers who do a reasonably good job of calendaring and having a tickler system for litigation, but do nothing about nonlitigation matters.

Your tickler system should come up five times, both on your calendar and on the calendar of your secretary or assistant or any other person who can nag you about your undone work.

If a job is tough to do, carve out an appointment with yourself of an hour or an hour and a half where you take no phone calls and talk to no one. If necessary, stay home and do the work at home or go to a law library with a laptop, or lock yourself in an empty office in your office.

If absolutely necessary, refer the matter and the client to another lawyer. If the work is not being done because it is beyond your ability, tell the client and help the client find another lawyer to do the work.

In most cases you can prevent late delivery and procrastination by using a good tickler system. When you call a client and tell the client you were able to finish his or her work a bit early, the client will love you.

If for no other reason, you should want to finish the job so you can get paid for the work.

Timely delivery of work is important, because the client may think you are delaying the matter in order to run up the bill.

An American Bar Association study showed that timely delivery of work was present in 83 percent of satisfied clients and that failure to timely do the work was a factor in 59 percent of dissatisfied clients.

Should You Use a Telephone Receptionist, Telephone Exchange, Mechanical Answering Device, Telephone Company Service, or Voice Mail?

Obviously, having your own secretary and/or telephone receptionist is nice. However, it may be a luxury that you can easily do without for the first several months. It is not likely that your phone is going to ring off the hook the first day, or even the first week, or possibly even the first month. After a couple of months, however, you can reasonably anticipate that you will have some telephone volume.

If you have an office in a suite with other lawyers, the receptionist is normally included in the cost of the suite.

As between using a telephone exchange with live operators, or a mechanical answering device, I strongly recommend the exchange. Try to find an exchange that services doctors and lawyers. These exchanges are experienced in handling emergency situations. They often are very well trained in calming the nervous or hysterical client until you can be contacted. From time to time, you should call your own number, pretending to be a client or potential client, to see what kind of service the exchange is giving your clients.

There is a saying that goes, "I needed you, I tried to get hold of you, I couldn't get hold of you, I don't need you anymore." This is self-explanatory as to the necessity of having a good telephone exchange to handle your calls when you are at lunch, or during nights and weekends.

Currently, there is a trend for executives and professionals to answer their own telephones. I personally do not feel that this should be done in a law office. If you are with a client, you should not have to interrupt your interview or conference to answer a telephone. When I call a lawyer, and the lawyer answers the phone, I do not assume that the lawyer is following a modern trend. I assume the lawyer cannot afford someone to answer the phone. Therefore, I recommend against this practice. The problem with this type of telephone answering becomes obvious: You would have to tell one client to hold on so you can answer the other ringing telephone. Therefore, do not answer your own phones if you can possibly avoid it. Even if you have to bring in your spouse or a friend to answer the phones for you, in my opinion, this is preferable to your answering your own telephones.

Be sure that every person in the office who answers phone knows how to do it. Print the instructions and tape them to the place(s) at which phones are answered.

If you tape the instructions at the places the phone is answered, everyone, including temporaries, will be able to properly answer the telephone.

How to Answer the Phone

Volumes have been written on how to answer the phones. I recommend that the phone be answered as follows: "Good morning, Carolyn Jones' office. This is Mary Moore speaking. Can I help you?" We use this method and get many compliments from clients. The State Bar of Wisconsin CLE has an excellent videotape on answering telephones, faxes, e-mail, etc.

Voice Mail

In general, you should not use voice mail during regular office hours unless you are truly on another call or out of the office. If you do use voice mail, immediately offer the caller the option of speaking to a live person. Have someone clean up your voice mail at the end of the day to be sure all calls have been returned. I know of one case where the lawyer had been dead for three weeks and his direct-dial number was being answered "Hello, I'm away from my desk right now. Please leave a message." Clients and lawyers were calling and leaving messages not knowing the lawyer was dead.

When clients consistently get voice mail they become upset and sometimes angry. They will take their next legal matter to a lawyer who is available to take a call.

Why You Should Use Investigators

As soon as possible after opening your office, ask several lawyers for recommendations for investigators. Meet with a few of them and choose one who really seems to want your business.

Investigators cost money, but they cost relatively little compared with what they will earn for you and your client or save you and your client.

When you tell your client that his or her case requires investigators and that investigators cost money, the client will be more than willing to pay you money "up front." The client will also be impressed by your professionalism. There will be a confidence that the case is being handled properly.

Investigators have the proper photographic equipment and recording equipment. They seem to have "friends" in places where you can only get a closed door. They know how to interview witnesses and to follow up leads. I've often gotten good settlements on cases by showing the insurance adjuster my investigator's reports and asking to see theirs.

As a new lawyer you'll need the investigator's help in evaluating the case. They've seen hundreds of cases and are more skilled than you in most of the areas in which they work.

Within limits, investigators will work with you on payment, sometimes deferring part or all of their fee until the case settles. Never let investigators or any other witnesses testify who are owed money by you or your client. Their testimony may be weakened due to a suspicion that their compensation is predicated on the results of the case.

Part VII
Ethics and Professional Responsibility

Professional Responsibility and Practice Management

Words such as "professionalism," "ethical," and "responsibility" are vague and must be defined in light of how and where they are used.

Professional responsibility does not mean just memorizing a list of dos and don'ts based upon ethical concepts that have lasted 500 years as modified by a recent court decision. Professional responsibility involves understanding the role and responsibility of the legal profession in our society and then further understanding the lawyer's individual role and responsibilities within the profession.

We in America have a legal system that gives Americans more political, religious, economic, and social freedoms than any system has provided to its citizens in the history of the world. Our system of freedom and liberty for the rich and the poor, the weak and the strong, the individual and the multinational corporation is based upon the legal rights and responsibilities found in our Constitution.

Our Constitution was created by a committee of fifty-five men, thirty-three of whom were lawyers. Our constitutional system is put into action daily in the courts by lawyers representing plaintiffs and defendants, the government, and the accused. The system is applied by lawyers sitting as judges and by other lawyers sitting as appellate judges. About two-thirds of the presidents of the United States were trained as lawyers. About one-half of all local and national legislators have been lawyers. We lawyers can take the credit for creating and maintaining the greatest system of constitutional freedoms in the history of the world. We can make a difference and we *do* make a difference in the quality of our clients' lives.

Our Constitution is a living document that changes in application and interpretation to meet the changing needs of a dynamic America. Some changes are made by amendment and some by interpretation, and from time to time we discard obsolete sections. Similarly, our professional responsibility is a changing responsibility that adapts our role to meet the needs of our society. The predecessor Canons of Ethics, adopted by the American Bar Association in 1908, was increased from thirty-two at origin with fifteen amendments. The Model Code of Professional Responsibility was adopted in 1969. The present Model Rules of Professional Conduct were adopted in 1983. There have been many piecemeal amendments to various parts of the Rules, especially during 2000, but the basic Model Rules have been the same since 1983.

We lawyers are accorded an elevated position within our society in recognition of the important function we perform in helping people manage the relationship between themselves and government. We are highly compensated as a profession. We receive great respect from the public, which adds titles such as "attorney" or "esquire" before or after our names. The public gives us the right to self-discipline and self-regulate our profession. In a manner, it is similar to the respect given to physicians and ministers. We have access to the powers of the court and to the decision makers in our society.

As part of the quid pro quo for occupying this respected position in our society, we have a professional responsibility to our society that arises because we are lawyers. If we were not lawyers, we would not have that responsibility. I have known lawyers who left the legal profession so they could conduct their profit-seeking ventures without the constraints of professional responsibility.

The American Bar Association's Model Rules of Professional Conduct and the rules of the various state bars are more than a list of ethical dos and don'ts. They are a strategic plan that addresses our relationship with our clients, the courts, the government, and other lawyers.

It is important to understand that ABA's ethical rules are not binding on anyone. Individual states and jurisdictions may adopt them by reference or modify them or refuse to enact them or parts of them. The ABA is a very complex organization with many diverse constituent lawyers and organizations having representation in the House of Delegates. Each of these organizations concerns itself with how proposed ethics rules changes will affect the practice of their fellow members. Accordingly, ethic rules changes and interpretations may change from time to time, reflecting the interests of the members. Proposed changes may benefit or harm the interests of member lawyers who practice certain types of law or in a large or small firm setting or in a given geographic area or political climate. Accordingly, pressures for proposed changes or interpretations that benefit one type of lawyer or firm may be opposed or rejected outright by others. Included within this relationship is competence, which itself includes the perception by our clients and the public of our professional competence, individually and collectively.

If we as lawyers are perceived not to be competent or if we are perceived not to be helping people or only interested in earning money, then we shall lose both our ability to maintain our American system of constitutional rights and responsibilities and our ability to be accorded a high level of respect by our society. We will also lose our right to self-regulate our profession.

Good office procedures and good client relations help us to deliver legal services competently, and help us in maintaining client and public confidence that we are in fact delivering competent legal services. It does little good for a lawyer to deliver technically competent legal services in a manner that alienates the client to the point where the client perceives the services to be incompetent, even though they are in fact competent.

A court system that causes parties two to three years of waiting for an available courtroom or judge, or that requires parties to pay for lawyers to come to the courthouse three or four times to be told there are no courtrooms available, will affect the clients' perception of the competence of the legal system. The clients will not blame the state or county for not voting for money for courtrooms and judges. The client will blame the lawyers and will lose confidence in the legal system.

Competent and efficient delivery of legal services not only benefits the clients who receive it, but also our society as a whole; because as we lawyers become more competent in delivering legal services, more members of the public will have access to our services and to the system.

The Profession of Law
Is Not the Business of Law

As a lawyer starting a law practice or starting a career as a lawyer, it is important to understand that the profession of law is not a business and to understand the reasons law is not a business.

In my opinion, those who call the profession of law a "business" insult and demean the legal profession and you as a lawyer, in addition to simultaneously displaying their own lack of knowledge of the differences between a profession and a business.

A business, by definition, has only one goal: the making of profits. As you may have learned in your course on Corporations, in many if not most or all jurisdictions, a corporation is prohibited from giving money or anything of value to a charity unless there is both an enabling law and a special provision in the corporation's charter or bylaws allowing the giving of funds or services to charity. A corporation's directors will be held accountable to prove that what they call "social responsibility" is in fact a tool to make more profits. The expression "Business is business" means that there is no room for public service or social responsibility or sentiment if it interferes with making profits.

In the profession of law, lawyers give substantial amounts of pro bono time in the pursuit of public service. A business, in contrast, has absolutely no social or pro bono responsibility unless it chooses to have one, and in many cases will have social responsibility only as a form of advertising to earn more profits. The public understands that the legal profession does pro bono work without expectation of monetary reward and respects the profession. The public would not ' look to a "business" of law for pro bono assistance nor respect a legal "business."

Helping the poor is an obligation to the lawyer. The poor can be ignored by a business if there is no money to be made from them.

Lawyers have "clients." A client, by definition, is dependent on the superior knowledge of the professional to give advice and act only in the client's best interest. The relationship is fiduciary and beneficiary. Businesses have "customers." The relationship is Caveat Emptor. The business in selling goods and services to the customer has no fiduciary obligation to the customer and is free to act in the best interests of the business's profits rather than the best interests of the customer.

A business can charge all it can get away with. A lawyer's fees must be reasonable; they cannot be unconscionable. A business can sell the names of its customers. A lawyer cannot divulge confidences or client names.

The legal profession is governed by ethical rules going back two thousand years in history requiring the lawyer to act in the best interests of the client. Failure to act in the best interests of the client can result in loss of license to practice. A business is free to do anything it wants to do, whether or not in the best interests of the client, subject only to the outer limits of lawsuits without any loss of license to continue its activities.

The legal profession has a responsibility to uphold and defend the constitution and to serve the public. A business has a responsibility only to make money.

Success in a profession is measured in excellence of performance in the broadest sense, service to the community and advancement within the profession. A large income may accompany you when you are successful as a lawyer, but income alone is not the measure of success

A professional has preliminary training and education, intellectual in nature, involving knowledge and learning in addition to skill. A business person has no intellectual or educational requirements. Only those skills necessary to making profits are required of a business person.

The profession of law seeks to resolve and end disputes rather than encourage and prolong disputes in the best interests of the client, even though ending the disputes may not be in the best financial interests of the lawyer. A business would be expected to prolong and exacerbate disputes to get more money from the customer.

Do not listen to the siren song of those who attempt to morph the profession of law into a business. They may be nonlawyers trying to sell some product or service to the new gullible lawyer, promising profits to the lawyer if only the lawyer will buy their goods and services. A few are lawyers not licensed to practice in any U.S. jurisdiction, who may or may not understand the history of our ethics and the reasons for the rules. A few may be apostate lawyers who may or may not find it easier to make money if not encumbered by legal ethics.

It is accurate to state that businesses have some things in common with professions. Businesses and professions both require efficient management of resources. Use and management of staff, technology, and capital are requisite to survival and success in both businesses and professions. A horse has some things in common with a mule and they may be similar in appearance. Having some things in common does not make a horse a mule or a mule a horse any more than having some things in common makes a profession into a business or vice versa.

You have been educated and trained and have been examined on matters of Constitutional Law. You understand and appreciate the importance of the 1st, 5th, 6th, and 14th Amendments, in addition to the basic Constitution. You understand our judicial system of courts and the role of courts and lawyers in preserving the confidence of the American public. You understand the words "Rule of Law" and all its benefits to America and the world, and the price we lawyers have to pay to preserve and improve it. You know the ethical prohibitions of the profession and their history, and you know the rules of court. It is unlikely that most of those who proclaim law to be a business like any other business are knowledgeable in these areas. If you allow others to violate the rules in a search for profits, they might lose a fee or a sale, but you stand to lose a license. You take regulated Continuing Legal Education courses to stay current, either voluntarily or because you have no choice. These courses are normally regulated as to content and quality.

People who have not been adequately trained in the American legal system cannot possibly understand all that is required. There is no reason they should. Unlicensed people have no Continuing Legal Education requirements, whether they are from a foreign jurisdiction or never did or no longer do have licenses to practice law anywhere in America.

Many occupations in their businesses have some form of continuing education requirements by various names and of varying quality, but not in those areas needed by lawyers.

I want you to earn a good living. I have always earned a good living and have educated my children and provided for my retirement. I have taken many good vacations, often to bar association conventions, accompanied by my family. I enjoy my life and career and have always made the time to "give back" to our profession. I want the same for you. That is one of the reasons I have written this book and may be one of the reasons you have purchased this book. Don't be misled by the false prophets of profit. Law is a profession not a business.

There are only three professions: Law, Medicine, and the Clergy. All three have in common the benefit of secrecy and confidentiality with the client, the patient, or the penitent, with immunity from process for communications. All three require putting the interests of the client, the patient, or the penitent ahead of our own. All three require helping people we personally would prefer not to help. Unlike a business, there is very little room for "We reserve the right to refuse service."

Other occupations and enterprises may call themselves "professional" (professional gardeners, professional barbers, professional musicians, professional accountants, etc.). Simply calling oneself or one's business or occupation "professional" does not make the activity into a profession.

I repeat: There are only three professions—Law, Medicine, and the Clergy, and for each there is a feeling of being called to help people and to make a difference in the lives of people.

If you treat the profession of law as a profession, you will be a happy person and you will earn a good living over a long period of time. You will make a difference in the lives of people and in our society. At the end of the day you will feel good about what you are doing.

If you believe that law is just a business with the goal of making money, ultimately you will be unhappy, no matter how much money you make. You would be happier and make more money by giving up your law license and doing something else without public service obligations and without ethical restrictions. If you don't feel a calling to help people and to make a difference, and are only interested in making money, you are in the wrong place.

If you do feel this calling, you are in exactly the right place.

Take issue with those uninformed people who would slander our profession and demean you by calling it a business.

I am confident that I have made my feeling and opinion quite clear. I am not a Pollyannish person or looking at the world with rose-colored or antiquated glasses. I am giving you the benefit of five decades of my experiences and knowledge, as well as the experiences of many other successful people.

Handling Anti-Lawyer Jokes and Comments

You have to learn how to deal with anti-lawyer jokes and comments. More and more lawyers, consultants, and sellers of products to lawyers talk about the "business" of law instead of the profession of law. The number of anti-lawyer jokes increase. Many people accordingly treat the law and lawyers as just another group of people looking to make money off others' misfortunes.

This is especially a problem when there is a group of people present and the "joke teller" is looking for an audience.

When an anti-lawyer joke or comment is made, you have choices:

1. Say nothing as though you admit the accuracy of the insult.
2. Say something to defend the profession (and yourself).

I don't agree that lawyers should "lighten up" and allow anti-lawyer jokes. Most of those who would want us to "lighten up" are not lawyers.

If you say nothing, others may think you lack the intellectual capacity to say something or that you agree with the statements made.

I believe that anti-lawyer jokes undermine the public's confidence in the legal profession and the legal system. Whatever negligible benefit they may have is far exceeded by the damage they can do to the American legal system if left unopposed.

If you agree with me (in whole or in part) and want to defend either your own personal reputation or the profession or both, you can easily respond as follows.

I personally have used the following retorts:

1. "OK, what's your question? Most people who tell anti-lawyer jokes are also looking for some free legal advice, so what's your question?"

2. "The next time you tell an anti-lawyer joke, you should thank the lawyers of America who in the past and today protect your right under the First Amendment to say what you want to say. Without lawyers defending your First Amendment rights, you might not have been able to tell that joke."

When some literary moron states, "Shakespeare said, 'First thing, let's kill all the lawyers,' " you might retort as I do:

"It's obvious you've never seen nor read the play where that line appears or you wouldn't have said what you just said. Shakespeare was, in fact, praising lawyers. Shakespeare didn't say that. A character in a play written by Shakespeare said that. The character was a revolutionary who wanted to install himself as King of England so he could dictate how people lived. He wanted to entice people to revolt. He knew that lawyers protected and defended citizens' rights and that he could never take power so long as lawyers defended people, so he wanted to kill them as a first step. In fact, his first step was to murder the town clerk whose only crime was that he could read and write. So when you use that phrase, you should know that you are quoting a murderer who advocated illiteracy as the first step to becoming a dictator. You really shouldn't quote what you never read."

I believe you should defend yourself personally and the profession by reacting to anti-lawyer jokes and comments.

Fifty-Two Ways to Win
or Avoid the Ethics War

   This chapter is based on my experience of four decades of practicing law and advising both new and experienced lawyers on ethical problems and matters of professional responsibility that arise in the day-to-day practice of law.

   The purpose of this chapter is to help a lawyer recognize common ethical or professional problems in the real world of practicing law. In some cases, I've made editorial comments based on my experiences, while in others I've suggested solutions. I've emphasized the applications to civil cases, although most of the rules relating to how you practice law apply to both civil and criminal practice.

   We lawyers are granted certain rights and privileges and access to the power of the legal system. In exchange for these rights and powers, there are rules as to how we can practice. These rules may be voluntarily self-imposed or may be imposed by others. These rules have various names and may be called rules of conduct or rules of ethics, or may bear other designations.

   There are various bodies promulgating rules that will affect how you must practice law. It is important that you learn what rules exist and whether you are governed by them, either directly or indirectly. You may be subject to rules issued by one or more of the following types of organizations:

1. State supreme court
2. State legislature
3. State voluntary bar association
4. Mandatory or unified state bar organization
5. County and local bar associations
6. American Bar Association

7. Various national and specialty bar associations

8. Individual local courts

9. Various federal, state, and local administrative bodies that promulgate and maintain their own rules

10. Various federal, state, and local courts that promulgate and maintain their own rules (some of these courts are technically administrative bodies).

Some of the bodies that issue rules create their own rules independently, and some simply refer to the rules of other bodies. One of the more common sets of rules referred to by other groups are those rules promulgated by the American Bar Association over the years. At various times these have been called the Canons of Professional Ethics, the Model Code of Professional Responsibility, and the Model Rules of Professional Conduct.

It was my original intent to append the current ABA Model Rules to this book in order to provide a guide for young lawyers, law students, and those lawyers who wanted continuing education. Unfortunately, the ABA Center for Professional Responsibility required payment of royalties for the right to repeat the rules. The Center would not allow reprinting, on a nonroyalty basis, of the rules as a whole in this book. The Center also refused to allow printing of the rules without the copious comments.

The cost of the royalties and the additional printing costs involved would have placed the price of the book beyond the reach of lawyers starting a practice. This chapter deals with practical problems faced in everyday law practice. If you want the Rules and Comments for your reference library, the Center for Professional Responsibility will sell them to you.

I have deliberately avoided making reference to any specific rules of professional responsibility, professional conduct, or ethics in this chapter because of the large number of these sets of rules currently in effect. I leave it to you the reader (or to your professor) to identify the rules in your jurisdiction(s) that are applicable to the situations described. You may be able to download them from a state bar Web site without copyright infringement.

Avoid the Ethics War

As my main point, I repeat here something that I've said elsewhere in this book and in the many articles and seminars I've authored in the last forty years. THE IMPORTANT THING IS NOT TO WIN THE ETHICS WAR, THE IMPORTANT THING IS TO AVOID THE ETHICS WAR. Fighting an ethics war is a lose-lose proposition. Even when a lawyer is totally and completely exonerated of any wrongdoing, an ethics complaint puts a permanent blot on his or her reputation. After that, the common misconception that "where there's smoke, there's fire" will apply. The lawyer is forced to spend time and money and attorney's fees to dig out old files and try to reconstruct records long after the event. The client has in most cases lost faith in the legal system. This disgruntled client will bad-mouth the lawyer and the legal system even though the lawyer is totally innocent. The client (and often the press) will treat the exoneration of the innocent lawyer as a cover-up or a whitewash. The lawyer will lose large amounts of money and otherwise billable time in defending himself or herself. The effect on the staff can be demoralizing. As a lawyer who has defended lawyers charged with ethics violations, I can attest to the tremendous cost in time and money in proving your innocence.

I repeat: *The important thing is not to win the ethics war. The important thing is to avoid the ethics war.*

Common Problems and How to Avoid Them

Keeping in mind that your goal is to avoid ethics wars by recognizing and solving ethics problems, let's proceed to examine the most common problems you are likely to encounter in the real world. These problems are not necessarily presented in the order that you will encounter them, nor necessarily in the order of their importance in your jurisdiction. In many cases these situations will apply to your adversary rather than to you. Being aware of unethical conduct on the part of your adversary can, in some cases, give your client's case an important negotiating or litigating position to the benefit of your client.

1. *Amount of Your Fee.* In some jurisdictions the amount of your fee must be "reasonable." In some jurisdictions the amount must not be "unreasonable." In some jurisdictions it must not be "unconscionable." In some jurisdictions, the fee is purely a matter of contract subject to the same rules as any civil contract. In some jurisdictions fees are limited to "*quantum meruit*" or for time actually devoted. Most jurisdictions have some sort of a list of factors to

be applied in determining how to classify a fee. Unfortunately for you as a practicing lawyer, everybody else can look at the amount of your fees with hindsight. Only you have the burden of needing foresight.

When you enter into an unusual situation, it's often a good practice to pick up the phone and call a couple of other lawyers with experience in the area of law involved to get their input. Be sure to take notes and document these calls in your time records. By getting input from other lawyers, you will simultaneously create an appropriate fee arrangement with the client and prepare a defense should a complaint later be made by an unhappy client.

You should also consider calling the bar ethics hotline or practice management advisor or committee of bar discipline personnel. Making these calls and considering the advice given may help demonstrate that you are an ethical lawyer trying to do the right thing in an unusual situation.

2. *Disclosure of Your Fee Agreement to Third Parties.* In some situations your fee agreement must either be disclosed to, or approved by, a third party. Failure to make the disclosure or get the approval may violate an ethical or court rule. And your failure may be deemed an indication of cover-up rather than ignorance. Depending on the forum or your jurisdiction, you may be required to make disclosure or get approval in the following types of cases. (This list is not intended to be all-inclusive.)

    a. Cases involving minors as clients.

    b. Probates (even though the fee is not related to probate assets).

    c. Family law matters such as adoptions, conservatorships, guardianships, dissolutions, and divorces.

    d. Insolvencies and bankruptcies. In some cases, trustees will try to recover fees paid to you prior to or during the proceeding.

    e. Criminal cases. Disgruntled clients are quick to file complaints from prison. Prosecutors may try to separate the client and the lawyer by attacking the lawyer to seize fees paid or to be paid.

    f. Contingency fees. Some courts and administrative bodies require disclosure and occasionally approval of contingent fee agreements as part of their administrative rules of practice.

    g. Cash fees. The law is unclear as to the extent, if at all, various government agencies are entitled to know the details of your fee agreements with clients when the fees are paid in currency. You must preserve the confidential relationship between yourself and the client. The government may press hard to get information on the source of your fee and the identity of your client's family or friends or business associates. You may find yourself in the uncomfortable position of having to resist government process and accusations until a court orders you to disclose information. Although contingent fees in criminal cases are normally unethical, the practical effect of these invasions of government into the attorney-client relationship may in fact be to make criminal cases contingent. That is, if your client is acquitted you can keep or get the fee, but if your client is found or pleads guilty, you may not get paid or you may have to refund or lose by forfeiture what has been paid. Various courts would provide a back-up arrangement wherein the lawyer would get paid what lawyers on the conflicts or indigent panels get paid. This would ensure that only the amount of the fee would be contingent.

h. Any fee where a complaint is made. Whether or not your fee agreement requires prior approval or disclosure to be effective, it will be reviewed by one or more authorities when a complaint is made by an unhappy client or a judge, and you'll have to prove your fee agreement meets all requirements.

In short, always keep in mind when you make a fee agreement that some unfriendly or skeptical third person may be reviewing it at a later time, at which point you'll have to defend it.

It is my experience, both as an arbitrator of fee disputes and after representing clients and lawyers in fee dispute litigation, that the most common reason lawyers lose their cases for fees is their failure to obtain a signed, written fee agreement that spells out what is expected of the client and of the lawyer. This lack of a clear agreement as to the scope of representation, coupled with poor time records, results in lawyers losing their cases for fees, in whole or in part, 64 percent of the time.

3. *Fee Splitting.* In some jurisdictions fee splitting with lawyers is permitted where the lawyers share both work AND responsibility. In some jurisdictions, fee splitting is permitted where the lawyers share work OR responsibility. In some jurisdictions the lawyers do NOT have to share either work or responsibility if the fee is purely a forwarding fee.

In most if not all jurisdictions, the client must be informed in writing that there is a fee-splitting agreement and the total amount of the fee to the client cannot be more than if there were no fee-splitting agreement. In some jurisdictions the client must also consent in writing to the fee-splitting agreement. In some jurisdictions the identity of all the lawyers dividing the fees must be made. In some jurisdictions the amount each will received must be disclosed. Be sure you know your local rule when you are sharing fees with another lawyer.

In some jurisdictions failure to follow the rules on fee division may result in not being paid for the work done, even on a quantum meruit basis.

In theory, a nonlawyer cannot receive any part of a fee. In a small firm, giving part of a fee to a nonlawyer for bringing in business or a particular matter would probably be considered unethical "capping." Small firms often divide the profits (theoretically not the fees) with nonlawyer employees. It is, of course, "coincidence" that the payment of bonuses coincides with the receipt of a fee. In a large firm, giving the same money to a nonlawyer might be permitted if the nonlawyer held some managerial or executive position, such as marketing director, and was entitled to the payment as a year-end or incentive bonus. In this case, avoid using the words "Performance Bonus," since this is often just simple fee splitting with nonlawyers.

Fee splitting with nonlawyers outside the firm is theoretically always prohibited. If your firm were economically strong enough to have nonlegal subsidiaries doing various forms of ancillary work such as environmental or other consulting or lobbying, if the fee splitting were indirect enough, and if the payment by the client were diverted from the law firm to the consulting firm, dividing the fees with the nonlawyer subsidiary or affiliate would probably not be questioned, even though you would in net effect be splitting fees with nonlawyers.

4. *Fees with Out-of-State Clients and Lawyers.* In many jurisdictions, an out-of-state or nonlicensed lawyer is considered a nonlawyer. Accordingly, you may ethically be unable to pay or receive fees from that lawyer. You may need two fee contracts with the client, with a separate fee agreement for each lawyer in each jurisdiction.

If your client is an out-of-state client, you may find that you are illegally or unethically practicing law in the state where your client is located.

If you are a solo or small firm and claim to have more than one office, you may be precluded from collecting a fee from a client even though you are licensed in the client's state.

If you or your adversaries are in a large firm with offices in more than one state, your local bar will probably either ignore the application of these rules or will find or create an exception.

5. *Fees Paid by Third Parties.* Your first duty is to your client, no matter who in fact is paying your fees. Often the legal fees are paid by a third party such as an insurance company, employer, union or trade association, or another organization or third party that seeks to advance its own interests through the medium of the client's case. Before accepting such a case you should make clear in writing, preferably both to the client and the payer, that your professional duty will be to the client should there be a conflict. These conflicts frequently arise as the case progresses. A common example is that the insured, your client, wants the case settled to be able to devote his or her time and energies to ordinary pursuits, while the insurance company, which is paying the fee, wants to drag the case out even to trial and appeals in order to suit its own economic interests. The need for experts often raises thorny problems. The payer of the fees may only be interested in cost containment and refuse to pay for needed experts that could exculpate your client, although at great economic cost. Another common example is that of an employee who is "taking a fall" for the employer who is paying the fees. A union, trade association, or activist organization may want to push or drop a case for its own interests or the interests of a larger group of parties. Any time a lawyer is looking to someone other than the client for payment of fees, the lawyer should check the rules and be careful.

A similar though not identical dilemma arises when the client is a corporate officer, director, shareholder, or employee of an organization and wants personal legal services billed to the business. The most the lawyer can do in such a case is to send bills to the individual at the business address and leave it to the client and the corporation's bookkeepers and auditors to make the appropriate bookkeeping allocations. Again, reread your local rules.

6. *Failure to Refund Unearned Fees.* A common problem arises from your agreeing to represent a client for a flat or fixed fee, often payable in advance. The client decides to change lawyers or is unhappy with your services. The client then demands a refund of the unearned fees.

7. *Dropping a Client or Case for Failure to Pay Fees.* Typically you can only drop a client for failure to pay fees if you have a writ-

ten fee agreement that spells out that you have the right to discontinue working if the client does not pay. In some types of cases (criminal and divorce, for example), you will not be allowed to withdraw for unpaid fees regardless of what your fee agreement says. You will never be allowed to withdraw from a case if your withdrawal would severely prejudice the client's case. These problems can, of course, often be obviated by applying "Foonberg's Rule," which is "Cash up front."

8. *False Billing Practices*. False billing practices are normally not grounds for disciplinary proceedings (with one exception). Firms sometimes lie to a client about the number of hours worked on a case (reputed to be a major problem with associates who are under pressure to record chargeable time). Firms also misstate who did the work, billing paralegal time as lawyer time and billing associate time as partner time. One form of false billing often condoned by clients is to inflate the amount of time to compensate for artificially low hourly rates. The client wants to look good by claiming to hire you at a low rate. This may explode in your face when the same client later sues you for overbilling, violation of fiduciary duty, etc., and files a complaint with your ethics body. It is my personal opinion that this type of false billing is not only a breach of the fiduciary and confidential relationship between a client and a lawyer, but is also grand theft and embezzlement. Fortunately (or unfortunately) this type of false billing is usually treated as a civil fee dispute rather than an ethics matter.

A common situation where a lawyer can be disciplined for false billing practices is when the lawyer accepts payment in advance to do work, does not do the work, and also refuses to refund the fee paid. This type of disciplinary proceeding can normally be avoided by the lawyer making prompt refund to the client of the unearned fee.

9. *Depositing Fees Paid in Advance*. When a client pays cash up front for fees and costs for the case, the lawyer should put all the funds into a trust account until the fees are earned or the costs incurred or the client receives a bill and does not object in a certain number of days. Many lawyers ignore this rule without consequence. The amount of the minimum or nonrefundable fee usually can be put directly into the general account, but the balance belongs in the trust account. Lawyers are particularly remiss in depositing money for future costs (rather than money for reimbursement for past costs incurred) into the trust account where it belongs. If a

client complains about your fee after payment, you may be required to return the disputed amount to the trust account until the dispute is resolved, unless your fee agreement "fixes" your right to withdraw the money if the bill is not objected to.

10. *Suing Clients for Fees.* There is normally no ethical prohibition against suing a client for earned and unpaid reasonable fees. Some codes caution that a lawyer should only sue a client for a fee in "exceptional situations."

As a practical matter, you can expect an often nonmeritorious cross-complaint for malpractice. You should not sue a client for fees unless your conduct has been exemplary and there is nothing in the file that you would feel awkward about explaining. Before considering a suit for fees you should ask another lawyer to review your case and file to point out areas where you may be at risk if you go to court. In some jurisdictions you must offer arbitration as a condition precedent to suing. Where available, mediation is often a good substitute for suits. Be sure to read all the applicable local rules before suing a client for fees. Be sure you have complete and accurate time records and that there is some evidence that the client understood the terms of the engagement, including what the maximum fee was likely to be or that there was no maximum fee discussed.

11. *Written Fee Agreements.* For more than forty years I have been a voice in the wilderness, advocating written fee agreements for the mutual protection of the client and the lawyer. I have written about what to put in a fee agreement in this and other books. Some professional rules now make a written fee agreement or a written fee memorandum mandatory. At a bare minimum, the agreement should cover what the lawyer is being hired to do, what the lawyer is not being hired to do, what the fees will be and/or how they will be calculated and charged, and when fees are payable. The right of the lawyer to stop working under specific circumstances and the right of the client to fire the lawyer under specific circumstances should also be covered. A letter to the client or a memo to the file is not as good or sufficient as a fee agreement signed by the client, but is better than nothing.

12. *Settlement Offers.* In some jurisdictions it is mandatory for a lawyer to communicate settlement offers to a client. In all jurisdictions it is good lawyering to communicate settlement offers to a client. You are perfectly free to recommend to a client that the settlement be accepted or rejected but you are not free to hide the offer from the client. You might wish to enclose an extra copy of the let-

ter containing the offer for transmission to the client when you send an offer for the adverse client to consider. You should be careful not to omit any of the terms of the offer to your client if you paraphrase or summarize it for your client. In most cases, the letter containing the offer will contain self-serving opinions of the merits (or lack of merit) of the other side's case, and for this reason, I don't recommend forwarding a letter from the other lawyer to your client. It is adequate to accurately summarize the other lawyer's offer to settle in your letter to your client. Be sure your client understands the difference between a gross settlement and the precise net amount the client will receive.

13. *Keeping Your Client Informed.* You have a professional obligation to keep your clients informed of the developments (or lack of developments) on their cases. Unfortunately (in my opinion) this may not be the law in your jurisdiction. In some jurisdictions you only have to respond to their requests for information when they ask. Failure to keep your client informed is, in theory, grounds for disciplinary action, although I've never heard of a disciplinary proceeding for failure to keep a client informed unless the failure to communicate was considered evidence of abandonment or cover-up or failure to respond when asked. Frankly, I think that failing to keep a client informed of everything happening on a case is bad lawyering, and is certainly just plain stupid from a client-relations point of view. Not keeping your client informed leads to unhappy clients who don't come back or refer more clients to you.

The best way to keep your clients informed is to bombard them with paper via mail, e-mail, and fax. Legal services are intangible, and lots of paper makes tangible the intangible. If you are concerned about clients calling you on receipt of information, mark the information "For your information; no reply necessary."

14. *Calling Yourself "Judge."* It is not uncommon for a lawyer, even a new lawyer, to serve as a *pro tem* or volunteer judge, often in small claims court. It is also not uncommon for a lawyer to serve as a full-time judge for a period of time and then return to private practice. In some jurisdictions, if you are a former judge you may not use the title "Judge" when the phone is answered, nor can you indicate on your professional cards or letterhead the fact that you are or were a judge. There appears to be concern that you would be intimating that your status as a judge or former judge would enable you to get special treatment for your clients in litigation. If this situation applies

to you or someone in your firm or another lawyer, you should check the rules to see if the conduct is permitted or prohibited. The public should never feel that the chances of winning or losing a case might be affected by a judge on the bench favoring a former judge.

15. *Listing Organizational Memberships on Stationery.* In most, if not all, cases you can list your membership in professional or nonprofessional organizations, provided the information is truthful. You will need to be careful, though, if your jurisdiction prohibits specialty listings. If you feel that it is important to let people know on your stationery that you belong to the National Aardvark Association, such a listing would probably be permitted if there is no claim on your part that this membership makes you a specialist in some area of law. As a Delegate at Large in the ABA (I was elected, not appointed as a delegate), I introduced a resolution recommending that the ABA members put the words "Member, American Bar Association" on their stationery and cards. The resolution was defeated for two reasons:

a. Firms would have to disclose which lawyers were not members of the ABA, and

b. There might be an inference by clients that lawyers who did not belong to the ABA were in some manner less qualified or credentialed than lawyers who do belong to the ABA.

16. *Listing Titles, Degrees, and Qualifications on Stationery.* Many of the same questions are also found in the area of listing organizational memberships. Some licensing authorities take the position that if you say anything more than "attorney-at-law," you are indicating that you have some specialty area and accordingly cannot do so in those jurisdictions that prohibit or regulate specialty designations. Since there is no fixed pre-law-school major in college and since many lawyers become lawyers after they have attained distinction in some field other than law, lawyers frequently have titles, degrees, and certificates other than a law degree and admission to practice as lawyers. (Interestingly enough, some lawyers have neither a baccalaureate or law degree from any university.)

I predict in time that the listing of all degrees and certificates will be permitted so long as the information is truthful. Clients and potential clients will have the right to know their prospective lawyer's qualifications and the lawyer will have the right to tell the client or prospective client who wants to know. Whether or not to provide this information (assuming it is truthful) will become a marketing question and not an ethics issue. You are, of course, cautioned to check your local rules. In some jurisdictions, calling yourself J.D. is a holding out that you currently are licensed to practice law in that jurisdiction. Lawyers who have failed the bar exam or have been disbarred or have given up their license to practice sometimes like to call themselves "J.D." to intimate that they are licensed to practice.

17. *Restricting Practice by Not Representing Other Clients with Similar Claims.* If you have done a good job in representing a client, the opposition may want to include in a settlement that you as a lawyer will not represent other clients with similar claims against that party or against other parties in the same industry. In most, if not all, jurisdictions you may not ethically make such an agreement even if you and your client are both willing. It may be unethical to ask opposing counsel to be party to such an agreement.

18. *Competence.* Competence is now included in the rules of professional conduct of most jurisdictions. This is relatively new and signifies one of the differences between ethics and professional responsibility. In the past, one could be both ethical and incompetent. Under most current rules you can be disciplined for undertaking or prosecuting work for which you or your firm are not competent. Your state (or whatever agency is involved in licensing or granting permission to practice) said that you were competent when you were admitted to practice. Lack of experience may be deemed lack of competence if you don't seek help.

With the ever-increasing public demand for specialization (or whatever name you wish to call it), the differences between competence and incompetence become even more fuzzy and difficult to define or identify.

My solution to the problem is to get help. When you truly don't feel comfortable that you know what you are doing, call another lawyer for his or her opinion on what you should be doing.

It's possible in some cases that you should associate with another lawyer or law firm to work behind or alongside you to give you ongoing help with the case. The choice of whether the other firm will work with you or alongside you may be determined by your relationship with your client and whether the other firm wants to accept professional responsibility to the client. If you are in over your head, it may be in everyone's best interest for you to simply tell the client that since additional facts and research have come to your attention, it now appears that the client's interests would best be served by calling in specialists, and that you will remain in the case to serve as liaison to the specialist. This will normally please most clients, and the truth is that you will feel better and breathe easier knowing that the client has the right lawyer for the problem. You may wish to put a clause in your standard fee agreement allowing you to engage additional counsel at your own expense.

Many, if not most, bar associations maintain a lawyer-to-lawyer directory listing lawyers available to help other lawyers. Even if your bar association does not have such a directory, you can network with other lawyers through the bar committees to find the right lawyer to help out. I have never been turned down in my entire career when I've asked other lawyers for help, and no lawyer will turn you down when you ask for a few minutes of their time by telephone. A truly caring lawyer will not want any fee for giving you a few tips to get you and the client down the right road. (Obviously there are limits to what any lawyer should ask another lawyer to do without compensation.)

There are many e-mail chat groups for lawyers that consist of large numbers of lawyers willing to give you help or pointers. Currently, "solosez" is an e-mail list serviced by the American Bar Association. I have witnessed hundreds of lawyers asking for and receiving help through this chat group. Your law school or a specialty bar or local bar association may maintain such a listserve. The Internet may lead you to lawyers willing to help you. A chat group for senior lawyers, including those starting or selling a practice, may soon be available at **www.SeniorLawyers.org**.

19. *Media Advertising.* Media advertising, for purposes of this section, will be defined as advertising by radio, television, billboards, bus placards, newspaper, magazine, or other print media; that is, advertising that is cleanly bought and paid for as advertising, as opposed to advertising that is indirectly bought and paid for through a public relations firm or other third party, whom you have paid to obtain free or indirect advertising disguised as news or public interest information. Internet marketing will be treated in a separate paragraph. There are publicists who do product placement; that is, for a fee they will get your name publicized in newspapers, airline magazines, airline audio channels, television and films, etc.

In general, media advertising has to meet the "three Ts" test. It must be Truthful, Tasteful, and Tentative. It must be truthful in that it cannot contain lies. It must be tasteful in that it doesn't offend the person who decides whether it is tasteful or offensive. It must be tentative in that you can't guarantee results. You may or may not be required to deposit a copy of your ad with a bar committee before or after using it. Read your local rules. Decide whether to comply, try to change the system, or forget about using direct media advertising and stick to indirect media advertising. (See next section.)

My personal feelings are clear and have never been subtle. I believe that all people and institutions should have access to the legal system and that we as individual lawyers and the legal profession as a group have a responsibility to help people and institutions with meritorious legal needs find the lawyer or firm for their needs by whatever means that get the job done. I have even written a book entitled *Finding the Right Lawyer* to help people find the lawyer they need.

It is far beyond the scope of this book or this chapter to repeat in detail all of the evidence that clearly demonstrates that media advertising does not create the need for legal services. The need for legal services exists or does not exist independently of media advertising. Media advertising does not stir up litigation. Clients do not contact a lawyer until after they need a lawyer. Most, if not all, of the firms and individuals who obtain lawyers through media advertising would not utilize media ads to find a lawyer if they could access the legal system by contacting a lawyer they knew or to whom they could be recommended.

Most of the complaints about legal advertising come from lawyers, not from clients. Most of the complaints deal with taste, not with whether the advertising helps the American public find the lawyer they need.

As mentioned, the current requirements for professional, paid-for media advertising for legal services are that it must be truthful, tasteful, and tentative. What constitutes truthful, tasteful, and tentative is, of course, a matter of both fact and opinion. Some lawyers would gladly abolish all media advertising. These lawyers normally have no problem with advertising that is bought and paid for through third-party sources, so long as it's disguised as information. In many cases, the person accused of violating the applicable rules is going to have an unfriendly judge or jury deciding whether the particular ad involved is truthful and tasteful.

If you are going to go heavily into paid-for media advertising you should include in your budget funds to have your materials reviewed by a lawyer who has experience in disciplinary proceedings and/or First Amendment law. In some jurisdictions, you may be required to deposit a copy of the materials with some committee or board before using the materials.

In summary, before you spend any significant amount of time or money on paid-for media advertising, be sure you know the current rules and understand that no matter what you do, you may have to invest time and money getting some sort of prior approval. The alternative is to take the risk of sailing through uncharted waters, which could cost you a lot of time and energy.

20. *Indirect Media Advertising.* I have heard statistics saying that more than 80 percent of all space in a newspaper is paid-for advertising or information planted by groups advocating their own economic interests through the guise of news. Less than 20 percent is true news such as current events, sports, and weather. Indirect media advertising is that type of paid advertising that finds its way into the media disguised as being newsworthy or as being some sort of public service. Rather than buy advertising space or time as such, you or any law firm can buy "high visibility." Rather than making a self-proclaimed statement of expertise in an advertisement clearly bought and paid for, the law firm can pay for and get a third party such as a newspaper reporter to claim that the lawyer or law firm are experts, when in fact the lawyer or firm may know little or nothing about the area of law involved. A public relations firm can set up individuals in your firm as experts to give an opinion on cases or laws in the news. Public relations firms are paid significant sums of money to keep a lawyer or firm in the public media. They have their own methods of getting information into the media by creating a seemingly newsworthy event out of the lawyer or law firm.

The line between publicity for the benefit of the client and publicity for the benefit of the lawyer is further blurred when litigants can hire public relations firms to flood TV, radio, and newspapers with coverage during a trial in an effort to influence the judge or jury. In major cases, the litigants who have enough money to spend or who have an important enough political motive to advance can spend unbelievable amounts of money, into the millions, on the theory that judges and jurors and their spouses, who may sincerely want to try to judge the case only by the evidence presented in the courtroom, still won't forget what they hear and see on television and in the newspapers. Accordingly, litigants may provide the media with food, drink, junkets, television remote-broadcasting facilities, and many other items to get favorable publicity.

While you as a new lawyer may not have the resources to wage a second front in the newspapers, you should keep in mind that your client may have the resources, and the apparent state of affairs currently is that bought and paid-for news coverage is not only ethical, but an important part of case management. If your client is trying to influence the trier of fact through media coverage, you may need help from a media consultant in trying to get some coverage for what your client wants the trier of fact to believe.

21. *Direct-Mail Solicitation.* The subject of direct-mail solicitation is a very heated one. As with other areas of advertising, the complaints come from lawyers, not from clients. The one major problem with direct-mail solicitation is that the mail may be reaching someone who is already represented by counsel. A letter counseling a person to do or not to do something may be contrary to the advice given by the current counsel. The mail could also be interfering with an existing attorney-client relationship in that it might be giving legal advice to someone represented by counsel. Both of these activities are usually proscribed by the various rules. Targeted direct mail should include a statement to the following effect:

> If you are already represented by counsel, it is not our intention to interfere with your relationship with your lawyer, and we ask that you seek appropriate advice from your lawyer. If you are not represented by counsel, we would be pleased to discuss the possibility of our representing you.

Another major problem is the intrusive or "in your face" type of advertising shortly after one has suffered a great loss and may not be in a rational state of mind.

The rules of your jurisdiction might require some sort of notice or warning in or on the letter that the letter consists of legal advertising. (See next section dealing with nonsolicitation mailings.)

22. *Nonsolicitation Mailings.* Nonsolicitation mailings, such as firm announcements, newsletters, bulletins, alerts, brochures, Christmas cards, seminar announcements, public relations mailings concerning published articles and firm activities, and a large variety of other mailings, may or may not have to carry a warning on or in the mailing. The warning usually must say something like "Legal

Advertising Enclosed" in big letters on the outside of the envelope. In some jurisdictions the warning must be printed in the contents. I believe one lawyer closes off the mailing by stating that the preceding message was legal advertising. You will have to check your current rules. Interestingly enough, lawyers report to me that words like "Legal Advertising Enclosed" whet the interest of the intended recipient and prompt the recipient to eagerly and carefully read what has been sent. Lawyers actually get better results when these words are prominently displayed.

23. *No Recovery, No Fee.* In contingency cases, lawyers often quote "no recovery, no fee" to a client. I believe that the problem with this type of fee quotation is that it often may be false and deceptive advertising, or may simply be lying to a client. Some lawyers fail to disclose that in the event the case is lost there may be a bill of taxable costs to be levied against the client. Clients have had to go bankrupt because of taxed costs. Lawyers often file a notice of appeal upon losing the case and then negotiate dropping the appeal for a waiver of costs. Obviously a lawyer should discuss the possibility of a bill for costs if the case is lost.

Lawyers rarely, if ever, discuss the possibility of losing a contingency case. I've never heard of a lawyer getting into trouble over filing a notice of appeal as an inducement to waiving costs. My problem is whether or not the client truly understands what is happening. There used to be an absolute prohibition against a lawyer advancing costs on a contingency case without such costs being considered a loan to be paid back by the client when the case was over, even when the case was lost. Many professional rules now allow a lawyer to openly advance costs on a contingency case with repayment to come only out of the recovery, if at all.

24. *Firm Name.* Unless you are going to call yourself JOHN DOE, ATTORNEY-AT-LAW, you'll have to find out what is or is not permitted in your jurisdiction. In some jurisdictions you cannot practice under a fictitious name; in other jurisdictions you can. In some jurisdictions, using the names of dead lawyers unknown to any human being alive is considered to be using a fictitious name. In other jurisdictions, it's not. In some jurisdictions you can use any name you wish to use. It is not uncommon in these jurisdictions to practice under names like "AAAA and AAAA, Attorneys-at-Law" in an attempt to be the first name in the telephone book. In some jurisdictions you can practice under a name like "American Institute

for the Defense of Drunk Driving Charges" (a name I created for this example). You can be disciplined for false advertising if you call yourself "Jones and Smith, Attorneys-at-Law" if Mr. Jones is not, in fact, a general partner, but an associate. Increasingly, law firms are using trade names descriptive of their law practice, which will lead potential clients to believe they are some sort of specialists. Names such as "The Business Litigation Group" or "High-Tech Law Group" or "The Environmental Group" could be used for this purpose. (Again, I made up the names.) The rules pertaining to firm name often are arbitrary and are not evenly applied to big and small firms. In common English, the words "attorney" or "lawyer" or "attorney and counsellor" or "attorney-at-law" are synonymous. I personally use what I feel comfortable using with the clients to whom I am speaking.

25. *Buying or Selling a Law Practice.* In many states it is still unethical to sell or buy a law practice if you are a sole practitioner. One has to use the guise of forming a partnership with the purchaser and then selling the goodwill connected with the partnership interest as indicated. Many states are now changing the rules to conform to what is happening in the real world. Some states now allow a sole practitioner or the spouse of a deceased sole practitioner to sell a practice rather than allow a lifetime of building a practice to go to waste. It is incumbent on the buyer and seller to carefully apply the existing rules to the transaction. In other words, it is now possible to buy and sell practices, but it must be done in such a way as to comply with the rules. A new lawyer would be wise to check the rules and then check the obituaries or special bar association committees to determine if it is possible to buy another lawyer's practice. The rules are changing rapidly in this area. If you have a sincere interest in buying a law practice or buying into a law practice, I suggest you take a look at **www.LawPracticeSales.net**.

26. *Coaching Your Client to Lie.* There are no jurisdictions of which I am aware that advocate a lawyer instructing a client to lie. Most if not all jurisdictions have express rules dictating that a lawyer may not counsel a client to lie. Some jurisdictions even want the lawyer to withdraw from the case and "turn in" the client to a judge or prosecutor if the lawyer knows the client is lying.

Some lawyers avoid this situation by prefacing important questions with a statement along the following lines: "The answer to the next question is critical. If you tell me the answer is 'yes,' you may win your case. If you tell me the answer is 'no,' you will definitely lose your case. Now what is the answer to this question?"

27. *Turning Over Files When You Are Discharged.* Generally, you must return to the client anything that is the property of the client. You must also turn over whatever the next lawyer will reasonably need to effectively represent the client. In most states, you cannot hold onto records because of an unpaid bill. You clearly do have the right to photocopy what you turn over in order to protect yourself for malpractice and tax purposes. You certainly can agree with your client beforehand (in your fee agreement) that the client must pay for these photocopy charges. A few states still allow "retaining liens" or "charging liens" that allow a lawyer to hold on to a client's file until all fees and costs are paid. Obviously such action could prejudice a client's case. Check your local rules as to whether charging or retaining liens are allowed.

A file may contain misfiled items that belong to other clients. You must protect the confidences of the other clients whose documents are erroneously filed by removing them before you turn over the file. Accordingly, it is necessary to review or screen the contents of a file before divulging the contents to a client or another lawyer or during discovery. Rules regarding turning over work product vary from jurisdiction to jurisdiction.

Special problems arise in multiclient representation. See chapter entitled How to Recognize and Handle Conflicts of Interest.

28. *Destroying Files.* The destruction of files is covered by professional rules due to the fact that the file may contain items that belong to the client or to others. There may be special rules concerning files on criminal cases. Some firms simply send everything off to the cheapest warehouse they can find, often hundreds of miles away, believing this to be the most economical thing to do. Some firms simply throw files away and cross their fingers that nothing will go wrong. Most firms seem to pick an arbitrary deadline of five or ten years, and then throw the files away, hoping that they won't ever need the files in the future. Putting files onto microfilm or other electronic media, such as CD-ROM, may provide economical solutions to the problem of the seemingly perpetual costs of file storage. As a new lawyer, you should plan to move files into storage as soon as possible to save rent costs, but don't destroy files until much later in your career. The subject of file destruction is of ethical concern because of the ethical mandate to protect property that belongs to the

client. Be careful about using electronic storage to replace paper storage. If you store information electronically, be sure to keep hardware and software to be able to reprint to paper what you stored. You may find that there is no longer support for the hardware or software needed to read the information. There is a special chapter in this book entitled Closing and Disposing of Files.

29. *Going Out of Practice.* Your jurisdiction may have special rules on file preservation if you decide to leave the practice of law on either a short-term or long-term basis. You may be required to make some sort of arrangement with another lawyer to take over your files. You may be required to give notices to clients. There is an excellent checklist for closing a law practice at **www.Seniorlawyer.org**. I intend to write a book on this subject in the near future.

30. *Turning Your Files Over to Third Parties Pursuant to Court Order.* There is an increasing tendency on the part of lawyers to attack other lawyers. Often a government agency will obtain some sort of court order such as a search warrant or a civil subpoena to seek the contents of a client's files. Some overly aggressive lawyers are quick to sue both the adversary client and the adversary's lawyers, hoping to get access to the lawyer's files through the guise of doing discovery on the lawyer. In these cases I would recommend simply refusing to comply by asserting attorney-client privilege, work product, etc., as reasons for not complying and respectfully requesting that the other side get a court order after giving the client an opportunity to assert all appropriate claims in court. As in other situations, you have to review and screen files beforehand to be sure you don't inadvertently turn over misfiled information concerning other clients.

31. *Inadvertent Violations of Attorney-Client Confidences.* Lawyers rarely violate attorney-client confidences deliberately. You must read the rules carefully to get a feeling of what information outside of the legal issues themselves are included and what practices constitute violations of attorney-client confidences. While you may not get disciplined for accidentally violating confidences, your reputation will suffer and you'll have a difficult time collecting on the unpaid balance of your fee. Special care should be exercised in sending copies of e-mail messages where a single key stroke can reach an infinite number of people.

32. *Sending Client Mail or Faxes or E-mail to the Wrong Address.* You should always ask clients where to send communications

concerning their legal matters. Some clients don't want their employees to know their legal problems and some don't want members of their families to know what's happening in their case. It's not too smart to send a strategy letter on a divorce case to the client's home where the spouse can get the letter and read it. Similarly, you don't want to send an e-mail concerning the company's high earnings to a place where the employee's union representative can see it and forward it to every employee in the company.

33. *Receiving Faxes and Copies or Mail Intended for Others.* I enjoy receiving copies of confidential letters and faxes sent by a lawyer to a client when the lawyer's mailroom erroneously sends me copies of all correspondence just because I'm on the mailing list to receive copies of pleadings filed with the court. Some bar associations recommend or require you to forward the document to the intended recipient without copying it.

34. *Sending the Wrong Enclosures by Fax or in the Mail.* I've often received the last page of a letter showing who gets the blind copies of correspondence. I've learned the identities of other clients and lawyers and law firms, which were meant to be confidential. I've also gotten original letters intended for the other lawyer's client. I suppose the other lawyer's client got the pleading I was supposed to get. Listing each enclosure or attachment at the end of each letter or e-mail can reduce this possibility.

35. *Failing to Put "Personal and Confidential" or "To Be Opened by Addressee Only" on the Mail Envelope or the Fax Cover Sheet.* Failure to use these words or similar wording such as "privileged and confidential information enclosed" on the outside of the envelope or on the fax cover sheet may make your mail fair game for whoever can get to it first. This problem is compounded by the widespread use of fax and e-mail transmissions. For reasons that I do not understand, many law firms do not indicate that a fax or e-mail communication is from a law firm on their cover sheet or in their sender ID code, which can appear at the top of each page of the document transmitted rather than at the end where it won't be read until after the confidential information is read.

36. *Not Protecting the Identity of Clients.* The identity of a client is as much a confidence as the nature of the legal work for which you are consulted. You won't get disbarred, but it won't help your reputation or the firm's when a client is upset because you've been using the client's name in public without permission. Lawyers

and nonlawyers in the firm have a tendency to want to advertise or brag about who their clients are. The identity of your client can be just as important to the client's case as the case itself. Accordingly, you should keep that identity confidential. Be careful about headers and footers disclosing a client's identity or who is the real party in interest when it is a secret.

You can understand that clients or the value of their companies' shares could be prejudiced if it were known that they had just become clients of a firm specializing in bankruptcy, or tax fraud, or divorce, or whatever. Individuals normally don't want anyone knowing they have legal problems.

37. *Failure to Teach Client Confidentiality to Family Members.* A lawyer should teach and reinforce client confidentiality to family members. You need to instruct your children or spouse not to repeat outside the house what they overhear on the phone or see in a document. Your family members did not take a course in professional responsibility, and unless you teach them what not to do, you run a serious risk that they will do just that.

38. *Failure to Teach Client Confidentiality to Independent Contractors.* A lawyer has to supervise and be responsible for what marketing directors, public relations firms, and other nonlawyers do for the firm. Most of these people have no knowledge about law or legal matters, except in how to sell their services to and for lawyers. Some of these people may simply be loose cannons rolling around on the deck who will eventually get the firm or a particular lawyer into deep trouble with a client or the bar or the public, simply because they didn't know that they were doing something unethical. You should at least tell them to buy a copy of the Model Rules of Professional Conduct from the American Bar Association or buy them a set yourself.

39. *Failure to Teach Confidentiality to Office Staff, Contract Lawyers, Of Counsel, etc.* You will be responsible and can be disciplined if members of your staff commit a blatant violation of the rules, and defend themselves by truthfully stating that they didn't know they were doing anything wrong. Your staff manual and the package you hand to new employees, contract lawyers, and others, both professional and nonprofessional, should include a copy of the rules of conduct applicable to your firm. It wouldn't hurt to have a once-a-year luncheon where the most common problems are taught or reinforced to the staff. You can buy or rent a videotape on this

subject to show once a year and to every new hire. Be sure to get a signed report from the employee or recipient of the staff manual or rules. The State Bar of Wisconsin CLE has an excellent videotape to teach law office confidentiality to staff. Contact me for a complimentary one-hour video on trust accounts.

40. *Trust Accounts.* Trust account violations make up a small percentage of complaints but a large percentage of disbarments. Some IOLTA "snitch rules" encourage banks to report lawyers for technical violations even when no client suffers any loss or harm. Trust account violations are easy to prove. Putting client money that belongs in a trust account into your personal or office account is an easy way to get disbarred, especially if you use the money for personal purposes and don't give it back to the client. The usual pattern is for a desperate lawyer to put money that should have gone into the trust account, such as a client's settlement money or unearned fees received from the client, into some account other than the trust account. Typically, the client is told that the case has not yet been settled or that the work has been done. Falling into this classic pattern is the simplest and fastest way I know of to get disbarred. The trust account should be clearly labeled as such and only the lawyer should have the power to write checks on the account.

In many, if not most, situations, trust account theft by an employee is not covered by malpractice or any other insurance. You can also be disciplined for failure to supervise employees who have access to the trust account.

Some lawyers who are in financial trouble put their own personal funds into the trust account and pay their personal bills from that account. They typically do this to hide money from creditors or spouses. It is clearly commingling to put your personal money in the trust account. I recommend you read the chapter entitled "Ten Commandments of Good Trust Accounts," and I also recommend *The ABA Guide to Lawyer Trust Accounts* (which I wrote), available from the ABA. On request, I will send you a free one-hour videotape on trust accounts management.

41. *Going into Business Deals with Clients.* An undercapitalized client may offer you a "piece of the action" in lieu of a fee or as part of a reduced fee. You may have visions of simultaneously doing the client a favor by conserving the client's cash flow and possibly getting rich on the investment. It is a "Foonbergism" to say "a lawyer who wears two hats has no head." You may be excluding

yourself from malpractice insurance coverage. These deals rarely produce anything but aggravation for the lawyer. If the deal turns out well, the client may want to renege on the basis that you were overreaching or that the fee is unreasonable. If you are tempted to take a piece of the action, be sure to send the client to another lawyer before finalizing the agreement. At the very least, put into writing your advice to the client that he or she has the right to see another lawyer before agreeing and that you recommend so. Get the client to sign a copy of the letter where you give this advice. If you suggest the possibility of taking a piece of the deal, you'll be in even worse shape when the client simultaneously files a lawsuit and an ethics complaint.

Historically, contingency fee agreements are excluded from the application of these rules. In some areas of law, such as entertainment law, lawyers get a piece of the deal in addition to a cash fee. I would assume this is allowed because the clients are presumed to be sophisticated and able to protect their own interests. Some people believe that overreaching lawyers getting a piece of the action were in part responsible for the practice and abuses leading to the dot com frauds and bad investments of the dot com companies.

42. *Alternative Billing Methods.* Many lawyers try to raise their effective hourly rates through ingenious alternative billing methods. These methods are frequently just a contingency plus an hourly rate. They are sometimes called "results-oriented" rates or "performance reevaluations." I've heard one client refer to them as begging for tips. In any event, if you are going to go for some exotic alternative billing method, you may face the identical problems you would face if you were to go into a business deal with your client. Be careful when you get innovative. You may get some good ideas from the ABA publication *Winning Alternatives to the Billable Hour*, Second Edition, edited by James Calloway and Mark Robertson. Just be sure your client is sophisticated and/or has another lawyer's advice before entering into some alternative method. I also recommend a book written by J. Harris Morgan and myself entitled *How to Draft Bills Clients Rush to Pay*, Second Edition, also available from the ABA. My portion of the book deals with tailoring fee agreements to make it possible for the client to pay the bill.

43. *Representing a Client with Zeal.* Many lawyers take this rule to be a blank check to win at any cost or to be hostile and unnecessarily aggressive. If it were up to me, I would limit application

of this rule to serious criminal cases or abolish it altogether. This rule may be a good rule in terms of helping a single client on a single case, but it may be doing the legal system more harm than good. I am seeing considerable overkill in civil litigation and in the "Rambo" atmosphere of hostility among lawyers toward each other. The public is lowering its opinion of lawyers and the legal system as they are asked to pay for this legal excess and as they witness the legal system and the courts becoming the instruments of those who have the resources to pay for this overkill. This rule can be a convenient safe harbor for you or your firm when you are accused of overkill or running up a bill with unnecessary work unlikely to add anything to the outcome of the case.

In serious criminal cases where human life is involved and in most serious criminal cases (you'll have to define "serious"), the rule may be a good one in theory but prove hard to apply. If every defendant pled not guilty and demanded a jury trial, our criminal justice system would probably come to a complete halt or reach the point where only the most serious cases were tried, leaving criminals free to attack society without punishment.

In applying this rule the lawyer will have to balance duty to the client, duty to the legal system, and duty to society. No matter what balance the lawyer reaches from a personal point of view, the lawyer will be forced to prove, after the fact, that the client was represented with zeal.

About the only advice I can give for this situation is to make sure that the client is aware of how much work you could do on a case and then let the client limit the amount of work to be done based on the client's view of the importance of the matter, relative to how much the client wants done or is willing to pay for.

Don't let your ego interfere with what is best for the client. It's the client's case, not yours.

44. *Prosecuting Nonmeritorious Cases.* You may not begin or continue to prosecute a case that you know to be nonmeritorious or to assert defenses based on knowingly false information. You may be subject to personal sanctions applied to you as an individual or to your firm, and you will face disciplinary proceedings when the court refers the matter for investigation and prosecution. This is one of the few areas where judges take the initiative in instituting disciplinary proceedings. They probably do so because they are eyewitnesses to the transgression and are angry about the waste of their

time and the waste of court facilities that could have been made available to clients with meritorious cases. If you feel or know that the case is nonmeritorious, get the opinion of a second lawyer (protecting the client's name), then tell the client that the case is *over* as far as you are concerned and that the client should substitute *in propria persona* or you'll make a motion to be relieved, thereby entering into the court record your opinion that the case is nonmeritorious, which might later hurt the client's case if the client is determined to prosecute. Recent cases in some jurisdictions hold a lawyer liable for abuse of process for maintaining a case after the lawyer learned that the case had no merit.

45. *Moral Turpitude*. In many jurisdictions, one can be disciplined for "moral turpitude" or "conduct unbecoming to a lawyer" or similarly vague transgressions. Typically, these transgressions are unrelated to the practice of law. The range of transgressions is unlimited. In some jurisdictions one will not be allowed to take the bar exam if one is in default on a student loan. In some jurisdictions, conviction of or pleading nolo to a felony means automatic disbarment, even though the felony is totally unrelated to the practice of law. In some jurisdictions, conviction of a felony is not grounds for disciplinary procedure unless the felony is related to the practice of law or deals with some particularly serious matter. I've heard of a lawyer being disbarred for moral turpitude for pleading guilty to a misdemeanor charge of having sex with a prostitute.

I can only suggest that if you are in trouble, you should consider whether the resolution of the matter will affect your license to practice law. An expedient or practical solution to the nonprofessional problem may create an unanticipated professional problem with the bar.

46. *Communicating with an Adverse Party Represented by Counsel*. It's basic that a lawyer cannot communicate with an adverse party who is represented by counsel. To do so will result in discipline. One cannot use the guise of communicating with the lawyer with a copy to the lawyer's client or vice versa. A serious problem arises when you want to do investigation either directly or through an investigator. Depending upon the jurisdiction you may be prohibited from contacting family members, employees, co-workers, expert witnesses, and a large variety of other people who have some special relationship to the adverse party. You will simply have to read the rules and the case law under the rules to decide each situation as it arises. One can communicate directly with an adverse person represented by

counsel only if you have the lawyer's permission. Based on my experiences with overzealous lawyers who interpret their mandate to represent a client zealously to include lying and who have thus lied about obtaining permission, you should confirm the permission in writing by mail or fax before contact. If the represented person calls you by telephone, hang up until you can confirm your right to contact the client. If the scope of what you can discuss is unlimited, the letter should so reflect. Some parties may claim they have fired their lawyers because of a fee dispute and want to talk to you directly to settle the case. Don't fall for this trick! In many cases you are being set up.

Be careful when communicating with a court. You can easily be accused of *ex parte* communications even when you call to ask a routine administrative question.

Some lawyers let the adverse person tell everything before asking if the person is represented by counsel. This is a dangerous technique and can backfire if the person claims later that he or she disclosed up front the fact that he or she was represented by counsel.

47. *Suppressing and "Sanitizing" Evidence.* I personally do not hide discoverable evidence in discovery proceedings, nor do I counsel clients to do so. It appears that I'm in a small minority. Many lawyers tell me that they have their clients screen evidence before turning it in to the lawyer for transmission to the other side. Apparently, the lawyer also screens the evidence. I get the impression that the only discovery that's worthwhile is when the other party and its lawyers accidentally leave something important in what was turned over, or when the source of the documents is from a third party. I totally disapprove of this conduct, but it's done and I'm not aware of any serious disciplinary proceedings resulting therefrom. If you can prove that opposing counsel has suppressed evidence, I ask you to make it a point to file a complaint. When a lawyer tells a client to suppress evidence, the client is justified in inferring that all lawyers suppress evidence.

48. *Turning in Other Lawyers for Violating the Rules and Failure to Do So.* Different jurisdictions have different rules governing a lawyer's obligation to turn in other lawyers for violations of the rules. In many jurisdictions, the authorities simply disregard complaints filed by lawyers, believing that there is a game going on and deciding that they don't want to be in the middle of a dispute between lawyers. (There's an old expression that it's the grass that gets trampled when elephants fight.) The same complaint will receive more serious attention if it is filed by your client rather than being

filed by you as the lawyer. Where adopted, this rule is sometimes referred to as a "squeal rule." Lawyers have also been disciplined for not squealing on another lawyer. As prosecutors and the public increasingly expect lawyers to expose financial fraud, this disciplinary area may grow.

49. *Preventing Your Client from Committing a Crime.* In some jurisdictions you are supposed to turn in a client who is planning to commit a crime. It can depend on whether the crime is one of violence against a person or of a threatening nature. You have to read the rule in your jurisdiction.

50. *Counseling Your Client to Commit a Crime.* You can never counsel a client to commit a crime. Such counseling can get you named as a co-conspirator in a criminal proceeding. No exceptions exist for those people who want to commit a crime through civil disobedience in order to get free publicity and attention for their cause. If you counsel a client to commit a crime or unlawful act to draw attention to a clearly unjust law or practice, you may find yourself in trouble with the bar as well as the criminal authorities, despite your good intentions. Only you as an individual can decide the price you are willing to pay to help a client make a point. There are some narrow exceptions and limitations in the area of challenging improper laws. Read the rules carefully before risking your license.

51. *Not Understanding Conflicts.* Many lawyers were never adequately taught about conflicts in law school. A client is entitled to total loyalty. Anything that does or that might impair that loyalty is a conflict. Any relationship, financial or otherwise, with any other person or entity that could impair that duty is a conflict and must be dealt with at the inception of a professional relationship.

52. *Getting Copies of All Applicable Rules for Your Personal Library.* Ethics is statutory. The rules change from time to time in an attempt to be responsive to the society we serve. The rules differ from body to body and jurisdiction to jurisdiction. You owe it to the public, yourself, your family, your clients, others in your firm, and, most importantly, to the legal system to practice ethically and professionally. You can't follow the rules or change the rules if you don't know the current rules. What you learned in law school may have been accurate when you were in law school, but may not reflect the current rules issued by those courts and administrative bodies where you will be representing your client.

What Are the Consequences of "Violating" the Canons of Professional Ethics, the Code of Professional Responsibility, or the Model Rules of Professional Conduct?

This is a difficult question to answer. The answer depends on the particular "violation" and upon your licensing laws.

A brief review of some basic definitions will be helpful.

Bar association usually means a voluntary group of lawyers. Associations are normally but not always organized on a geographic, specialty, or special interest basis and may be on an international, national, state, county, city, or neighborhood basis. A state or local bar association may have its own "canons" or "code," or it may adopt in toto or by reference the canons or codes of another association. In some states, the bar association can "recommend" a license proceeding against a lawyer.

"State bar" usually means a mandatory bar group that you must belong to to practice law in the state. This type of bar is often called an "integrated bar" (having nothing to do with civil rights) or a "uniform bar" or a "unified bar." "State bars" can sometimes do more or less than "bar associations." In some cases bar associations started as voluntary associations that became mandatory, but kept the word "association" in the name. Some states have both a voluntary and mandatory bar existing at the same time.

The ABA *Canons of Professional Ethics* are the pronouncements of the American Bar Association adopted in 1908, which remained in effect until 1970.

The ABA *Code of Professional Responsibility* contained nine Canons (general statements) that were subdivided into 128 Ethical Considerations and 39 Disciplinary Rules. The Code was adopted in 1970.

The ABA *Model Rules of Professional Conduct* were adopted in 1983, superseding the Code of Professional Responsibility. They consist of 52 rules on seven broad topics (see the chapter that follows on The ABA Model Code of Professional Responsibility and the ABA Model Rules of Professional Conduct). Copies are sold by the American Bar Association's Center for Professional Responsibility.

State Rules of Professional Conduct are rules promulgated by licensing bodies such as the Supreme Court or legislature of a state. Not every state has adopted both the Code and the Model Rules. Most states have variations on the Code and the Rules that take into account local practice standards. The local practice standards are sometimes more stringent or less stringent than the ABA Code or Rules.

The American Bar Association modifies or changes its rules of ethics through its House of Delegates, which is composed of a mixture of voluntary and mandatory bar associations and other groups. The ABA House can add, obliterate, or modify ethical rules. The ABA rules have no legal effect anywhere. Other bar associations and state bars can copy them, ignore them, adopt them with modification, or refuse to be governed by them in whole or in part.

With some of the definitions in mind, we can go back to the basic question of the effect of violation of accepted standards of ethics.

The ABA Code and the Model Rules, in my opinion, represent the sincere efforts of well-meaning lawyers and nonlawyers to develop standards of conduct for lawyers on the highest level for the benefit of the public. Some of the rules may not be practical or enforceable and there are other objections. Notwithstanding all of the criticisms of the rules, on balance, it is a good work and deserving of respect and following.

The new lawyer should not be frightened or awed by the rules. Violations of some of the provisions will cost you your license. Violations of other provisions could result in disciplinary proceedings such as a reprimand or being expelled from the association.

Is unethical conduct per se also illegal? Some unethical conduct can be illegal, such as trust fund violations or fee splitting with the laity, and could result in criminal prosecution as well as disciplinary proceedings. Some unethical conduct could result in disciplinary proceedings only, such as telephone book advertising violations.

Some violations probably have absolutely no effect in some states, such as fee splitting. Some unethical conduct may have civil or malpractice implications. Some courts allow ethics rules into evidence when expert witnesses testify. Some courts incorporate ethics rules into jury instructions. The law is in flux in this area. Does unethical conduct give a client legal rights? This is an incredibly complex question with differing and inconsistent results. Even though the rules might specifically state they are not intended to create or defeat civil causes of action, the rules are often admitted as standards in attorney-client disputes. They may be part of an expert's testimony or read by the judge as a standard of conduct or information to be considered or simply admitted as evidence.

In summary, "violating" the Code of Professional Responsibility or Model Rules of Professional Conduct can have either serious consequences or lesser consequences, depending upon whether the rules are or are not part of your disciplinary system and upon the powers of your state bar or bar association.

As a new lawyer, you do not have enough sophistication or experience to decide selectively not to observe portions of the rules. You should initially observe the rules in their entirety, both in letter and in spirit. When you are an established lawyer and better understand the needs of the public, you can and should attempt to modify the local application of the rules to meet the local needs of the public.

Remember that even if you do not lose your license to practice law, expulsion from a bar association or a nonmeritorious ethics complaint against you can leave an ugly stain on your career and can cost you money by loss of referrals.

I must strongly advise that you thoroughly understand exactly what the situation is in your state or community before you begin your practice. If you're in sole practice there may be no one to review your work and you may be inadvertently doing something unethical, without realizing it. Somewhere in your legal education you were taught or exposed to legal ethics. Be sure you understand the interrelation of ethics, licensing, and malpractice liability.

Ten Rules for Avoiding Disciplinary Complaints

It is estimated that every year about one disciplinary complaint is filed for every ten lawyers. Very few of these complaints result in any discipline against the lawyer, either because the nature of the complaint is not covered by the disciplinary system or because the lawyer is innocent of any wrongdoing. But the complaints are made. Most complaints are made by clients, some are made by lawyers, and a few by judges.

More than half of all disciplinary complaints result in no action taken against the lawyer, but the lawyer must defend himself or herself at emotional and financial cost.

The important thing with disciplinary complaints is not to win the war, but rather to avoid the battle. A nonmeritorious complaint against you can hurt you no matter how innocent you are of any wrongdoing.

Surveys I've done indicate that more than 50 percent of all ethics complaints are caused by poor or nonexistent client relations, including poor or nonexistent communication with clients. Poor client relations skills result in lost income to the lawyer, unnecessary work for bar counsel, and an erosion of the public's opinion of lawyers and of the legal system.

There is a very basic defect in almost all disciplinary systems in that the file on the lawyer that contains nonmeritorious complaints often stays open forever, or at least as long as the lawyer lives. Assume, for example, that a totally nonmeritorious complaint is made against you. Assume that a full investigation is made and that you did absolutely nothing wrong. Assume it turns out that the client is mentally disturbed or unhappy about a divorce, and in a moment of anger files a complaint that is a "pack of lies." Assume you are completely and totally innocent of any wrongdoing legally, morally, ethically, or otherwise, and that you are totally exonerated.

That nonmeritorious complaint may stay in your file forever. It is possible that additional complaints will be made over the thirty to forty or more years you are in practice. These complaints may also be nonmeritorious, but they will be cumulative files of prior complaints and there may be a "where there's smoke, there's fire" mentality on the person or committee investigating the complaint. You may be prejudiced by prior nonmeritorious complaints.

A convicted felon who pleads guilty and goes to jail may have a right to expunge his record, but an innocent lawyer often has no right to expunge any records. This is the system in many, if not almost all, states. I think it is grossly unfair, but it is the system. Accordingly, the important thing for you to do is to avoid the complaint, not to win the war with the complaining client.

Although what follows may be duplicated in other parts of this book, it is worthwhile to repeat it here in this most vital chapter.

To avoid many, if not most complaints, you should:

1. Discuss fees and expectations and the legal process at the first meeting with clients so that they have an opportunity to understand clearly what you can and cannot do for them, what it will cost, and how long it should take. Use estimates, if necessary.

2. Have a written fee agreement clearly stating what you will do, what you will not do, what is or is not covered by the fees, and any other factors you feel are important to you and to the clients as outlined in Rule 1.

3. Bombard your clients with paper mail, faxes and e-mail, keeping them informed of what is happening, including letters explaining why nothing is happening. The client's file should almost duplicate your file.

4. Return all telephone calls promptly (within two hours, if possible) or have someone take them and return them for you, but never ignore them. If you are unable to make telephone contact with the party, leave a voice-mail message or send an e-mail, postcard, form letter, or fax indicating that you tried to return the call. Put the ball back into their court.

5. Be honest and open when a case is lost. Tell the client as rapidly as possible after you find out. Never lie to a client. The client may come back in the future or refer other clients to you.

6. Be "holier than thou" when handling a client's money. To quote an old proverb (which I just created), "It is better to see your kids without new clothes than to touch the client's trust money." You may wish to use *The ABA Guide to Lawyer Trust Accounts*, which I wrote, or ask me for a complimentary copy of a videotape on trust accounts.

7. Cooperate fully with the next lawyer and the client if you are discharged.

8. Respond immediately to communications from disciplinary boards or investigators. Offer immediate access to yourself and to your files. If you have any questions concerning an investigation, hire an ethics or professional responsibility lawyer. You may wish to call me for a "gut reaction" to your situation. It is possible that if you or your lawyer respond rapidly enough, a file will not be opened on the complaint.

9. Keep accurate time records detailing what you did and when you did it. Retain old records, including notes of telephone calls and conferences, until the statute of limitations for malpractice expires.

10. Read, reread, and remember the ABA Model Rules of Professional Conduct as adopted by your state.

Practicing Professional Responsibility

Legal scholars debate about whether legal ethics and rules of professional conduct are absolute rules of conduct that must be obeyed and that if violated, result in penalties, or whether they are ideal lofty goals that are commendable, but not to be taken seriously in day-to-day practice of the law.

Depending on where you practice, a given rule can be either, or both, or neither. As a practicing lawyer, you must remember that the rules can be imposed by any combination of organizations, including but not limited to the following:

1. American Bar Association
2. Other national bar associations
3. Mandatory or voluntary state bar groups
4. City bar association
5. County bar association
6. Specialty law groups
7. State supreme court
8. State intermediate and lower courts
9. United States Supreme Court
10. United States circuit and district courts
11. State legislature
12. County and city governments
13. Federal, state, county, and city administrative bodies

Some of these groups have their own rules, independently considered and adopted. Some of these groups simply incorporate by reference the rules issued by other groups. As with any law, one body and another body can apply the exact same rule to the exact same set of facts and come up with an opposite result. An ethics professor claimed to have counted the number of independent rules of ethics or rules of practice in the United States governing the conduct of lawyers and found 1,003 different sets of rules that could apply to a lawyer depending on where the lawyer was practicing. I have never confirmed this figure but have no reason to doubt it.

Due to the overlay and interplay of the rules of the various promulgating bodies, you would be wise to contact each group you have contact with on a periodic basis to get a copy of their current rules. You should get the current versions about once a year, but in no event less frequently than every three years. When you ask for the current rules, you should ask if there have been any changes since the last time you updated the rules. You should also ask whether or not there is a mailing list or other distribution list, which will automatically notify you of changes made or under consideration.

While it may seem that this will require an unnecessarily large amount of time and effort, you should remember that it's your license to practice law that you're protecting. You should do at least as good a job for yourself as you would do for a client. If you don't want to do all this work for yourself, then think of your doing all the work to protect those of your family members who depend upon you to provide their sustenance. If you wish, you can think of yourself doing the work to protect the rights of clients of yours and clients of other lawyers who are protected by the rules.

Regardless of your motivating reasons—to protect yourself, your family, your clients, or the legal system generally—the message is rather obvious, which is *get copies of all applicable rules of conduct for your office.*

By having copies available in your office or elsewhere, you will at least have the reference materials to consult when you have a question.

Having copies of the rules that apply to you is the first step in practicing law ethically.

Although most rules are independently considered and adopted, there are more similarities than differences in the various rules.

Many of the organizations that have promulgated rules have made them available on the Internet. As with any Web site, some sites are up-to-date and some are too old to be relied on. The important thing to remember is that there is often more than one set of applicable rules.

A Short History of Our Ethics

It is important to keep clearly in mind that your primary duty of loyalty is to the client rather than to the government or the accuracy of the document. You must have regard and respect for the courts and the government and the transaction, but you must never forget that professionalism and ethics begin with your professional and ethical duty to the client.

It is sometimes helpful to understand a little of our background, as a profession. Scholars have spent lifetimes writing libraries about what is condensed here in a few words.

In 1836, seventy years after our independence, David Hoffman of the Baltimore Bar, wrote "50 Resolutions in Regard to Professional Deportment." In the 1850s, Judge George Sharswood of Pennsylvania used the fifty resolutions in a series of lectures at the University of Pennsylvania and collected the lectures as a scrics entitled "The Aims and Duties of the Profession of Law." After the Civil War, lawyers could become lawyers without going to any law school. They simply opened their office or "read the law" or apprenticed. Abraham Lincoln, a great lawyer, never went to high school or college or law school. He "read the law" under the tutelage of a lawyer. Bar associations came into being to regulate the practice of law and to influence who could or could not become a lawyer. Their rules were normally called "Ethics." In 1887, Thomas Goode Jones of Alabama took the fifty resolutions as modified by Mr. Hoffman, and put them together as the "Alabama Code of Ethics." In 1908, at its first Annual Meeting, the ABA copied the "Alabama Code of Ethics" and called it the "ABA Canons of Professional Ethics." In 1970, the ABA replaced the 1908 "Canons of Professional Ethics" with the "Model Code of Professional Responsibility." In 1983, the ABA replaced the "Model Code of Professional Responsibility" with the "Model Rules of Professional Conduct."

In 1776, the United States revolted from England, adopting the Common Law but rejecting much of the English Law, substituting uniquely American revolutionary concepts of personal freedoms and rights. The United States then adopted our present Constitution, creating the uniquely American system that has lasted into the millennium long after other legal systems in and out of the United States have flourished and died.

It is also important to understand that in the 1500s, England rejected the Civil Law system, which was based on Roman Law. Under the Civil Law, the church controlled much of the wealth and many of the governments of western civilization.

In rejecting the Civil Law, the English Common Law system, which still exists and flourishes in modified form, rejected the role of the Notary.

In existing Civil Law systems throughout the world, Notaries and nonlawyers do about 60 percent of what lawyers do in America. The loyalty and duty of the Notary is not to the individual client, but rather to the government and the transaction.

In ancient Roman Law the advocate did trials and nothing else. Notaries did transactional and what we would call "office law," will, corporations, marriage contracts, deeds, mortgagees, etc. England adopted the Common Law rather than the Roman or Civil Law, but called the two kinds of practitioners "barristers," who did what advocates did and "solicitors," who did what notaries did.

At the American Revolution many lawyers were loyalists and fled to Canada, the Caribbean, or to England, leaving a shortage of lawyers in America. Lawyers were needed to write new laws, handle transactions in a growing economy, and do trial and appellate work. There never was a division in the U.S. between barristers and solicitors as in pre-revolutionary England. Many of the ethical restrictions on what advocates or barristers could or could not do were not carried over into our unified system.

The ABA Model Code of Professional Responsibility and the ABA Model Rules of Professional Conduct

When you start your own law practice, you must know the ABA Model Rules of Professional Conduct to protect your clients and to avoid claims of unprofessional conduct, suspension, or, worse, disbarment. You must also learn your state's version of the rules.

I am justifiably proud of the role of *How to Start and Build a Law Practice* in making lawyers understand they have a professional responsibility. In earlier editions of this book, I refer to the ABA Model Code of Professional Responsibility and the Model Rules of Professional Conduct. Many young lawyers ask questions about problems they face in their everyday practice of law. A large percentage of the questions they ask are answered at least preliminarily in the Model Rules of Professional Conduct. I use the word "preliminarily" because the "final" authority is, of course, the rules of their own state licensing authority.

On the one hand, I am proud that my readers recognize the problem areas as they arise. On the other hand, I am concerned that these lawyers frequently don't have a copy of the Model Code or of the Model Rules in their offices.

I recommend that you reread this section on Professional Responsibility including the preceding short history after you read the other sections of the book. You then will have a clearer understanding of how and why following the suggestions of this book will help you practice law within the limits set forth in the Model Code and the Model Rules.

You may wish to observe the rules out of a sense of obligation to our profession and our society or out of fear of being disciplined or disbarred for violating the rules or fear of malpractice liability. In any case, you must know the rules so you can observe them. Naturally, the rules may be modified in your state or jurisdiction. You must take it upon yourself to learn the history and the interrelation of the Model Rules and the rules of your jurisdiction.

As you go through the rules, you will see that many areas are covered or at least touched upon in this book. Such areas as competence, scope of representation, diligence, communications with clients, fees, procedures to preserve confidentiality, conflict of interest between your clients, conflict of interest with your clients, conflicts with former clients, clients under disability, safeguarding property through trust accounts, declining representation, withdrawing from a case, and many others that appear in the Model Rules are covered in this book.

New lawyers (and, indeed, older lawyers) are sometimes confused by references to "ethics" or "Codes" or "Rules." Although this chapter contains overgeneralizations, I hope it will clear the air a bit.

The original Canons of Ethics of the American Bar Association were adopted in 1908. (I leave you to your law school professional responsibility class notes and other chapters in this book as to the long version of what happened in England and America prior to 1908.) A short history is found elsewhere in this book. The Canons set forth high ethical conduct. Some would say they were goals rather than standards of actual law practice. If you "violated" the Canons you could be kicked out of the voluntary bar associations you belonged to, but you rarely, if ever, got disbarred or disciplined for violating the Canons unless trust funds were involved. The number of lawyers in America was relatively small both in absolute numbers and in proportion to the general population. Law firms were small. Almost all lawyers went to court on occasion, even in the big cities, and the lawyers and judges pretty much knew one another. If they did not actually know one another, in fact, they knew of one another by reputation. If a lawyer did something "unethical," the other lawyers and judges quickly knew about it and the resulting ostracism and damage to reputation were probably more effective in disciplining the lawyer than any formal proceedings, which in some cases were designed simply to give the lawyer a chance to present his side of what did or did not happen in an attempt to clear his name and reputation.

The "judges" of the lawyers were volunteer members of the association who were practicing lawyers and who understood the practical day-to-day problems that arise in a law office. These lawyers preferred a "quiet" type of discipline without publicity that might undermine public confidence in the bar or the legal system. When lawyers were disciplined, they simply were referred to as "Lawyer A" or "Lawyer B," using no real names. Expulsion from the voluntary bar association was often tantamount to being disbarred. This system worked reasonably well to protect both the bar and the public in an America that was rural and where everyone in the legal profession knew one another, either in fact or by reputation. Some bar associations or licensing authorities still have a Canon of Ethics.

By the 1960s the number of lawyers had increased greatly, the lawyers and judges still knew one another but not very well, and lawyers began specializing so that some did not go to court. Firms began getting bigger and anonymity could protect an errant lawyer from the peer pressure of other lawyers and judges. The Canons simply no longer did the job of protecting both the bar and the public. A series of court decisions began eroding seriously the ability of the bar to protect itself or the public through the Canons.

In 1969, the ABA adopted the Model Code of Professional Responsibility to replace the Canons of Ethics. The Model Code contained canons worded in broad statements. It also contained disciplinary rules, violations of which could lead to lawyer discipline, and lofty ethical goals like the old Canons. By the 1970s many states had adopted a mandatory bar (sometimes called "unified" or "integrated").

The mandatory bar by definition is not optional. You cannot practice law without belonging to it and paying "dues," which, in fact, are license fees.

The mandatory bars exist alongside voluntary bar associations, but the mandatory bars have the power directly on their own, or indirectly through the court system, to discipline and disbar lawyers. A lawyer or judge could not escape discipline simply by resigning from a voluntary bar association.

By 1983, the number of lawyers in America had exploded both in regard to the absolute number of lawyers and relative to the population of the country. Law firms had mushroomed in size and numbers of offices to the point that the lawyers in a community did not know one another, and often, even the lawyers in a firm did not know one another. Additionally, by this time, many lawyers never expected to go to court during their entire careers. The ability of the legal profession to police itself through peer pressure, judicial pressure, or general reputation clearly had collapsed.

Lawyers who specialized either never knew why some of the rules existed or, if they had once known, forgot through lack of contact with the area of law or client relations involved in the rules.

Peer pressure and a sense of *noblesse oblige* could no longer protect others, the rights of clients, or the role of the bar within our society.

Accordingly, by 1983, it became necessary for the ABA to adopt the Model Rules of Professional Conduct. These Model Rules are intended to lead to disciplinary action when violated. (There have not been any major revisions since 1983, although I was on the advisory council that considered major changes in the rules that were to take place after the year 2000.) Some changes have been made (e.g., no sex with clients or staff; requiring certain client agreements to be in writing and signed), but very few major changes have been made since 1983.

Allegations of violations of the Model Rules often are investigated by nonlawyers and administered by referees or judges who may have become judges without ever having had a fee-paying (or nonfee-paying) private client in their entire lives. They may come from government service where they neither considered nor dealt with the rules they are now applying to other lawyers.

This is not to suggest they are not serious or competent. This is to warn you that, unlike the judges in the disciplinary hearings of bar associations under the Canons, your judge under the Model Rules may never have had the problems you have. They may have no experience, feeling, or understanding of why you did or did not do what you are accused of. They may never have had to deal with a weeping spouse or parent or family member begging you to help by doing something or not doing something that at the time seemed the human thing to do but that, upon cool, detached study with good hindsight, appears possibly to have violated a disciplinary rule. A practicing lawyer might have compassion and be forgiving, but your judge might not. The body that applies disciplinary conduct may be under pressure, like a district attorney's office, to administer discipline, prosecute a large number of lawyers, and get a high percentage of disbarments to justify the funds being spent on the office and staff.

The ABA Model Rules of Professional Conduct are intended to be the minimal standards that must be followed to avoid disbarment or discipline. Most states have adopted, or will adopt, some form of these Model Rules. Accordingly, the new lawyer must know them.

Again, I recommend most strongly that you read and periodically reread the Model Rules of Professional Conduct. Unfortunately, as of this fifth edition, you cannot get a set of the Model Rules for free. You can, however, contact the ABA Center for Professional Responsibility, which will sell you a set. You may be able to download them for free by going to the Web site of a state that has adopted them.

Ten Commandments
of Good Trust Accounts

New lawyers, without any business courses or training, are expected to manage trust accounts with no experience, necessitating this minimal coverage in this chapter.

Trust account violations are the fast track to disbarment. Most trust account violations are the result of poor management rather than evil intent, but will still be punished.

I have written the book *The ABA Guide to Lawyer Trust Accounts,* which is available from the American Bar Association's Law Practice Management Section. You may have used the book in your law school class on Professional Responsibility or used it in a CLE ethics course. There is also a videotape based on the book entitled "Dos and Don'ts of Lawyer Trust Accounting." I highly recommend reviewing both the book and the videotape as being well worth the time. You should have copies of the book and the videotape or DVD in your current library for new lawyers and office manager education. A complimentary copy of the videotape can also be obtained from me.

The book and tape are practical, not theoretical. They present real-life trust account situations faced by real-life clients with real-life problems.

In this book, I have excerpted and modified two parts of the book, entitled "Ten Rules of Good Trust Account Procedures" and "Ten Steps to Good Trust Account Records."

The book contains many forms and form letters you will find helpful.

Ten Rules of Good Trust Account Procedures

These ten rules are generic. They will apply anywhere in the United States. It is also important to know your local rules and where to get help locally. Get a copy of your local trust account rules. Learn where they can be found on the Internet. Learn the telephone number of the ethics hot line maintained by your state and local bar associations. Learn the name and phone number and e-mail address of the chair of the bar association ethics committee. Don't be afraid to call as many people as you can when you have a trust account question. There are no foolish or stupid questions when it comes to trust accounts.

If you follow the general rules set forth in this section, you'll go a long way toward staying out of trouble.

Rule 1
Have a trust account.

You can't properly use what you don't have. Be sure it is clearly identified as "Client Trust Account" or use some other language that makes it clear that the account is a trust account. At the very least, you should have a checking client trust account, a client trust safe deposit box, and, when appropriate, a savings client trust account. You should have these even though you have no immediate need for them. When you do need them, you'll be ready to go. The account should be in a federally insured institution within the geographic boundaries of your state.

Rule 2
Never let anyone else sign your trust account.

Never allow another person to sign trust account checks. Do not use mechanical or rubberstamp signatures. Do not allow your bookkeeper or secretary or paralegal or spouse to sign on the account. If the trusted secretary or bookkeeper of many years opts for early retirement down in Brazil some Friday afternoon using the latest trust account deposit as the funding for retirement, you will have civil and disciplinary responsibility, including possible loss of license, if you don't cover the defalcation. An intervening defalcation won't relieve you of responsibility.

Rule 3
Obtain and understand your IOLTA (Interest On Lawyers' Trust Account) rules.

Almost every state, if not every state, requires that lawyers put trust account funds into special accounts where the interest on the account goes to fund some activity such as legal aid or a client trust account protection fund. Your state will have such a mandatory system, your bank will have an agreement with the bar organization, and you will have no option but to use the IOLTA account in most situations. Most IOLTA banks are obligated to notify the bar disciplinary authorities if one of your checks is presented against insufficient funds, even if it doesn't bounce. The bar may send out auditors to investigate your trust account. They may investigate your account for many years, looking for mistakes. They might not limit their investigation to the single transaction that caused the bank to notify the disciplinary authorities.

If the amount of interest is likely to be significant because of the amount of money or the length of time, you should not use an IOLTA account, but rather you should open another special trust account for that one client, giving the interest to the client.

The technical issues of whether the interest does or does not exist and whether or not it has been "taken" and who took it has been up and down before the U.S. Supreme Court at least twice and is beyond the scope of this book.

Rule 4
Immediately notify the client every time something is added to the client's account balance and every time something is taken from the account balance.

For your purposes, assume that the interest does or will exist and must go to IOLTA or to your client, and that your client is entitled to accountings even if they are not entitled to the interest.

Rule 5
Unearned fees and unexpended costs belong in the trust account until earned or spent.

Calling the fees a "retainer" or "deposit" or "advanced funds" doesn't change anything. A nonrefundable or minimum or retainer fee can only go to your general account and be spent by you if expressly permitted under your local rules; otherwise, it must go to the trust account. When the fee is earned, you must withdraw the earned fee, notifying the client of the withdrawal and the remaining balance in the account. You do not have to wait for client permission to withdraw the funds, but if the client complains about the fee taken, you must immediately return the funds to the account until the disagreement is resolved. In some cases, the disputed fee need not be entirely returned to the trust account if your fee contract is properly written. Costs expended in accordance with your written fee agreement normally need not be returned to the account if the client complains.

Rule 6
Do not commingle your funds with the client funds in the trust account.

Your funds must be removed immediately upon being earned. You probably may leave a "nominal amount" of your funds in the account to cover check printing and miscellaneous charges to the account. Ask your ethics hot line how much you may keep in the account. Typically, the amount allowed, if any, is $50 to $200.

The IRS will be especially interested in whether you left earned fees in the account on December 31 in order to defer fees into the next taxable year.

Do not pay personal or office expenses from the trust account even if earned. Transfer the earned fees to the general account and spend from there. If you are going to be writing both business and personal checks from the same account, it is better practice to pay your personal bills from a "personal account."

Rule 7
Be sure you understand the exact nature of the item deposited or credited to the trust account.

Do not write checks against the deposit or make advances out of the account until you are positive the deposit is good. If the deposit bounces or is not honored, checks that clear will be cleared against the funds of other clients and you will have compounded the rules violation and created new rules violations.

Rule 8
Reconcile the bank trust account monthly.

If your CPA or office manager does the reconciliation, be sure you have personally examined the reconciliation and are satisfied that your records and the bank statement reconcile to each other. Trust account responsibility cannot be delegated to anyone else. You and your license to practice are personally responsible for others' mistakes.

Rule 9
Reconcile and examine the individual client trust account balances monthly, and do not delay giving the clients their money.

Trust accounts should liquidate in a month or two in most cases. If the funds are in the account more than ninety days, there should be a good reason. By notifying the clients monthly of the balance in their account, the clients will normally inquire as to when they will get their money.

Rule 10
Be alert to third-party claims.

In some states, failure to honor a third-party lien on trust accounts is an ethics violation. In other states, only trust account disputes between the client and the lawyer are covered by ethics rules. If there is an unresolved dispute between third parties or between you and third parties over funds in the trust account, get an ethics opinion and consider interpleading the money into court.

Following these ten rules will help you avoid some of the most common trust account problems.

Ten Steps to Good Trust Account Records

This is a short summary of longer chapters in *The ABA Guide to Lawyer Trust Accounts* describing mandatory trust account records and documents. Use this list for a quick review of how to maintain good trust account records.

1. Get a copy of your current local rules and read them.
2. Give a copy of the rules to your CPA along with a copy of this book and *The ABA Guide to Lawyer Trust Accounts*, so the CPA can set up a "no brainer" system for your office.

3. Be sure you reconcile everything at least monthly.

4. It's all right to use a computer to write checks, record bank deposits, maintain balances, do reconciliations, etc., but be sure you make a hard-copy printout once a month for easy examination at a later time.

5. Maintain a journal. The journal can be the client trust account checkbook. The starting point and main focal point in your system should be the trust account checkbook. A simple, ordinary handwritten checkbook is adequate if you record all deposits, checks, dates, and amounts and explain each item. This will be the source document for all subsequently prepared required records.

6. Keep a client ledger. This is a trust account term, not an accounting term. It is the statutory name (in many states) for a simple running balance by client with all checks, disbursements, dates, amounts explanations, etc., on the card with a running balance calculated after each transaction.

7. Track client balances. This is simply a list of every client trust account balance as of month's end by client name and amount. The total of this list should equal the total of all the individual ledger cards.

8. Do regular bank reconciliations. This is nothing more than the old-fashioned bank reconciliation found on the back of most bank statements on which you reconcile cash per checkbook to cash per bank statement.

9. Do regular triple reconciliations. To be in perfect balance, the reconciled bank balance must reconcile to the client balances total, which must reconcile to the total of all the ledger cards.

10. Keep your financial statements separate. Do not combine or include client trust account cash with other cash balances on the financial statements you give to creditors. It's not yours.

If you follow these ten steps, you should have no difficulty in producing most, if not all, of the required documents and reports when needed.

What to Call Yourself

What you call yourself and put on your cards and stationery and e-mail signature is a matter of combining personal preference and local custom. I will list some of the more common designations.

Whatever you finally decide should make clear that you are a lawyer in order to protect the attorney-client privilege.

You might ask other lawyers in the community what they feel is appropriate.

Some possibilities follow:

1. *Law Offices* or *Law Office of.* This is my favorite. It says you are a lawyer and that you have an office from which you practice.

2. *Lawyer.* This is clear, but for some reason is not common.

3. *Esq.* (not Esquire). This suffix is increasingly being used. At one time there was concern over whether "Esq." might be gender-biased. It is now commonly used by both male and female lawyers.

4. *Attorney-at-Law.* This is common but is looked upon with great disfavor by many foreign lawyers. If your work will have international aspects, you might not wish to use it.

5. *Attorney.* See number 4 above.

6. *Counselor* or *Counselor at Law.* I have never seen this description used without being joined to "attorney" (see below).

7. *Attorney and Counselor at Law.* This is a very common description in New York and New Jersey. It goes back to the ancient distinction between lawyers who only went to court (trial lawyers) called "Advocates" or "Barristers" and nonlawyers who did what lawyers in America do (transactional work) called "Notaries" or "Solicitors."

8. *Honorable.* I have seen this prefix used primarily in smaller Southern cities. It is confused with the prefix used by judges.

9. *Attorney* as a title: "Attorney Jones." This also seems to be used primarily in the South, but is sometimes looked upon with disfavor by foreign lawyers.

10. *A.B., B.S., M.A., M.S.,* etc. I would avoid listing nonlegal degrees as they are not commonly used except by people who have not passed the bar or have obtained a law degree from a "diploma mill" or for some reason are not admitted to practice in the state where they work.

11. *L.L.B, J.D.,* or other law degrees. It is common for people who have gone to some law school somewhere or who have obtained a law degree from a "diploma mill" but who are not licensed to practice to use these descriptions. In my opinion, they often are trying to mislead people into thinking they are licensed lawyers. In some states, one can be criminally prosecuted for calling oneself "J.D." (even if true) if one is not licensed to practice in that state. They carefully avoid the word "lawyer" or "attorney" on their cards or stationery to avoid criminal prosecution for the unauthorized practice of law. If you are a licensed lawyer, there is no reason to list these legal degrees. I would avoid using these designations in order not to be lumped in with the unlicensed people.

12. *Other businesses or professions.* You should be very careful about putting other businesses or professions on your cards and stationery. There may be serious questions as to whether your communications and advice were legal and protected by attorney-client privilege or not legal without the privilege.

13. *Fictitious names.* I have seen lawyers call themselves the "AAAAAA Law Firm" to get their name listed first in alphabetical telephone directory listings. I have seen names that are indicative of a type of practice, such as "The Litigation Firm" or "The Litigation Association Firm" or "The Family Law Firm." I have seen names that apparently get people's attention but don't indicate what kind of law is being practiced. "Bitches from Hell," I guess, is intended to convey the image of an aggressive, all-female law firm.

14. *Military and Civilian Decorations.* Americans may not use "Sir" in their titles. It goes back to Benjamin Franklin. Accordingly, although I have, in fact, been knighted, I may not use "Sir" as a prefix. I cannot use my foreign government decorations (which I do have) or military decorations (which I don't have).

Note: There may or may not be a problem if a solo practitioner calls himself or herself a "Firm." It's up to you to learn the local customs where you intend to practice.

Dealing with Foreign Lawyers

If you are going to have communications with foreign lawyers, you must be careful and must advise your client to be careful.

Almost every foreign lawyer hired by major foreign law firms in the last ten to twenty years speaks and writes fairly well in English. They probably spent a year in the U.S. or U.K. or other English-speaking country to improve their spoken and idiomatic English. They may have taken a course at an American law school in comparative systems or some other subject.

Do not assume that because they speak English well, they are knowledgeable about U.S. laws.

In civil law countries, what we in America call the practice of law breaks into two or more categories:

Attorneys—Advocates—only go to court. Normally communications with them are privileged.

Notaries—Notaries do transactional work. They may or may not have some legal education but they are not advocates. Communications with them may not be privileged, even though they are affiliated with lawyers. Often drafts of contracts are discoverable as well as communications to and from the client. A notary may have gone to law school and might even have been licensed as a lawyer, but if he or she is practicing as a notary, the attorney-client privileges may be lost or deemed never to have existed.

Consultants—Many nonlawyers call themselves "consultants" to avoid charges of practicing law without a license. Communications are probably not privileged in commonwealth countries (former British Colonies, etc).

In other countries the word may be an umbrella for what in America would be practicing law.

Taxation and Tax Consultants—Again, communications probably are not privileged and are attainable on discovery.

In order to protect your client's interests and your malpractice exposure, you should ask the person with whom you are dealing whether communications will or won't be privileged from process.

Buying and Building a Law Practice

This is a new concept that might work for you if you are going to start your law practice after leaving a job where you have been exposed to the practice of law or if you already have about a year or two of practice under your belt. You might consider buying into an existing law practice and using that existing practice as a platform for building your own law firm.

The practice of most solo senior lawyers begins to taper off when they reach age 55 to 65. Their clients die, the people who referred them work retire or die, and the practice normally begins a slow process of withering, often leaving only probate and trust work.

Consider making an arrangement with a senior lawyer where you buy into his or her practice at a very slow pace while building your own practice.

Purely as a hypothetical, after determining price, you might want to buy in at 10 percent down and thirteen annual payments with interest, you would be compensated at an hourly rate for any work done on "his" or "her" clients and contribute a small percentage on a sliding scale toward overhead from the work done on "your" clients. After ten years, he or she is paid in full and continues to get some income for another three years. He would continue to be compensated at an hourly rate for the work on either your clients or his clients. In summary, each of you receives compensation from the work you do, and your percentage of the practice increases as the senior's decreases. After thirteen years, the senior (or elder) is cashed out. (The time periods could be shortened.)

The foregoing is a hypothetical fact situation we are just beginning to deal with in open market practice sales and procedures.

You may wish to visit **www.lawpracticesales.net** for a list of opportunities. Hopefully, it will be functioning by the time this edition is out.

Avoiding Disciplinary Problems

In preparing an earlier version of this book, the National Academy of Law, Ethics & Management (**www.Nalem.org**) conducted an informal survey of Bar Counsel and Professional Liability Lawyers to determine the areas where lawyer deficiencies in client relations and office management were present in disciplinary complaints.

Between 98 and 100 percent of the respondents listed fifteen areas as being "very important" or "important" areas of management and client relations deficiencies present in bar complaints.

This book has addressed all fifteen areas and has given the reader some help and guidance in avoiding these problems and or resolving the problem areas.

The top fifteen most important areas of deficiency (in order of ranking) are as follows:

Topics 1 through 11 tied at 100 percent:
1. Trust accounts
2. Managing telephone communications
3. Managing written communications
4. Written fee agreements
5. Fee disputes
6. Unconscionable fee agreements
7. Conflicts problems
8. Accepting work when underwater with existing unfinished work
9. Withdrawal and attorney substitution problems
10. Illegal fees
11. What to do when the State Bar knocks on your door

Topics 12 through 15 tied at 98 percent:

12. Calendar, tickler, and case review systems

13. Delays or untimely length of case (alleged incompetence or procrastination)

14. Unconscionable fees (padding of bills)

15. Nonperformance of work after accepting fees

Although the ranking of problem areas may change a bit from year to year, the basic problems are the same.

When you have a problem or think you might have a problem in any of these areas, you should get some help in order to avoid the filing of a complaint against you.

Part VIII
Resources and Advice

Where to Go for Help

Most lawyers reading this will have almost no knowledge of how to manage a law practice. Therefore, you should increase your knowledge immensely just by reading this one publication.

This publication should go a long way toward getting you started in the creation and building of your law practice.

This book is only intended to get you started. You may soon find that you need more resources than are available here.

When I first decided to write this book I spent several hours in a university law library looking for sources of materials for new lawyers. I then had one of my law clerks spend weeks going through the sources that I had found, plus finding additional sources I had missed.

I soon realized there was no one single book that could help new lawyers and so decided to write this book. The current catalog of recommended ABA publications for solo and small firm lawyers includes more than 300 books and materials costing many thousands of dollars and requiring a huge amount of time to absorb. I have tried to create this one single book that will satisfy the needs of lawyers starting a practice.

Join the American Bar Association's Law Practice Management Section and you'll receive the periodical *Law Practice*, and also consult back issues. On balance, *Law Practice* will be an investment, not an expense.

There are many other good publications available. As with the law library, it's a question of balancing the value of the publication to a new lawyer against the expenditure of cash, which is in short supply to the new lawyer.

593

This book is intended to teach basics, which do not ordinarily change radically in a short time. However, law office management and administration is now mushrooming as an occupation, and there are major changes occurring due to technological advances in computer technology, communication, document reproduction, increasing use of nonlawyers in the office, etc.

Therefore, until you are established, as a general rule, you should stay away from hardbound publications that may become rapidly obsolete and dated; and as a general rule, you should concentrate on bar-sponsored periodicals during your first few years.

Books, Pamphlets, Etc.

I hesitate to recommend a book today that may be obsolete or out of print by the time you need it; however, I strongly recommend that you keep current on those materials available through the publications of the American Bar Association Law Practice Management Section. For relatively few dollars you can have a library that is up-to-date, with systems that in most cases are easily adaptable to your office.

Courses, Conferences, Etc.

It should be kept in mind that there are many opportunities during the year to attend programs and workshops put on by various organizations. Some of these have a service-to-the-profession aspect. (I try to present my programs as lawyers helping lawyers) Some are simply infomercials being put on by organizations with something to sell. I personally believe that courses taught by practicing lawyers free of infomercial sales motivations are the best and most sincere. On the other hand, some prefer the programs put on by consultants believing that they may have a broader exposure to different practices and can better recommend systems to replace your systems even if the recommendation is for something they sell. A little careful planning will enable you to combine these programs with your vacations, getting at least a partial income tax deduction for the travel expenses involved. (See chapter on "The Importance of Continuing Education.")

Getting Free Management Help from Your Local Law Practice Management Advisor

Law practice management advisors provide free or low-cost unbiased telephone advice to lawyers who call for help. There may or may not be one available to you in your state. Depending on their setup, they may or may not make office visits. They often can help you with quick answers to common questions in your particular state or area. They are known by a variety of titles. They normally are funded by the state bar, but are sometimes funded by malpractice carriers. In some cases they are funded or supported by the solo and small firm sections of their state or local bars.

As of the time of this writing, there were advisors of one sort or another in many states. The first Law Office Management Advisory Service (LOMAS) in the United States was created in 1976 in Florida under J.R. Phelps, and as of this writing, there are advisors in the states of Florida, New York, Washington, Oregon, Arizona, New Jersey, South Carolina, North Carolina, Georgia, Connecticut, Colorado, Oklahoma, Texas, Alabama, Tennessee, Missouri, Virginia, and the District of Columbia, as well as several Canadian provinces.

They are fairly current on what's hot in technology. They are sometimes able to help in a variety of management areas including computer hardware, software, noncomputer equipment, staff management, staff training and compensation, filing systems, local file retention rules, trust accounts, impaired lawyer problems, various insurance coverage and costs, vendor support numbers, and purchasing. No one person or consultant or salesperson could possibly be current in all areas of management. These advisors can communicate with one another through an e-mail listserve provided by the Law Practice Management Section of the ABA. They also have periodic meetings to share problems and solutions. At the present time, these meetings are funded by the ABA LPM Section. Currently, the e-mail listserve is closed, but hopefully it will open up as a listserve to benefit all lawyers, both inside and outside of the ABA.

I personally am proud of my role in organizing and promoting this source of management help for new and experienced solo and small firm lawyers. (They will also help government, large firm, and corporate lawyers, but they predominantly help solos and small firms.) I personally wrote and presented the resolution to the House of Delegates of the ABA encouraging the creation of these management advisory services. I helped create the first management advisory service in 1973 after a visit from the bar's first management advisor, Carrie Rubin of New South Wales, Australia. I recommended Carrie visit the office of Sam Smith and Charlie Robinson in Florida. Sam became President of the State Bar of Florida and a Chair of the ABA Law Practice Management Section. Charlie also later became a Chair of the ABA LPM Section. Sam and Charlie got Florida Bar to be the first American group to start a practice management advisory group, and they interviewed and hired J.R. Phelps. I also helped the funding of their organizational meetings by getting financial support for them to meet and organize from the ABA Standing Committee for Solos and Small Firms during my membership on that committee.

The help you get from your local advisor should be independent advice free of influence from the various for-profit vendors who sell their products and services to lawyers. If your state does not yet have a law practice management advisory service, you should actively lobby to create the positions within your bar.

The following list spells out many but not all of the ways a practice manager can help a sole practitioner or small-firm lawyer:

1. Suggest computer software to meet lawyers' needs.
2. Suggest hardware to meet lawyers' needs.
3. Provide CLE speakers and subjects and plan programs and Town Hall meetings on law office management.
4. Answer questions about starting a law practice alone or with others.
5. Answer questions about dissolving a law firm.
6. Answer questions about leaving a law firm.
7. Advise on closing a law office.
8. Advise on equipping and opening a new law office.
9. Advise on noncomputer equipment.

10. Answer trust account management questions.

11. Help install tickler systems.

12. Do staff training.

13. Answer general accounting questions.

14. Answer questions concerning possible conflicts or direct the lawyer to the appropriate ethics hotline or agency.

15. Answer ethics questions, or direct the lawyer to the appropriate "hot line" or agency.

16. Answer questions about client relations.

17. Answer marketing questions (getting clients).

18. Answer questions about profit distribution.

19. Answer lawyer compensation questions.

20. Answer staff compensation questions.

21. Suggest solutions to personnel problems.

22. Help with filing systems.

23. Answer questions concerning file retention.

24. Answer questions concerning records retention.

25. Answer quality-control questions.

26. Answer impaired-lawyer questions.

27. Install loss prevention programs.

28. Suggest damage control in malpractice situations. (Called claim intrusions or claim instruction.) (In those states where the program is malpractice-claim-prevention driven.)

29. Suggest commercial private consultants or vendors where appropriate to the size or needs of the firm.

30. Answer library questions.

31. Assist with purchase and provisions of malpractice insurance from competing companies. (In some states.)

32. Assist with purchase and provisions of medical insurance.

33. Assist with purchase and provisions of life insurance.

34. Assist with purchase and provision of liability insurance.

35. Help design forms.

36. Assist with disaster preparedness.

37. Help with real-time "fix-it" problems.

38. Recommend currently appropriate equipment and software support hotlines provided by vendors.

39. Do malpractice prevention audits. (In those states where program is malpractice-claim-prevention driven.)

40. Mandatory visits subsequent to discipline complaints or malpractice claims.

41. Write management articles and columns for bar journals.

42. Obtaining bar association and third-party funding for speakers and programs similar to my CLE program on "How to Make Money and Stay Out of Trouble."

How Practice Management Advisors Deliver Information

1. Telephone communication is the most common method of assisting lawyers with their questions. Florida Bar LOMAS and others provide a toll-free 800 number available to every lawyer in the state.

2. E-mail is used when the lawyer wants e-mail.

3. U.S. mail is used for reprints of lengthy articles.

4. Fax and e-mail are commonly used for short documents.

5. Town Hall CLE conferences are used to attract large numbers of solos and small-firm lawyers to one time and place.

6. On-site single-firm consultations are sometimes done subject to available resources.

7. Multifirm workshops for firms in the less-populated or more-remote geographic areas are commonly done.

8. Multifirm retreats are held.

9. CLE programs are produced on law practice management subjects, in live format and videotape format, for multiple presentations throughout the state and at annual conventions.

10. CLE speakers and subjects are provided for local bar association meetings.

11. Mandatory visits are made to law offices when directed by disciplinary authorities or to assist impaired or deceased lawyers.

Getting Management Help from the Internet and Discussion Groups

There are many discussion groups open to you to give you help with specific management and substantive law problems.

A list of some of the discussion groups currently open to you can be found on the Internet at **http://www.abanet.org**. There are also discussion groups open to you through many state and local bar associations.

The listserve **solosez@abanet.org** is especially worthwhile for new lawyers. The questions and responses found there are typical of the problems faced by new lawyers and lawyers in solo and small firms facing a problem for the first time. Some of the materials in this edition of *How to Start and Build a Law Practice* had their origins in solosez.

The listserve found at **www.SeniorLawyers.org** is helpful for starting, maintaining, or closing a law practice.

A new lawyer, or a lawyer considering going into practice alone or with others, would benefit greatly from spending a few minutes each day on solosez.

There are literally hundreds, if not thousands, of Web sites and various legal resources available on the Internet. Many are very dated. It is difficult, if not impossible, to recommend specific Internet resources.

Law schools and law firms and governments provide huge amounts of information. When you surf the Internet looking for help, you could get lucky or waste huge amounts of time.

I would recommend you ask for help from a discussion group as to the problem(s) you have before you spend a lot of time on the Internet looking for help with management problems.

You might wish to visit one of my Web sites to get an idea of how you might use other Web sites or create your own. My Web sites currently include: **www.FoonbergLaw.com, www.HowtoStartand Build.com, www.estatecontests.com, www.fractionaljetownership. com**, and **www.gettingclients.com**. My **www.FoonbergLaw.com** Web site will direct you to free management tips and other information.

As the Internet continues to expand, you will find it to be of more and more help to you.

The Importance
of Continuing Education

If on January 1 of a given year you know all the law there is to know in any typical area of law, and if for one year you make no attempt to "keep current," at the end of the year you will be an expert on what the law used to be. You went to law school to learn legal principles and to spot legal issues. If you learned well, your legal education will probably last you about five years. You must keep up with the law.

The First Two or Three Years of Your Practice

There are many courses and seminars offered by universities and various institutes. In the main, these courses are too expensive for the new lawyer and are not suited to your needs. The costs run as much as several hundred dollars. The basic courses are too far below your level of experience, and the sophisticated courses are too far above your level of experience. In some states, the state university with the state bar puts on low-cost programs with excellent textbooks. Fees of $65 to $95 for a two- or three-hour program, including the book, are reasonable and worth the price. Therefore, although continuing education is important, getting it cheaply can be difficult. In my opinion, the cheapest and easiest ways to keep current are as follows:

1. *Daily Legal Newspaper.* These papers are often free or low in cost your first three to six months. They normally contain cases of interest to practicing lawyers.

2. *Bar Association Committee Luncheons and Programs.* You can get the benefits of experienced lawyers' views and a meal and help for the price of a luncheon or an hour or two out of the office.

3. *Bar Association Journals.* The state and local bar journals are excellent low-cost sources of new legislation and major cases as well as "How-to-Do-It" articles.

4. *Audiotapes and CDs.* Audiotapes and CDs run anywhere from a few dollars to $25 or $35 for a one-hour tape. The advantage to audiotapes and CDs, in my opinion, is that you can listen to them in places where it's not practical to read, such as your automobile on the freeway or on public transportation.

Unfortunately, some performances are dull and boring. The panelists or speakers often read prepared papers into a microphone with all the emotion and feeling of a log. The tapes and CDs sometimes constitute a traffic hazard by putting you to sleep on the freeway. Some refer to charts and overhead displays without repeating orally what is seen visually. I suggest that you try a few and form your own opinion. The audiotapes are normally available from or through various state bar associations as well as through other commercial sources. The bar journals will usually contain information on the availability of the tapes. When you can afford it, get my audiotape series on *How to Get & Keep Good Clients* or the set on *How to Make Money and Stay Out of Trouble.* I've tried to make them both informative and interesting. (For information go to **www.Foonberg.com**)

5. *Videotapes.* Excellent videotapes are available from varied sources on varied subjects. The commercial tapes are normally best because they use speakers who are interesting as well as informative. They often are truly infomercials trying to get you to hire the speaker or the speaker's sponsor. The American Bar Association Section of Law Practice Management videotapes, for example, use only entertaining speakers. University tapes and local bar association tapes are often a waste of time and money because you can't stay awake for the dull, boring speaker. As of the writing of this chapter, DVDs have not yet replaced videotapes for CLE.

The State Bar of Wisconsin has excellent videotapes.

You could make your own videotapes or DVDs or CDs for training lawyers and secretaries, and for informing clients. Additionally, you can "write off" or deduct for income tax purposes video equipment that you use in your practice.

After Two or Three Years

1. *Non-Practice Areas.* After you have been out of school two or three years, you will have started your downhill decline in those

areas in which you haven't had any practice. Therefore, some of the institutes and seminars that would have been below you right out of law school are no longer below you and are worth the expense if you want to keep some familiarity with the area.

2. *Practice Areas.* If you are, in fact, doing some work in the subject area of the seminar or institute, then these courses are worth their weight in gold. You must, however, undertake the courses with the proper perspective. In most courses, you should already know 85 to 95 percent of the material before you attend. Your purpose in attending should be to pick up a few "pointers" or tips. I've never yet attended a seminar where I didn't pick up one or two tips or techniques.

I've traveled many thousands of miles and spent many thousands of dollars to attend seminars and institutes that lasted from one to five days. I've never been disappointed because I maintained the proper perspective. To put it another way, if you don't know 85 to 95 percent of what you'll hear before you get there, then perhaps you're not as sharp as you think you are.

Follow the Leaders

If you don't believe that continuing education is important, look around you when you go to a program. You'll see the "specialists" and lead lawyers in the big law firms. They know the importance and value of continuing education.

Time Records

Record your continuing legal education under a category entitled "Continuing Legal Education." You may need this time record for CLE or certification or specialization programs.

Getting Maximum Tax Dollar from Your Educational Expenses

Amounts spent to maintain your skills as a lawyer are deductible for income tax purposes, including transportation, meals, and lodging away from home as well as the tuition charges.

With a little careful planning, you can combine your educational expenses with a rest away from your office. Courses today are offered on cruise ships and resorts as well as in hotels and classrooms. Another advantage in attending courses away from home is the opportunity to meet lawyers from other areas of the state or country who can give you new or different approaches or perspectives in areas you deal with. From time to time, you may get some referral business from these lawyers, but this should be a minor factor in attending the program.

Continuing Education—Technology

A new lawyer usually is more technologically advanced than most practicing lawyers. Over a period of time, your knowledge may become obsolete, yet technical competence is a major factor in the cost-effective delivery of legal services. About three years out of law school, and every three years thereafter, you will inevitably need to refresh and update your technical knowledge and skills.

Analyze what you are getting before you spend your money. CLE has become a multi-million dollar business. There are hundreds, perhaps thousands, of CLE providers all seeking your CLE dollar. Some CLE courses are essentially worthless; in some cases, the provider is simply selling credits. Attendees often do knitting, work on their notebooks, and read newspapers during the course. In some cases the presenters are simply doing infomercials trying to establish themselves as experts in order to sell you something. In general, CLE courses presented by currently practicing lawyers and local bar associations will provide the biggest bang for the buck, but in all cases, an analysis must be made of expected benefits. If you don't feel you received the program as advertised, complain and you may get your money back or a credit for another seminar. CLE organizations are very sensitive to complaints, especially when their program is not as advertised.

The Wheel Has Been Invented

At several places in this book I have emphasized that as far as the new lawyer is concerned, the basic principles of starting and building a law practice remain constant over the years. I spent a lot of time and money and made a lot of mistakes learning the lessons I've tried to teach you in this book. This book simply attempts to put the things a new lawyer in practice has to know into one place.

Each edition of this book has taken about two to four years to write. It has been updated five times over a period of more than thirty-five years. It contains useful information gathered from my more than forty years of practice and the experiences of thousands of lawyers, both new and experienced. I've written parts of it on airplanes and in hotel rooms on every continent. On one trip to Morocco and Kenya, I met John P. Clark, a lawyer from Winslow, Arizona. John was interested in this book and told me about an incident that occurred in 1932. An itinerant bookseller approached John in 1932 and offered to show him how to increase his income for a $5 fee. Things were bad during the depression and Winslow, Arizona, was no exception, so John paid the $5.

The sales rep printed up some forms and gave them to John for the $5 fee, telling him to fill out the form at the end of the interview and to give it to the client with the charge filled in. A copy of the form was placed in the client file. (A copy of the form follows this chapter.)

On reflection I'm not sure that the most current computer technology or surveys have given us much new information that wasn't sold for $5 by the itinerant bookseller in Winslow, Arizona, in 1932.

The handwritten original is given to the client at the end of the interview, two copies are kept by the lawyer, one for accounts receivable, one for the client's file.

LAW OFFICES

JOHN P. CLARK

ATTORNEY AT LAW

WINSLOW, ARIZONA

CLIENT'S LEGAL ADVICE MEMO

CLIENT—

FACTS BY CLIENT—

DATE—
ARRIVAL—
DEPARTURE—
FEE—

LAW AS READ—

SEE _____

OPINION BY ATTY.—

Handwritten original given to client at end of interview, two copies kept
by lawyer, one for accounts receivable, one for client file.

How to Manage and Collect Accounts Receivable

Effective management and collection of your accounts receivable is critical for a lawyer, but especially for the new lawyer.

Most accounts receivable problems are the result of credit that never should have been given to begin with. Nonetheless, since you will already have done work for which you have not been paid, you must now face the problem.

What Is an Account Receivable?

Very simply, an account receivable is money people owe you for work done or costs advanced after you have sent them a bill. Until you send a bill, you don't have an account receivable. You have work in process or, if you wish to be fancy, you can call it deferred time, or unrelieved time, or any other number of fancy titles, but it is not an account receivable until after you send a bill.

Professional credit managers and consultants have written volumes of information on this subject. In this chapter I'll try to convey what a lawyer, especially a new lawyer without formal training in accounts receivable collection or management, has to know. Although this chapter may appear lengthy, it contains only the bare minimum of what you have to know.

Reasons for Accounts Receivable Management

1. *Your own cash flow.* You can't pay bills at home or in the office with warm feelings and professional satisfaction. You need cash.

Landlords, secretaries, student loan creditors, booksellers, super-markets, auto repair shops, stationery supply stores, credit card companies, etc., all will insist on cash for payment. The best source of cash is "cash up front." The second best source is your accounts receivable and in-process cases.

2. *To recognize the danger signs at the earliest possible point for those cases that are or may become problem cases for any number of reasons.* Sometimes people don't pay because they can't, or think they can't. Sometimes they don't pay because they don't want to pay. In either case, you may have a problem that can only get worse as time goes on. Your client may be dissatisfied with you or with the way the case is being handled. In either case, you had better find out as soon as possible.

Sometimes a client simply ignores the bill rather than telling you of his or her dissatisfaction. You must find out what is wrong.

3. *To have facts upon which to decide to terminate the professional relationship when the client can't pay the bill or refuses to pay the bill.* It is better to say: "Mr. Jones, you now owe $1,775. You still need $3,500 more work. You haven't paid anything since March when you paid $100 and before that, December, when you paid $100. I'm asking if possibly we should make an arrangement or terminate the case," than it is to say: "Mr. Jones, your bill is overdue. And if you don't pay, I can't work." As a Canadian lawyer said to me, "If you are going to eat crow, it's better to do so when the crow is young and tender than to wait when this crow will be old and tough.

4. *To keep your bad receivable losses as low as possible.* Every business and profession has some bad accounts receivable. You can't avoid them (unless you only work for cash up front). The secret is to keep them as low as possible and to prevent small losses from becoming big losses.

5. *Because every dollar of accounts receivable is 100 percent profit or loss.* Collecting an account receivable is 100 percent profit and not collecting it is 100 percent loss. It is right on the bottom line. Your income as a lawyer is heavily dependent on your not having bad accounts receivable. I have practiced as a CPA and as a lawyer for more than a quarter of a century. I've lost more money on uncollected receivables for good work done than I've lost because a contingency case was lost or because the case was a bad case. In

almost every case my mistake was either in granting credit to begin with or not ending the matter before the client found himself with a huge debt that could not be paid.

Definitions

1. *Bill.* The bill is the document you send wherein you first inform the client that you did the work or advanced the costs and that you expect payment now! The bill is the first communication asking for money for work previously done. The bill might be for a period of time (monthly, etc.), or for a quantity of work done (stages in a proceeding), or work to be done in the future.

2. *Billing.* Billing is the process of preparing and sending the bill.

3. *Statement.* A statement is the document you send after you send the first bill and you are still owed all or part of what you asked for on the first bill. In some cases there will be an overlapping or combining of the statement where you ask for money for work previously billed and a new bill where you ask for money for the first time for new work or costs.

4. *Account Receivable.* What the client owes you after you have sent a bill.

5. *Work in Progress.* A case or matter that is not completed and not ready for billing (probate, contingency case, etc.).

6. *Deferred Time.* The work is done. You could bill the client, but you don't want to just yet. (The case will be over next month and you'll send a final bill, or the client is temporarily upset with the bill and it's better to wait, etc.)

7. *Delinquent.* It is easier for me to give an example than to explain. The time sequence is as follows:

    a. Send Bill no. 1 for work done or to be done (at this point not delinquent).

    b. Send Bill no. 2 for additional or different work done or to be done along with statement for first bill unpaid (at this point still not delinquent).

    c. Send Bill no. 3 for new or additional work done or to be done along with statement for first bill unpaid in whole or in part. *You now have a delinquent account receivable that demands immediate attention.*

Note that I have defined "delinquent" in terms of the number of times you have told the client you wish payment rather than in terms of days, weeks, or months.

8. *Accounts Receivable Listing*. A list of all accounts receivable, normally in alphabetical order.

9. *Accounts Receivable Aging*. A list of all accounts receivable normally showing a "spread" of amounts due by time periods (often combined with a listing).

10. *Priority Accounts Receivable List*. These are the ten or fifteen largest receivables and must be reviewed weekly. These are important clients and cases that must be monitored continually as to whether they are current or delinquent.

11. *Delinquent Accounts Receivable*. This is a case where you and the client have a problem that must be faced. (See definition of "delinquent.")

How to Analyze and Use Account Receivable Information

1. Get the information on all accounts receivable *monthly* (weekly for your ten largest receivables) so you can, in a timely manner, recognize the problems that are developing and have developed. Normally, you get this information when you do billings.

2. Get the information on your ten most serious problems (if you have that many) weekly so you don't forget about them or lose sight of their importance.

3. Always get your accounts receivable information in terms of dollar size, not in terms of alphabetical listing. Pay the most attention to the "biggest," whether or not it is delinquent. Always be aware of whom your major debtors are so you can respond accordingly.

4. Define what a "delinquent" account is for your purposes. I have my own definition, which I consider a "softie" approach, but which works. (See definition no. 11 above.)

5. Decide whether or not you can continue working on the case without payment and, if you can, under what arrangement.

6. Contact client. (See "How to Collect Accounts Receivable" section below.)

    a. First contact: short note from secretary, bookkeeper, or office manager;

    b. Second contact: telephone call from you to client;

     c. Third contact: letter from you to client setting forth telephone call summary.

     7. Decide whether this would be an appropriate time to allow client to make some other lawyer rich before you get in deeper.

     8. Consider refunding all money paid by a client as fees to get out of a bad case before it becomes a serious case. It is better to refund $750 and not collect $1,500 more than it is to do $3,000 more work you'll never get paid for because the client can't or won't pay.

     9. *Never forget* you are your client's lawyer, not the client's partner. You have no obligation, moral or legal, to go under financially just because your client is going under or can't or won't pay for services. Legal aid does exist. There is nothing wrong with your budgeting a percentage of your time for pro bono work (not to exceed 5 percent), but you, and not the client, must decide when you can or should do pro bono work.

How to Manage Accounts Receivable

     You manage accounts receivable by getting the proper information and then acting on that information. Simply knowing about your accounts receivable isn't adequate if you don't do something about them. Obviously, you can't do something about them if you don't have the information. Collecting the accounts receivable is 100 percent profit, since you already have invested the time and money to earn the accounts receivable.

Information Needed

     To maintain a simple, effective account receivable management system, you must have the following information before contacting a client:

     1. How much all of your clients owe you, by dollar amount, largest amount first.

     2. How much a client owes on this matter.

     3. How much a client owes on other matters.

     4. How much work (in dollars) has been done.

     5. How much work (in dollars) remains to be done and over what period of time.

     6. History of payments made (especially dates and amounts of last two payments).

7. When you last discussed fees with the client and what the client said and what you said (you should have a memo to the file on this).

8. What your fee agreement (preferably in writing) requires the client to do and whether or not the client is in default on the agreement.

9. Other factors (client sent you a $25,000 case, or is the brother-in-law of the president of your best corporate client, etc.)

10. The priority accounts receivable list: these are the biggest accounts receivable you have (typically ten to fifteen) and warrant review at least once a week even though not delinquent.

11. The delinquent accounts receivable list: these are accounts receivable that are delinquent.

12. The action accounts receivable list: these are the delinquent receivables that require immediate action. (Don't waste time on a $300 receivable when someone is delinquent $2,200.)

How to Collect Accounts Receivable (Accounts Receivable Collection Technique in Chronological Sequence)

1. Have the bookkeeper (or some person other than yourself) sign and send a short note included with the bill but not typed on the bill to the effect, "It has come to our attention that your account is overdue. If there is a problem, please call me."

2. Have the secretary or bookkeeper call client's bookkeeper or accounts payable person. Be helpful, not threatening: "We notice that your May account of $_____ has not been paid and I'd like to know what to tell Mr. Foonberg." Write down and date the response.

3. Always send the bill to both a company name and a person's name. People don't like seeing their own name on an unpaid bill.

4. The lawyer should call the client and say something to the following effect: "Joe, I'm very concerned that our bill is being ignored, and we're wondering if there is a problem with you. You owe $_____. Nothing has been paid since _____ and there's more work to be done and we want to know what you want to do. I can either concentrate on your problems or my problems, but not both."

Say nothing more. No matter how long the silence, no matter how awkward the silence, say nothing more. The next move is up to the client.

5. Get a commitment. "I'll send you $_____ by _____ and $_____ every week thereafter."

6. Send a letter to the client confirming the new arrangement to be sure there is no misunderstanding.

7. If the client refuses to make a commitment, begin the process of dropping the client.

8. Try to match the client's payment to you with the client's income (pay days, contract or case closing, etc.).

9. If you have a loser, face up to the fact as soon as possible and begin to devote your energies more to the clients who honor their agreements.

10. Remember "Foonberg's Rule"—It is better not doing the work and not getting paid than doing the work and not getting paid.

11. Every lawyer should do some pro bono work, but the lawyer, not the clients, should decide which clients don't pay. The decision should be made before the work is done.

12. The billing is the process of preparing and sending the bill.

13. A statement is the document where you ask for money after you have sent the first bill. In some cases you will be overlapping.

a. Send bill—*not* delinquent.

b. Send statement following the month with first unpaid bill—be aware that a problem may be developing.

c. Send statement the following month with first unpaid bill. You have a problem that demands immediate attention.

14. Decide whether or not you can continue working on the case without payment and, if you can, under what arrangement.

15. Contact client about discontinuing your relationship as his or her lawyer.

Where to Get Cost-Effective Help to Build and Expand Your Practice

As far as I was aware, *How to Start and Build a Law Practice* was the first book devoted to building a law practice. In 1968, when I began doing programs on starting and building a law practice, the subject was considered to be unethical. There was objection to using law school facilities for such programs and we held them in the basement of a savings and loan. The county bar association refused to announce the availability of the programs to new admittees because they thought it was unethical. I had to print the first copies of the first edition of this book at my own expense because its subject matter was considered controversial and possibly unethical.

Today the world has changed. Bar associations, law schools, law firms, and national and international organizations now invite me to speak and lead workshops on practice development. *How to Start and Build a Law Practice* is the all-time bestseller of the American Bar Association and is deemed a classic. I was told that the Law School Library Association has classified this book as the title most stolen from law school libraries in the U.S.A.

My book *How to Get and Keep Good Clients* is the standard reference work for marketing experts. My audiotapes are required listening for associates in megafirms. I have been given CLE's highest honor, the Harrison Tweed Award, for my work. I have been honored by the ABA with the Donald C. Rikli award for lifetime achievement in helping solos and small firms.

Law firms of every size, including the largest and most prestigious law firms in the world, now have marketing directors as part of the administrative staff and marketing committees. They often invite me to lead in-house seminars. These marketing directors are organized into many different legal marketing companies and associations.

There are now many experts on practice development. There are now also many books on the subject. Some of these books have some value. There are many "consultants" who will help you design a firm brochure, television advertising, Internet Web sites, or other media advertising. Public relations experts will get your photo on the society and business pages. Other experts will tell you how to dress, what artwork to hang in your office, etc. There are other experts, besides myself, who will lead "in-house" marketing seminars or workshops for your firm. There are universities that provide seminars and lectures on lawyer marketing; there also are periodicals on lawyer marketing. There are many personal "coaches," trainers, and other individuals who promise you riches if only you will hire them.

I list the foregoing sources not to recommend them, but to advise you that they exist in the event you wish to use them. In the main, I advise great caution in choosing them for the following reasons:

1. They are often directed toward the larger firm that has an established practice and lots of time and money to invest. They often are not responsive to smaller firms and sole practitioners. Those techniques that work for a small firm or sole practitioner are normally applicable to larger firms, but not vice versa.

2. They may require a large "up front" cash outlay now and promise long-term cash results later. New lawyers, sole practitioners, and small firms can't afford the impact on cash flow.

3. They are excellent in helping you self-inventory your problems and self-define your goals, but they don't help you solve your problems or give you the techniques and tools you need to actually get results. (It has been said that a consultant borrows your watch to tell you what time it is and breaks your watch in the process.) They often stir up ambition and desire but leave you unfulfilled in terms of the end product needed.

At the risk of being immodest, I am recommending to you a book I have written, *How to Get and Keep Good Clients,* which took more than fifteen years to complete in its most recent revision because of the rapid changes in defining permissible and nonpermissible practice development methods. The book is now in its third edition. It has received praise from the *New York Times,* the *ABA Journal,* and many other authorities. It is cost-effective and immediately usable for every lawyer in America, especially the sole practitioner and small firms that have limited cash but need immediate results.

All my books are based on four sources:

1. What I have learned from other lawyers in doing more than 1,000 programs and workshops for tens of thousands of practicing lawyers (as well as doctors, architects, dentists, small businesses, etc.) in every state of the Union, every Province in Canada, and on every one of the 7 continents and many foreign countries over a period of more than four decades. Most of these programs were done at bar association conventions where I got input from lawyers from all over the United States and the world. My input is literally from every possible size and type of law practice. Many lawyers from all over the world send me letters and e-mail messages with their success stories, and sometimes their failures, with suggestions. My alumni association is large.

2. Those things that I have applied in my own practice and are successful.

3. Those things that I have advised others to do, which have worked in their practices as reported by their unsolicited reports to me over the years.

4. Those things that are found to be immediately feasible and successful, based on my consulting for law firms and their feedback to me. The book I am recommending, *How to Get and Keep Good Clients,* has been heavily borrowed from and used by many of the nation's leading "consultants" and law firms. Just as this book is the most stolen law book in the United States, I believe the book *How to Get and Keep Good Clients* has been heavily stolen.

How to Get and Keep Good Clients assumes an existing practice and deals only with marketing and getting paid for work done. This book, *How to Start and Build a Law Practice*, devotes itself to both management and entry-level practice development. It assumes a starting point of zero experience. Most of the work, then, has to be done by the lawyer and indeed can be done by the lawyer prior to opening his or her doors. This book also provides a master plan where all of the actualities are integrated. The basic concepts and lessons of *How to Start and Build a Law Practice* would apply to any lawyer in America.

Much of the work detailed in *How to Get and Keep Good Clients* can be done and indeed should be done by either lawyers or nonlawyers. *How to Get and Keep Good Clients* uses some of the same fundamental concepts as *How to Start and Build a Law Practice*, but recognizes that the existing law practice has the demands of clients, staff members, and family members co-existing with the desire to get and keep better clients. Each of the techniques in *How to Get and Keep Good Clients* can be applied one at a time in any sequence that the particular lawyer wishes to implement. Many of the techniques can be used or not used by an individual lawyer, depending on whether or not he or she feels comfortable with the technique. There is no need for every lawyer in the firm to do the same thing at the same time. Those who are comfortable utilizing the most number of techniques will become the better "client-getters." Others may still remain good technicians, who can just "get along" with existing clients, as their success or failure may not be dependent on client-getting abilities. *How to Get and Keep Good Clients* also assumes a practice/experience frame of reference so that the individual lawyer can understand why some prior activities were successful and some were not.

Although there is a small amount of common ground in the two books, I recommend that every lawyer have both books and that they periodically re-read each one.

How to Get and Keep Good Clients is the most cost-effective practice development investment you can make. My agreement with the American Bar Association provides a 100 percent refund to any purchaser who is not happy with the book for any reason. *How to Get and Keep Good Clients* is a runaway best-seller because it works and lawyers recommend it to each other. If you are interested, contact the American Bar Association, or The National Academy of Law Ethics and Management (1-800-556-2536), or contact my office at 310-652-5010 or my Web site at **www.FoonbergLaw.com**. The book is also available in an audiotape and audio disc series consisting of tapes or discs as you wish. I guarantee it will help you make more money and improve client satisfaction with very little effort.

If you or your CPA or bookkeeper want to learn how to manage your trust account to avoid disbarment, I recommend my book *The ABA Guide to Lawyer Trust Accounts*.

I will also suggest *How to Draft Bills Clients Rush to Pay*, Second Edition, which I have coauthored with J. Harris Morgan. My part of the book suggests different billing methods to help the client afford your fee.

Foonberg's Short Course in Good Client Relations

If this chapter looks familiar to you, it may be because it has been reprinted in many bar journals both within and outside the United States.

This chapter is intended to give you a five-minute course in good client relations. It also is intended to be a teaser to entice you to buy my book *How to Get and Keep Good Clients* when you can afford it.

Each of the sixty-seven tips here on what to do or not do is expanded and is a part of my other book, in a two- to five-page chapter on how to do it.

How to Get and Keep Good Clients, subtitled "Fundamental Techniques of Lawyer Marketing for Solo Practitioners and Small Law Firms," contains more than 200 different techniques with how-to-do-it checklists and forms. I sincerely recommend to you this compendium of techniques for busy lawyers. I insisted, as a condition of my contract with the publishers, that it be sold with a money-back guarantee.

Why 67 Rules? 67 is the number representing all 10 Canadian provinces, all 50 US states, and all 7 continents where I have done presentations for law firms, bar associations, law societies, law schools, and others. (50 plus 10 plus 7 equals 67.) I believe I am the only person in the world to have had this opportunity to teach and learn from other lawyers what does and what does not work.

In June of 2003, I had the honor of addressing the Law Society of Newfoundland-Labrador, Canada; hereby reaching a milestone on a journey that began thirty-seven years ago, when I began doing

Marketing and Practice Development programs for CLE and law firms. At each program there were questions and other panelists. I not only taught, I learned what works and what doesn't work. I have learned that these Rules apply in many languages, many legal systems, and many cultures. Fads come and go, but basics remain the same. These 67 rules are among the basics.

On my more than forty-year journey, which still continues, I have learned that these 67 rules work. They have worked for other lawyers and firms throughout the world and they will work for you.

1. Always carry high-quality professional cards.

2. Always offer clients and other visitors coffee or a soft drink while they wait in the reception area.

3. Be sure your reception area contains periodicals indicative of the kind of practice you want people to think you have.

4. Be careful when you answer the question, "What kind of law do you practice?" Don't limit yourself or your firm.

5. Always send thank-you letters when someone refers you a client.

6. Always send thank-you letters to the witnesses who testify for your side (if the local rules permit).

7. Either return all calls yourself or be sure that someone returns them for you. Return all calls before the end of the day and preferably within two hours.

8. Always send clients copies of all "correspondence in" and "correspondence out."

9. Dress the way you would expect your lawyer to dress if you were a client paying a fee.

10. Always get as much cash up front as possible from new clients. This is known as "Foonberg's Rule" and is a modification of Lincoln's statement that when a client has paid cash up front, the client knows he has a lawyer and the lawyer knows he has a client.

11. Always be sure that your fee agreement is in writing.

12. Always send your clients Christmas cards or Seasons Greetings cards.

13. Remember that your invoices are a factor in your clients' opinion of you.

14. Dump the dogs. Get rid of the "Bad News" cases and clients as soon as you know you have a problem before they really give you problems.

15. Learn how to convert "social consultations" at weddings, etc., into paying clients by being attentive, letting the person know they may have a serious problem and suggesting they come into your office where you have facilities for helping them.

16. Remind the nonlawyers in the firm that they can also refer their friends' legal matters to the firm.

17. When a staff member refers a client, give the staff member a praise in a memo that goes to everyone in the office to remind them that they can also refer clients to the firm.

18. Remember that immediate availability is the single most important factor in your being selected or not being selected after you are recommended.

19. Always send a tax news letter in November, reminding clients of new tax laws that might affect them. Be sure you remind them that cash basis taxpayers can only deduct legal fees if they pay them before December 31st. Show the client how a bill can be tax deductible if possible.

20. Send clients "no activity" letters when a case is inactive for ninety days or more.

21. Always discuss fees and payment schedules at the first meeting and confirm your discussion in writing.

22. Always remind the client that the firm has a good reputation in the community.

23. Always reassure the client that you have handled similar cases to theirs (if true). Clients don't like being used for educational purposes.

24. Calendar ahead and remind clients of the need for annual minutes of shareholders or directors meeting, lease renewals, judgment renewals, etc.

25. Recognize and appreciate that clients have a high anxiety level when they go to see a lawyer. Be prepared to meet it.

26. Be careful if you adjust a bill downward so that the client doesn't think that you were deliberately overcharging to begin with.

27. Be sure that you and not the clients decide which clients are going to get free legal work before you do the work.

28. When collecting fees, try to match clients' payments to you with clients' receipt of money or cash flow.

29. Always be firm and in control in your manner with clients when discussing the case or discussing fees. If you act wishy-washy

or wimpy, your clients will quickly lose confidence in you and stop using you and stop recommending you.

30. Don't complain about how hard you're working. The prospective client may feel you have no time to devote to their matter and go elsewhere.

31. Always use high quality legal stationery for client communications with your address clearly legible. Use large-sized fonts for correspondence with senior clients.

32. Always have some hard-back, firm chairs in the reception room for injured or elderly clients.

33. Always introduce your clients to your secretary and to paralegals and/or associates who will be working with them or on the case.

34. Always get new clients into the office to meet them before giving them any legal advice whenever possible.

35. Be wary of clients who have lots of complaints about their former lawyers. It is probably just a matter of time until you are on that list of lawyers.

36. Always communicate to a new client that what the client tells you is normally covered by attorney-client privilege and that you won't discuss the client's affairs with other people.

37. When an interview is over, stand up, walk to the office door, and tell the client that the interview is over and walk them back to the reception area or elevator.

38. When the case is over, send a letter to the clients thanking them for the opportunity to have been of service to be sure they are not expecting you to do more work on the case.

39. When a client offers you a cash fee saying "nobody will know," don't forget that the client knows and may be setting you up for blackmail.

40. When a case is lost, be simple, direct, and honest. Tell the client by phone or in person as soon as possible and follow up with a letter.

41. When quoting settlements, be sure the client understands the difference between gross settlements and net settlements after fees, costs and liens and acknowledges the difference in writing.

42. When quoting fees, be sure to cover (in your fee agreement) the difference between fees and costs and what the fee does and does not cover.

43. When collecting fees, remember that people are more willing to pay for what they desperately need and don't have now than

for what they used to desperately need and already have. Clients are more eager and willing to pay before the work is done than after the work is done. They will feel better and you will feel better if you get an advance retainer check before you do the work.

44. Always ask a client whether to send mail and e-mail to the home or the office or if the client wants to pick up the mail (to keep information from getting into the wrong hands).

45. Keep a photo of your children or family on your desk facing you to remind you of your unpaid bills and your need to be sure that the clients clearly understand and can meet their financial obligations in the case.

46. Have someone call your office for you while you listen in and see if you are satisfied with the way your phones are handled. See if the receptionist projects a helpful attitude or is simply functioning as a human answering machine. Remember, people can and do hang up and call other lawyers when they're not happy with the way their call is handled.

47. Remember to give the client a road map of the matter at the first meeting, telling the client what will happen, when it is likely to happen, and what it is likely to cost.

48. Remember the clients want you to listen to them tell their story. Remember you have 2 ears and 1 mouth. It was intended that you listen 2/3rds of the time and only talk 1/3rd of the time. Otherwise you would have two mouths and one ear.

49. At the end of an interview, always ask the question, "Is there anything you want to ask me or tell me?" Tell the client, "I don't want you to leave here upset that you never had a chance to tell me something you wanted to tell me or ask me something you wanted to ask me."

50. Limit your pro bono work to 5 percent of your time or you may become pro bono yourself. Tell clients and potential clients that you do pro bono work, but must limit it to 5 percent of your time.

51. Be very careful of conflicts when you have more than one client in a matter. Be sure to get appropriate waivers and consents to avoid being conflicted out of the matter without getting paid. Clients will appreciate your strict compliance to ethical rules. If there are two or more people in the room, ask yourself (and them), "Who is the client and why are the others in the room?" Have forms ready to cover the various situations.

52. Be flexible and creative in helping the client figure out ways to pay for the legal services they need. They will appreciate your

working with them and both you and the client can avoid unreasonable expectations. They might appreciate and be receptive to alternate billing methods.

53. Be sure you have a web site. When you are recommended, clients will often check you out on the Internet before deciding to call you. Include your areas of practice. Try to include your full name in your web site URL and in an e-mail address, so that clients can contact you by simply remembering your name.

54. Consider having a Web site that includes your geographic area of practice for potential clients looking for a lawyer in a particular city, county, state or neighborhood.

55. Be sure a caller can immediately reach a live operator without several minutes of voice-mail hell. Clients are often nervous or upset and often do not have the patience for voice-mail prompt systems. If you are not in the office, the receptionist should ask callers if they wish to speak to another person or leave a voice mail message. This may deter a potential client from calling another lawyer when you are not immediately available.

56. Remember that a client or potential client is more likely to choose you based on your friendliness and demeanor than on your legal skills.

57. Remember that Yellow Pages are extremely effective in attracting certain types of work in certain communities. Do not advertise in the Yellow Pages unless your staff is trained on how to handle the calls which the ads produce.

58. Add clients' names to your spell checker to reduce the possibility of misspelling their name.

59. Keep a written list of who refers clients to you and to whom you refer clients and review it at least once a year.

60. Calendar client birthdays, anniversaries, or other important events to send cards or e-mail greetings when appropriate. Be sure to have the names of your own spouse and children and clients' secretaries on the list.

61. Prepare a written document to be given to the receptionist on duty listing the most important clients and the difficult clients and how to work with them. Include how the clients' names are pronounced. Indicate who covers for whom when the called person is not available.

62. If you have not spoken with a client in ninety days, call the client just to say hello. Start the call with: "I'm not calling on any

specific legal matter. I'm just calling to see how things are going as we haven't spoken in a while." These calls often result in a new legal matter that needs attention.

63. Protect your mailing addresses (postal and e-mail) if you move or your zip code or domain are changed. Have mail forwarded even if you will also get junk mail and spam. Clients get very upset when they get mail returned "return to sender" or "undeliverable." Be sure to renew the forwarding services and notifications when they would otherwise expire and keep a stack of notices to send out every time you receive a forwarded item.

64. Protect your phone number and fax number if you move or if the area code changes. Have your phone calls and faxes forwarded to the new numbers. Clients get upset when they hear "This number is no longer in service." They may simply call lawyer #2 on their list rather than spend time and money calling information to get your new number.

65. Remember, you have a sales force consisting of yourself, your firm, your family, your friends, those who refer you clients and your former and existing clients. You are only one person. They are hundreds. Utilize the leverage of your entire sales force instead of trying to do everything yourself.

66. Send clients alerts as to new laws and cases which may affect them or their business. Utilize e-mail or fax blasts to be the first person with the news ahead of printed formats.

67. Always shake hands with a client when saying hello or goodbye. Touching by way of handshake, cheek to cheek kiss, or other means appropriate to the client's age, gender, and station is a basic human trait of friendship.

The Importance of Doing It Right

My very first client was the man who installed my telephone. He installed my telephone at the end of March. He looked on the wall and saw my CPA license. He told me that he had prepared his own income tax return and would like me to review it for $5. In those days $35 was a reasonable minimum fee for an income tax return. I told him that I would need about an hour of his time for an interview to ascertain whether the income tax return was correct. He begged me to please look it over for $5 and he wouldn't hold me responsible for any mistakes. I told him that I wouldn't do anything unless I did it right and that $35 was my minimum fee. He said he wouldn't pay that much and we talked about something else until he finished his work. (Multiply these prices by five for the 2004 equivalents.)

Two days later the phone rang and it was the installer. I said hello and told him that the phone was working fine because my wife had already called twice. He said he was calling me for professional help and would I see him that evening in the restaurant of the building. I asked him the nature of the problem. He explained that his wife had a daughter by a prior marriage and that the father was a drunken bum. He had promised the wife that if anything happened to her, he would do his best to keep the child away from the natural father. He had not adopted the child. His wife had just died in an accident and he wanted to keep the child from the natural father.

I discussed the case with a couple of lawyers in the building who told me the case was an absolute loser because the natural father would get the child unless it could be conclusively proven that the father was unfit. They also told me that in those days $2,500 would be a reasonable fee and to be sure to get $2,500 for investigators, deposition costs, child psychiatrists, etc. (Remember to multiply the numbers by five for 2004.)

I met the client that night in the restaurant and told him that he had a losing case and not to waste his money, and that I needed my fee and costs paid in advance before I would begin work. Truthfully, I was trying to dissuade him from proceeding with the case. He told me he had already been to another lawyer who told him essentially the same thing but who was a little more optimistic and who would charge less. I said nothing. He said he would drop by the next morning.

The next morning he came by with a cashier's check for $2,500 and fourteen $100 bills and asked if I could wait a few days for the next $1,100. As a phone company employee he had accumulated a large amount of AT&T stock and was borrowing against it to get money for my fees. I could have waited six months.

I then got cold feet and told him that I had never handled this type of case before and in fact had never handled any kind of case before. He told me that he knew this was my first time but that he had promised his wife that if anything happened to her he would do his best. He said that when I refused to do his tax return for $5 I had told him that I wouldn't do anything unless I did it right. Therefore he was confident that even though the case was a loser and I had no prior experience, I would do whatever could be done and he would have fulfilled his promise to his late wife.

I won the case (by default) after lining up all sorts of witnesses and devoting all of my time day and night to the case. The other lawyer caved in when he and his client saw the huge array of evidence I had prepared.

I got a $2,500 fee on the custody case, and a $3,000 fee on his wife's industrial accident case, all within a short time of opening my practice, because I turned down a low fee and told a prospective client that I wouldn't do something unless I did it right.

That one case led to additional cases with several hundreds of thousands of dollars in fees.

Believe me, over the years you'll do better and get more clients and fees if you make it clear that you'll only do things the right way. Always do your best. Even when you underestimate the fee, do your best. When the client is not worthy of your best, give your best anyway.

Checklist for Opening
Your First Law Office

Foreword

This is a checklist for opening a law office. It was initially prepared at the request of the Young Lawyers Division of the American Bar Association through its then-President, David Weiner of Cleveland, Ohio, and its then-Law Practice Management Section representatives, Kenneth Rice of Everett, Washington, and Karen Feyerherm of Seattle, Washington. Sam Smith of Miami Beach, Florida, then-Chair of the American Bar Association's Law Practice Management Section, encouraged its preparation, and Bob Wilkins of Columbia, South Carolina, gave me valuable suggestions and advice as he has so often done in the past. Bill Blaine of the California Continuing Education of the Bar was most helpful in suggesting its dissemination by CEB. Curt Karplus, Assistant Director of CEB, served as editor.

This list is as comprehensive as I can make it based upon my experiences in doing programs for young lawyers throughout the United States and Canada and as Chair of the New Lawyers in Practice Committee of the American Bar Association. The list has been updated with comments and suggestions from letters I receive from lawyers who have read this book. I welcome your comments and suggestions for revisions.

Make a Timetable and Priority Checklist

After learning of the approximate lead time you'll need for each step in the checklist, make a priority checklist. Do the things first that will require the longest time. This checklist reflects upon my experiences with the difficulties in decision making and getting things done. The things requiring the most lead time should be at the top of your list; the things that require less lead time should be toward the bottom. You will have to rearrange many of the items into your own list, depending on your personal situation and local circumstances.

Consider the Area in Which You Wish to Practice

1. Where are your friends and relatives?

2. Pick a growing rather than decaying area. Watch out for blight and decay. Consider possible changes in economic patterns due to escalating energy costs. Increasing sales and payroll taxes indicate a growing area while decreasing taxes indicate an area that is in fact declining.

3. Do you want an urban, rural, or suburban practice? Analyze whether you can really be happy in a rural or small-town atmosphere or in an urban atmosphere. This is a matter of your personality and background.

Consider Quality-of-Life Factors

1. *Quality of professional life*: What kinds of cases and clients can you expect to get where you will practice?

2. *Quality of social life*: Do you want proximity to museums, symphonies, young intellectual people, etc.?

3. *Quality of atmosphere*: Is there smog and pollution, or clean air and water?

4. *Quality of recreational life*: Do you want proximity to swimming, skiing, boating, hiking, hunting, etc.?

5. *Quality of home life*: Is the area safe for your spouse and children? Will you be afraid to go out at night or to sleep with the windows open?

6. *Quality of economic life*: What kind of money can you earn there?

Consider Miscellaneous Factors

1. Proximity of office to public transportation for staff and clients.

2. Proximity to eating places for client entertainment and meetings.

3. Proximity to law library.

4. Proximity to major anticipated clients.

5. Type of practice you are planning. For personal injury, workers' compensation, and criminal law, proximity to courts and administrative hearing locations or jails may be important.

6. Proximity to other lawyers for possible consultation, referral of overflow work, or library sharing.

7. Will office and building be accessible for people on crutches or in wheelchairs, or elderly people?

What Size Office Will You Need?

You'll need 400 to 600 square feet of office space per lawyer, as follows: personal office, 150 to 200 square feet (smaller is OK if you have access to a conference room for meetings with clients); secretarial area, 150 to 200 square feet (try to defer this for a few months, if possible); reception area, storage, copy machine, etc., 100 to 200 square feet.

Consider Office Sharing

Office sharing can be very economical. Shared suites are becoming common. You give up some individuality, but you save a lot of agonizing and decision making. It is obviously cheaper to divide costs for receptionist, library, reception area and furniture, secretary, photocopy equipment, conference rooms, etc. You also have access to experienced lawyers for assistance and possibly some referral work. Ask the lawyers already in the suite how long they have been in the suite and what they like or dislike about the arrangement. Be careful to control your own phone number. (See the separate chapter on Shared Offices.)

Consider Cheap Space in an Expensive Building

Inside, nonwindow space is very cheap. With imaginative drapes, lighting, and decorating, the client won't realize that the offices are inside offices. Cost savings in rent can be very significant. Indicate that you are willing to accept inside space for price or other considerations.

Make Contacts to Find Space

Helpful sources of information include your local legal newspaper, nonlegal local papers, and local bar association journals. A commercial broker may be a good source, if the space you require is not too small. Other lawyers can be of assistance. If there is a particular building in which you want space, try a form letter sent or delivered to every existing tenant and to the building manager. This is a good source of leads on sublet space that becomes available when offices move or firms break up, which often creates opportunities for reduced rent.

Determine the True Rental Cost

Always ask for the net square footage figure from the broker or landlord, and put it into the rental agreement. Divide the monthly or annual rent by net total square footage to get cost per net square foot, which is the only true way to measure rent cost for comparison shopping. There can be a 20 percent difference between net square footage and gross square footage, due to poles, beams, corridors, window sills, ducts, stairwells, irregularly shaped premises, etc.

What to Negotiate and Include in Your Rental Agreement

1. Parking for yourself, staff, and clients at fixed prices. Don't automatically accept the story that parking is controlled by a separate concessionaire. If pushed, buildings often grant parking as a part of the lease.

2. Access to office at night and on weekends. Will air conditioning, heating, and lights be available then at no extra cost? Is building security provided after hours?

3. Any desirable furniture from the outgoing tenant you might have.

4. Right of first refusal on additional space in the building if you expand.

5. Air conditioning and heating thermostat controls for your part of the suite.

6. Are electric and telephone outlets where you need them? If not, get the landlord to install them.

7. Carpet cleaning or replacement.

8. Painting, replacement, or cleaning of wall coverings.

9. If old drapes can't be cleaned, insist on new ones.

10. Janitorial services such as trash removal, vacuuming, etc., and frequency of service.

11. A one-year term, with two one-year renewal options is best for a starting lawyer. You can stay or move after a one- or two-year experiment.

12. Try to delay the effective date for as long as possible to gain time for delivery of furniture, mailing of announcements, etc., before you have to start paying rent.

13. Don't commit malpractice on yourself before you get your first client. Whether you lease space, share space, or enter into any other arrangement, be sure to *get it in writing* before you move in or spend money on furniture or announcements. Don't depend on a handshake deal.

Start on Announcements

1. Prepare mailing lists.

   a. Law school class (get addresses from alumni association).

   b. Undergraduate classmates (get addresses from alumni association).

   c. High school classmates, if appropriate (get addresses from alumni association).

   d. Church members, if appropriate.

   e. Family.

   f. Organizations such as sports clubs, social clubs, philanthropic clubs, etc. you belong to (get addresses from club secretary).

   g. Professional associations you belong to.

2. Get sample announcements from printer.

3. Get time and cost estimate from printer.

4. Decide on style; for example whether to list your principal areas of practice.

5. Order professional cards, and enclose one with each announcement.

6. Use engraved announcements and cards, on good stock.

7. Get cost and time estimate from professional addressing service for addressing, stuffing, and mailing.

8. Start addressing the envelopes while the announcements are being printed.

9. Consider buying old postage stamps from a stamp dealer to attract attention to the announcements.

10. Decide on whether or not to send e-mail announcements, especially to people you don't know well.

Order Stationery

1. Allow up to two months' delivery time for high-quality stationery.

2. Get catalogs with samples.

3. Order letter-size bond letterhead and second sheets, blank letter-size bond, letter-size envelopes, professional cards, announcements, paper and covers for wills, billing stationery with window envelopes, and other items suitable to your own practice.

4. Separately buy inexpensive envelopes to use when paying bills.

Get Telephones and Internet-Ready

1. Estimate number and kind of instruments needed, and number of lines needed by meeting with phone company marketing representative. Don't forget that your secretary, receptionist, and clients will also be using your phones. Consider a second extension in your office for your clients' use. Be sure to include adequate dedicated lines for fax and computer equipment.

2. Order equipment, get estimate of waiting time for delivery.

3. Order installation, which may require several days.

4. Reserve telephone number in advance of opening office, so you can give it to printer to put on announcements, cards, and stationery.

5. Consider shopping long-distance carriers if you will have a lot of long-distance calls and faxes.

6. Consider Yellow Pages advertising, and listings in directories for other localities.

7. Try to negotiate low cash deposit on telephone equipment.

8. Get an answering service used and recommended by other lawyers or by doctors.

9. Get a domain name and e-mail addresses.

10. Determine what broadband is available at the location. There may be delay or impossibility of getting anything but dial up.

Order Furnishings

1. By subletting a furnished office you may be able to postpone many of these capital expenses.

2. Determine if major items can be rented instead of being purchased.

3. Determine if used furnishings are available. These cost about 60 percent of the price of new furnishings. Also keep in mind that new furniture often takes from two to six months to deliver. Use a conference room to meet your clients if your office is shabby or incomplete.

4. Read ads in local legal newspapers for used furnishings.

5. Minimum furniture for your office:

   a. Picture of family members for desk.

   b. Your desk should be at least six feet wide with overhang in front, and treated to protect against scratches and spills. Consider putting your computer or keyboard or monitor and a printer on a separate desk behind you or alongside you.

   c. Your chair. Try it out next to the desk you have selected.

   d. Two to four straight-back chairs.

   e. Wastebasket to match desk.

   f. Clear floor pad for chair if office is carpeted. Don't skimp on pad size, or chair will roll off the edges.

   g. Floor lamp, if additional light is needed.

   h. Potted plant.

   i. Bookshelves.

   j. Table for computer, computer supplies, and periodicals.

6. Minimum furnishings for reception room:

   a. Four straight-back chairs.

   b. Magazine rack or table.

   c. Reading light.

   d. Bookshelf.

   e. Coat rack and umbrella stand.

Order Equipment

1. Determine if secretarial service can provide you with dictating systems as part of its service.

2. Determine if equipment can be rented rather than purchased.

3. Determine if used or refurbished equipment is available. Should be about 60 percent of new equipment price.

4. Read ads in local newspapers for used equipment and for equipment specials.

5. Minimum equipment:

    a. Secretarial desk, with return.

    b. Secretarial chair. If possible, let secretary choose own chair.

    c. Small copy machine, unless one is available nearby.

    d. Dictating equipment including dictating unit, transcription unit, and two portable tape recorders, or digital recorders, one for your briefcase or purse and one for your car.

    e. Word-processing system. This requires serious study. Don't depend on vendors to advise you. Consult secretaries, office administrators, and other lawyers. Read the publications listed in this book. In general, go with what you know. Don't change if you don't have to. Historically, Corel WordPerfect has been preferred by lawyers and is still heavily used in lawyer to lawyer transmissions of drafts, etc. Clients historically have preferred Microsoft Word. Most law firms are able to use both systems and, when necessary, convert files from one format to the other or send and receive both versions. You should have and be able to use both systems.

    f. Accurate postage scale and postage meter. This will save you considerable money over the years.

    g. I recommend a stand-alone fax machine with a dedicated phone line, not one that is integrated into your computer system.

    h. Second desk or table for computer and peripherals.

Order Office Supplies

1. Get catalogs from several nearby office supply stores.

2. Open charge accounts with these stores. Negotiate for a discount from the list prices in the catalogs.

3. Ask your secretary or another lawyer's secretary to help you make up an initial order list. Consider such items as staplers, paper clips, scissors, two-hole punch, three-hole punch, telephone message pads, rubber stamps with inking pads, scratch pads, legal pads, paper cutter, felt-tip markers, staple removers, adhesive tape, desk calendars, pens and pencils, manila envelopes, Rolodex™ files, coffeemaker and cups, check protector, fireproof safe, etc.

Order Insurance

Engage an insurance broker or agent who is likely to refer you business, or buy from several brokers:

1. Malpractice insurance against errors and omissions. Get occurrence rather than claims-made coverage, if possible.

2. General liability insurance.

3. Workers' Compensation insurance.

4. Nonowned automobile insurance.

5. File replacement and valuable papers coverage.

6. Fire and theft insurance, for replacement value.

7. Get "umbrella" coverage, if available.

8. Check with broker or bank for financing of premiums through monthly payments.

9. Check if "office block" policy available.

Start Secretarial and Nonlawyer Hiring

1. Check with local high schools, junior colleges, business colleges, and universities for trainee secretarial and clerical help who will work without pay or for low pay to get work-training credits. Excellent source of capable trainees.

2. Publications are available from the American Bar Association Section of Law Practice Management. New materials are continually being published.

3. Allow three weeks for advertising and interviewing of applicants, and an additional two weeks' notice, which the successful candidate may have to give his or her present employer.

Start a Filing System

1. Get help from a legal secretary or office administrator or practice management advisor in setting up a filing system. The file folders are just part of the system.

2. Allow six to eight weeks for delivery of supplies.

3. Install a numerical system rather than an alphabetical system, using vertical rather than horizontal files. Various systems are suggested in the publications listed below.

Start an Accounting System

1. Engage a CPA to be your accountant. Have the accountant install a system for bookkeeping and for timekeeping, and order accounting supplies for you.

2. If you choose not to use a CPA, review the systems suggested in the publications below, and adopt a system appropriate to your practice.

3. Consider contracting an outside source for timekeeping and billing.

4. Again, contact the American Bar Association Section of Law Practice Management for appropriate publications.

Prepare Business Plan Budgets

1. Get help from a CPA in preparing business plans and budget statements that can be used in applying for loans for credit from a bank. Many business plan budgets and marketing plan budgets are available for free on the Internet.

2. A practice cash budget should be prepared for the first year, by month, estimating your expenses. Include such items as rent, telephone, insurance, furnishings and equipment, copy equipment charges, stationery, office supplies, bar dues (including lawyer reference service fees), legal newspapers, lawyer service, salaries, announcements (including postage and addressing), continuing education seminars and programs, diploma framing, automobile, parking (if not included in rent), estimates of costs to be advanced, and business development (lunches, entertainment, etc.).

3. A personal living expense cash budget should also be prepared by month for your first year. Allow money for some recreation and for medical expenses.

4. To cover these expenses, consider:
    a. Estimated income from fees for services.
    b. Savings accounts.
    c. Working spouse.
    d. Relatives who may offer help.
    e. Bank loan.
    f. SBA-guaranteed loan.
    g. Credit union loan.
    h. Bar association credit union loan.

Licenses, Permits, Etc.

1. Obtain federal and state employer identification numbers and sales or services tax numbers where applicable.

2. File federal and state quarterly income tax estimates for personal income taxes.

3. Obtain city or county licenses or permits, as required.

4. Notify state bar of address.

5. Join local bar association.

6. Join Young Lawyers Association or section of your state bar.

7. Join lawyer referral services.

8. Notify possible sources of court-appointed work of your availability.

Open Bank Accounts

1. Open office account and get checks printed.

2. Open client trust account and get checks printed.

3. Open credit line with banker.

4. Arrange for a safe-deposit box for wills and other client valuables.

Buy Only Essential Library Items

A library is a bottomless pit, which should be avoided during the first year of practice to the extent possible. Unannotated codes and some legal journals are probably essential. Use other libraries, at least at the start. Don't try to build your own until you can afford it.

Where to Get More Answers

Every law office should have the publications listed below as its basic reference library for management suggestions. In this basic library you will find the solution to almost any problem you will have to face. This may be the best investment in your practice you can make.

1. *Law Practice*, bimonthly publication of ABA Law Practice Management Section, 750 N. Lake Shore Drive, Chicago, IL 60611. Buy all back issues available and subscribe currently. Almost any problem you have can be found in one issue or another. Section dues include subscription to this publication.

2. Articles by J. Harris Morgan of Dallas, Texas, in back issues of *Texas Bar Journal*. In my opinion, J. Harris Morgan is the great-

est mind and personality in the management of a law office and practice.

3. *The Bottom Line*, bimonthly newsletter of the Law Practice Management Section of the State Bar of California.

4. Your Bar Association Practice Management Advisor

Keep Up with New Developments

The least expensive and most comprehensive way to keep current in this field is by belonging to the Law Practice Management Section of the American Bar Association and of your state bar. For further information, write to: Law Practice Management Section, American Bar Association, 750 N. Lake Shore Drive, Chicago, IL 60611, or see **www.lawpractice.org**.

Part IX
Quality of Life

Quality of Life—Dealing with Difficult People

I am deeply indebted to Zora Speert, B.S., L.C.S.W., a psychotherapist who practices in West Los Angeles, California, for her assistance in formulating this chapter of the book. Ms. Speert and I have worked together on several bar association programs dealing with quality of life. We feel that lawyers are sometimes different from other professionals because of their training and the nature of the practice of law.

The quality of your life as a lawyer will to a large extent be the result of how you avoid and/or control stress. By finding and maintaining the equilibrium that you need in your life, you will be happier, and healthier, and still enjoy your life and your practice, and probably make more money.

Law is the most stressful of 204 occupations studied by Johns Hopkins.

Stress is good until it becomes excessive. Excess stress causes physical illness and even premature death.

You cannot control other people, but you can control how you do or do not react to people.

Dealing with Difficult People

Dealing with abusive and hostile lawyers. As lawyers we were taught always to respond whenever the other lawyer does something. If the other lawyer files a complaint, we immediately file a responsive pleading. Using the process of narrowing the issues, we always respond to the other lawyer's actions. It's part of our basic training as lawyers. Medical studies have proven that hostile, aggressive lawyers are literally committing suicide with their hostility and aggressiveness. They die prematurely of arterial blockage, stroke, heart attack, etc. Refrain from responding to their taunts and aggressiveness. Think to yourself, "You are a jerk. You are committing suicide. I'm not going to respond to your personality. I will coolly and calmly respond, if at all, with appropriate pleadings and appropriate legal argument in the appropriate place at the appropriate time."

Dealing with hostile clients. Fire them as clients. You may lose some legal fees, but your mental and physical health will be worth the cost. Often a hostile client can be controlled by simply telling the client in no uncertain terms what is expected. Your initial interview and fee letter will be very important in setting forth what is expected. Many clients can be controlled by not being afraid to tell them what you are expecting them to do or not to do. If that doesn't work, fire them as clients. Our profession or our employment sometimes requires us to help people who are not worthy of help. Don't let it bother you excessively.

Dealing with hostile judges. Judges are a special problem because we can't strike back, even if the judge deserves it and we want to. The key is to ignore the tone of voice of the judge and respond calmly to the judges' words.

Dealing with incompetent staff. Fire them. You will have to micromanage everything they do and they will cause you to worry about whether they did something right or wrong.

Dealing with new technology. Don't try. Review what you have at two- or three-year intervals. You can't keep up with every new thing. Don't try. Many of them will become obsolete before the three-year period is reached.

Getting rid of excess stress. There are many books and systems for getting rid of excess stress. Regular exercise, closing your eyes for fifteen minutes, getting out of the office for a fifteen-minute walk, or having a good friend or even a pet to listen to you are all tried-and-true methods of getting rid of excess stress.

If you feel totally overwhelmed, overworked, or out of control, a good therapist may be just what you need.

Quality of Life for the New Lawyer Starting a Practice

When you start a new practice, your quality of life may take a back seat for a couple of years. I don't know anyone who successfully started a law practice working thirty-five hours per week with no evenings or weekends. It has been said that a lawyer needs forty hours a week just to survive, fifty hours a week to get ahead, and sixty hours a week to build a practice. You will never have enough time or enough money to do what you want to do or what you have to do. Learn to accept this situation for two or three years, knowing in your heart that the sacrifice is only temporary, and will benefit you and your family and even your clients in the long run.

In this chapter, I'll give you a few tips that may help you keep your career and your life in balance. Any one of these tips is probably worth a whole chapter, but pick out as many as you can to enrich your life and the lives of those who love you.

1. Understand that you will never have enough time for career, spouse, children, parents, house, community, and self.

2. Set your priorities in ninety-day or six-month time periods. Be willing and able to change priorities from time to time as your situation changes.

3. It's OK to feel guilty about not spending enough time or money where you feel you should. Don't let the guilt feelings linger. Talk it out with a loved one or another lawyer or colleague or friend or a psychotherapist.

4. Starting a new practice takes a huge amount of time to market by establishing and reestablishing relationships with new people and people you already know. Try to devote as much of your marketing activity to people and events and groups where you will feel

good in the activity. Thus you will be making some time for self at the same time.

5. Look for opportunities to involve your family in your professional activities. Take your spouse and children or other family members to bar association conventions and meetings. Look for places where the rest of the family will enjoy themselves in the day when you are in meetings and where they can join you for the social activities at night. My children grew up knowing all about bar association conventions. (They loved the exhibits.) The whole family traveled together to places we would never have otherwise gotten to. Bar associations typically negotiate low rates for hotels and travel in connection with conventions and continuing education and often plan family and children events. We all had fun and Uncle Sam subsidized part of the vacation.

6. Try not to schedule any meetings for Friday afternoons or even all day Friday. Look to take three-day weekends when you can.

7. If a trial or other matter is rescheduled or settled, look to use the open time for a surprise vacation.

8. Don't feel guilty about doing work at home, especially if doing it at home saves you a trip to the office.

9. Take care of your body. It's the only one you have. You can't help anyone if you are disabled or dead. Get regular medical examinations and follow your doctor's advice. Exercise and control your weight. Don't be embarrassed or ashamed to take a five-or-ten minute "power nap" in the afternoon.

10. Get adequate or at least minimal malpractice and medical insurance. Knowing you have protection will eliminate much of the day-to-day stress that arises when you don't have adequate insurance and a problem arises.

11. Go for quality, not for affordability, in selecting people to work for you. People who can't spell, make mistakes, and seem unable to learn things after you've explained it three times are people who will stress you out every day and eventually get you in trouble. On the other hand, having people whom you trust and who can "take charge" in your absence allows you to relax when you are not in the office.

12. Go for gadgets. Many of them will save you or make you a lot of money and allow you to intervene at the important first moments of a matter.

13. Build a network of other lawyers from your office or local bar association with whom you can test legal strategies and theories. It's important to have other professionals to bounce ideas off of. This is especially true if you are a solo or small firm. Lawyers are control freaks and don't often seek help until they feel isolated and at the last minute.

14. Don't be afraid to revamp and revolve your priority of quality of life issues. An excellent time to reevaluate your priorities is when you have your first child. When you have to plan your children's education and plan your pre-retirement are other excellent times.

15. Share parenting with your spouse or partner. The children grow up and are gone quickly. Put kids ahead of all else, except possibly spouse or parents, as soon as you can. I never heard of a lawyer who went to his or her grave with the last words "I should have spent more time with the clients and less time with the family."

16. Don't miss your children's tee-ball or soccer games or piano recitals. Schedule them with the same sanctity as a deposition or court appearance.

17. Make time for your parents (if you are fortunate enough to still have them with you).

18. Never forget, your clients come and go. Family is forever. Don't let your priorities get turned upside down.

19. When in doubt, take the high road. You might make a little less money, but you will be a happier person, sleep well, and avoid the illnesses associated with stress.

Quality of Life—September 11, 2001

On September 11, 2001, almost 3,000 people got up, got dressed and went to work never dreaming that this would be their last day on earth.

They died in burning buildings and on airplanes. Many of them had cell phones or access to telephones and they made calls.

Whom did they call? They didn't call their office to say they would be late for work. They didn't call their clients to tell them their work would be delayed. They called members of their families; they called spouses and parents and children.

In the final moments of life, what was important to them was their family.

Clients come and clients go, but family is forever. I have often said I wouldn't mind dropping dead doing client work on a Sunday, if I thought the client would come to my funeral, but the probability is that the client will simply be concerned about his or her legal matter, and there's a good chance that the only contact will be the client asking how to get his or her file.

You are probably a young person. It is hard to understand that when you lose a parent, it's forever. When you lose a parent you are losing someone you have known your entire life. It's like losing a part of your body—an arm, or a leg. Your children change every day, and then they are gone.

When you are standing at the grave site, what's the difference who was right and who was wrong?

As a lawyer building a practice, you will have to work many long hours for the benefit of a client. Your family will be the loser and pay a price.

My message is rather obvious. Family comes first. Clients come second. Don't get your priorities mixed up.

Don't try to find time for your family, rather make time for them.

Foonberg's Rule: Clients come and clients go, family is forever. Time with family will enrich your quality of life and their quality of life.

Epilogue
Proof That This Book Works

For many years, Professor Rick Rodgers taught a course in Law Office Management at Campbell University in North Carolina using this book as the text. From 1994 until 2002, when he left the school to return to private practice, he taught an extension of that course known as the North Carolina "Start Your Own Law Firm" project. During those eight years, more than one hundred Campbell graduates went straight from law school to starting a practice. I met with many of them at a reunion at Campbell. All of them have been successful, earning a good living and enjoying their practices. Most have located their law firms in communities where they previously had no friends or family, based on the economic demographics of the community.

These lawyers universally appreciated the help they received from this book, and most keep their copy in their desk drawer for reference. Prior graduates of Campbell have advised them to reread the book at least once a year. Several brought along their dog-eared copies, asking me to autograph their books.

I am proud that this book is part of their success story.

It can be part of your success story.

Index

651

About the Author

Jay G Foonberg was sworn in as a lawyer in January of 1964 and immediately opened his own practice. Today he is Of Counsel to Bailey & Partners in Santa Monica, California. He lives in Beverly Hills, California, and practices probate litigation, trust litigation, and business litigation.

Mr. Foonberg has been awarded the Harrison Tweed Special Merit Award by the American Law Institute–American Bar Association (ALI-ABA) Consortium on Continuing Professional Education for his long-term efforts in continuing legal education. He has also received the Gold Key, Platinum Key, and Highest Honors awards from the ABA Law Student Division and the Award of Merit from the ABA Young Lawyers Division. Mr. Foonberg has also been honored by the ABA General Practice, Solo and Small Firm Section with the Donald C. Rikli Lifetime Achievement Award for his ongoing work with small firms and solo practitioners. He has been a member of the Executive Council of the ABA Law Practice Management Section and was the first Chair of the Law Office Economics Committees of the Inter-American Bar Association and the State Bar of California. Mr. Foonberg has been decorated by the governments of Brazil and Argentina in honor of his work to stimulate and increase trade between the United States and these countries.

He has lectured for law firm continuing legal education and bar associations in all fifty states and the District of Columbia, as well as all ten Canadian provinces and on every one of the seven continents. He is the author of numerous articles and books, including *How to Get and Keep Good Clients, Finding The Right Lawyer*, and *The ABA Guide to Lawyer Trust Accounts,* and co-author (with J. Harris Morgan) of *How to Draft Bills Clients Rush to Pay,* Second Edition, all available through the American Bar Association. He can be reached on the Internet at **www.FoonbergLaw.com**.

CUSTOMER COMMENT FORM

Title of Book: _____

We've tried to make this publication as useful, accurate, and readable as possible. Please take 5 minutes to tell us if we succeeded. Your comments and suggestions will help us improve our publications. Thank you!

1. How did you acquire this publication:

☐ by mail order ☐ at a meeting/convention ☐ as a gift

☐ by phone order ☐ at a bookstore ☐ don't know

☐ other: (describe) _____

Please rate this publication as follows:

	Excellent	Good	Fair	Poor	Not Applicable
Readability: Was the book easy to read and understand?	☐	☐	☐	☐	☐
Examples/Cases: Were they helpful, practical? Were there enough?	☐	☐	☐	☐	☐
Content: Did the book meet your expectations? Did it cover the subject adequately?	☐	☐	☐	☐	☐
Organization and clarity: Was the sequence of text logical? Was it easy to find what you wanted to know?	☐	☐	☐	☐	☐
Illustrations/forms/checklists: Were they clear and useful? Were there enough?	☐	☐	☐	☐	☐
Physical attractiveness: What did you think of the appearance of the publication (typesetting, printing, etc.)?	☐	☐	☐	☐	☐

Would you recommend this book to another attorney/administrator? ☐ Yes ☐ No

How could this publication be improved? What else would you like to see in it?

_____

_____

_____

Do you have other comments or suggestions? _____

_____

_____

Name _____

Firm/Company _____

Address _____

City/State/Zip _____

Phone _____

Firm Size: _____ Area of specialization: _____

We appreciate your time and help.

Fax your Customer Comment Form to: 312-988-6030

ʌning Alternatives to The Billable Hour: ʌrategies that Work, Second Edition
:dited by James A. Calloway and Mark A. Robertson

Find out how to initiate and implement different billing methods that make sense for you and your client. You'll learn how to explain—clearly and persuasively—the economic and client service advantages in changing billing methods. You'll discover how to establish a win-win billing situation with your clients no matter which method you choose. Written for lawyers in firms of all sizes, this book provides valuable examples, practical tools, and tips throughout. The appendix contains useful forms and examples from lawyers who have actually implemented alternative billing methods at their firms.

Flying Solo: A Survival Guide for the Solo Lawyer, Fourth Edition
Edited by K. William Gibson

More and more lawyers, both new and seasoned, are opting to start their own practice. This book will give solos—as well as small firms—all the information needed to build a successful practice. This book is a must-have reference for the solo or small firm in any area of law practice. This comprehensive guide contains 55 chapters that tell you how to make the decision to go solo, determine the best kind of practice, handle money issues, choose a location for your office, work with other professionals, organize and run your business, manage billing and cash flow, choose computers and equipment, and much more. Cutting-edge issues such as Web ethics, telecommuting, and the best technology for a solo or small office are also covered.

Law Office Procedures Manual for Solos and Small Firms, Third Edition
By Demetrios Dimitriou

This concise manual provides everything you need to set policies and establish procedures that will keep your office operating efficiently and productively. It provides an organized and flexible format for customizing your own office procedures manual, and acts as a step-by-step guide to building and maintaining a thoroughly professional staff and practice. There are a variety of forms and reports ready to be customized to your firm's specifications, including a partnership agreement; trust account protocols; instructions on file and electronic records retention; billing protocols; office docket control system; sample court transmittal letter; client data sheet; and much more. An accompanying diskette contains the entire text for easy revision and implementation.

The Essential Formbook: Comprehensive Management Tools for Lawyers
By Gary A. Munneke and Anthony E. Davis

Volume I: Partnership and Organizational Agreements/Client Intake and Fee Agreements
Volume II: Human Resources/Fees, Billing, and Collection
Volume III: Calendar and File Management/Law Firm Financial Analysis
Volume IV: Disaster Planning and Recovery/Risk Management and Professional Liability Insurance

Useful to legal practitioners of all specialties and sizes, these volumes will help you establish profitable, affirmative client relationships so you can avoid unnecessary risks associated with malpractice and disciplinary complaints. And, with all the forms available on CD-ROM, it's easy to modify them to match your specific needs. Visit www.lawpractice.org/catalog/511-0424 for more information about this invaluable resource.

Making Partner: A Guide for Law Firm Associates Third Edition
By John R. Sapp

Many factors come into play in achieving the goal of making partner: the quality of your work; how you relate to your superiors, fellow associates, and staff; how you entertain your clients; your choice of outside activities; even publications you read. Do you know what you should and should not be doing? Do you really know what your chances are at your firm? This concise, straightforward book looks at all these factors and provides detailed advice on how to create your own strategic plan for success.

The Lawyer's Guide to Marketing on the Internet Third Edition
By Gregory Siskind, Deborah McMurray, and Richard P. Klau

The Internet is a critical component of every law firm marketing strategy—no matter where you are, how large your firm is, or the areas in which you practice. Used effectively, a younger, smaller firm can present an image just as sophisticated and impressive as a larger and more established firm. You can reach potential new clients, in remote areas, at any time, for minimal cost. To help you maximize your Internet marketing capabilities, this book provides you with countless Internet marketing possibilities and shows you how to effectively and efficiently market your law practice on the Internet.

The Lawyer's Guide to Fact Finding
on the Internet
Third Edition
By Carole A. Levitt and Mark E. Rosch
Written especially for legal professionals, this revised and expanded edition is a complete, hands-on guide to the best sites, secrets, and shortcuts for conducting efficient research on the Web. Containing over 800 pages of information, with over 100 screen shots of specific Web sites, this resource is filled with practical tips and advice on using specific sites, alerting readers to quirks or hard-to-find information. What's more, user-friendly icons immediately identify free sites, free-with-registration sites, and pay sites. An accompanying CD-ROM includes the links contained in the book, indexed, so you can easily navigate to these cream-of-the-crop Web sites without typing URLs into your browser.

The Lawyer's Guide to
Marketing Your Practice
Second Edition
*Edited by James A. Durham and
Deborah McMurray*
This book is packed with practical ideas, innovative strategies, useful checklists, and sample marketing and action plans to help you implement a successful, multi-faceted, and profit-enhancing marketing plan for your firm. Organized into four sections, this illuminating resource covers: Developing Your Approach; Enhancing Your Image; Implementing Marketing Strategies and Maintaining Your Program. Appendix materials include an instructive primer on market research to inform you on research methodologies that support the marketing of legal services. The accompanying CD-ROM contains a wealth of checklists, plans, and other sample reports, questionnaires, and templates—all designed to make implementing your marketing strategy as easy as possible!

The Legal Career Guide:
From Law Student to Lawyer
Fourth Edition
By Gary A. Munneke
This is a step-by-step guide for planning a law career, preparing and executing a job search, and moving into the market. Whether you're considering a solo career, examining government or corporate work, joining a medium or large firm, or focusing on an academic career, this book is filled with practical advice that will help you find your personal niche in the legal profession. This book will also help you make the right choices in building resumes, making informed career decisions, and taking the first step toward career success.

Also by Jay Foonberg

How to Draft Bills Clients Rush to Pay,
Second Edition
By J. Harris Morgan and Jay G Foonberg
The authors take you, step by step, through the process of building the client relationship, setting the appropriate fee agreement, and drafting the bill that will get you paid. You'll find, in plain language, a rational and workable approach to creating fee agreements and bills that satisfy your clients, build their trust, and motivate them to pay. Comparisons and samples of fee agreements and invoices are integrated throughout the text, along with a clear explanation of which methods work best—and why.

The ABA Guide to Lawyer Trust Accounts
By Jay G Foonberg
Avoid the pitfalls of trust account rules violations! Designed as a self-study course or as seminar materials, with short, stand-alone chapters that walk you through the procedures of client trust accounting, this indispensable reference outlines the history of applicable ethics rules; how you could inadvertently be violating those rules and exposing yourself to discipline even where no one is harmed; ways to work with your banker and accountant to set up the office systems you need to avoid trust account problems; numerous forms that you can adapt for your office (including self-tests for seminars and CLE credits); plus Foonberg's "10 rules of good trust account procedures" and "10 steps to good trust account records"—intended to work with whatever local rules your state mandates.

NOTE:
Additional publications, including CDs, DVDs, and downloadable PDF documents, by Jay Foonberg are available by visiting the ABA Web store at www.ababooks.org.

30-Day Risk-Free Order Form
Call Today! 1-800-285-2221
Monday–Friday, 7:30 AM – 5:30 PM, Central Time

Qty	Title	LPM Price	Regular Price	Total
___	Winning Alternatives to the Billable Hour, Second Edition (5110483)	$129.95	$149.95	$_____
___	Flying Solo, Fourth Edition (5110527)	79.95	99.95	$_____
___	Law Office Procedures Manual for Solos and Small Firms, Third Edition (5110522)	69.95	79.95	$_____
___	The Essential Formbook: Volume I (5110424V1)	169.95	199.95	$_____
___	The Essential Formbook: Volume II (5110424V2)	169.95	199.95	$_____
___	The Essential Formbook: Volume III (5110424V3)	169.95	199.95	$_____
___	The Essential Formbook: Volume IV (5110424V4)	169.95	199.95	$_____
___	Making Partner: A Guide for Law Firm Associates, Third Edition (5110576)	49.95	59.95	$_____
___	The Lawyer's Guide to Marketing on the Internet, Third Edition (5110585)	74.95	84.95	$_____
___	The Lawyer's Guide to Fact Finding on the Internet, Third Edition (5110568)	84.95	99.95	$_____
___	The Lawyer's Guide to Marketing Your Practice, Second Edition (5110500)	79.95	89.95	$_____
___	The Legal Career Guide: From Law Student to Lawyer (5110479)	29.95	34.95	$_____
___	How to Draft Bills Clients Rush to Pay, Second Edition (5110495)	57.95	67.95	$_____
___	The ABA Guide to Lawyer Trust Accounts (5110374)	69.95	79.95	$_____

*Postage and Handling	
$10.00 to $24.99	$5.95
$25.00 to $49.99	$9.95
$50.00 to $99.99	$12.95
$100.00 to $349.99	$17.95
$350 to $499.99	$24.95

**Tax
DC residents add 5.75%
IL residents add 9.00%

Subtotal	$_____
*Postage and Handling	$_____
**Tax	$_____
TOTAL	$_____

PAYMENT
❏ Check enclosed (to the ABA)
❏ Visa ❏ MasterCard ❏ American Express

Account Number   Exp. Date   Signature

Name _____ Firm _____
Address _____
City _____ State ___ Zip ___
Phone Number _____ E-Mail Address _____

Guarantee
If—for any reason—you are not satisfied with your purchase, you may
return it within 30 days of receipt for a complete refund of the price of the
book(s). No questions asked!

Mail: ABA Publication Orders, P.O. Box 10892, Chicago, Illinois 60610-0892
♦ Phone: 1-800-285-2221 ♦ FAX: 312-988-5568

E-Mail: abasvcctr@abanet.org ♦ Internet: http://www.lawpractice.org/catalog